eila Silver Library

Exploring the Professional Identity of Management Consultants

LEEDS BECKETT UNIVERSITY
LIBRARY
DISCARDED

A volume in
Research in Management Consulting
Anthony F. Buono, *Series Editor*

Leeds Metropolitan University

17 0589957 3

Exploring the Professional Identity of Management Consultants

edited by

Anthony F. Buono
Bentley University

Léon de Caluwé
Vrije Universiteit

Annemieke Stoppelenburg
University of Tilburg

INFORMATION AGE PUBLISHING, INC.
Charlotte, NC • www.infoagepub.com

Library of Congress Cataloging-in-Publication Data

A CIP record for this book is available from the Library of Congress

Library of Congress Control Number: 2012953964

LEEDS METROPOLITAN
UNIVERSITY
LIBRARY

1705899573
MK-B
CC-143019
8.4.14
658.46 EXP

Copyright © 2013 Information Age Publishing Inc.

All rights reserved. No part of this publication may be reproduced, stored in a
retrieval system, or transmitted, in any form or by any means, electronic, mechanical,
photocopying, microfilming, recording or otherwise, without written permission
from the publisher.

Printed in the United States of America

CONTENTS

SECTION I

THE MULTIPLE IDENTITIES
OF MANAGEMENT CONSULTANTS

SECTION II

CONSULTANTS AS AGENTS OF CHANGE

SECTION III

ACQUIRING AND DISSEMINATING CONSULTING SKILLS

SECTION IV

SHIFTING IDENTITIES AND CHALLENGES
IN MANAGEMENT CONSULTING

INTRODUCTION

Anthony F. Buono, Léon de Caluwé and Annemieke Stoppelenburg

This volume in the Research in Management Consulting (RMC) series is one of the outcomes of the presentations and discussions from the Fifth European Conference on Management Consulting sponsored by the Management Consulting Division of the Academy of Management, which took place June, 2011 at Vrije Universiteit in Amsterdam, the Netherlands. The conference theme—Exploring the Professional Identity of Management Consultants—attempted to capture the highly ambiguous social status of this young and emerging profession. As other volumes in the RMC series have explored (e.g., Adams & Zanzi, 2012; Buono, 2001, 2004, 2009), management consulting does not have professional standards or accreditation criteria like those found in medicine or law, there are low barriers to entry, and a broad range of tasks are undertaken in the name of consulting. As a result, a crucial aspect of what constitutes such a loosely defined profession is the identity of its members. The professional identity of management consultants is continuously developing through the interplay of how consultants are seen and valued by clients as well as in the larger society, and how consultancy firms and consultants identify and position themselves.

This theme includes a variety of topics, ranging from the interaction between consultants and their clients, consultant rhetoric and self-presentation, and the plethora of books, media and public discourse on consulting, to human resource (HR) policies and practices, knowledge development

Exploring the Professional Identity of Management Consultants, pages ix–xx
Copyright © 2013 by Information Age Publishing
All rights of reproduction in any form reserved.

activities of consultancy firms, career and life stories of consultants and consultancies, and consulting associations, accreditation bodies, and education programs. All of these factors contribute, either directly or indirectly, to identity construction in the field of management consulting.

The Amsterdam conference was attended by 157 participants from across the globe. Overall, the program consisted of 44 paper presentations, four symposia, and 13 professional development workshops over three days. As the volume's editors, we carefully examined the conference papers and presentations, selecting 16 papers that were further developed and rewritten for this book.

EXPLORING THE PROFESSIONAL IDENTITY
OF MANAGEMENT CONSULTANTS

Beginning with a general chapter that sets the context and tone for the volume, the book is divided into four sections that deal with different aspects of the professional identity of management consultants, focusing on the multiple identities of consultants, consultants as agents of change, the processes involved in acquiring and disseminating consulting skills, and shifting identities and challenges in management consulting.

The opening chapter by Hans Strikwerda—"Setting the Context"—presents a series of critical reflections on management consultancy in the 21st century. Strikwerda traces the history of the profession, drawing in critical observations about differences between consulting in the 20th and 21st centuries, with insight into consultancy's present status and standing and recommendations for the profession's development as we move further into the second decade of the 2000s.

THE MULTIPLE IDENTITIES OF MANAGEMENT
CONSULTANTS

In the first chapter in this section, Anthony F. Buono and Flemming Poulfelt examine the interaction between consultants and their clients and the relationship that develops between them, both of which are critical dimensions of the consulting process and the professional identity of consultants. As their analysis underscores, the role of the management consultant can range from objective outsider, maintaining an "arms-length" relationship with the client to that of "trusted advisor," creating almost a sage-like bond between consultant and client. The chapter explores the varied nature of this relationship through the lens of different perspectives of consulting and the consulting process, drawing out different patterns, challenges, dilemmas, and possibilities that shape the role and identity of the management consultant.

The chapter captures the various views, roles, and functions of consulting through four basic perspectives—functional, behavioral, critical, and experience-based—that shape much of the orientation and subsequent identity of consultants and the consulting process. These perspectives are used to examine and explore the dynamics surrounding the consulting process, the client–consultant relationship, and the various ways in which the identity of management consultants is constructed. The analysis includes an assessment of the lingering problems and challenges faced by management consultants and their clients, drawing out related research questions that still need to be explored.

The next chapter by Annika Schilling and Andreas Werr seeks to develop a more multifaceted understanding of the nature of professional competence, focusing on variations across different types of professional services. Their research focuses on recruitment criteria in 28 professional service firms in eight different sectors, which are analyzed and compared in order to identify patterns within and between the professional service sectors. The findings—across all sectors—indicate the limited importance of formal knowledge. Instead, the skills and attitudes of the professionals themselves are emphasized, including such generic professional characteristics as "ambition/drive" and "team working skills."

Schilling and Werr found that other kinds of skills and attitudes are more sector-specific. Based on their analysis, they argue that the more well-defined the formal knowledge base in a service sector, the less elaborate are other competence criteria. In contrast, in those sectors in which the formal knowledge base is less clear, with employees from a broad range of educational backgrounds (e.g., as found in advertising or communication consulting), the image of necessary skills and attitudes for successful professional performance is more elaborate and multifaceted. They also found a prevalence of "balancing acts" in the promotion of professional competence. While Schilling and Werr point to a number of key attitudes and skills, their research underscores that in addition to the availability of these skills/attitudes, emphasis is placed on the ability to balance opposing skills and attitudes, such as individual ambition and teamwork or creativity and structure.

The final chapter in this section, by Yvette Taminiau, Liselore Berghman, and Petra den Besten, examines the way in which consultants employ informal contacts in order to create a sustained bond of mutual trust with a client. Drawing on established theories of consultant-client relationships and the literature on informality, the authors describe how consultants use informal activities with clients and the underlying contradictions they can face. The analysis, which is based on 125 interviews with consultants in seven European countries, distinguishes five paradoxes that are related to two types of consultants—the *star player* and the *natural.*

Taminiau and her colleagues argue that informal client contact is increasingly regarded as an essential distinguishing criterion within professional service organizations. As a consultant advances into the higher levels of an organization, informal client contact becomes progressively more important, particularly as a way of acquiring new or ensuring subsequent assignments. The analysis delves into the underlying paradoxes—for instance, insider versus outsider roles, the blurring of the professional with the personal, and adapting to client needs and demands while maintaining authenticity—providing insights into the tensions related to informal client contact.

CONSULTANTS AS AGENTS OF CHANGE

Focusing on the growing prominence of group work for innovation in organizations, Karin Derksen, Léon de Caluwé, and Robert Jan Simons examine the underlying complexities, focusing on the requisite range of talents, experiences, and knowledge that are required. Yet, as they argue, even when a group is formed with the "right" talent, experience, and knowledge, it still may not be successful. Drawing on Coenders' (2008) work as the starting point for their research, they argue that groups working on innovation must have sufficient "developmental space"—the social and mental space that emerges from the interaction of group members—to be successful.

Management consultants, especially those involved in organizational development (OD) work, often facilitate these innovating groups as process consultants. Derksen and her colleagues suggest that while Coenders' model can be a useful starting point, it is incomplete, and as a model for analyzing and influencing the developmental space it is too complex. As part of an exploratory research project, they refined and adjusted the model with the goal of creating a more comprehensible and practical model of developmental space as a starting point for groups and consultants to analyze and influence that space. Drawing out the four key dimensions and processes of developmental space—dialoging, reflecting, creating future, and organizing—they argue that in their interventions consultants must ensure that all four dimensions receive appropriate attention.

In the following chapter, Karen Somerville and Dawn-Marie Turner underscore that the requirement for change skills has become a global issue as organizations around the world continue to face significant challenges in managing and leading change initiatives. Yet, they argue that surprisingly little information is found in the literature about the specific skills needed for successful organizational change. Based on interviews with 42 leaders from different industry sectors and organizational levels in Canada and the United States, they identified an array of change skills that organizations seek to develop—from a general ability to conceptualize and manage the change process, to the ability to deal with resistance and conflict, to the capability to build coalitions and networks and establish trust throughout the system.

Although their research identified 11 categories of such organizational change-related skills, they also found that most managers, when not presented with this list, did not realize the broad range of skills required for successful organizational change or were not actively thinking about the specific skills needed when seeking help from management consultants. When organizations do seek the help of consultants, the most frequently cited roles included working with C-Level executives, knowledge transfer, education and training, and project management. Somerville and Turner also concluded that the vast majority of managers (90%) from organizations that use management consultants in change-related projects were generally positive about their contributions.

In the last chapter in this section, Susanna Alexius and Frida Premer focus on the work of seven professional associations involved with setting standards for the profession. Given the present situation in consultancy—an ambiguous profession with a lack of any clear definition of the work of the consultant—they argued that one would expect that increased formalization within the consulting industry would be welcomed by both clients and consultants.

Their research, however, shows quite a different picture. In fact, standard-setting has become a high-risk project for the professional associations, creating a balancing act that could cause them to lose both their legitimacy and members. Facing skepticism and resistance, these professional associations have re-prioritized their standard-setting ambitions, even "hiding" them behind what were seen as more attractive informal initiatives and offers (e.g., breakfast seminars, insurance options). As Alexius and Premer argue, the resultant rule-setting ambivalence is likely to further damage the already frail authority of the associations as rule-setters rather than to help sustain the existing informal field order. Their findings and discussion add to our understanding of why attempts to standardize the profession have, thus far, fallen well short of intentions.

ACQUIRING AND DISSEMINATING CONSULTING SKILLS

In Chapter 7, Sonja van der Arend, Bertien Broekhans, and Sebastiaan Meijer examine professionalism in consulting work, drawing out the relationships among institutionalization, reflective learning, and performance quality. They argue that given the open and loosely demarcated occupational field of consulting, the roles and identities of those doing advisory work are under continual adaptation and negotiation. The resultant efforts to adapt or negotiate what it is that consultants do can be conceptualized as efforts to professionalize the trade, in essence, focusing on the need to enhance the quality of advisory work.

As part of their analysis, they distinguish between different forms of professionalization—practice formation, knowledge development and legitimation, and professionalization on the individual and institutionalization level—and their ramifications for practice. Looking at the development of consultancy in the Netherlands, they argue that a number of traditional mechanisms for professionalism have emerged—for instance, standardized training and education, professional associations, codes of conduct, and performance indicators—but these are loosely coupled and implemented on a voluntary basis. Given these limitations, they point to the need for reflective learning, as they argue that high quality performance occurs through deeply reflective consultants and consultancy firms. Yet, van der Arend and her colleagues underscore that although institutions contribute to leveled performance, their actions could also hamper quality improvement efforts with individual consultants. They conclude with a number of thoughtful insights into the apparent balance that is needed between institutional and reflexive mechanisms within the context of professionalizing consultancy work.

The next chapter, by Sebastiaan Meijer, Geert Roovers, Tanja Verheij, and Ivo Wenzler, discusses an experiment that included management consulting professionals in an academic teaching program as part of an initiative to bridge the gap between the university and practitioners. Their analysis illustrates how senior consultants can add substantial context and knowledge to the program, especially through the active mentoring of groups of students, a critical component of consultant development that cannot be taught by theory itself.

The authors reflect on the contribution to learning in four areas: the planning process, understanding client expectations, development of solutions, and the role of the consultant in these areas. Examining the experiment, they point to the need for both traditional academic approaches and practitioner experience. As they argue, "co-teaching" is very important, with academic teachers providing students with context, background, and theories to begin their work, helping them *apply* and partially *analyze* problems in the consultancy domain. The senior consultants, in turn, can provide guidance for students to bring their levels of learning towards *synthesis*, working with the students so they are better able to create new advice and creative solutions that would be useful for real clients.

Noting that skill development in the executive coaching field remains more of an art than a science, John Bennett and Kelly Rogers present a qualitative, descriptive study involving 26 executive coaches, with and without formal coaching credentials. Building on the Dreyfus (Dreyfus & Dreyfus, 1980; Dreyfus, 2004) model of skill acquisition and expertise development, data from the advanced beginner and expert level coaches were thematically analyzed. The results indicate that there are discernible differences between advanced beginner and expert executive coaches that are evident as individuals progress through the framework's five levels of proficiency.

Bennett and Rogers argue that this framework is useful in distinguishing between the skill of acquiring theoretical insights in an instructional setting and the context-dependent decisions and choices one has to make in "lived-experiences." Their interview data reveal the developmental stages that individual coaches experience as they progress toward mastery of a particular skill, advancing from abstract principles that are needed at the novice level to the more intuitive, less self-conscious state possessed by expert coaches. Other results include that self-awareness and client-centered focus increase with skill level, coaching presence is more confident and the coaching role itself is clearer as skill level increases, and expert coaches seek knowledge and experience in distinct ways. As they conclude, coaches develop through honing their skills, testing competencies, increasing capabilities, putting theories into practice, and reflecting on those experiences.

The following chapter by Elsbeth Reitsma continues the emphasis on reflection as an essential part of learning by professionals, drawing out how the self-reflecting capabilities of consultants affect client evaluation. She argues that a guiding assumption is that clients prefer consultants with a high level of self-reflecting capabilities compared to consultants with a low level of such capabilities. However, drawing on a qualitative study of 18 management consultants involved in two educational programs—one in a large Dutch consultancy and the other in a Dutch business school post-graduate program—her research raises questions about that assumption.

Reitsma found that all of the consultants in the study who were evaluated positively by the client had high self-reflecting capabilities, and those consultants who received moderate evaluations had lower self-reflecting levels. However, she also found that there were consultants with high levels of self-reflecting capabilities who received negative client evaluations. As she concludes, although self-reflection is an important dimension of consultancy, it is not automatically effective. In fact, more training and guidance on the nature and quality of client–consultant relationships, the ways in which clients interact with their clients, and their resultant effectiveness requires more attention in the professional development of consultants. The chapter provides insights into the nuances and complexities associated with such self-reflection, from when the reflection itself takes place (e.g., during, after an intervention), to reflecting (and learning) with others, to self-monitoring.

The final chapter in this section, by András Gelei, Balázs Heidrich, and Gergely Németh, examines the challenges involved with cross-fertilization between the worlds of practice and academia, drawing out views about theory and practice in the work and thinking of OD consultants. As part of their analysis, the authors reflect on the current "rigor-relevance" debate and related questions about the actual utility of this work for practitioners. In essence, should academic research in this field have practical "relevance" or should it seek to only satisfy scientific criteria ("rigor")? Can rigor and relevance be achieved at the same time?

Gelei and his colleagues argue that OD goes beyond the practice of intervention, change and consultancy per se, as it is not solely an intervention theory or methodology. As they note, as originally envisioned, OD should be viewed as the *constant reflexive relationship* between theory and practice, in essence between rigor and relevance. In the past, the academic- and practitioner-oriented worlds of OD overlapped significantly, and the key figures in the field were scholars *and* practitioners themselves, building on both dimensions. Drawing on their experience organizing the World OD Summit, however, the authors argue that dialogue between diverse OD approaches, intended to build on each other's insights, seems far less likely in the current environment. In fact, the present-day sentiment appears to be that different approaches and methods to handle organizational issues should be kept in different "camps." Moreover, they note that when there are attempts at blending traditions and change methodologies, the results are too often chaotic or superficial in nature. They conclude with a call to put the focus on praxis once again—emphasizing practice informed by theory and theory informed by hands-on practice. As they argue, to be of ongoing value, the OD field needs to achieve mastery in both action and reflection at the same time, practicing the essence of dialogue and the ability to question ourselves and our methods.

SHIFTING IDENTITIES AND CHALLENGES IN MANAGEMENT CONSULTING

The final section in the volume contains four chapters that look at ongoing challenges and shifting identities within the management consulting profession. Valentin Bejan and Léon de Caluwé examine the comparative image of management consultants through the lens of three of its main stakeholders—academics, consultants themselves, and the public. Drawing on interviews with subject area experts and a questionnaire focusing on key content areas (advice, roles, competencies, personal characteristics, effectiveness), their research suggests that the image of management consulting is an overall positive one, although academics remain the biggest critics of both consultancy and its practitioners. The results also reflected the Gelei, Heidrich, and Németh chapter findings about the lingering gap between theory and practice.

As Bejan and de Caluwé argue, management consulting is a practical, highly-intensive knowledge producing discipline, diffusing expertise and knowledge. Although academia also produces knowledge, that knowledge is seen as more conceptual and theoretical. In order to cooperate effectively, the image that the two groups have about each other must improve—consultants need to be less skeptical about the value of university research, moving toward evidence-based knowledge in their work, while academics must create increasingly relevant results and guidance for practice. Ongoing research on the perceptions of clients, which is not included in this chapter, is currently in progress as part of their larger research project.

The next chapter focuses on the challenges of international expansion. Flemming Poulfelt, Kåre Christiansen, and Irene Skovgaard Smith present a case analysis of Valcon A/S, a Scandinavian management consulting firm that entered the Indian market, to examine the firm's process of international expansion and how that process resulted in a significant organizational identity change. As the authors underscore, encounters within India significantly changed Valcon, reversing the stereotypical process of globalization as a one-way exportation of Western products, knowledge, and ideas. A new Valcon emerged from this experience, a firm that was not only more international but an entity that was more clearly differentiated and differently positioned in the Scandinavian consulting market. Using the notion of "reverse consulting," Poulfelt and his colleagues show how the value that Valcon gained from its entry into India was related to new business development and organizational learning, not just about how to operate in India, but also how to more effectively position the firm in Scandinavia.

John Bennett and Mary Wayne Bush look at executive coaching as a form of management consulting, noting that both fields are relatively new disciplines, early in their development as professions—they share ambiguous social status, a lack of clearly defined and agreed-upon professional standards or accreditation criteria, and low barriers to entry. This experience-based chapter explores how the professional identity of management consultants incorporates or includes a coach role, with particular respect to work with organizational change interventions.

The concluding chapter by Andreas Drechsler, Peter Kalvelage, and Tobias Trepper draws on Hamel's (2009) call for radical changes in the practice of management, looking at his proposed "moon shots" within a consultancy context. Although they argue that consultants can play a role in helping to translate these "moon shots" into practice, they suggest that traditional consulting approaches are not well fitted for the challenge. Drechsler and his colleagues compare three kinds of consulting—traditional, systemic, and complementary—looking at their compatibility with Hamel's "moon shots for management."

As part of their analysis, they provide comparative insights across these approaches, placing them within the context of a general theory of social systems by the German sociologist Niklas Luhmann (2008). Their analysis illustrates how complementary consulting attempts to combine the best elements from traditional and systemic consulting approaches, integrating technical and process know-how based on a common value system. They conclude that although all three consulting approaches have some merit for putting the "moon shots for management" into practice, if consultants will be truly able to effectively assist clients in such transformative change, consultancy itself might also need its own accompanying and complementary "moon shots."

ACKNOWLEDGEMENTS

We would like to thank our colleagues for their rich insights and thoughtful work participating in the 2011 conference and in completing this volume. Our goal was to further stimulate the debate among researchers, educators, consulting practitioners, and executive clients on the role and professional identity of management consultants.

Building upon the conference itself, our goal with this volume was to add to our continuously developing insight into the professional identity of consultants by presenting and examining the underlying dynamics and multiple ways in which this identity is constructed and reinforced. As with all the volumes in the RMC series, our hope is that this book continues to further our insights in our young and emerging profession.

REFERENCES

Adams, S. A., & Zanzi, A. (Eds.). (2012). *Preparing better consultants: The role of academia.* Charlotte, NC: Information Age Publishing.

Buono, A. F. (Ed.). (2001). *Current trends in management consulting.* Greenwich, CT: Information Age Publishing.

Buono, A. F. (Ed.). (2004). *Creative consulting: Innovative perspectives on management consulting.* Greenwich, CT: Information Age Publishing.

Buono, A. F. (Ed.). (2009). *Emerging trends and issues in management consulting: Consulting as a Janus-faced reality.* Charlotte, NC: Information Age Publishing.

Coenders, M. (2008). *Leerarchitectuur: Een exploratief onderzoek naar de relatie tussen ruimte en leren in werksituaties en het ontwerpen voor leren dichtbij de praktijk* [Learning architecture: An explorative research for the relation between space and learning in work situations and the design of learning near practice]. Delft, The Netherlands: Eburon.

Dreyfus, H., & Dreyfus, S. (1980). *The five-stage model of the mental activities involved in directed skill acquisition.* Berkeley, CA: Operations Research Center, University of California.

Dreyfus, S. (2004). The five-stage model of adult skill acquisition. *Bulletin of Science, Technology & Society, 24*(3), 177–181.

Hamel, G. (2009). Moon shots for management. *Harvard Business Review, 87*(2), 91–98.

Luhmann, N. (2008). *Soziale systeme* [Social systems]. Frankfurt: Suhrkamp.

SETTING THE CONTEXT

Reflections on Management Consultancy in the 21st Century

J. Strikwerda

It is an obvious thing to ask about the challenges and issues for the management consultancy profession in the 21st century. What will the new issues be with respect to organization, strategy, management, leadership, followership, processes, change management, and so forth? What new roles, new forms of cooperation with clients, and new ways of solving *de novo* problems are likely to emerge? Which paradigms will we need to shed, and which will be, or perhaps already are, the new paradigms to embrace? One could also question whether there is a need to reinvent the profession of management consultancy, applying the principle of creative destruction to the field of management consultancy before others do so.

QUESTIONS AND ISSUES FOR 21ST CENTURY CONSULTING

There are a number of thought-provoking questions and challenges facing the management consulting profession as we enter the second decade of the 21st century, ranging from the extent to which management consul-

Exploring the Professional Identity of Management Consultants, pages xxi–lvi
Copyright © 2013 by Information Age Publishing
All rights of reproduction in any form reserved.

tants are truly indispensable, to whether what we do as consultants is sufficiently examined, to how we conduct research in the field. This section attempts a modest view into these challenges and the myriad unanswered questions that face us as we explore the professional identity of management consultants.

Are Management Consultants Indispensable?

As management consultants, we prefer to present ourselves as a profession without which firms and institutions, even society at large, would not be able to function. We present ourselves as the knighthood of change. As a profession, we like to brag about our contributions to the growth of welfare in the 20th century—from making decentralization possible, to applying methods to increase labor productivity, and adapting organizations to respond to sometimes fundamental changes in society.

Despite this attempt at image management, the underlying question that needs to be asked is whether management consultants are truly indispensable. Perhaps society, clients, and/or members of client systems have or may soon develop a perception that is different than—even incompatible with—the self-perception held by consultants. Shouldn't we ask ourselves whether the role of management consultancy in society, in the economy at large and with respect to single organizations, might be subject to the law of diminishing returns, like most economic activities? The earliest management consultants came to the market at the end of the nineteenth century (e.g., Arthur D. Little), roughly around the start of the second industrial revolution. Why should management consultancy be a part of the third industrial revolution?

Is Management Consulting Suffering from Its Own Dominant Logic?

Why shouldn't management consultants be governed by laws of psychology, like belief conservation, belief persistence, or dominant logic? Why should we, as human beings, be different from those to whom we give advice? Pride goes before the fall, also for management consultants. Might it be that our own paradigms, the way we are organized, the way we work, creates a lens that makes us fail to see what changes are going on and thus disables us to adapt or even to transform ourselves? Do we take heed to the lessons Prahalad tried to teach us with respect to the issue of dominant logic (Prahalad & Krishnan, 2008)?

Are Management Consultants Sufficiently Scrutinized by Others?

An adequate measure whether a profession plays a significant role in society might be whether such a profession is the object of academic research, journalism, and political debate. Indeed the profession of management consultancy enjoys the interest of academics; for example, those academics who do research into the economic ratio of the consulting industry as part of the wider context of the economic process (e.g., Baaij, Van den Bosch & Volberda, 2005; Canback, 1998, 1999) analyze the role of the management consultant through the lens of transaction cost theory. Baaij et al. (2005) apply the perspective of resources, dynamic capabilities, and competences, in their case especially with respect to the strategy consultant. Another example of an academic who applies the transaction cost theory as well as the perspectives of competences to at least a part of the consulting industry is the British researcher Chris McKenna. In his book *The World's Newest Profession* (2006), the first chapter presents a theory of consulting, in which consulting is explained from the perspective of economic theory, especially transaction cost theory. This perspective, of course, is not without critics, and it might be that, due to the vanishing costs of information and communication, transaction cost theory is losing its relevance. But if so, perhaps such a theory helps us to understand changes with respect to the role, work and position of management consultancy.

Is There Sufficient and Innovative Self-Searching?

Publications in the *Journal of Management Consulting*, a book like *Critical Consulting* (Clark & Fincham, 2002), and research programs on consulting (e.g., Vrije Universiteit in Amsterdam) suggest there is significant research on various aspects of the consulting industry by consultants themselves. Focus has been placed on researching the competences required for those who want to be professional consultants, the innovations consultants pursue, how clients experience consulting, and so forth.

Much of the research on management consultancy, however, is conducted to identify preferably ever-lasting factors for success, and how to change organizations and leadership to achieve high performance. Even worse, much research aims to develop "products," that is, solutions and methods to be exploited in a commercial way. Much research is placed on how we can do better, not on whether management consultants really are necessary or which alternatives clients have available. Most research tries to be scientific in nature, trying to define positive, engineering type knowledge, whereas the characteristic thinking of entrepreneurs is neither induction or deduction, but abduction—what else might be possible?

Most research fails to address what is most typical in business and institutions: which assumptions underlie, in most cases unconsciously or even pre-consciously, theories-in-use on how to organize, how to manage, how to change, and even on how to consult. Assumptions, which are being eroded with an increasing speed and effect (e.g., by technology, demographic changes, cultural change), requiring new ways of organizing, new strategies, and new ways of managing, must be constantly questioned.

As a result of this narrow scope of research, we lack proper methods and understanding about how to design organizations fit for the 21st century. We even lack a proper theory both for organization and organization design (Davis & Marquis, 2005; Lewin & Volberda, 2003).

LOOKING AT MANAGEMENT CONSULTING IN HISTORICAL CONTEXT

Management Consulting and Scientific Management

Frederic Taylor usually is seen as the founder of scientific management, although the expression *scientific management* was introduced by his lawyer, Louis Brandeis (Kanigel, 1997). Taylor basically elaborated on the idea of utilitarianism dating back to the eighteenth century. According to Deutsch (2011), utilitarianism acted as a liberating focus for the rebellion against traditional dogmas (e.g., on how to work, how to organize), making possible improvements in efficiency, which were until then limited by social dogma. The idea of scientific management was to fight non-scientific management.

Through systematic time and movement studies, Taylor, Gilbreth and industrial engineering consultants made significant contributions to efficiency improvement and subsequently increased labor productivity and capital productivity, essentially by ignoring, eliminating, or sometimes fighting routines and dogmas, especially with managers and foremen at the shop floor.

Scientific management was not a movement on its own. Its success was determined by the context within which it was applied. Three context variables seem especially important. The first was the change in the labor law system, especially that part that eliminated foremen. Until then an entrepreneur hiring a foreman had no say on work methods deployed by that foreman. The foreman hired his own workers, and workers themselves decided how to work. Company law, establishing the institutional corporation as opposed to the firm as a partnership, provided a second relevant institutional change. This corporation, as the legal organization form of the firm, made the legal entity the owner of all of the assets organized in the firm.

This was not the case in the partnership, in which the worker often used his own tools. Subsequently the board of the corporation was authorized to issue instructions to its workers, now employees of that corporation, based on the corporation being the owner of all the tools to be used by the worker, including the work methods. The third factor scientific management depended on was the capital provided by investors like Carnegie. To create the highest possible return on investment capital, equipment needed a high utilization rate, which, among other factors, required rationalized working methods, logistics, and supply of raw material and efficient distributions of finished products. In most cases managers did not hire scientific management-type consultants to improve labor productivity on their own initiative; they were forced to do so by their investors.

The gains of the application of scientific management principles turned out to be of macroeconomic importance and thus of political relevance. By 1929 virtual all "modern" economies embraced the principles of scientific management to stimulate economic growth and to increase family income of workers, including Lenin for his communist system (Guillén, 1994). This political context in its turn legitimized the profession of consultancy.

An Explanation of the Contribution of a Specific Subset of Management Consultants

McKenna's (2006) examination of the economic contribution and legitimization of the McKinsey-type management consultant in the first quarter of the twentieth century was substantial because the (then) consultants transferred new solutions for management and organization from more advanced, innovative firms (e.g., DuPont, General Motors) to other firms. This knowledge transfer proved to be much faster than would have been the case through normal channels of knowledge exchange—publications, education, hiring of experienced staff, and so forth (Davenport, Prusak, & Wilson, 2003). It should be noted, however, that the knowledge that was transferred by the early consultants was applied to single problems or incidental problems; it was not worthwhile for the receiving firm to establish its own departments to develop such knowledge or solutions. This transfer of knowledge of proven solutions, from advanced firms to followers, is highly appreciated in economic theory. In this way an important production factor, knowledge on management and organization as a semi-public good, was exploited on a larger scale, with reduced costs and investments for the following firms. In economics it is assumed that especially in the first quarter of the twentieth century this transfer of knowledge by consultants was a significant factor in the growth of labor productivity in the United States and thus in the growth of its economy.

The Role of Law

Transaction cost theory does not provide the only explanation of the role and contribution of management consultants in the first quarter of the 20th century. The U.S. legal system also played its part. The U.S. Banking Act of 1933 outlawed banks from offering their clients advice usually linked to loans for investments. This linking of advice to loans was a common practice, as it was in other countries such as Germany (today it is widespread in the financial industry, especially by investments banks). The combination of the Banking Act and the opinion of the Securities and Exchange Commission (SEC) resulted in the general opinion that lawyers, engineers and accountants were prohibited to act also as management consultants. This enforced limitation of the scope of activities of those professions was due to the loss of trust by the larger public in banks like J. P. Morgan & Co. due to the crash of 1929. Also the anti-cartel laws made it illegal for firms to directly exchange knowledge, forcing them to do so through management consultants. In 1950, the U.S. Justice Department outlawed IBM from consulting to firms on how to apply computers—a law that would only be revoked in 1991. As a result, Arthur Anderson stepped into the consulting business, focusing on the application of computers in business. Following the change in the law in 1991, IBM regained its position in consulting on information technology (McKenna, 2006).

Images of Man, the Use of Psychology, and the Economy

Both McKenna's analysis and the emergence of scientific management do not provide a complete picture of the profession of consultancy. With the rise of the large firms at the end of the nineteenth century, industrial psychology came into being. Initially industrial psychologists concentrated on testing individuals to achieve the best fit between individual and function or task. Also physiology and stress were objects of research, and issues of ethics and dignity of the human being in work situations soon followed. Mayo's Hawthorne experiments revealed the role of attention and acknowledgement of the individual workers and the group in motivation and productivity. This work sparked the human relations movement in organization theory and management. Mary Parker Follett emphasized the role of empowerment around 1900, and Chester Barnard was the first executive to acknowledge and promote the idea of human relations in organizations, drawing out the role of psychology or, as it would be labeled in later years, organizational behavior in organizations and in management.

Human relations continued in the 1950s as the human resource movement. The essential contribution of this movement was McGregor's Theory X, Theory Y, those sets of assumptions about human behavior that influenced the mindset of most managers, going from the image of man (workers) from being predominantly negative to a far more positive image. Workers were seen to be self-motivated, working not only for a paycheck but for higher fulfillment or purpose in that work had a value beyond its monetary rewards.

The introduction of a positive image of man was not only a value in itself, it was also a condition to achieve further decentralization of decision rights in organizations, as pleaded by the Austrian-British economist Hayek in his 1945 paper *The Use of Knowledge in Society*. This decentralization of decision rights was needed to increase the information processing capacity of organizations as needed in a continuously and increasingly differentiated economy. Apparently, morality with respect to human dignity met economic necessity. Whereas McKenna's type of consultants transferred innovation from firms to firms, and scientific management helped to rationalize work methods and shop floor level organization, behavioral science educated consultants, bringing new academic insights as well humanistic values to firms.

The Context of Management Consulting: The MBE

The Modern Business Enterprise (MBE) was shaped by law at the end of the nineteenth century—through a change in property rights, the corporation was created as a legal persona in itself with a strict separation of capital and labor. Combined with the axiom of neo-classical economy to maximize utility, MBEs were the micro-institutional context within, or perhaps even the basis of which the profession of management consultancy developed.

The separation of capital and labor—as compared to the craft system and system of day laborers—severed the direct relationship between effort and results as well as the direct entitlement to the monetary rewards following those efforts and their results. In addition, scientific management, with its separation of thinking and doing, also denied the role of tacit knowledge and the idea of human capital. These two factors, of course, were ultimately acknowledged to be of importance, but any economic power based on tacit knowledge was contained by using idiosyncratic work methods and tools, and firm specific idiosyncratic standards. Task specialization as implied by scientific management, although having its roots in the shipbuilding in medieval Venice and Barcelona and documented by Adam Smith, also severed the relationship among effort, results, and rewards.

Tasks for Management Consultants Induced by MBEs

The severing of the direct relationship among effort, results, and rewards required a system of job descriptions and job evaluations (based on time-motion studies) in order to install a compensation system to prevent the continuous negotiation of labor contracts. This change created another demand for consultants to design and to implement such systems.

Stated in more abstract terms, systems for job descriptions and job evaluation reduced uncertainty and complexity for both employers and employees. Management consultants played an important role by applying more or less uniform methods, or at least a restricted number of methods, to reduce such uncertainty and complexity for both employers and employees.

Changes Induced by the Capital Market

The emergence of change management in the 1970s is best viewed within the context of the changing economy of that period. The most important change that took place in the 1970s is not the emergence of the discipline of change management per se, but rather the change with respect to the capital market and the way firms were financed. The U.S. stakeholder society ran into a wall as a result of managerial practices that were far from entrepreneurial, including the cash flow trap, blind trust, a lack of innovation, a tendency to keep too large cash reserves, not being accountable, and so forth. As a result, the U.S. economy stagnated. The combination of the new discipline of corporate finance and a new generation of shareholders, not having experienced the 1929 crisis, changed performance criteria and the way firms were financed. This so called control revolution, because the management of firms was denied the discretionary power over the cash flow of the firm, structured and restructured industries and individual firms. In the 1980s, this control revolution restructured the U.S. economy, creating the basis of the strong growth in the nineties (Donaldson 1994).

Within this structural change at the industry level, organization development (OD), a typical tool employed by consultants, was used to increase self-coordination within organizations. It was also within this restructuring by corporate finance that strategy consulting (e.g., portfolio management) started to flourish, as reflected in the work of the Boston Consulting Group with its famous growth-share matrix.

Resistance to Change

The economist Hayek (1945) stressed that the first task of the management is adaptation, in other words, to adapt the organization of the firm and its strategy to changing circumstances of whatever nature. After the Second World War, in a dominantly manufacturing economy, in most cases it happened to be managers trained as engineers who were supposed to manage the required adaptation of their organizations or departments. In doing so they met resistance. Resistance to change has many causes, but basically the issue that is often overlooked is that firms not only produce products and/or services, but that through their organization they also produce identities, roles, power, discipline, and other social constructions in society. Attempts to adapt an organization for rational economic reasons often conflict with interests of individuals or groups in the organization with respect to identities, power, and other factors related to the individual or group.

The sociologist Talcott Parsons (1962) copied the paradigm of market equilibrium from the economists and applied it to the concept of the organization. Parsons acknowledged the need for change in an organization, but this necessary change constituted a disturbance of the organization's equilibrium. This disturbance needed to be brought under control as quickly as possible to create a new phase of equilibrium.

Economists themselves did not show any particular interest in the issue of adaptation. Their reasoning was based on the ecology paradigm—firms that do not adapt in a timely manner to changing circumstances in the market will become inefficient, be eliminated from the market, and replaced by (new) more efficient firms (Baum, 1996). Sociologists, behavioral science-based consultants, sensed that this economic approach to change implied a loss of what decades later would be labeled human and social capital. Therefore they focused on changing existing organizations in order to preserve human and social capital.

Change consultants still base themselves—explicitly or implicitly—on Bennis, Benne and Chin's (1962) work, which was based on Parson's (1962) AGIL paradigm, for what they called planned change. This movement developed in a context of high growth in the economy, which required further decentralization of decision rights and changes at the shop floor in terms of semi-autonomous tasks group, job rotation, and so forth. These changes in the structure of the organization at the shop floor level served to facilitate growth, higher productivity, and an increase in the information processing capabilities of the firm in view of an increasingly differentiating economy and market. Change therefore focused on people and their processes, and changes in the structure of the internal organization within the context of a non-changing economic or business model of the firm.

Meanwhile, at the level of the firm itself, the required change in organization forms, especially the change from the functional organization to the multidivisional organization (M-form), was catered by consultants like McKinsey. This work was based on the pioneering insights of Alfred Sloan, CEO of General Motors. Sloan's ideas were documented by Peter Drucker in his (1946) *Concept of the Corporation*. Sloan (1962) later wrote about the organization form he implemented in *My Years with General Motors*, which he published because in his opinion Drucker had not explained his model correctly (Freeman, 2005).

Management Consultants: Acting within a Larger Economic Agenda?

In general, management consultants, whether focusing on strategy, organization design, human relations, or culture, act within the context of economically defined changes, in essence acting as an instrument within the larger economic agenda. Similar to the way in which Frederick Taylor served capitalists (for example, Carnegie) to enhance capital productivity through improvements in labor productivity, later generations of consultants made contributions to economic development through behavioral interventions.

Management consultants picked up and carried out those aspects of economic organization that are made invisible by economists by defining these as residual factors in the production function. These "invisible" factors, however, turned out to be material to achieve improvements in labor productivity and economic growth.

The Role of Institutional Context for Management Consultants: The Dutch Case in the 1950s

The historical development of the role and position of management consultants, although usually labeled organization consultants, in the Netherlands is an illustrative case. After the Second World War, Dutch society managed to organize a restructuring and development of its economy, which resulted in a level of labor productivity second to that of the United States, far higher than countries like Germany and Japan. This development was planned in a 1949 whitepaper, "Policy for the Manufacturing Industry in the Netherlands." The policy created a set of measures that defined how to restructure the Dutch economy, attract foreign investments, and increase labor productivity. It was based on tripartite cooperation among the Dutch government, the Dutch employers' associations, and labor unions and institutionalized in the Social-Economic Council. Search teams composed of government representatives, employers, and the unions visited other countries, especially the United States, to learn new methods for industrial engineering, efficiency, organization, and management.

One of the elements in this economic policy was a centrally-guided contract wage policy based on increases in labor productivity—contract wages would not increase beyond an increase in labor productivity, but increases in labor productivity would be translated into increases in contract wages. It was within this context, in the 1950s, that Dutch management consultancy firms (e.g., Berenschot) enjoyed great prestige and respect for their work on improving efficiency in organizations—in for-profit firms, non-profit organizations, and government agencies alike. As noted above, this program and its execution resulted in the Dutch economy having the highest labor productivity per hour, after the United States, of any other country in the world. It is understandable that the success of this economic program was also a success on other dimensions. For years the Dutch economy was the highest beneficent of foreign direct investments and achieved a high level of quality in its vocational training. This success also reflected on the profession of management consultants in terms of appreciation, acknowledgement, authority, and income. Management consultancy enjoyed a high level of acceptance, with managers and workers alike, not in the least because, precisely in line with Taylor, it was arranged ex ante that and to whom the gains from increasing labor productivity would be distributed. This example shows that an institutional embedding of management consultants does mater. With an eye toward the 21st century, one might question the present institutional embedding of management consultant—and what it should be.

Management Consultants: De-contextualized

The present generation of management consultants work on the assumption that clients who are limited in their alternative actions are best helped by consultants who understand that their own knowledge is limited as well (Sloterdijk, 2005). In many cases, however, consultants have lost their consciousness about the context within which they operate, including the ideological context. Over time, many management consultants became literal "errand boys," carriers of the ideology of neo-liberalism (or the Washington Consensus), denying the AGIL paradigm framed by Talcott Parsons.

Some First Lessons

Sloterdijk's (2005) analysis has a number of lessons for consultants with respect to the roles and positions they might have or should have in the twenty first century. A first lesson from the foregoing analysis is that the role of consultants is defined and redefined by the (institutional) context in society. Both scientific management and the case of Dutch management consultants suggest that management consultants make the best contribution to society, and thus to individual firms, when they act on a higher agenda.

A second point is that the object of management consulting depends on structural economic conditions (e.g., transaction costs). The transfer of knowledge as described by McKenna (2006) explains the role of knowledge transfer together with the legislation at that time. Since the costs of information and communication are vanishing (Alberts & Hayes, 2006; De Kuijper, 2009), and the level of education of managers is increasing, it is understandable that the comparative transfer of knowledge by consultants has been reduced. It also explains why transaction theory has lost much of its value and that transaction costs, contrary to Williamson's (1991) claim, no longer play a dominant role in organization design. According to Simon (1945/1997), organization design no longer is about structure, but about the organization of information and the factoring of decision making.

A third lesson is that specific types of consultants (e.g., behavioral science trained consultants) have different views compared to economists about what is important. Social capital and positive images of the individual seem to conflict with economist views, yet in pursuing their "ideology" they still serve an economic agenda. A growing and differentiating economy implies the need for a higher capacity for information processing in firms, which also requires decentralization of decision making and, in turn, a positive image of co-workers (trust). The behavioral approach was thus quintessential for economic growth. The immense success of the human relations movement, moving beyond its humanistic values, is explained by its economic utility.

Deal and Kennedy's (1982) work on corporate culture also served, in their own words, economic purposes. Traditional coordination mechanisms within the firm were running against their capacity, and imposed coordination needed to be replaced with self-coordination. The programming of the thinking of workers by bosses and structure was replaced by organizational culture. Culture is about the collective programming of the mind of individual members of the firm (Hofstede, 1980), which ultimately serves an economic purpose—to maximize the information processing capacity of organizations.

The solutions management consultants proposed were outside the scope of economics itself. Yet, although their solutions originated from psychology and sociology, the questions that triggered experiments were, as in the Hawthorne experiments, economic questions (e.g., how to improve labor productivity). Other questions, for example how to improve information processing capacity, were more implicit.

These lessons suggest that to understand possible roles and issues for management consultancy in the 21st century, we must focus on questions about an economic agenda for growth and increases in labor productivity—non-economic constraints that must be addressed in order to achieve this growth.

Differences between the 20th Century and the 21st Century

To understand the challenges that might be ahead for the management consulting profession, we first need to explore a number of differences—some that are already manifest and others still latent—between the 20th and 21st century. These differences, which can be seen at the societal, organizational, and even individual levels, set the context for examining consultancy in these two centuries. The profession of management consultancy has been shaped by the institutional context of the modern business enterprise. But we also need to have an open mind for the roles that other institutions of the 20th century have played, perhaps in the background, with respect to the profession of management consultancy. Of course, we cannot be complete on this as the 21st century is only a decade old, yet looking back to the second Industrial Revolution (circa 1975), there is a longer period of change we are able to assess.

A number of differences should be taken into consideration. First, as already noted above with the modern business enterprise, the 20th century assumed an absolute separation of capital and labor, especially in corporate governance. In the 21st century it is acknowledged, especially by the practice of corporate finance, that uncodified, personal knowledge is material for the performance of the firm and its value creation (Bryan & Joyce, 2007; Brynjolfsson, Hitt, & Yang, 2002; Jensen, 1998).

A second element is openness. The vertically and functionally integrated firm has yielded to open business models (Chesbrough, 2006), open standards, access to knowledge, and especially a mobile labor market. Third, high transaction costs, due to vanishing costs of information, communication, better education, and market liberalization, changed to low transaction costs. This is reflected in the open business models, in line with Coase's (1937/1991) theorem and in the demise of the traditional, popular unit-organization.

A fourth element is that corporate culture, which produces collective programming of the minds of organizational members, has to compete with a media culture, professional training, part-time workers, and interim managers, which this chapter will further explore. A related reality is that since the late 1980s clients are far better trained, especially with respect to strategy, management, and organization, than their predecessors.

Sixth is that management consultants in the 20th century helped to reduce uncertainty and complexity by applying a limited number of organization forms, strategies, and work methods. In the information economy, uncertainty and complexity cannot be mastered through reduction, but by exploitation. Seventh, which is probably the most important and least understood change between the 20th and 21st centuries, is the vanishing costs of information and communication and the immense effects this has on a vast array of aspects of organizational and societal life.

Information Society

Many authors (e.g., Castells, 1996, 2002; Castells & Himanen, 2002; Himanen, 2001; Webster, 2006) have proposed definitions of an information society, drawing contrasts to the second industrial revolution. Webster (2006) argues that there may be something like an information society, but the various attempts to define "information society" or even to prove that we live in an information society are questionable. Nevertheless the idea of an information society is useful, as it serves to ask questions concerning differences between what we are experiencing today and the era of the second industrial revolution. As Webster (2006) has argued, "The concept has helped scholars to focus attention on, and to collect together, a wide-ranging and diverse number of phenomena, from occupational shifts, to new media, to digitalization, to developments in higher education" (p. 263).

One of the most intriguing problems is the idea of information itself. Often its definition is based on the theory of Shannon and Weaver (Gleick, 2011). Sociologists like Luhmann (1984) have argued that Shannon and Weaver's mathematical theory at best is about signaling between two machines with finite structures; their theory has little to do with information in a society of human beings. A far richer definition of information, or more precisely different types of information, is provided by cybernetics (Garfinkel, 2008). It turns out that the types of information as defined by cybernetics are highly relevant for Drucker's (1988) idea of information-based organization as opposed to "command and control" organizations.

Lash (2002) has added to this the difference between discursive information and disinformation. Management science typically is based on discursive information, whereas disinformation (e.g., YouTube movies) appears to play a far more important role in shaping and defining perceptions and judgments of individuals, even within organizations. The vanishing costs of information, availability of information, and the abundance of communication have an immense effect on the idea of organization, command, control, and leadership (Alberts & Hayes, 2003). But whether this is being noticed by management consultants is yet to be discussed.

Sloterdijk

The foregoing sketch of the influence of the institutional environment for the role, position, and acceptance of the profession of management consultant is still of an operational nature. It fails to provide us with a deeper understanding of the role of the management consultants in society.

The American writer and philosopher Ralph Waldo Emerson (1803–1882) wrote "In every society some men are born to rule, and some to advise."[1] Why does this division of roles exist in each of the societies known to us? Most likely it has to do with *la condition humain*, what has been labeled by Herbert Simon (1945/1997) as our bounded rationality, bounded awareness, and bounded knowledgeability. As a human being, executive, manager, worker, or consultant, we have difficulty being aware of all that we could be aware of or even we should be aware of, even if we want to. Our thinking often is constrained if not trapped by our interests, including the self-interest of reputation, status, property, and power, be it position power or personal power. This point is well phrased by the German philosopher Jürgen Habermas (1990) in his *Erkenntnis und Interesse*. Because management consulting has become a multibillion dollar worldwide business, it has interests of its own, interests that constrain our thinking, our awareness, and our perceptions.

It can be added that it may be in the interests of specific interests (e.g., that of shareholders or an executive) to suppress particular insights, values, or even a common or public consciousness. Often interests are best served by the naturalness of non-articulated interests. Utilitarianism and thus scientific management was presented as a natural value to pursue. Its consequences on the social fabric of society were not discussed. Some in society have the feeling that the achievement of the high levels of efficiency after the Second World War, as well as the high growth of the economy in the 1990s, was at the expense of the quality of democracy and even civil society. As a result, which is expressed in post-modern movements, distrust developed with respect to efficiency-based organizations.

According to the German philosopher Peter Sloterdijk (2005) the deeper cause of this feeling of distrust is found in a swing in our culture: our modern culture of activity resists the heteronomy of hierarchy and command. For a long time, hierarchy and command helped individuals to do what they failed to do themselves—the disinhibiting (*Enthemmung*) of action.

The resistance against hierarchy and command produced a quest for a method by which command and instruction are experienced by receivers as if they were solely and purely following their own inner voices. This method, expressed in phrases like empowerment, competence management, and cultural control, became absorbed in the discipline of change management. With that, change management has become one of the instruments in our culture to form and shape subjectivity—because, as the modern discourse reasons, the individual should be prepared to be willing to change from his or her own free will, to free oneself from inhibitions to change. In doing so, management of change as a discipline nurtured programmatic individualism—the individual was represented as free and equal to all others. Reality was and is that individuals are shaped and constrained by formal and informal institutions in society, but these were kept out of the change equation.

In this way of thinking about change, no use is made of real theories or institutional frameworks, but interests are used to achieve practical purposes. Sloterdijk noted that in the discourse of the entrepreneur, the bridge to the act is constructed from (self) interest. But in this argued concentration on the self, the actor will not act without support (by a consultant) in his self-consultation and self-belief. Behavior is guided and constrained by institutions (Picot, Dietl, & Franck, 2005). In the traditional and modernistic society of the 20th century, trust was not about the other as an individual; trusting the other was based on institutional trust. The dilemma of freedom versus predictability cannot be solved by a request to trust the other. Those who have to deal with others who follow their own motives and beliefs never understand the precise source of these motives because what is being presented as one's own motives has been indoctrinated. It evolves through oblivious processes and anonymous powers, with honorable or less honorable motives, in a non-trivial complex of ambitions, reflections, energy, and slyness. The modern, subjective individual, according to Sloterdijk, approaches others with an attitude of distrust. Sloterdijk observes that management consulting as a profession has let itself be captured in the discourse of postmodernism and, as a result, has let itself become an instrument of it. Management consultants were deployed to achieve this change in the individual because management consultants themselves were not aware of the deeper motives to achieve this.

The Role of Management Consulting: Sloterdijk's Disinhibiting

Despite this critical note, Sloterdijk's concept of disinhibition is the core of the function of management consulting in the society of the 20th century: to assist individuals, groups, and organizations to become aware of conventions, routines, and beliefs that have become dysfunctional and to throw these off in order to make new growth and new developments possible. With a single stroke of the pen, Sloterdijk positions this function of disinhibiting in a cultural historical perspective. He describes how the Jesuits, by combining science and obeisance to the Pope and making use of liturgical symbols of the church, were able to transform the passive suffering of the individual into an acting ability and willingness.

Later generations of lawyers, consultants, and therapists organized this inhibition by making use of evidence, morality, and decisionism. According to Sloterdijk this disinhibition was pursued in the name of progress. Increasing labor productivity and economic growth was seen as progress. In the 1970s the idea of progress was narrowed to the growth of shareholder value. Yet, as Porter and Kramer (2011) have recently acknowledged, running a firm is not just for shareholder value. To do so assumes that the value a firm creates is equal to created shareholder value. Due to the increasing role of personal knowledge in business models (input of human capital), created shareholder value no longer equals the value created by the firm, apart from the fact that a firm does not create value in splendid isolation, but does so in a network of partners (Porter & Kramer, 2011). Jensen (2000) further states that corporate governance is not about maximizing shareholder value: "the real issue is what corporate behavior will get the most out of society's limited resources" (p. 56), to which is to be added, in a sustainable way. The focus on shareholder value has been useful to disinhibit some executives from their habits of the cash flow trap, satisficing behavior, rule following decision making (instead of pursuing innovation), not being accountable, and so forth. But due to its success, at least for some in society, this focus on shareholder value has become an inhibition in itself, not in the least for all types of consultants.

So most likely we need a continuation of this disinhibition, but it is of importance from what perspective, in whose interest, to which purpose this disinhibition is being pursued and achieved. Related questions include the extent to which such inhibition resides in the individual or the institutions.

MANAGEMENT CONSULTANTS IN THE ERA OF THE SECOND MODERNITY

Within the field of management consulting a fine-grained specialization exists, mirroring the specialization of functions especially in large firms, and partly mirroring the overspecialization in academia. With this specialization in consultancy, the profession organized itself on the basic institutions of the era of modernity with the defining clear cut dualities of that period—for instance, clear distinctions between family and non-family, paid-for work and not paid-for work, hierarchy and market, scientific knowledge and non-scientific knowledge, nature and non-nature, and indeed between consultants and clients. Modernity was the era in which experts were perceived and trusted as a source of eliminating risks and uncertainty.

Basically risk and uncertainty in the modern era were dealt with through institutions. As North (1991) noted:

> Institutions are the humanly devised constraints that structure political, economic and social interaction. They consist of both informal constraints (sanctions, taboos, customs, traditions, and codes of conduct), and formal rules (constitutions, laws, property rights). In consequence they structure incentives in human exchange, whether political, social, or economic. Throughout

history, institutions have been devised by human beings to create order and reduce uncertainty in exchange. (p. 97)

Sloterdijk's disinhibition and the work of management consultants, especially their work with respect to human relations, human resources and organization development, was applied within the institutions of the modern era. Management consultants operated specifically within the institutions of capitalism: property law, corporation law, labor law, industrial relations and within the concept of the modern business enterprise. Neither Sloterdijk's disinhibition nor the work of management consultants touched upon those institutions.

The protest against modernism, with its positivism that rejected the grand narratives in western culture (e.g., Christianity, redemption, enlightenment, utopian thinking), did not touch upon those institutions either. Post-modernism mainly was and is a play of language, which denies much of positivism and certainly has induced subjectivism to the individual. The changes in the individual with respect to relations to the institutions of modernism (e.g., capitalism, paid-for-work, careers, hierarchy, employment, scientific knowledge, authority, government, democracy) were imbued by the media, radio, movies, television, and the Internet. There were also significant improvements in the welfare of most families in Western economies, including paid vacations and less dependence on employers. Through adopting the language of post-modernity, some management consultants made themselves part of post-modernism if not the carriers of this movement. But in doing so they still did not touch upon the role of institutions in the development of organizations, and the changing institutions being a cause of issues within and with respect to organizations.

Management Consultants and Their Competition

The constraints induced by some of the institutions of the modern era— economic development and growth, the U.S. stakeholder society, regulation of markets, trade barriers, lack of standards, price regulations—were not removed by management consultants but by economists. Whereas Frederick Taylor provided with his scientific management the tools to apply utilitarianism at the shop floor level to remove taboos, conventions and habits restraining the growth of labor productivity, the economists with their shareholder value, market liberalization and corporate finance-based techniques for valuation and decision support subjected societal institutions to utilitarianism. Rules became disembedded from their institutional context. This fact, combined with the media culture and materialism of the twentieth century, weakened 20th century institutions.

During this period, management consultants operated within and on the basis of those institutions. Within these institutions, management consultants helped to reduce complexity and uncertainty by applying a limited number of organization forms and other organization techniques. This function of management seemed to be lost as a result of a meta-change in our society. As Böschen and Wehling (as quoted by Beck & Lau, 2005) noted:

> in the sphere of science and technology it has become clear that the elimination of boundaries from institutionalized nature-society distinctions and the elimination of the difference between scientific and non-scientific knowledge is leading to situations marked by crisis. Science is itself developing into a source of uncertainty, lack of knowledge and categorical ambiguity. (p. 529)

The post-modernism school proclaimed to abandon modernism, whereas philosophers like Habermas and sociologists like Beck plead that the promise of modernism was not yet being fulfilled—hence the idea of a second modernity. The core of the second modernity is a conflict between continuity of basic principles and discontinuities of the basic institutions of society. While there will be new institutional configurations, they will co-exist with most of the old institutions of society (Beck & Lau, 2005). The issue is that other professions, such as auditors and lawyers, became competitors for management consultants with respect to issues of corporate governance, risk management, control systems, and so forth. These competitors do so from the context of the old institutions. Management consultants, in order to answer this emerging competition, tended to offer solutions, techniques and methods also based on these old institutions, except for those consultants working on business model innovations. Others, such as Kaplan and Norton (2004, 2008), offered relevant tools for the 21st century, but carefully cloaked them in terms and language of the old institutions. The latter may be needed especially to win over controllers for new approaches against compliance criteria set to them. Many consultants though fail to see the message that Kaplan and Norton basically are telling, although they themselves also seem to be trapped in the competitive game in management consulting.

The Changing Balance of Power in the Consulting Market

Executives do not want to be dependent on consultants to fulfill their responsibilities. Although it may contribute to the reputation of an executive to have hired the "right" consultant for the "right" problem at the "right" moment, to be known to be completely dependent on consultants erodes the executive's reputation.

Except for Austria, the governments in all countries have declined to set legal requirements for the profession of management consultants. There are no entry barriers to our profession. Although we may be proud of our certification system, clients rarely, if ever, ask for it. The assumption is that management consultants who do not qualify will be eliminated from the market by the market mechanism. Unfortunately, markets don't always act as a clearing mechanism—not because there is a demand for under-qualified consultants, but clients often fear that a consultant knows better, or attempt to use an under-qualified consultant to legitimize and protect their own position: "You can't blame me—the consultant was unable to solve the problem."

Because of the increase in the supply of consultants, demand in combination with higher price elasticity has resulted in lower prices (Niewiem & Richter, 2004). This dynamic, in turn, evokes a process of commoditization, leaving consultants less time and resources to think and to make themselves independent from clients. This outcome is problematic because the core activity of the consultant is thinking—thinking that is independent of clients and their interests, independent of what is in vogue in popular publications, and independent of the current ideology in economics or what politicians may prefer. Consultant thinking should be independent of the media culture, of what communication consultants and journalists think people want to read or to hear or not.

Conflicts Between Schools of Management Consulting

Within the management consulting profession a number of conflicts can be observed. Within different management consulting schools, some perspectives condemn old organization forms, attempting to get rid of siloed organizations and moving toward post-modern forms (Alvesson & Deetz, 1996; Gergen, 1992; Hatch, 1997; Linstead, 2004). At the same time, other perspectives continue to emphasize modernism and its positivism, such as is found in performance management (Merchant & Van der Stede, 2003), competing on analytics (Davenport & Harris, 2007), and evidence-based management (Pfeffer & Sutton, 2006), as well as decision support, information management and others. Consulting with respect to corporate governance and related audits and controls is also based on principles and institutional configurations of the twentieth century. As Beck and Lau (2005) have noted:

> This is what we mean when we speak of "reflexive modernization": radicalized modernization consumes the foundations of first modernity and transforms

its institutions and its frame of reference, often in a way that is neither desired nor anticipated. Or, in terms of systems theory: the unforeseen consequences of functional differentiation can no longer be controlled by further functional differentiation. In fact, the very idea of controllability, certainty or security—so fundamental to first modernity—collapses. (p. 526)

Especially in fields like risk management, control, audit and performance management, functionally differentiated tools that as part of reflexive modernization have both been simplified and have been detached from their institutional, value laden context, are applied to solve the problems created by the application of the same tools. And as a consequence, a consulting industry has emerged around governance issues, risk management and control.

But even the postmodern school in management consulting, despite Schön's (1991) work on the reflective practitioner, responds often in a reflexive way to new situations and problems. Many suggest that in the era of second modernity, individuals and groups, mostly informal through Internet-based social media, have a higher capacity to solve problems compared to the institutions in society (Tapscott & Williams, 2006). Yet to which category does management consulting belong—to the individuals or, as professionals, to institutions?

A weakness of the profession of management consultancy lies in its intellectual weakness. Certainly, impressive academic work exists. However, there is a difference between trying to create a deep academic foundation for existing issues, methods, and paradigms used by management consultants, and using academic tools to both scrutinize the validity of such tools and to create and maintain a collective consciousness on the role in society of management consultants and its defining (institutional) context. There is a difference between the question of whether what we do we do in the right way, and the question of whether we are working on the most relevant issues for society, irrespective of what questions clients ask. Within this context, it could also be argued that the profession of management consulting is itself an expression of the conflicts of the second modernity.

Inhibition: Where does it Reside?

Beck (1999) made an interesting observation when he remarked, "People are better adapted to the future than are social institutions and their representatives..." (pp. 10–11). The emphasis from the field of economics, expressed in Friedman's Washington Consensus (Kay, 2003), suggests that the limits of the next wave of economic growth are in institutions and the role of government. Meanwhile the 2007–2010 crisis suggests that over-deregulation of markets has destabilized the economic and the social system with huge social costs. Consultants played their part in this over-deregulation and became part of the problem. The underlying question is whether consultants are the ones who are better adapted for the future—or whether they have become representatives of our social institutions.

Beck's observation suggests that resistance to change is not so much with the individual worker, but with managers and other representatives of social institutions. This would be consistent with Prahalad and Krishnan's (2008) concept of dominant logic as an object of change, rather than the resistance to change by workers in the organization. If the dominant logic is the object of change, then most likely quite different tools for change need to be applied compared to those used for overcoming the traditional resistance to change.

Innovation in the Functions

Although functions in the organization—human resource (HR) management, management accounting, corporate finance, management control, information and communication technology (ICT), strategy, audit—have become professions in themselves, there is a basic lack of academic research leading to innovations in those functions. Certainly, for example, corporate finance has deep mathematical underpinnings. But much of the academic research in these fields consists of either refining existing tools or trying to legitimize the function itself. Some of the academic publications in these fields, especially in HR and ICT, are defensive in nature. At the same time, due to the decline of the modern business enterprise—which in part is due to the changing nature of assets—new business models, changes in the basis of motivation of the workforce, and changes in the role of work in life need to be redefined themselves if we are to have efficient organizations in the 21st century. Management consultants must also shift their focus in order to assist firms in reinventing these functions.

Consultants as Killers of Intuition?

A deeper intellectual understanding by management consultants of questions asked by clients is necessary. In the 1990s, writing mission statements, in conjunction with inspiring visions, became popular as a way to inspire and to motivate workers and to achieve teamwork and coherence. It can be argued that this need for a clear mission statement was a rightfully, if intuitive, response to changes in the environment of the firm, the changing nature of the firm, its organization, and especially the changing nature of the workforce (see Abrahams, 1999).

Clients, however, became increasingly cynical about such mission statements, especially because of their similarities, trivial content, and posturing, in essence, placed on wall rather than in the minds of managers and workers. In many cases management consultants and communication consultants who assisted organizations in defining their mission simply did not understand the true nature of a mission, its role, or how it could be integrated into the workings of an organization. This problem emerged because of two basic errors made by consultants. First, consultants mistook mission statements as an issue of communication and inspiration. In terms of organization theory, a mission is goal information, one of the six types of information defined by cybernetics (Garfinkel, 2008). Second, a mission, due to its function in the control of the organization, needs to be codified in the objective functions in the organization. In one company, which had redefined its mission due to a change of control and market liberalization for its industry, consultants suggested to implement its new mission in the organization by having each department, based on the corporate mission, write its own mission. This plan resulted in a pile of papers, inconsistent sub-missions, confusion, and frustration. The consultants created a mess, which was ultimately cleaned up by translating the corporate mission in the objective function of all of the departments, in financial and non-financial objectives and constraints.

A similar observation can be made with respect to the role of values. As Lash (2002; Lash & Urry, 1994) has argued, values are needed by individuals and by organizations to cope with the increasing availability of and access to information. What values are, and are not, is clearly explained in the professional literature (Cha & Edmondson, 2006; Rollinson & Broadfield, 2002), including the fact that a hierarchy of values is needed (Cha & Edmondson, 2006). In terms of cybernetics, values are axiological information, which need to be codified in multi-objective multi-criteria objective functions. Yet despite these available professional insights, one is appalled to see in case after case how management consultants have undermined client intuition of the role of values in organizational life.

Control by Culture

Management consultants, other than those consulting on the level of corporate finance and corporate strategy, were tasked to assist in the implementation of the restructuring of firms as enforced by the capital market. This included the idea of corporate culture, as it turned out that management by objectives had clear limitations in achieving required changes. Traditional control techniques (Anthony & Govindarajan, 1995; Merchant & Van der Stede, 2003), which are based on the use of generic codified knowledge, also lost their effectiveness. But the Total Quality Management movement implied a shift to specific knowledge (Wruck & Jensen, 1994). In addition tacit, uncodified personal knowledge was seen as playing an increasing role in the firm, as a result of which the basis of management control (the idea that the firm has full control over the alienation rights of its assets) became impaired (Furubotn & Richter, 2000; Jensen, 1998). But in the 1980s, due to lack of fundamental research on management control and management accounting, the real cause of this impairment remained obscure.

Earlier Juran (1995), one of the founding fathers of quality management, had discovered the role of culture in implementing quality programs. Management control, in essence, is about influencing behavior, and culture was sought after as a solution to repair the problems with traditional management control approaches (Deal & Kennedy, 1982). Deal and Kennedy themselves linked corporate culture to control with the objective to improve productivity. But many consultants viewed culture programs from the perspective of organization development as a behavioral science intervention. Many of them lacked a deep understanding of culture and overlooked its relation with control. In most cases, when members of an organization talk about culture, in reality they talk about the psychological climate (Schein, 2000). It is often overlooked that traditionally the business model of a firm included assumptions on markets and customers, which codified in culture, and through that culture were being transferred to new members of the organization. Academics and consultants working on performance management issues sensed there was something like culture that was playing a role in their field. As Merchant and Van der Stede (2003, Chapter 3) noted, in addition to action controls and personnel controls, cultural controls were useful to encourage mutual monitoring and increase group pressure. Within the field of organizational behavior, cultural control is defined as a way to control hearts and minds, inducing employees to think in the way that their managers wanted them to think (hegemonic control). Cultural control is also defined in terms of achieving control over employee emotions (Rollinson & Broadfield, 2002). As Bradley, Schipani, Sundaram, & Walsh (2000) underscore, there are ethical issues in culture control—"... cultural control is problematic in the best of times, and scholars have pointed out that this kind of hegemonic control insidiously robs individuals of their humanity" (p. 16). In an era of explicit business models (Johnson, Christensen, & Kagermann, 2008; Kaplan & Norton, 2004; Osterwalder, 2004) and competing by innovating business models, in combination with big data and widely available analytical tools, and a workforce that for a large part is on temporary contracts, Schein's concept of culture no longer is relevant.

Knowledge Transfer, Knowledge Creation and Knowledge Exploitation

In McKenna's model, management consultants are not really a source of knowledge and insights. Instead management consultants pick up knowledge of leading, innovating firms, with respect to organization and management, and transfer this knowledge to follower firms (Davenport et al., 2003). Even the popular Balanced Scorecard was discovered by Kaplan in a U.S. midwestern firm, although the idea was also embedded in the earlier work of Fayol (1918/1999) and Drucker (1958).

It is to be expected that this role has diminished to a minimum if it still exists. This change is due to the improved education of managers—the sheer increased numbers of managers in MBA and executive programs—which offers a flourishing system of tools, frameworks and case studies. Many consultants use their consulting experience to deepen and broaden their views, knowledge, and understanding as a step to achieve an executive-level position. Moreover, many clients of management consultants have been consultants themselves and are therefore well-versed in the tricks and tools of consultants.

The Internet has also changed the behavior of clients when they need an answer to a question. Routinely the first consultant to be sought out is Google or another search engine. A number of sites offer Q&As on various issues, as illustrated in the Netherlands in which www.tql.nl is visited ten thousand times per month by managers and staff members for insights with respect to HR, strategy, organization, fiscal affairs, contract management, and change management among many other subjects.

An overwhelming plentitude of trade books on management, leadership, change, organization, and strategy are also published each year. Consultants themselves, largely for marketing purposes, write many of these books. Some are extremely popular; most do not catch attention. Clients have armed themselves more or less against these books by displaying cynicism—except for regarding that one specific book that serves their purpose.

When consultants seem to bring in new ideas in organizations today, they do not enlighten management, but they execute a set agenda by management. And management selects from the varied offerings in the market the ideas that fit their agenda. Within this context, it is important to note that there is a strong herd mentality among executives and managers, that an idea carries the "truth" because so many firms are using it. An example is Economic Added Value (EVA), applied by all large banks in the Netherlands, sourced from the same New York based consulting firm. Unfortunately, with hindsight, EVA is now viewed as one of the concepts responsible for perverse behavior in the financial institutions. The concept was seriously flawed and is now abandoned.

Even worse, management consultants by their knowledge creation by case-based-empirical-research-turned-into-publications undermined Boisot's (1995) learning cycle, which collapsed because the process of selection, abstraction, and validation of the abstract model was left out, and therefore the assumptions underlying these "theories" and their limitations were not specified.

Another of the economic developments of importance, which was not understood by management consultants, is knowledge management. The intuition that uncodified personal knowledge is of importance was correct. But the idea that knowledge is created by turning tacit knowledge into codified knowledge (Nonaka & Takeuchi, 1995; Nonaka, Toyama, & Nagata, 2000) was simply wrong—it is a modern variant of scientific management. New knowledge is created by applying existing knowledge to new, original problems and challenges, with a mixture of inductive thinking, deductive thinking, abductive thinking, and trial and error (Jensen, 1998). Also because of the institutional limitations of management consultants, they failed to see that turning tacit, uncodified personal knowledge into codified knowledge to be managed by the firm was also an issue of property rights. So knowledge management died a silent death, whereas growth of knowledge remains the main driver of growth and development in society (North, 2005)

We do, of course, have insights into how to exploit knowledge—as evidenced by firms like IBM and captured in Foss's work (Foss, 2005a, 2005b, 2007; Foss & Mahnke, 2003; Foss & Pedersen, 2004)—but not by management consultants.

Management Consultants: Reflective or Reflexive?

The system disturbance in the early 2000s—Enron, WorldOnline, Parmalat—in which, especially in the case of Enron, management consultants played a dubious role, resulted in legislation (e.g., SOX) and greater attention to risk management. In this case, management consultants, especially the works of Tversky and Kahneman (1981) and Bazerman (Bazerman & Moore, 2009; Kahneman, 2003; Tversky & Kahneman, 1981), could have provided firms with deeper insights with respect to risks and the psychological processes that cause risk events in firms. However, while management consultants jumped on the elephant of risk management, they did so as a reflex, in an instrumental way, without providing deeper insights based on rigorous academic research. A similar movement can be seen the fields of performance management and financial management. Management consultants often respond to needs and problems of managers as a reflex, in essence, making themselves part of the problem instead of the solution.

Another remarkable phenomenon can be observed in the field of HR. The traditional system of management control, as defined by its main authors (Anthony & Govindarajan, 1995; Merchant & Van der Stede, 2003), has met its limitations. By happenstance, a consultancy firm (Hay) stumbled on competence management, turning it into a consultancy hype. In this case, a market for competence management emerged—not as an economic need, but instead because HR was losing ground to management control systems and was looking for ways to legitimize itself. Competence management was being presented as a tool to develop people, whereas in reality, it is another control technique (Durand, 2004). As with programs for talent management (real talent by definition does not need programs), we see that consultants offer ideas and concepts that appear to serve an economic agenda, but in reality serve to maintain the status quo of functions like HR.

A development within consultancy is a specialization mirroring the specialization within firms. The HR manager is consulted by consultants specialized in HR, the CIO is consulted by consultants specialized in IT, the CFO is consulted by consultants specialized in (separately) corporate finance, management accounting, performance management, data logistics for consolidation, and so forth.

In many instances, the CEO does not directly hire a consultant to change or improve the organization; instead the hiring is delegated to a staff department. The staff department will select a consultancy firm that will confirm and reinforce the role and contribution of the staff department hiring him. The consultancy industry being responsive to this demand, unwittingly perhaps, blocks the integration of the various aspects of the organization and even, following Beck and Lau, reinforces the functional specialization beyond its efficiency. As an example, a couple of years ago I consulted with a multinational on how to implement corporate social responsibility (CSR) and sustainability objectives. Our firm was hired by the head of the corporate staff department for sustainability. Our proposal was to integrate the objectives and constraints for CSR and sustainability, based on thorough research, at the lower-level decision-making processes in the organization. This change would also redefine functions as part of the system of performance management, resource allocation and objective setting, and reporting and control. The goal was to integrate the objectives and constraints induced by CSR and sustainability into the genes of the management control system of this multinational, with reporting on social responsibility and sustainability being integrated in the overall reporting system. The head of this corporate staff department did not accept this proposal because he wanted to maintain separate reporting lines and functional authorities. The manager was more concerned about his personal position than about the objectives and performance of the firm. As consultants, we terminated this relationship because we felt we could not serve the company.

Kant's Imperative: To Consult to Oneself

After the philosophers Descartes, Kant, Fichte and Marx, man no longer acts from his mortality, rather man acts from a theory (Sloterdijk, 2005).

Not theories for reflection, but theories for achieving success. The enlightenment philosopher Immanuel Kant, who anchored the highest level of self-consulting—the categorical imperative—in the individual, intended the measure for justified practical actions. It was Kant who made man his own consultant, when he stated the imperative: I consulted with myself. After de-contextualizing objectives in economic life by accepting the utilitarianism, the profession of management consultant definitely made itself part of the modern society by applying Kant's imperative at the level of the individual.

This subjectivist individualism carries the benefit of advancing the development of society by pushing aside restrictive hierarchies, in either an evolutionary or revolutionary way. After 1968 consultants took on the role of the ideological thinkers by defining the world no longer in terms of enemies, but in terms of competition. In the name of the free market and success as a form of human rights, consultants disinhibit their clients towards new strategies, organizational forms, processes, styles of leadership, and labor relations. Consultants do so by applying a restricted arsenal of infallible tools and methods, based on not knowing the limitations of those tools and methods. But consultants do so from a limited set of solutions or focus on a limited aspect of organizations, for example, the attitude of the individual. At face value, management consultants appear to be innovators, even revolutionaries. From a perspective of systemic change, however, it is often much ado but little real change.

Management Consultancy in a Media Culture

In order to understand why management consultants sometimes kill intuition, we need to take into the equation the role of the media, or the interaction between the media culture and management consultancy. Management consultancy, right or wrong, is often associated with management books. U.S. management books dominate the market, in first place in the media culture, as a significant mechanism to transfer knowledge. In a media culture, life is composed of pseudo-events, existing in stories, images, and experiences. Everything that is seen or heard must immediately be understood, preferably in an unconscious way. All expressions, images, sounds, and writings should exert a maximum influence on a mass audience. Within this philosophy, U.S. management books are edited with great care (Clark & Greatbatch, 2004).

The style in which U.S. management books are written and edited is based on a formula developed by *Readers Digest* around 1900. The U.S. historian Daniel Boorstin (1969) wrote on this theme in *The Image*: "In this new world, where almost everything can be true, the socially rewarded art is that of making things seem true" (quoted in Clark & Greatbach, 2004, p. 404). As a consequence, images are replacing reality. The image of an idea makes what it stands for. Creating such images is the core task of management books, not technical descriptions of how problems should be solved in the reality of a firm. As a result most management books are written in an apodictic style, and amplification of an image is emphasized over argumentation without reflection. This media style is not restricted to management books, but also is applied to the performance of management consultants.

The profession of management consultants should ask itself the question: to what extent has it let itself get trapped in this media culture philosophy?

Management Consultants: Infallible Popes?

The philosophy that legitimizes disinhibition is pragmatism, the philosophical basis of business administration. Sloterdijk (2005) quotes William James, one of the founders of pragmatism, writing about practical, empirical, not theory inclined practitioners: "They dogmatize like infallible popes" (p. 100). The idea of an infallible pope is not a monopoly of the Catholic Church, it is a ubiquitous psychic function that needs to be activated whenever the subjective individual starts to doubt. The task of this inner pope is to suppress doubt, which always is gnawing in the individual, to enable the individual to act in the uncertainty of the society of chances and opportunities.

These infallible popes are especially found in management books. Precisely management books present prescriptions, stripped from all uncertainties, as disinhibiting theories. Especially the apodictic U.S. management books provide contextless apodictically phrased recipes, even on how to reflect. This includes most books written by management consultants; if not, consultants are the errand boys of such ideas.

FINAL THOUGHTS ABOUT MANAGEMENT CONSULTING IN THE 21ST CENTURY

In accordance with the philosopher Emerson, I assume that advising or consultancy will remain a function in society. The lingering question concerns the nature of consultancy's subjects, organization, tools, legitimization, and advertising objectives. The 20th century suggests that these parameters will be, to a high degree, if not completely, defined by the needs and institutions of society. The 20th century also suggests that consultants may be deluded as much as their clients were by the loss of public consciousness and words being used as signs rather than communication. Talking about organization and organization issues has become "throwing words-as-signs" at each other, each individual projecting his own meaning and understanding in those thrown signs, carefully not asking what analytical content the thrower assumed in the thrown signs.

The client has also changed and will continue to change. Clients are better educated, with access to all and everything. It seems to be that in the 21st century the conflict that needs to be addressed is between entrepreneurial intuition and rules, regulation and tools supplied by management consultants based on the economy, technology, and institutions of the 20th century.

The challenge for management consultants is to be independent thinkers, to assist clients to achieve their objectives in a confused world that is continuously losing its public consciousness. A lesson to be learned especially from the last twenty years is that the impartiality and independence in thinking needed for this should be in view of the interests of society at large, as today it is understood that firms have not only the task to produce goods and services, but also have the task to play institutional roles in society. And so do management consultants.

Habermas (1990) and Sloterdijk (1999) have observed that individual and public consciousness is being lost in society as a result of a *Verschränkung der Sphäre*. In order to be effective and to make a contribution, management consultants need to be outsiders with respect to the client in their thinking. An outsider orientation should permeate the consultant's relationship with the client's system, as well as the systems of the functions, professions, and governance. Consultants also need to be outsiders with respect to the media and the media culture—which is especially the case for their own books.

In the 20th century, capital was core in the economic system, and exploitation of knowledge was done through embedding that knowledge in physical products. The free individual as created by the enlightenment needed to be adapted to the new production system of capitalism and within the production system, specific subsystems were needed to coordinate between the production system and the individual. The HR and management consultant took care of this.

In the 21st century there will be a less clear core. It can be argued though that knowledge, tacit uncodified personal knowledge, information, both discursive and disinformation, are sufficiently more important as will be physical capital in the process of the creation of consumption. The basic conflict structure of the 20th century between capital and labor is being replaced by the conflict between knowledge and decision rights, with the latter conflict structure carrying more ambiguity.

So most likely the challenge for management consultants will be to assist in achieving systemic change with respect to the functions and professions within the firm and to challenge the vested interests of those functions and professions, including the vested interests in the profession of management consulting itself. As with other professions, our ultimate client must be society.

NOTE

1. See "The Young American," February 7, 1844, a lecture delivered to the Mercantile Library Association, Boston (published in *Addresses and Lectures*, 1849).

REFERENCES

Abrahams, J. (1999). *The mission statement book: 301 corporate mission statements from America's top companies.* Berkely, CA: Ten Speed Press.

Alberts, D. S. & Hayes, R. E. (2003). *Power to the edge: command, control in the information age.* Washington, DC: CCRP Publication Series.

Alberts, D. S. & Hayes, R. E. (2006). *Understanding command and control.* Washington, DC: CCRP Publications.

Alvesson, M. & Deetz, S. (1996). Critical theory and postmodernism approaches to organizational studies. In S. R. Clegg, C. Hardy & W. R. Nord (Eds.), *Handbook of organizational studies* (pp. 191–217). London: SAGE Publications.

Anthony, R. N. & Govindarajan, V. (1995). *Management control systems* (8th ed.). Chicago, IL: Irwin.

Baaij, M., Van den Bosch, F. A., & Volberda, H. W. (2005). How management consulting firms influence building and leveraging of client competences: Towards a conceptual framework. ERIM Report Series Reference No. ERS-2005-079-STR. Retrieved from http://papers.ssrn.com/sol3/papers.cfm?abstract_id=871124

Baum, J. A. C. (1996). Organizational ecology. In S. R. Clegg, C. Hardy & W. R. Nord (Eds.), *Handbook of organization studies* (pp. 77–114). London: SAGE.

Bazerman, M. H. & Moore, D. A. (2009). *Judgment in managerial decision making* (7th ed.). Hoboken, NJ: John Wiley & Sons.

Beck, U. (1999). *World risk society.* Cambridge: Polity Press.

Beck, U. & Lau, C. (2005). Second modernity as a research agenda: Theoretical and empirical explorations in the 'meta-change' of modern society. *The British Journal of Sociology, 56*(4), 525–557.

Bennis, W. G., Benne, K. D., & Chin, R. (Eds.). (1962). *The planning of change: Readings in the applied behavioral sciences.* New York, NY: Holt, Rinehart and Winston.

Boisot, M. H. (1995). *Information space: A framework for learning in organizations, institutions and culture.* London: Routledge.

Boorstin, D. J. (1969). *Het imago; of: Wat is er met de Amerikaanse droom gebeurd?* [The image] (Y. Foppema, Trans.). Den Haag: Leopold.

Bradley, M., Schipani, C. A., Sundaram, A. K., & Walsh, J. P. (2000). The purposes and accountability of the corporation in contemporary society: Corporate governance at a crossroads. Retrieved from http://scholarship.law.duke. edu/cgi/viewcontent.cgi?article=1136&context=lcp

Bryan, L. L. & Joyce, C. I. (2007). *Mobilizing minds: Creating wealth from talent in the 21st-century organization.* New York, NY: McGraw-Hill.

Brynjolfsson, E., Hitt, L. M., & Yang, S. (2002). Intangible assets: How the interaction of computers and organizational structure affects stock market valuations. *Brookings Panel on Economic Activity, 33*(1), 137–198.

Canback, S. (1998). The logic of management consulting, Part 1. *Journal of Management Consulting, 10*(2), 3–11.

Canback, S. (1999). The logic of management consulting, Part 2. *Journal of Management Consulting, 10*(3), 3–12.

Castells, M. (1996). *The rise of the network society* (Vol. I). Hoboken, NJ: Blackwell.

Castells, M. (2002). The cultures of the internet. *Queen's Quarterly, 109,* 333–343..

Castells, M. & Himanen, P. (2002). *The information society and the welfare state: The Finnish model.* New York, NY: Oxford University Press.

Cha, S. E. & Edmondson, A. C. (2006). When values backfire: Leadership, attribution, and disenchantment in a values-driven organization. *The Leadership Quarterly, 17*(1), 57–78.

Chesbrough, H. W. (2006). *Open business models: How to thrive in the new iInnovation landscape.* Boston, MA: Harvard Business School Press.

Clark, T. & Fincham, R. (2002). *Critical consulting: New perspectives on the management advice industry.* Hoboken, NJ: Blackwell Publishers.

Clark, T. & Greatbatch, D. (2004). Management fashion as image-spectacle: The production of best-selling management books. *Management Communication Quarterly, 17,* 396–424.

Coase, R. H. (1937/1991). The nature of the firm. In O. E. Williamson & S. G. Winter (Eds.), *The nature of the firm: Origins, evolution, and development.* New York, NY: Oxford University Press.

Davenport, T. H. & Harris, J. G. (2007). *Competing on analytics: The new science of winning.* Boston, MA: Harvard Business School Press.

Davenport, T. H., Prusak, L., & Wilson, H. J. (2003). *What's the big idea: Creating and capitalizing on the best management thinking.* Boston, MA: Harvard Business School Press.

Davis, G. F. & Marquis, C. (2005). Prospects for organization theory in the early twenty-first century: Institutional fields and mechanisms. *Organization Science, 16*(4), 332–343.

De Kuijper, M. (2009). *Profit power economics: Aa new competitive strategy for creating sustainable wealth.* Oxford: Oxford University Press.

Deal, T. E. & Kennedy, A. A. (1982). *Corporate cultures: The rites and rituals of corporate life.* Reading, MA: Addison-Wesley.

Deutsch, D. (2011). *The beginning of infinity: Explanations that transform the world.* New York, NY: Viking Adult.

Donaldson, G. (1994). *Corporate restructuring: Managing the change process from within.* Boston, MA: Harvard Business School Press.

Drucker, P. F. (1946). *Concept of the corporation.* Piscataway, NJ: Transaction Publishers.

Drucker, P. F. (1958). Business Objectives and Survival Needs: Notes on a Discipline of Business Enterprise. *The Journal of Business, 31*(2), 81–90.

Drucker, P. F. (1988). The coming of the new organization. *Harvard Business Review, 66*(1), 45–53.

Durand, J. -P. (2004). *La Chaîne invisible: Travailler aujourd'hui: flux tendu et servitude volontaire* [Invisible chain: Constraints and opportunities in the new employment]. Paris: Éditions du Seuil.

Fayol, H. (1999). *Administration Industrielle et Générale* [General and industrial management]. Paris: Dunod. (Original work published 1918)

Foss, N. J. (2005a). The knowledge governance approach. Retrieved from http://ssrn.com/abstract=981353

Foss, N. J. (2005b). *Strategy, economic organization, and the knowledge economy: The coordination of firms and resources.* Oxford: Oxford University Press.

Foss, N. J. (2007). The emerging knowledge governance approach: Challenges and characteristics. *Organization, 14,* 29–52.

Foss, N. J. & Mahnke, V. (2003). *Knowledge management: What can organizational economics contribute?* Copenhagen: Danish Research Institute for Industrial Dynamics.

Foss, N. J. & Pedersen, T. (2004). Organizing knowledge processes in the multinational corporation: an introduction. *Journal of International Business Studies, 35,* 340–349.

Freeman, A. (2005). *The leadership genius of Alfred P. Sloan.* New York, NY: McGraw-Hill.

Furubotn, E. G. & Richter, R. (2000). *Institutions and economic theory: The contribution of the new institutional economics.* Ann Arbor, MI: University of Michigan Press.

Garfinkel, H. (2008). *Toward a sociological theory of information.* Boulder, CO: Paradigm Publishers.

Gergen, K. J. (1992). Organization theory in the postmodern era. In M. Reed & M. Hughes (Eds.), *Rethinking organization: New directions in organization theory and analysis* (pp. 226–245). London: Sage Publications.

Gleick, J. (2011). *The information: A history, a theory, a flood.* New York, NY: Vintage.

Guillén, M. F. (1994). *Models of management: Work, authority and organization in a comparative perspective.* Chicago, IL: University of Chicago Press.

Habermas, J. (1990). *Strukturwandel der Öffentlichkeit: Untersuchung zu einer Katergorie der bürgerlichen Gesellschaft.* Frankfurt am Main: Suhrkamp.

Hatch, M. J. (1997). *Organization theory: Modern, symbolic, and postmodern perspectives.* Oxford: Oxford University Press.

Hayek, F. A. (1945). The use of knowledge in society. *The American Economic Review, 35*(4), 519–530.

Himanen, P. (2001). *De hacker ethiek en de geest van het informatietijdperk* [The hacker ethic, and the spirit of the information age] (M.-C. v. Spaendonck, Trans.). Amsterdam: Nieuwezijds.

Hofstede, G. H. (1980). *Culture's consequences: International differences in work-related values.* Beverly Hills, CA: Sage Publications.

Jensen, M. C. (1998). *Foundations of organizational strategy.* Cambridge, MA: Harvard University Press.

Jensen, M. C. (2000). Value maximization and the corporate objective function. In M. Beer & N. Nohria (Eds.), *Breaking the code of change* (pp. 37–57). Boston, MA: Harvard Business School Press.

Johnson, M. W., Christensen, C. M., & Kagermann, H. (2008). Reinventing your business model. *Harvard Business Review, 86*(12), 50–59.

Juran, J. M. (1995). *Managerial breakthrough* (revised ed.). New York: McGraw-Hill.

Kahneman, D. (2003). Maps of bounded rationality: Psychology for behavioral economics. *The American Economic Review, 93*(5), 1449–1475.

Kanigel, R. (1997). *The one best way: Frederick Winslow Taylor and the enigma of efficiency.* New York, NY: Viking Penguin.

Kaplan, R. S. & Norton, D. P. (2004). *Strategy maps: Converting intangible assets into tangible outcomes.* Boston, MA: Harvard Business School Press.

Kaplan, R. S. & Norton, D. P. (2008). *The execution premium: Linking strategy to operations for competitive advantage.* Boston, MA: Harvard Business Press.

Kay, J. (2003). *The truth about markets: Their genius, their limits, their follies.* London: Allen Lane.

Lash, S. (2002). *Critique of information.* Thousand Oaks, CA: Sage.

Lash, S. & Urry, J. (1994). *Economies of signs and space.* Thousand Oaks, CA: Sage.

Lewin, A. Y. & Volberda, H. W. (2003). The future of organization studies: Beyond the selection-adaptation debate. In H. Tsoukas & C. Knudsen (Eds.), *The Oxford Handbook of Organization Theory: Meta-theoretical perspectives* (pp. 568–595). Oxford: Oxford University Press.

Linstead, S. (2004). *Organization theory and postmodern thought.* Thousand Oaks, CA: Sage.

Luhmann, N. (1984). *Soziale Systeme: Grundriß einer allgemeinen Theorie* [Social systems: Writing science]. Frankfurt am Main: Suhrkamp.

McKenna, C. D. (2006). *The world's newest profession: Management consulting in the Twentieth Century.* Cambridge: Cambridge University Press.

Merchant, K. A. & Van der Stede, W. A. (2003). *Management control systems: Performance measurement, evaluation and incentives.* London: Prentice Hall.

Niewiem, S. & Richter, A. (2004). The changing balance of power in the consulting market. *Business Strategy Review, 15*(1), 24–36.

Nonaka, I. & Takeuchi, H. (1995). *The knowledge-creating company: How Japanese companies create the dynamics of innovation* (2nd ed.). New York, NY: Oxford University Press.

Nonaka, I., Toyama, R., & Nagata, A. (2000). A firm as a knowledge-creating entity: A new perspective on the theory of the firm. *Industrial and Corporate Change, 9*(1), 1–20.

North, D. C. (1991). Institutions. *The Journal of Economic Perspectives, 5*(1), 97–112.

North, D. C. (2005). *Understanding the process of economic change.* Princeton, NJ: Princeton University Press.

Osterwalder, A. (2004). *The business model ontology: A proposition in a design science approach.* Docteur en Informatique de Gestion, Université de Lausanne, Lausanne. Retrieved from http://www.hec.unil.ch/aosterwa/phd/osterwalder_phd_bm_ontology.pdf

Parsons, T. (1962). The problem of the theory of change. In W. G. Bennis, K. D. Benne & R. Chin (Eds.), *The planning of change.* New York, NY: Holt, Rinehart and Winston.

Pfeffer, J. & Sutton, R. I. (2006). *Hard facts, dangerous half-truths, and total nonsense: Profiting from evidence-based management.* Boston, MA: Harvard Business School Press.

Picot, A., Dietl, H., & Franck, E. (2005). *Organisation: Eine ökonomische perspektive* [Organization: An Economic Perspective] (4th ed.). Stuttgart: Schäffer-Poeschel Verlag.

Porter, M. E. & Kramer, M. R. (2011). Creating Shared Value. *Harvard Business Review, 89*(1/2), 62–77.

Prahalad, C. K. & Krishnan, M. S. (2008). *The new age of innovation: Driving cocreated value through global networks.* New York, NY: McGraw-Hill.

Rollinson, D. & Broadfield, A. (2002). *Organisational behavior and analysis: An integrated approach* (2nd ed.). New York, NY: Prentice Hall.

Schein, E. H. (2000). Sense and nonsense about culture and climate. In N. M. Ashkanasy, C. P. M. Wilderom & M. F. Peterson (Eds.), *Handbook of organizational culture and climate* (pp. xxiii–xxx). Thousand Oaks, CA: Sage Publications.

Schön, D. A. (1991). *The reflective practitioner: How professsionals think in action.* Aldershot: Arena.

Simon, H. A. (1997). *Administrative behavior: A study of decision-making processes in administrative organizations* (4th ed.). New York, NY: Free Press. (Original work published 1945)

Sloan, A. (1962). *My years with General Motors.* New York, NY: Doubleday.

Sloterdijk, P. (1999). *Globen (Sphären II)* [Spheres]. Frankfurt am Main: Suhrkamp.

Sloterdijk, P. (2005). *Im Weltinnenraum des Kapitals: Für eine philosopische Theorie der Globalisierung* [The inside of capitalism: A philosophical theory of globalization]. Frankfurt: Suhrkamp Verlag.

Tapscott, D. & Williams, A. D. (2006). *Wikinomics: How mass collaboration changes everything.* New York, NY: Portfolio.

Tversky, A. & Kahneman, D. (1981). The framing of decisions and the psychology of choice. *Science, 211*(4481), 453–458.

Webster, F. (2006). Theories of the information society Retrieved from http://www.loc.gov/catdir/toc/ecip069/2006006404.html

Williamson, O. E. (1991). The logic of economic organization. In O. E. Williamson & S. G. Winter (Eds.), *The nature of the firm: Origins, evolution, and development* (pp. 90–116). New York, NY: Oxford University Press.

Wruck, K. H. & Jensen, M. C. (1994). Science, specific knowledge and total quality management. *SSRN eLibrary.* doi: 10.2139/ssrn.47731

SECTION I

THE MULTIPLE IDENTITIES
OF MANAGEMENT CONSULTANTS

CHAPTER 1

CONSULTANT–CLIENT INTERACTION

Shaping the Identity of Management Consultants

Anthony F. Buono and Flemming Poulfelt

Management consulting continues to be a fast growing business, with an average double-digit growth rate over the past decade, evolving into a more than 250 billion dollar global industry. The consulting field has not only turned into a huge professional service industry, it has also developed into a cultural force, exerting a major influence on corporate life as well as the public sector. Indeed, there appears to be a basic consensus that management consultants have become key players in the knowledge creation and transfer process, pushing their insights across firms, industries, and even countries (e.g., Clark & Fincham, 2002; Davenport & Prusak, 2009; Kipping & Engwall, 2002; Mills, Dukeov, & Fey, 2007; Sahlin-Andersson, & Engwall, 2002). The reality is that in most cases where consultants have been involved, the outcome clearly reflects their footprint, shaping to varying degrees how the client organization will perform in the future (Buono,

Exploring the Professional Identity of Management Consultants, pages 3–16
Copyright © 2013 by Information Age Publishing
All rights of reproduction in any form reserved.

3

2009; Buono & Poulfelt, 2009). Such influence is also reflected in an analysis conducted in the UK showing that consultants on average added value to their clients ten times the fees paid (Management Consultancies Association, 2010).

Paralleling the growth and influence of the business, however, management consulting is also in flux. Both the consulting business and the profession itself are undergoing rapid changes, and if anything is clear, it's that literally nothing will be the same again (Greiner & Poulfelt, 2009). Client demands reflect higher and more specialized expectations, which, on one level, means that the ways clients have to be served are constantly being challenged (Czerniawska, 2007). Client needs and their situations have also become more complex and ambiguous, and, as a result, consultants are being faced with increasingly demanding mazes to navigate. And clients themselves are becoming more sophisticated in the ways in which they engage and utilize consultants, partly due to their accumulated experiences from working with consultants over a long time span. A related force challenging the management consulting realm is what appears to be growing skepticism among client organizations about consultants and their wares (Stewart, 2009).

THE CLIENT–CONSULTANT RELATIONSHIP

A useful way to conceptualize and explore the dynamics underlying these trends draws on the nature of the client–consultant relationship. As recent research has reinforced (e.g., Buono & Poulfelt, 2009; Schwarz & Clark, 2009; Todorova, 2004), the interaction between consultants and their clients and the relationship that develops between them are critical dimensions of both the consulting process itself and the professional identity of the consultants themselves. The role of the management consultant, of course, can be quite varied, ranging from objective outsider, maintaining an "arms length" relationship with the client (cf. Antal & Krebsbach-Gnath, 2001; Sturdy, Clark, Fincham, & Handley, 2008; Uzzi, 1997), to that of "trusted advisor," creating almost a sage-like bond between consultant and client (Maister, Green, & Galford, 2001; Nadler, 2009). This chapter explores the nature of this relationship through the lens of different perspectives of consulting and the consulting process, drawing out various patterns, challenges, dilemmas, and possibilities that shape the role and identity of the management consultant.

As a way of exploring these issues, this chapter presents a comparative assessment of consultants and the consulting process. Drawing on the management consulting literature (see, for example, Buono, 2009; Clark & Finchham, 2002; Clark & Salaman, 1996; Poulfelt, 1999; Sturdy et al., 2008;

Sturdy, Werr, & Buono, 2009; Werr & Styhre, 2003), the various views, roles and functions of consulting can be captured in four basic perspectives. As summarized in Table 1.1, the functional, behavioral, critical, and experience-based perspectives capture much of the identity and orientation of consultants and the consulting process. The *functional perspective*, which reflects a rational and logical approach to consultation, takes a prescriptive approach, comprised of principles and models for how the consultant role *can* and *should* be exercised, and how the consulting process *should* be planned and implemented. The underlying assumption is that consultants add value to a client organization (Solomon, 1997) and that such value is created through a planned and systematic problem-solving process. The *behavioral perspective* is rooted in the social sciences and portrayed in the organization development (OD) literature. It is based on a classic therapeutic paradigm focused on how to increase the "patient's" (client's) self-awareness and knowledge on how the person acts (Schein, 1969, 2009). The *critical perspective* includes observers who dissect and challenge the function of consulting, characterizing consultants as "management gurus" and "witchdoctors" (e.g., Clark, 2004; Clark & Salaman, 1996; Kam, 2004; Micklethwait & Wooldridge, 1996), suggesting that consultants are often little more than merchants of meaning, surrounded by a certain kind of mystique and power. Finally, the *experience-based perspective* is grounded in practice and the knowledge acquired through several years of consultancy. This view, which shares some similarities with the functional perspective, is highly reflective and introspective, reflecting almost a sage-like quality (e.g., Biech, 2007; Buono, 2000; Nadler, 2009; Schaffer, 1997).

TABLE 1.1 Perspectives on Management Consulting

	Perspectives			
Characteristics	**Functional**	**Behavioral**	**Critical**	**Experience-based**
Ideology	Normative/ Prescriptive	Facilitation/ Process-oriented	Skepticism/ Illusion	Reflective/ Introspective
Knowledge Base	Multi-disciplinary	Behavioral/ Social Sciences	Critical Management Theory	Past Experience
Consultant Role	Expert in a Broad Sense	Facilitator	Management Instrument	Sage/Trusted Advisor
Problem-solving Processes	Insight/ Understanding	Prompting Self-insight	Sense-making	Action Orientation
Results/Outcomes	Managerial Solutions	Self-driven Solutions	Manipulation	Guided Improvements

These four perspectives can be used to examine and explore the dynamics surrounding the consulting process, the client–consultant relationship, and the various ways in which the identity of management consultants is constructed. The overview in Table 1.1 is meant to capture and illustrate certain role-related ideal types within consulting practices and the literature. As this brief comparative assessment suggests, one of the characteristics of the consultant universe is its diversity and range in both time and space in relation to professional standpoint (e.g., management vs. psychological basis), role perspective (e.g., content-driven vs. process driven), problem-solving orientation (e.g., normative vs. explanatory), and experiential platform (e.g., full-time vs. part-time consultant), as well as the broader ideology associated with the utility of consultation (e.g., consultant supporter vs. consultant critic). This latter point is an important consideration when examining the professional identity of management consultants, as critics and skeptics abound—as reflected in the comments of a manager when he noted, "The reason for not using consultants is sometimes fear-based. If one slips something like that into the pot, one is risking an unpredictable outcome."

The discussion that follows focuses on the ways in which the relationship between consultants and their clients are framed and shaped, drawing on the contrasting perspectives and views in Table 1.1. The analysis then turns to an assessment of the lingering problems and challenges faced by management consultants and their clients, drawing out related research questions.

The Functional Perspective

The functional perspective reflects a series of principles and models for how the consultant role *can* and *should* be pursued and how the consulting process *should* be organized and implemented. The starting point is that consultants do contribute something of value to clients, and that this value-added service can be created and enhanced through a planned and systematic problem-solving process (Kubr, 2005). Although the functional perspective is characterized by a high degree of diversity with respect to actual consultant roles, it is based on a premise of rationality in the client's perception of reality. It reflects a broad range of theoretical fields and disciplines, from management and behavioral science, to marketing, systems theory, philosophy, and the sociology of knowledge. The consultation process is mainly grounded in a conception of the consultant as a professional in solving generic corporate problems and subject to standards from classical occupational theory. The consultant's professional behavior and ethics therefore have a prominent position within this perspective.

With regard to the actual roles of the consultant, this view, as suggested above, is quite varied, comprising a broad spectrum ranging from consultant as classical expert, to facilitator, to a clinical process role (though this latter dimension blurs into the behavioral perspective). As suggested by the literature (e.g., Williams & Woodward, 1994), consultants by definition fulfill an expert role through their professional insight and experience. The role of consultant is therefore more specifically linked to how this professionalism manifests in a concrete problem-solving context. The *1 + 7 model*, for example, is based on an expert role (1) supplemented by 7 corresponding role components covering analysis, project management, integration, political influence, conflict management, teaching, and coaching. Each of these roles is seen as being based on insight, prudence, and understanding, oriented to outcomes and results as essential ingredients in the collaboration with the client. At the same time, there is an underlying goal that client problem-solving skills should be improved, looking to the future, enabling clients to solve similar or analogous problems on their own.

The majority of contributors to this view of consultation have a constructive attitude toward consultants and the consulting process. The functional approach reflects what can be construed as "best practice"—and in some instances suggested "next" practices—based primarily on cases and personal experience, with an inspirational orientation. Additional examples of key proponents within this perspective include Block (2007), Greiner and Metzger (1983), Greiner and Poulfelt (2009), Guttmann (1987), Margerison (1988), Metzger (1988), and Turner (1982).

THE BEHAVIORAL PERSPECTIVE

This view has its roots in the social sciences and its methodology, and is based on a classic therapeutic problem, namely the question of how to increase the "patient's" self-awareness and ability to take action. The overall philosophy, which is portrayed in the organization development (OD) literature, has a kind of "help to self-help" character (see, for example, Schein, 1969, 2009). Although the consultant's role is depicted in many different versions, the core is embedded in process more than content per se (a key distinction with the functional perspective), where the goal is to increase client understanding of the complex problems they are dealing with. It is therefore a matter of being inquisitive to a greater extent and allowing space for reflection, more than (over)steering the process and acting as "the expert" in the traditional professional sense. The resulting problem-solving process is grounded in the behavioral scientific framework bearing the imprint of hermeneutics and phenomenology, as well as dialogue and discourse-based methodology.

The content dimension of this process-focused role has gained renewed importance through an increased focus on "corporate emotions" (Fineman, 1996) and "emotional intelligence" (Goleman, 2006), which includes a more explicit emphasis on the expressive dimension in organizational and personal contexts. From an organizational perspective, it reflects a move away from the myth of rational behavior—and the presumption of rationality in the functional perspective—in that the behavior of actors is acknowledged to be influenced by their individual needs, wishes, and unconscious fears and desires (Fineman, 1996). Thus, while the prevailing rhetoric about management and change is typically grounded in rationality, logic, and analysis shaping the processes underlying problem identification, diagnosis, planning, and intervention, this perspective underscores that such rational views are typically "mocked by actual practice" (Lundberg, 2004, 2010).

Common to the behavioral perspective is the idea that the consultant role is primarily developed in connection with solving problems related to individual, group, and organization dynamics, which all have a behavioral element (French & Bell, 1973). The roles range from diagnostician, to facilitator, change agent, and conflict solver, to clinical therapist. The main perspective within this view is the importance of creating understanding as a basis for action, in essence creating the conditions for self (as well as organizational) learning. Relationships, attitudes, processes, and related interventions are key foci. Examples of key contributors include Schein (1969, 2009), Bennis, Benne, and Chin (1969), Argyris (1970, 2000), French and Bell (1973), Lippitt and Lippitt (1978), and Nevis (1987). It is striking that all of the contributors within the behavioral field have a clear belief in the usefulness of consultants and the consulting process, presumably because of their ideology about people and, for many, their years of clinical practice.

The Critical Perspective

In stark contrast to both the functional and behavioral perspectives, the critical perspective includes contributors who dissect the function and role of consulting from the vantage point of what, in fact, constitutes its value. Questioning whether the consulting process adds real value to the client, the consultant role is described as an "organizational witch doctor" (Clark & Salaman, 1996; Micklethwait & Wooldridge, 1996), doing little more than transforming knowledge and learning into fads and fashion (Contino & den Hond, 2009; Venard, 2001) that lead to "naïve, superficial and overly commercialized ideas" (Clark, 2004). The background of this metaphor in the consultant universe is linked to "performance" as being relevant to both parties. However, the consultant's goal, much like that of the witchdoctor, is to produce results through a process that is shrouded in mystique and power, in spite of formal contracts, declared transparency, and stated commitments to collaborative processes. In more instances than are typically realized, critics contend that consultants themselves are the actual learners, taking knowledge *from* their clients to sell to others (Walsh, 2001).

The ability to influence and convince clients to pay large sums to support the introduction of new management principles is also part of this worldview. The idea of "management gurus"—consultancy's elite—is used with both admiration and disdain, the latter reflected in analyses that suggest editors and ghost writers often drive the process far more than the so-called gurus themselves (see Clark, 2004). Instead of real performance, the consulting process is described as a "performance art," in essence little more than image management and attempts at "selling professionalism" (Kam, 2004), promoting best practices that are not necessarily "best for practice" (Lalonde, 2011; Ngayo, 2009).

With similar focus, others emphasize the consultant's role as a merchant dealing in words (Czarniawska-Joerges, 1988), where the aim is to create meaning through the use of language, labels, and metaphors. Through this process, the consultant helps to define the power arena and accompanying action set for those in power—in essence the management. Consultants thus gain considerable power through this position, an assessment that has long been recognized in a power-base philosophy (see Borum, 1976; Johnsen, 1978). An underlying concern is that consultants are often not sufficiently aware of the long-term impact of their efforts, suggesting that significant reflection should be prioritized in the consultant's camp. There is, however, a whiff of double standards within this perspective, which partly puts forward positive interpretations of the relevance and usefulness of the role and partly presents critical opinions of the way the role is managed in practice. As counter critics suggest, "Theories don't pull companies in conflicting directions. Managers do" (Shapiro, 1997, p. 142).

The spectrum of roles that emerge from the critical perspective include expert, translator, redeemer, guru, and magician. In addition to the contributors noted above, other prominent proponents of this view are Abrahamson (1996), Baxter (1996), O'Shea and Madigan (1997), and Sturdy (1997).

The Experience-Based Perspective

The fourth perspective is rooted in practice and in the experience gained through several years of consultancy work. This view illustrates how different types of problems and assignments have been handled, providing advice on how consultants should act, partly in relation to clients and partly in relation to their own business. Examples like "build your own practice" and "develop a successful marketing plan" are frequent headlines in the relevant literature. In addition, this perspective also includes a variety of mini-portraits of exemplars, such as the consultant biography of James O. McKinsey (Wolf, 1978), who established McKinsey & Co., Harrison's (1995) *Consultant's Journey*, a personal biography of the author's development on the consultant front, and Tepper's (1985) *Become a Top Consultant*, which outlines a series of consultant styles and ways of handling client assignments.

This contribution primarily describes how different types of problems and interventions have been handled, providing advice to consultants on how they should act both in relation to their clients and in relation to the development of their own business. This category consists of contributions written by practicing consultants, who attempt to explain and substantiate their various experiences (cf. Bell & Nadler, 1979; Bellmann, 1990; Biech, 2007; Schaffer, 1997). Characteristic of a range of presentations with a distinct technique orientation, this approach contains a wide variety of checklists and similar support materials. Although this view shares some similarities with the functional perspective, this approach is more reflective and, in many instances, highly introspective (see, for example, Buono, 2000).

It is also notable that only very few contributions within this group include actual theoretical illumination or insight into basic fundamentals (which are more characteristic of the functional perspective). As for the more person-oriented descriptions, ultimate conclusions are primarily left to the reader.

Experience-based perspectives are generally characterized by a less critical approach, focused more on introspection and reflection about the contributor's own role and related behavior. As with the other perspectives, the experience-based view includes a range of roles, including specialist and process adviser. This view also includes critical assessments of failure, from being in the unfortunate position of working with "neurotic" and "toxic" clients (e.g., Goldman, 2009; Motomadi, 2009) to admitted shortcomings of the consultancy itself (e.g., Harris & Wang, 2003). Yet, despite the fact that much can be learned from less than successful engagements, this latter role is rarely portrayed in the literature. In addition to the contributors noted above, other examples of this approach include Holtz (1999), Kelley (1981), Greenfield (1987), Metzler and Metzler (2010), Nadler (2009), Weinberg (1985), and Weiss (2001, 2002).

REFLECTIONS ON PROFESSIONAL IDENTITY

The growing body of research on management consulting during the past decade has clearly enhanced our insights into and understanding of the dynamics involved in consultation and the consulting process, drawing out a fuller understanding of the complexities, nuances, and limitations associated with this fast changing field. Yet, there are plenty of "dark spots" that remain on the consultancy map. Especially as clients, their needs, and the consultancy profession itself continue to evolve, there is need for greater understanding and additional insight into how consultants see themselves and how others see consultants. Indeed, juxtaposed with the ongoing influence of the management consulting profession, there is a growing disparity between consultant expectations for engagements and client expectations for outcomes, and between consultant expectations for compensation and market realities, to the point where an increasing number of management consultants report that they do not see themselves working in the industry in the near future (see Kennedy Information, 2011).

We suggest that the four perspectives summarized in this chapter provide different glimpses into the myriad ways in which the professional identities of management consultants are constructed. Yet by themselves each of the perspectives provides a useful but limited view. While the functional perspective provides insight into what could be characterized as best practices, and often has an inspirational orientation and positive view of the profession, it is clear that its normative models fall well short of the realities of context-bound engagements. Similarly, while the behavioral perspective adds needed insight into client–consultant relationships, their underlying dynamics, and self-development problem-solving capabilities, lingering tensions between process versus content foci and the need to ensure that business imperatives are given sufficient attention raise questions about the overall utility of this approach. Moreover, emphasis in both the functional and behavioral approaches is placed on the role and perspective of the consultant, minimizing views of other key stakeholders in the process—including the client. Even though the behavioral approach places a greater emphasis on the variety of clients in an engagement (Arnaud, 1998; Schein, 1997) and recognizes the range of client involvement along an activity-passivity dimension (Sturdy et al., 2009), the client is still identified as someone (or some entity) "in need." The consultant is the one who is identified as the savior, perhaps a reflection of a pre-MBA business world, where people in organizations were seen as lacking the knowledge, diagnostic abilities, and professional insights that were identified with the consultant (see Sturdy et al., 2009).

Within this context, the critical perspective—although this approach is not an actual applied perspective and reflects more of an "arm's length," external view—raises key issues about the legitimacy of the consulting profession, an important factor in identity construction. Even though the consulting business has developed into a more mature business, there are still numerous myths and folktales about consultants and their work. These depictions might be due to the fact that consulting is a profession in a non-traditional sense, as its members come from various other professions (such as economists, accountants, lawyers, engineers, sociologists), and the product itself is essentially a non-tangible and less transparent service.

The views of the experienced–based consultancy reflects a self-perceived identity of the actors, as the experiences outlined primarily illustrate what consultants themselves see as "good" consulting behavior and performance, often described in a positive but also to a certain extent superficial way. However, this too illustrates that consultants primarily report on successful assignments and less about the root challenges and experiences from less than successful consulting projects. This omission often limits the learning that can be distilled from consultants, making their experiences that much more explicit and insightful.

As suggested by Kitay and Wright (2007), occupational identity is a multifaceted phenomenon rather than a consistent whole. Such identities are constructed from imagery—both positive and negative—and used to both interpret and manage situations that are commonly experienced by members of a particular occupation. As a profession, management consultants must grapple with questions about their legitimacy, their role in relation to their clients and the client organization, and their overall impact and effectiveness. The four perspectives outlined in this chapter—and the related roles that consultants play within each approach—highlight the varied ways in which this identity is conceptualized and exposed in practice.

REFERENCES

Abrahamson, E. (1996). Management fashion. *Academy of Management Review, 21*(1), 254–285.

Antal, A. B., & Krebsbach-Gnath, C. (2001). Consultants as agents of organisational learning. In M. Dierkes, A. Berthoin, J. Child & I. Nonaka (Eds.), *Handbook of organizational learning and knowledge* (pp. 462–483). Oxford, England: Open University Press.

Argyris, C. (2000). *Flawed advice and the management trap: How managers can know when they're getting good advice and when they're not.* New York, NY: Oxford University Press.

Argyris, C. (1970). *Intervention theory and method: A behavioral science view.* Reading, MA: Addison-Wesley.

Arnaud, G. (1998). The obscure of demand in consultancy: A psychoanalytic perspective. *Journal of Managerial Psychology, 13*(7), 469–484.

Baxter, B. (1996). Consultancy expertise: A postmodern perspective. In H. Scarborough (Ed.), *The management of expertise* (pp. 66–92). New York, NY: MacMillan Business 1996.

Bell, C. R., & Nadler, L. (1979). *The client–consultant handbook.* Houston, TX: Gulf Publishing.

Bellman, G. M. (1990). *The consultant's calling.* San Francisco, CA: Jossey-Bass.

Bennis, W. G. Benne, K. D., & Chin, R. (1969). *The planning of change.* New York, NY: Holt Rinehart & Winston

Biech, E. (2007). *The business of consulting: Basics and beyond.* Hoboken, NJ: Pfeiffer.

Block, P. (2007). *Flawless consulting: A guide to getting your expertise used.* San Francisco, CA: Jossey-Bass.

Borum, F. (1976). *Strategies for organizational changes.* Copenhagen, Denmark: CBS Press.

Buono, A. F. (2009). Introduction. In A. F. Buono (Ed.), *Emerging trends and issues in management consulting: Consulting as a Janus-faced reality* (pp. vii-xx). Charlotte, NC: Information Age Publishing.

Buono, A. F. (2000). When the client dies: Reflecting on the personal and professional ramifications of a sudden tragedy. In R.T. Golembiewski & G. H. Varney (Eds.), *Cases in organization development: Four perspectives on value-guided consulting* (pp. 145–155). Itasca, IL: F.E. Peacock Publishers.

Buono, A. F., & Poulfelt, F. (2009). Introduction. In A. F. Buono & F. Poulfelt (Eds.), *Client–consultant collaboration: Coping with complexity and change* (pp. vii–xx). Charlotte, NC: Information Age Publishing.

Clark, T. (2004). Management fashion as collective action: The production of management best-sellers. In A. F. Buono (Ed.), *Creative consulting: Innovative perspectives on management consulting* (pp. 3–25). Greenwich, CT: Information Age Publishing.

Clark, T., & Fincham, R. (2002). *Critical consulting: New perspectives on the management consulting industry.* Oxford, England: Blackwell Publishers.

Clark, T., & Salaman, G. (1996). The management guru as organizational witchdoctor. *Organization: The Interdisciplinary Journal of Organization, Theory and Society, 3*(1), 85–107.

Contino, C., & den Hond, F. (2009). Sense and sensibility in managerial advice. In A. F. Buono (Ed.), *Emerging trends and issues in management consulting: Consulting as a Janus-faced reality* (pp. 207–238). Charlotte, NC: Information Age Publishing.

Czarniawska-Joerges, B. (1988). *Att handla med ord [Merchants of Meaning].* Stockholm, Sweden: Carlssons.

Czerniawska, F. (2007). *The trusted firm: How consulting firms build successful client relationships.* Hoboken, NY: Wiley.

Davenport, T., & Prusak, L. (2009). Knowledge management in consulting. In L. Greiner & F. Poulfelt (Eds.), *Management consulting today and tomorrow: Perspectives and advice from 27 leading world experts.* New York, NY: Routledge.

Fineman, S. (1996). Emotions and organizing. In S. Clegg, C. Hardy & W. R. Nord (Eds.), *Handbook of organization studies.* London, England: Sage.

French, W. L., & Bell, C. H. (1973). *Organization development.* Englewood Cliffs, NJ: Prentice-Hall.

Goldman, A. (2009). Toxic downsizing inc.: Deconstructing a dysfunctional consultation. In A. F. Buono (Ed.), *Emerging trends and issues in management consulting: Consulting as a Janus-faced reality* (pp. 255–268). Charlotte, NC: Information Age Publishing.

Goleman, D. (2006). *Emotional intelligence: Why it can matter more than IQ.* New York, NY: Bantam.

Greenfield, W. M. (1987). *Successful management consulting.* Englewood Cliffs, NJ: Prentice Hall.

Greiner, L., & Metzger, R. O. (1983). *Consulting to management.* Englewood Cliffs, NJ: Prentice-Hall.

Greiner, L., & Poulfelt, F. (Eds.). (2009). *Management consulting today and tomorrow: Perspectives and advice from 27 leading world experts.* New York, NY: Routledge.

Guttmann, H. P. (1987). *The international consultant.* Washington, DC: Wiley & Sons.

Harris, M. E., & Wang, G. (2003). Building sustainable networks: An action research strategy for management consultants. In A. F. Buono (Ed.), *Enhancing interfirm networks and interorganizational strategies* (pp. 239–258). Greenwich, CT: Information Age Publishing.

Harrison, R. (1995). *Consultant's journey.* San Francisco, CA: Jossey-Bass.

Holtz, H. (1999). *The concise guide to becoming an independent consultant.* New York, NY: Wiley & Sons.

Johnsen, E. (1978). *Consulting roles.* Copenhagen, Denmark: FDC.

Kam, J. (2004). Selling professionalism? Image making in the management consulting industry. In A. F. Buono (Ed.), *Creative consulting: Innovative perspectives on management consulting* (pp. 51–72). Greenwich, CT: Information Age.

Kelley, R. E. (1981). *Consulting: The complete guide to a profitable career.* New York, NY: Charles Scribner's Sons.

Kennedy Information. (2011). *Consulting compensation data, trends, and strategies.* Peterborough, NH: Kennedy Consulting Research & Advisory.

Kipping, M., & Engwall, L. (Eds.). (2002). *Management consulting: Emergence and dynamics of a knowledge industry.* Oxford, England: Oxford University Press.

Kitay, J., & Wright, C. (2007). From prophets to profits: The occupational rhetoric of management consultants. *Human Relations, 60*(11), 1613–1640.

Kubr, M. (Ed.). (2005). *Management consulting: A guide to the profession.* Geneva, Switzerland: International Labour Office (ILO).

Lalonde, C. (2011). Challenging universal criteria in management consulting: When practices meet prescriptions. In A. F. Buono, R. Grossmann, H. Lobnig, & K. Mayer (Eds.), *The changing paradigm of consulting: Adjusting to the fast-paced world* (pp. 279–307). Charlotte, NC: Information Age Publishing.

Lippitt, R., & Lippitt, G. (1978). *The consulting process in action.* La Jolla, CA: University Associates.

Lundberg, C. C. (2010). Consulting processes for organization change: A belief system, situation centered, sensemaking perspective. In A. F. Buono & D. W. Jamieson (Eds.), *Consultation for organizational change* (pp. 209–232). Charlotte, NC: Information Age Publishing.

Lundberg, C. (2004). Toward an emotion nuanced sensemaking perspective of organizational consultation: Consulting as frame sharing and frame changing. In A. F. Buono (Ed.), *Creative consulting: Innovative perspectives on management consulting* (pp. 245–265). Greenwich, CT: Information Age Publishing.

Maister, D. H., Green, C. H., & Galford, R. M. (2001). *The trusted advisor.* New York, NY: Free Press.

Management Consultancies Association. (2010). *The value of consulting.* London: MCA

Margerison, C. J. (1988). *Managerial consulting skills.* New York, NY: Gower.

Metzger, R. O. (1989). *Profitable consulting: Guiding America's managers into the next century*. Reading, MA: Addison-Wesley.

Metzler, R., & Metzler, J. (2010). *The Wisdom of wizards: Insights from leading consultants*. New York, NY: Trove Publishing Company.

Micklethwait, J., & Wooldridge, A. (1996). *The witchdoctors: Making sense of the management gurus*. Portsmouth, NH: Heinemann.

Mills, T., Dukeov, I., & Fey, C. F. (2007). Russian competitiveness in the global economy. *Journal of East-West Business, 13*(4), 97–138.

Motomadi, K. (2009). Neurotic styles of management. In A. F. Buono (Ed.), *Emerging trends and issues in management consulting: Consulting as a Janus-faced reality* (pp. 241–253). Charlotte, NC: Information Age Publishing.

Nadler, D. (2009). Consulting to CEOs and boards. In L. Greiner & F. Poulfelt (Eds.), *Management consulting today and tomorrow: Perspectives and advice from 27 world experts* (pp. 199–225). New York, NY: Routledge.

Nevis, E. C. (1987). *Organizational consulting*. New York, NY: Gardner Press.

Ngayo, C. B. (2009). Organizational change management: When is a "best practice" not best for practice? In A. F. Buono (Ed.), *Emerging trends and issues in management consulting: Consulting as a Janus-faced reality* (pp. 141–170). Charlotte, NC: Information Age Publishing.

O'Shea, J., & Madigan, C. (1997). *Dangerous company: The consultancy powerhouses and the businesses they save and ruin*. New York, NY: Random House.

Poulfelt, F. (1999). Konsulentrollens anatomi [The anatomy of consulting]. *Nordiske Organisasjons Studier, 1*, 25–48.

Sahlin-Andersson, K., & Engwall, L. (Eds.). (2002). *The expansion of management knowledge: Carriers, flows and sources*. Stanford, CA: Stanford University Press.

Schaffer, R. H. (1997). *High impact consulting*. New York, NY: Prentice Hall.

Schein, E. H. (1969). *Process consultation: Its role in organizational development*. Reading, MA: Addison-Wesley.

Schein, E. H. (1997). The concept of 'client' from a process consultation perspective: A guide for change agents. *Journal of Organizational Change Management, 10*(3), 202–216.

Schein, E. H. (2009). *Helping: How to offer, give, and receive help*. San Francisco, CA: Berrett-Koehler Publishers.

Schwarz, M., & Clark, T. (2009). Clients' different moves in managing the client–consultant relationship. In A. F. Buono & F. Poulfelt (Eds.), *Client–consultant collaboration: Coping with complexity and change* (pp. 3–28). Charlotte, NC: Information Age Publishing.

Shapiro, E. (1997). Managing in the age of gurus. *Harvard Business Review*, (March-April), 142–147.

Solomon, A. L. (1997). Do consultants really add value to client firms? *Business Horizon*, (May-June), 67–72.

Stewart, M. (2009). *The management myth: Why the experts keep getting it wrong*. New York, NY: W. W. Norton & Company.

Sturdy, A. (1997). The consulting process: An insecure business. *Journal of Management Studies, 34*(3), 389–413.

Sturdy, A., Clark, T. Fincham, R., & Handley, K. (2008). Rethinking the role of management consultants as disseminators of business knowledge: Knowledge flows, directions, and conditions in consulting projects. In H. Scarbrough (Ed.), *The evolution of business knowledge* (pp. 239–258). Oxford, England: Oxford University Press.

Sturdy, A., Werr, A., & Buono, A. F. (2009). The client in management consultancy research: Mapping the territory. *Scandinavian Journal of Management, 25*(3), 247–252.

Tepper, R. (1985). *Become a top consultant.* New York, NY: Wiley & Sons.

Todorova, G. (2004). Exploring knowledge issues in the consulting relationship: A client-centered perspective. In A. F. Buono (Ed.), *Creative consulting: Innovative perspectives on management consulting* (pp. 73–98). Greenwich, CT: Information Age Publishing.

Turner, A. N. (1982). Consulting is more than giving advice. *Harvard Business Review, 60*(5), 120–129.

Uzzi, B. (1997). Social structure and competition in interfirm networks: The paradox of embeddedness. *Administrative Science Quarterly, 42*(1), 35–67.

Venard, B. (2001). Transforming consulting knowledge into business fads. In A. F. Buono (Ed.), *Current trends in management consulting* (pp. 171–188). Greenwich, CT: Information Age Publishing.

Walsh, K. (2001). The role of relational expertise in professional service delivery. In A. F. Buono (Ed.), *Current trends in management consulting* (pp. 23-42). Greenwich, CT: Information Age Publishing.

Weinberg, G. M. (1985). *The secrets of consulting.* New York, NY: Dorset House Publishing.

Weiss, A. (2001). *The ultimate consultant.* San Francisco, CA: Jossey-Bass/Pfeiffer.

Weiss, A. (2002). *How to acquire clients—Powerful techniques for the successful practitioner.* San Francisco, CA: Jossey-Bass/Pfeiffer.

Werr, A., & Styhre, A. (2003). Understanding the ambiguous consultant–client relationship. *International Studies of Management and Organizations, 32*, 43–66.

Williams, A., & Woodward, S. (1994). *The competitive consultant.* London, England: Palgrave.

Wolf, W. B. (1978). *Management and consulting: An introduction to James O. McKinsey.* Ithaca, NY: ILR.

CHAPTER 2

WHAT IS PROFESSIONAL COMPETENCE?

A Study of Assessment Criteria in Eight Professional Service Sectors

Annika Schilling and Andreas Werr

The nature of competence in professional services has been heavily debated for some time. The classical professions such as law and accounting as well as newer professions such as management consulting and advertising put strong emphasis on a formal and unique knowledge base in legitimizing their existence. In the established professions, this knowledge base, in combination with a code of ethics/conduct and criteria for certification testing this knowledge and values, are defining characteristics (Abbott, 1988; Alvesson, 2001; Jones, 2003). The well-defined knowledge base, as well as a defined education leading to it, serves as the grounds for protecting the profession, creating a monopolized labor market for professionals. This professional knowledge base is thus regarded as a prime regulator of professional practice. It has also been argued to be a foundation for professionals' identification, where loyalty to the profession, its mission, knowledge

Exploring the Professional Identity of Management Consultants, pages 17–49
Copyright © 2013 by Information Age Publishing
All rights of reproduction in any form reserved.

base, and clients are assumed stronger than loyalty to a specific employing organization (Løwendahl, 2005). While management consulting, as one of the more recent professions, lacks several of the protecting characteristics of a formal knowledge base, it mimics the classical professions in legitimating its existence on the basis of specific and unique knowledge and expertise (Alvesson, 2001; McKenna, 2006; Morris & Empson, 1998).

Such a focus on the formal knowledge base as both a regulator of practice and a source of identification has, however, been questioned for some time. Research on how professionals form their actions (e.g., Schön, 1983) and what kind of "knowledge" is developed, enacted, and valued in professional service firms (e.g., Alvesson, 2001) gives reason to question the predominant importance of the formal knowledge base in understanding professional work. Instead, aspects such as rhetorical skills, adaptability, flexibility, and social skills have been highlighted as key to understanding action and success in the performance of professional services. Also in relation to identification, the role of the profession and its formal knowledge base has been questioned. Research has argued for a gradual replacement of professional values and norms by a more commercial orientation among professionals and professional service firms. A focus on applying the best available knowledge to each problem is replaced by a focus on staff utilization and profitability (see, for example, Cooper, Hinings, Greenwood, & Brown, 1996).

That professional competence goes beyond a formalized knowledge base is thus well established. Numerous key skills and attitudes have been suggested in addition to formal knowledge, such as communication skills, social skills, personal drive, and so forth (see the discussion in the next section). Most previous discussions of professional knowledge have, however, neglected the variations among different kinds of professional services. Studies have focused on specific professions, and their findings have been presented as generally valid for all kinds of professional services. Similarities have been emphasized over differences.

Although the importance of impression management over formalized knowledge is often motivated by specific aspects of professional services (in contrast to other kinds of services and products), such as their intangibility and their lacking standardization (Clark, 1995), variations along these dimensions within professional services are seldom discussed. However, professional services are by no means a homogeneous category in terms of intangibility, standardization, delimitation, and "technicality" of the knowledge base (see Von Nordenflycht, 2010). A technical consulting service resulting in a construction that works—or doesn't work—may be argued to be something different in terms of competence enacted than a management consulting service producing a new strategy, the quality and success of which is much more difficult to assess. Still, previous research argues for a homogeneous treatment:

> Where knowledge-intensity is central, so is ambiguity and, contingent upon this ambiguity, issues of image, rhetoric, orchestrating social relations and processes. (Alvesson, 2001, p. 876)

While we agree with this statement on an aggregate level, we can also see that professional services vary on knowledge intensity and ambiguity as well as other potentially important dimensions. Against this background the current chapter aims at elaborating the notion of professional competence by investigating constructions of professional competence in different kinds of professional services. More specifically, we focus on the nature of competence that is sought for and promoted by Professional Service Firms (PSFs) in different service industries.

This guiding question is investigated through an interview-based study focusing on assessment criteria in recruitment in 23 organizations in eight different service industries in Sweden. We assume that these criteria are valid reflections of central competence within these industries as they regulate the entrance to practice at the same time as they are central in shaping subjectivities and normalized practices within the respective firms and industries (Alvesson, 2001; Alvesson & Kärreman, 2007; Covaleski, Dirsmith, Heian, & Samuel, 1998).

The chapter proceeds as follows. The next section reviews the literature on competence in professional services, discussing key knowledge, skills, and attitudes identified in previous research. This section is followed by a description of the methodology underlying the current study. The chapter then turns to the empirical findings on different competence constructions in different professional service industries. The competence constructions in the different industries are compared in the "discussion" section. Main findings are summarized and conclusions drawn in the final section of the chapter.

CONCEPTIONS OF PROFESSIONAL COMPETENCE IN THE LITERATURE

Investigations into the nature of competence in professional services have been focused on a rather limited number of professions, especially management consulting (e.g., Alvesson, 1995; Clark, 1995) and accounting (Covaleski, Dirsmith, Heian & Samuel, 1998; Grey, 1998). These studies identify a number of different knowledge bases, skills, and attitudes as central drivers of success in their respective professions.

Knowledge

A formal knowledge base is a defining characteristic of professions and professional services (Abbott, 1988; Løwendahl, 2005), and it is acknowledged as an important foundation of professional practice. The formal knowledge base may, however, be more or less well defined and protected. Law and accounting are examples of services with more well-defined knowledge bases, linked to a specific (academic) education and a certification procedure ensuring possession of this knowledge base by professionals. Management and communication consulting are examples of professions with a less well defined knowledge base. The educational background of management consultants varies widely, and the group may include psychologists, medical doctors, priests, literature majors, and so forth. In between these extremes of the classical, regulated profession and the more loosely knit management and communication consultants, we also find technical consulting and architecture, in which practice is generally linked to a specific academic educational background, but without a legal requirement.

While the existence of a formal knowledge base is acknowledged, its role as the key basis for professional practice has been questioned (Alvesson, 1993, 2001; Schön, 1983). Rather, formal professional knowledge is depicted as one of several resources professionals may apply in their work, either in problem solving or in impression management in relation to a client. Schön (1983) highlights the role of formal knowledge as a resource in problem solving, providing a "language from which to construct particular descriptions and themes from which to develop particular interpretations" (p. 273). Formal knowledge provides concepts and relations that help represent, make sense of, and communicate about complex realities as a basis for dealing with them (Schön, 1983; Werr, 1999).

The formal knowledge base of professionals has also been attributed a role in establishing and maintaining the credibility and elite status of professionals. Given the lack of tangible proof of competence in many professions, claims of formal knowledge in the form of education and background become important proxies of competence, especially if they are backed up by a certification system like in law and accounting (Alvesson, 2004; Armbrüster, 2006). Formal knowledge may also be represented by methods and tools that can be used to signal competence to clients (Bloomfield & Danieli, 1995; Jones, 2003; Sturdy, 1997; Werr, Stjernberg, & Docherty, 1997). Common to these characterizations of formal knowledge in the performance of professional services is their secondary position in driving success of professionals. It is not the formal, professional knowledge as such that makes the (successful) professional, but rather its skillful application in problem solving or persuasion.

Skills

While downplaying the role of formal professional knowledge, conceptualizations of professional competence have highlighted the importance of skills in professional performance. When it comes to problem solving, Schön (1983) highlights the practitioner's ability to reflect in action and bring together an understanding of the problem situation with formal knowledge and previous experiences. What is in focus is the professional's ability to creatively adapt to new situations and apply existing knowledge (both formal and experience based) in creative and flexible ways (Jones, 2003; Visscher, 2006, p. 258). This highlights the importance of the professional's previous experiences (rather than the profession's formal knowledge base) as an important foundation of professional practice.

Professional practice is seldom an individualistic endeavor, but in many cases involves interaction with both colleagues and a client. As argued by Hargadon (1998), knowledge in consulting is created through a skillful integration of one's own knowledge and experience with that of others', such as the knowledge and experience of colleagues and clients (see also Hicks, Nair, & Wilderom, 2009; Morris & Empson, 1998). Against this background, "social skills," which are highlighted by previous research (Alvesson, 2004; Armbrüster, 2006; Hicks et al., 2009), enable interaction and knowledge creation as well as the clients' impression of value. Given the intangibility of management consulting services, the ability to orchestrate the social interaction process is defined as a key skill (Alvesson, 2001). Given the lack of tangible evidence of professional competence, value is claimed to be assessed based on subjective impressions created in the interaction process. If the interaction feels good, value is assumed to be created (Clark, 1995).

The probably most commonly mentioned skills in previous research on professional competence are communication, rhetoric, and persuasion skills (Alvesson, 2001; Berglund & Werr, 2000; Bloomfield & Danieli, 1995; Czarniawska, 1990). Given the difficulties to assess the quality and value of professional services in advance, and in the case of, for example, management and communication consulting services also after delivery, the professionals' ability to create impressions of value is highlighted as central. Creating this impression of value involves two key aspects. The first concerns creating and maintaining the need for the service, answering the question why, for example, management needs external help from management consultants rather than dealing with the problem themselves. The second aspect involves creating and maintaining trust in a specific professional and his or her competence. Both these aspects are rhetorical accomplishments in most professional services, involving communication, persuasion, and social skills (Furusten & Werr, 2005).

Attitudes

Beyond knowledge and skills, professionalism has been attributed to certain values and attitudes. Traditional professional values include vocation, altruistic service to the client, loyalty to the profession and its mission, self-regulation, and civility (Løwendahl, 2005). It is, however, argued that these values are increasingly replaced with, or at least complemented by, other more commercially oriented values such as punctuality, style, dynamism, business-mindedness, and entrepreneurialism that instead of the public good focus on "business," based on responding to the needs of a specific client, thus questioning the existence of specific, unique values in professional services (Alvesson, 2004). This claimed shift in professional attitudes is reflected in the central skills identified above, where the persuasion and social skills geared at creating the client's need and trust in professional services are founded on a more entrepreneurial and commercial professional logic (Cooper et al., 1996).

Although attitudes are identified as a key aspect of professional competence, studies provide relatively little insight into exactly what attitudes are ingrained in professional competence. Among those identified are a strong internal motivation (Alvesson, 2001) as well as self-confidence (Jones, 2003).

Identity/Subjectivity

Rather than focusing on isolated knowledge, skills, and attitudes, research has increasingly focused on professional identity/subjectivity as a key concept in understanding professional competence. Such a conceptualization of competence emphasizes the integrated nature of knowledge, skills and attitudes (Alvesson, 2004; Sandberg & Pinnington, 2009). Attitudes are an important element of this way of understanding competence, but they are complemented by an overall understanding of the task/role as well as the different aspects of performing it (see also Schön, 1983). Competence is not so much related to any specific knowledge, skill, or attitude but to the way these are integrated in the performance of professional work (Sandberg & Pinnington, 2009).

This perspective identifies certain specific behaviors that are attributed with professionalism in certain fields (Starbuck, 1992), such as "tightly disciplined, accountant like, clean, proper, impersonal, objective, standardized, predictable, reliable" and so forth in accounting (Covaleski et al., 1998). It also points at physical attributes such as dress and appearance as indicators of professional competence. In the advertising industry, for example, professionals are expected to be fashion conscious, wear casual but elegant clothes, and frequently change dress (Alvesson, 2001). In line with such a perspective on professional competence, Armbrüster (2006) argues that the selection procedure, based on case interviews, in the management consulting industry "is not a test of aptitude, skill or talent but, rather, of attitude, identity and subjectivity" (p. 188).

METHODOLOGY

To gain a broad understanding of the variations in competence construc-tions among different professional service sectors, our study targeted PSFs in Sweden offering professional services within eight different professional areas—advertising, architecture, auditing, communication consulting, IT consulting, law, management consulting and technical consulting. Within each of these professional service industries, one larger, one medium-sized and one smaller firm in terms of number of employees relative to the typi-cal firm's size within the industry were approached for interviews (except for in law where access only was gained to a large and a medium-sized firm). In this way we have attempted to capture variation both between and within different professional service sectors, since conceptualizations of compe-tence may vary also within the industries (see Alvesson, 2002).

Interviews were conducted with the person responsible for human re-source (HR) management in each of the firms. In the larger firms, these were often HR specialists, sometimes with a background in the respective profession. In the smaller firms, interviewees were typically the CEO or a professional with part-time HR responsibilities. All were actively involved in the recruitment process. In total, 23 interviews lasting between one and a half to two hours each were conducted. See Table 2.1 for a summary of the firms and interviewees included in the study.

The interviews focused on HR practices in general, including recruit-ment practices and processes as well as what kind of person is considered to fit in and able to be successful in the firm. The analysis is based on how the respondents conceptualized the competence of the professionals, mainly in response to the question "what do you look for in the candidate when you recruit?" The interviews were transcribed and thematically analyzed using the software tool NVivo. Competences emphasized were coded into nodes, which were inductively integrated into the three broader categories: (1) education, experience, and expert knowledge; (2) skills; and (3) attitudes and personal characteristics. These categories provide the foundation for the presentation of the empirical patterns below.

TABLE 2.1   Summary of Firms and Interviews Included in the Study

Professional Service Industry	Relative size of the firms[a]	Number of employees	Person interviewed/responsible for HRM
Advertising	Large	150	HR director
	Medium-sized	67	Founder and CEO
	Small	10	Consultant
Architecture	Large	300	HR director
	Medium-sized	50	CEO
	Small	30	CEO
Auditing	Large	2,000	HR director
	Medium-sized	250	HR director
	Small	20	Partner
Communication Consulting	Large	130	HR manager
	Medium-sized	80	HR and consultant manager
	Small	20	CEO
IT Consulting	Large	5,500	HR director
	Medium-sized	1,200	HR director
	Small	50	Partner and consultant manager
Law	Large	670	HR director
	Medium-sized	500	HR director
Management Consulting	Large	110	HR manager
	Medium-sized	25	Consultant manager
	Small	10	Consultant and CEO
Technical Consulting	Large	4,800	HR director
	Medium-sized	1,250	HR director
	Small	30	CEO

[a] Number of employees in the organizational unit the respondent was responsible for.

CONSTRUCTIONS OF PROFESSIONAL COMPETENCE IN PRACTICE

This section examines the patterns of emphasized recruitment criteria in eight different professional service industries in three dimensions of competence: education, experience and expert knowledge; skills; and attitudes and personal characteristics. The discussion begins with the classical professions (e.g., law, architecture), which have a rather clear knowledge base, and gradually moves on to the less regulated "new" professions such as management consulting, communication consulting, and public relations (PR) consulting.

Law

When talking about the need for *education, experience, and expert knowledge* in law firms, there are strict requirements. Most of the recruitments are targeted at selecting new professionals directly from law school. In both law firms included in the study it is stressed that the primary goal in recruitment is to attract and select "the best," both in knowledge and in character and potential. In order to select "the best" students, the law firms look mostly at the students' grades, since grades are considered to tell a lot about the individual's abilities and potential. Also, since the candidates often have little other experience, the firms have little else than grades to rely on in the first round of selection.

Besides the grades of the law students the law firms look at their *attitude and personal characteristics.* In the large law firm a list of preferred characteristics is given. Good grades are supposed to give a hint on the "ambition," "abilities," and "interests" of the candidates, important characteristics for being successful in the profession. Furthermore, they look at the personality of the candidates, if he or she will "like it here and fit in," what they "believe and see," "how they will handle being a consultant," and "maturity."

In the medium-sized firm they also look at personal characteristics in order to select "the best," those who are "ambitious" and "who want to work hard" and "who like to develop relationships with a lot of people." There is an underlying tension as pointed out by the HR director, who noted that the kind of person who would be considered to be "the best" is still debated among the partners of the firm. Until this point is agreed upon, the selection is based on the discretion of the partners involved in the recruitment process:

> And then it is, of course, what personal characteristics you should have and there, I must admit, we could do more. What are we looking for? Here we have 44 partners who think we should get "the best." But, what do we mean by "the best"? (Medium-sized law firm)

Technical Consulting

In the technical consulting firms in the sample, most of the emphasis was put on criteria around *education, experience, and expert knowledge.* Mostly the candidates are engineers, but with different engineering specializations depending on the department within the firm for which they were recruited. Overall, the recruitment process tended to be decentralized in this industry, meaning it is up to the local manager to make decisions on what is important in candidates and who to recruit. Therefore the HR directors in the two larger firms stated that they could not exemplify the criteria used in recruitment more than that they are looking for "the best people" and "the most knowledgeable." The dream candidate is described as someone with experience, who "has a good CV," and who is relatively self-reliant because of his or her previous experience. Experience could come either from having worked as an engineer or manager within industry, or as a consultant, as long as you have acquired good knowledge of the technology you are specializing in and about the situation and needs of the clients:

> It's what you know. Experience and what you know. That is what they look at. When it comes to engineers we don't go so deep into the individuals' social abilities but focus mainly on the knowledge. We don't care if the person is white or black, a woman or a man, short or tall, but it's the knowledge we look at. Knowledge and experience. That you have a specific degree, what you have worked with until now. (Medium-sized technical consulting firm)

Some specific *skills* were mentioned as important, specifically relating to the ability to act as a consultant, "helping clients," having a "focus on the client," and gaining the trust of the client:

> Of particular importance is to have the ability to focus on the client. This means individuals who can get the client to feel heard, that you can see the need of the client and listen and then deliver. Often the clients want to get answers quickly on complex questions, so an ability to provide that, without hesitating and questioning yourself, is an important characteristic. (Small technical consulting firm)

Less is said about the need for the right *attitude and personal characteristics* of the candidates. In the small technical consulting firm, the ability to learn from one's experience is emphasized. The CEO mentioned how he asks candidates to mention three things they could have done better in previous projects. If they can't mention anything they will not be considered for the job. In the large firm, the respondents noted that it was important that the people you hire fit into the work group and would get along with their colleagues.

Architecture

In the architecture firms, although the respondents did not focus on needed *education, experience, and expert knowledge,* having a degree in architecture or other relevant technical field was described as a requirement. At times, the architecture firms rely on recommendations from their network at the architecture schools to find promising and talented new hires. It was mentioned in all three firms that they looked at previous experience as well, whether it was for a more senior hire or a hire directly from architecture school. Judgment of the candidates is partly done by looking at their work portfolios, for example, samples of projects they have undertaken either at school or if they have worked for another firm previously. Focus was also placed on whether they had been involved with what were seen as "interesting projects." Previous work was viewed as an indicator of the potential of the candidates as described below:

> You need to feel that there is a potential that is a little different. Partly you see that in their portfolio; if they have a drawing in front of them you can make a judgment of the project and if it looks professional or if it looks a bit sloppy. (Medium-sized architecture firm)

However, having the right educational background and knowledge is described as merely a prerequisite for a hire, while "getting a feel for the human" is what provides the basis for the final selection.

Some *skills* mentioned as important in the small architecture firm are to be able to balance the aesthetic, technical, and human aspects of architecture. It is further described as an important skill to be able to "acquire new knowledge and competence" and to turn this into the best value for the client.

Emphasis was also placed on the *attitude and personal characteristics* of the candidates. As one of the respondents noted, "having an eye on the person" was important. Particularly in the large firm, the need to balance the knowledge perspective with the human perspective in the recruitment process was emphasized. It was important that the candidates have not "forgotten themselves as humans" when writing the application letter. It was further described as important to try to select individuals who have a good and relatively accurate self-image and who can take feedback well. Based on some of their own bad experiences, they stressed that they try to avoid hiring people with a skewed self-image.

In the medium-sized firm, reliance was put on recommendations of candidates from others in the industry, for example, teachers at architecture school. The architecture industry, particularly in Stockholm, is quite small and everyone knows each other, so it is not hard to have a sense of what competence is out there. They are particularly looking for persons who are "curious," "alert," and "interested." A good candidate was described as someone who one feels has a "potential to be a little different."

In the small architecture firm, they have an eye out for "somewhat odd people" as an extra flavor, if the quality in the work is also there. As the CEO of the firm remarked, however, "eccentrics" may be expensive. Furthermore, it was emphasized that a good architect should be able to balance the architectural and artistic values against the needs and wants of the clients:

> We are not artists who work for ourselves but artists who work for others. At least some of us are artists. But we work for others in assignments. We don't design a house and then sell it. We are more like advisors. (Small architecture firm)

It is interesting to note that in all three architecture firms some kind of reference was made to the feeling one gets of the candidates in the recruitment situation. This implies more vague criteria, which seem to be hard to put into words. The CEO of the medium-sized firm, for example, talked about how her long experience of recruiting people has enabled her to rely on "the feeling." In the small firm, the CEO further emphasized that "the personal chemistry" with the candidates was important, a good indicator that the person would fit in and won't be "dull." In the large firm, the HR director talked about how his long experience has made him "trust his gut feeling" about people when deciding if a candidate was right for the company.

Auditing

In relation to *education, experience, and expert knowledge* in auditing, a common practice is to recruit candidates directly from the business schools. The educational requirements are strict and regulated by the audit association. The candidates must have a master's degree in business with a specialization in accounting in order to eventually take the exam to become a licensed auditor. The auditing firms' internal training courses for junior auditors take up where the business school ends. Because of these strict requirements, recruitment is described as "quite simple." Some reference was made to the grades of the newly graduated students. In the medium-sized firm, they wanted the candidates to have "good enough" grades but they "need not be the best" since just because "you are successful in school doesn't automatically mean that you will be successful at work."

When it comes to *skills,* all three auditing firms mentioned good social skills and that candidates could "easily communicate" as important criteria. The social skills are needed in the interaction with the clients, where it is important to be able to explain difficult things. It's important to be able to "develop the cooperation with the client" and that the client doesn't feel that they are audited but that the auditors are there to help them improve. This dynamic is important in order to get the client to share the right information with the auditors. Therefore it was also important that the auditor is someone the client gets along well with and enjoys the company of:

We look at social skills since it's according to us the most important thing. Even if knowledge is important, the personality is important. The only way we can make sure to keep the client is to get a feel for the person that you get along well together and like to work with him or her. It makes no difference how competent and knowledgeable this person is if you don't like the company of him or her. (Medium-sized auditing firm)

The representatives from the three auditing firms also mentioned a number of *attitudes and personal characteristics* they value in candidates. In the large auditing firm, "drive" and "brilliance" were described as something they look for specifically. Brilliance, logic and analytical and verbal ability are also something they test, particularly with the younger recruits. In the small auditing firm, they were looking for candidates who are "analytical" and "thorough," but "not too thorough" since they also need to get the work done quickly. The auditors were seen as needing to balance thoroughness and efficiency in a "wise way," something that also requires good judgment:

At the same time you should not be too thorough either. It's a balancing act. You must not spend your time on small errors because if you do you go in the wrong direction. Instead you need to be able to let go a little. (Small auditing firm)

In the medium-sized firm it was emphasized that they do not have a particular personal profile in mind when they are recruiting, but instead are looking for professionals who complement the others. The respondent also noted that the firm needs people with different kinds of personalities, since the clients have quite diverse personalities.

IT Consulting

Concerning *education, experience, and expert knowledge,* the need for a specific educational background or experience was only mentioned in the small IT consulting firm. Since the company specializes in IT solutions in banking and insurance, the typical background of hired candidates is to have a degree in information systems management and to have extensive experience either in a bank or in an insurance company or as a consultant in these industries. However, it was stated that it is just as important to look at the person as at their technical competence.

In the medium-sized IT consulting firm, the HR director stressed that they are increasingly starting to prioritize sector knowledge over IT competence. The basic premise is that with the right attitude IT can be learned; however, experience from the world of the client takes time to develop:

> If you have the right mindset you will also be able to understand this IT thing, you can understand and apply IT well in order to improve the processes. IT in itself is not that interesting any more for our clients. Instead it's this combination. (Medium-sized IT consulting firm)

Interestingly, not a lot of specific *skills* were explicitly mentioned. The importance of social skills, as indicated both in the medium-sized and small IT consulting firm, was reinforced but not developed further.

Finding professionals with the right *attitude and personal characteristics* was noted as important in all three IT consulting firms. Some of the personal characteristics the recruiters were looking for in the medium-sized IT consulting firm were "drive," to be "proactive and not reactive," someone who "can cooperate" and who has the ability to think analytically and logically. The candidates undergo in-depth interviews with a psychologist alongside tests of their analytical and logical abilities. One of the characteristics that was also stressed was the ability to easily learn new things, something needed in the consulting role. As the HR director explained:

> When we recruit it is not only a certain type of competence we are looking for. Instead we say that 50 per cent is attitude and personal characteristics. We find that this is at least as important. If you learn easily you can always learn new things, and this you need to be able to do in the role of a consultant. But to change the attitude, that is harder. (Medium-sized IT consulting firm)

Having the right attitude is important, and it's a balancing act to find people who are both ambitious with an internal drive and who "can cooperate":

> It is really important that you can cooperate, that you put the team or the project as a first priority, before your own results. Sometimes this is in conflict with having a lot of very ambitious people, because they want to shine. But in order to do a good job in the role of a consultant we believe that, first of all, it is the client who should shine and second it is the result of the project which is most important. It's important and something we test. So, there could be potential colleagues who are really competent in a specific area but who have the wrong attitude. In that case we cannot hire that person. (Medium-sized IT consulting firm)

The small IT consulting firm also used an external psychologist who creates a personality profile of the candidates. Particularly, the psychologist looks at how well the candidates can handle different kinds of situations, how they handle themselves in a leadership situation, how they handle stress, and if they will be able to work autonomously in the assignments. In the small firm, they were looking for people with "social competence" and "business mindedness." Such a person was described as someone who "spreads enthusiasm," is "receptive to change," and "wants to move forward." However, the feeling the recruiter gets about the candidate was also said to be a guide for the final recruitment decision. In essence, how well the candidate does in the interview situation was seen as mirroring how well he or she will be able to gain the trust of a client.

In the large IT consulting firm, the recruitment process and decisions were decentralized to the middle managers who were in need of adding new competence in their areas. Thus, there weren't any explicit checklists for what the managers should look at, only a general request to consider that the candidate should fit into the whole company, not only the particular work group of the recruiting manager.

Management Consulting

Education and previous experience were emphasized as important in two of the management consulting firms. In the large firm, "academic merit" in terms of good grades was seen as important since they are viewed as an indicator of "analytical ability," "ambition," and the "desire to perform well." Yet despite this focus, the academic field in which such merit was achieved was not specified.

In the small management consulting firm, where all consultants were hired on a senior level, everyone in the company holds an academic degree, some even with a PhD. However, the academic disciplines varied widely, from political science, information systems management, and business management to psychology and behavioral science. Behavioral science was mentioned as the most common academic background. Having academic experience was said to be important since "it's a foundation to stand on" and it shows that you can "take on theories and literature."

When it comes to experience in general, the large firm looked at, as they put it, "the CV of the candidates," focusing on what they have done. Particularly, it was stressed that it was important for candidates coming directly from a university to have combined their studies with other kinds of experience while at school. In the small firm, they reported that they only hire people with at least five years of relevant work experience. It was a merit to either have worked as a manager at the operational level of some company or as a consultant elsewhere.

Among the *skills* mentioned as important in the small management consulting firm were having previous work experience, the ability to act as consultants, be successful in selling assignments, and conducting the business itself. Given the small size of the firm, it was also seen as critical that newcomers be able to contribute to the development of the company internally, as well as their own professional development and that of their colleagues.

Attitude and personal characteristics were described as important in all three management consulting firms, and the tendency is that they list a lot of preferred characteristics. In the small firm they are looking for people who have a stable and well developed self-image. They also need to be "autonomous," "put quality first" in the services they deliver, and "be good at helping others." Other characteristics mentioned as important were to be: "a good communicator," "interested," "curious," "playful," and "brave." The new person was expected to "bring something to the group."

In the medium-sized firm, they underscored that they were looking for people who were: "hungry for knowledge," "hungry to do a good job," "not someone you feel you need to delegate tasks to all the time," "proactive in selling themselves," "eager to be a project leader," and "eager to take initiatives." The firm was also looking for candidates that had "drive," "social competence," and "some kind of empathy," as well as a sense of curiosity." Given case exercises as part of the recruitment process, candidates were also tested on how "smart" they were and if they had the "analytical ability to solve logical problems." This practice was also described as a test to see if the candidates could "reason themselves to what is interesting." In the large firm, it was also briefly mentioned that it is important that the person fits into the culture of the firm, which was said to be "very unpretentious with a high ceiling."

In both the large- and medium-sized firms, references were made to what happens in the relationship between the interviewer and candidate in the recruitment process. According to the representative of the medium-sized firm, an important factor when making recruitment decisions is "whether you get a good feeling":

> And then you have this aspect which is about if it's a nice guy or girl. Again, if you feel this is someone you can sit and have a beer with or sit and talk to on an airplane when we travel for six hours. The classic question to ask—is this a guy or a girl I'd want to play a round of golf with? (Medium-sized management consulting firm)

Advertising

Not a lot of emphasis was placed on *education, previous experience, or expert knowledge* in any of the three advertising firms. Requirements for educational background were mentioned but not specified in the smaller advertising firm. They also noted that good grades were something they valued. Relevant previous experience, however, was mentioned in all three firms. In the large firm experience was seen as specifically relevant for more senior hires. The small and medium-sized firms, which claimed they restricted hiring of more senior professionals to those who could bring new knowledge and competence into the company, also put more emphasis on previous experience. It was described as too time consuming to hire candidates who need to be trained.

Some specific *skills* were mentioned as important in the large advertising firm, such as "being able to read the client" and "being a consultant," suggesting the importance of understanding client needs, the ability to adjust solutions as needed, and effectively arguing for solutions that were believed to be the "right ones":

> You should be able to read the client in an intelligent, wise, and warm way. You should dare to be a consultant, both when it comes to the problems of the clients but also when it comes to what the market needs, that is, in order to meet the client in different ways. You need to be a consultant, you need to be sensitive and dare to push the ideas you believe in. This we must have. (Large advertising firm)

Emphasis was also placed on selecting professionals with the "right attitude" and appropriate personal characteristics. It was stressed that it was important to find "the right person," independent of previous experience, based on the assumption that the right person can always be taught missing knowledge.

In the large advertising firm the ideal recruit was described as "down to earth," "humble" but also temperamental. As the HR director noted:

> People are welcome to scream and shout here. Nothing happens. We are Latinos in a way in this place. Stir the pot now and then and bang the doors and stir things up a bit. That is okay. (Large advertising firm)

The HR director also argued that, as an advertising professional, the right individual needs to be a person who "dares to show who you are" and "dares to show what you do," someone who is not afraid to make a fool of him or herself. It was stressed that the profession was no place for shy people or people who were afraid "to get out there," since this would not work in relation to clients with high demands and expectations. As the HR director for the large firm explained, "You must remember that this is life or death for the clients."

Other preferred characteristics mentioned in the large advertising firm were that candidates should be "adaptable" with the ability to potentially change their role in the company, that they were not "intrigue makers" who fake deliveries or do not do the homework about the client's wishes and needs. Desired applicants were seen as individuals who were "centered and stable," who "trusted themselves."

In the medium-sized advertising firm, "the personal attitude" of the candidates was emphasized as something they look at very closely. It was also more important to look at "whom than what," that is, to look more at the personal characteristics than prior experience. A specific aspect of the personal attitude mentioned as important was "how you function in the team."

Another aspect emphasized in the medium-sized firm was the balance between talent and experience relevant for the work with a specific client. Client relations are often long-term, but specific talent may also be used in other client projects.

In the small advertising firm the representative also talked about selecting the right person. It was important to be "smart" in business, be "fast in thought," and to "have a clue." Other characteristics that were valued were that the applicant was "driven and hungry" and "on," with the ability to "roll up your sleeves and work hard if needed" and to show "commitment." Against the background of some bad hiring experiences, the representative also spoke about the need to balance creativity with the ability to align professional creativity with the structure of the project. It was further emphasized that the cultural fit of the candidates was important in order to build the culture of the small firm. In the past, the company had turned down "really competent people" because they felt that they would not fit the culture.

Communication Consulting

When talking about the need for *education, experience, and expert knowledge,* there was a varied picture of whether previous experience was important when recruiting in communication consulting firms. In the smaller firm, previous experience was said not to be important at all. In the medium-sized firm, the HR director described the guidelines for recruitment as basically "hire for attitude, train for skills." In the larger firm, the CV with relevant previous experience was said to be very important. However, it was not primarily experience in communication consulting that was promoted, but rather experience in general, from junior politics or a summer job in journalism, to management consulting. Particular emphasis was placed on the type of experience that showed that the candidate had an interest in public debate, and that he or she was well read in public issues and politics, the latter of which was described as a merit.

Higher education was also emphasized in the large firm; however, the range of relevant academic fields was quite wide—from business and political science to engineering and law. Interestingly, an educational background within media and communication was described as less likely to lead to an employment offer. An active and proven interest and engagement in society and its development (as demonstrated by, for example, engagement in politics) was seen as more important than a theoretical understanding of communication.

In communication consulting one *skill* stood out as particularly important in all three firms—the ability to write well and fast. The CEO of the small communication consulting firm even mentioned that this ability was the primary thing he looks for in an application, that it is one of the main criteria he uses to select the candidates he will even consider inviting for an interview:

> I try to find out if this is a person who can write at all, for example. And I have done a judgment of that already based on the application letter, the e-mail and the CV. In nine cases out of ten they fall out already there. (Small communication consulting firm)

In the large communication consulting firm it was also emphasized that the professionals they recruited needed to have good general knowledge and good insight into politics and the business industry in Sweden. This latter area was something they also tested candidates on.

Also in the communication consulting firms there were some preferred *attitudes and personal characteristics* of the candidates. In the large firm the HR director noted that they were interested in "genuine people," who have "talent," are "smart and alert," "ambitious," and curious with a genuine interest in politics and public debate. Analytic ability, creativity, and the extent to which the person was seen as structured and a good planner were also tested in the interview process.

In the medium-sized firm they reported that they look for people who fit into the culture and who believe in the basic values of the firm. Having the right attitude was particularly stressed:

> We have a bigger problem if a person is really competent but doesn't want to be a part of the culture, doesn't want to be a team player and doesn't want to talk about ambassadors—see the big picture and sell other business areas—than if a person is less competent but has the right attitude. (Medium-sized communication consulting firm)

They also work with a personality profiling tool in order to get a better feel for the candidates. However, it was described as more useful in order to see how well the candidates know themselves and how well they can take feedback about themselves than to select individuals with a specific personality profile. They are looking for people who "are aware of how others perceive them" and who do not have "a wide gap between self-image and others' perception" of them. The HR director in the medium-sized firm also mentioned that the profession puts a high demand on "flexibility and "adaptability," and that you can "work with a lot of people."

The CEO of the small firm also mentioned how he needed to get "a feeling for how [the candidate] is as a person" during the interview. Emphasis is placed on finding people who have "drive," who "radiate energy" and can be "an energy source in relation to their colleagues," someone who is not likely to become "an energy taker." They also reported looking for someone who can "create trust," "a strong and warm person" who "radiates competence" and who is relatively open about his or her weaknesses. Therefore it is important that the candidates are also open about themselves in the interview situation and not appearing to try to "sell themselves" to the recruiter.

DISCUSSION

Drawing on the construction of competent professionals in the professional service companies discussed in the preceding section, it is apparent that there are similarities and differences across the industries. The following discussion examines these dynamics in greater detail.

Formal Knowledge: A Hygiene Factor

Formal knowledge in terms of a specific educational background or knowledge of specific theories, methods, approaches, and so forth was seldom mentioned as an important variable in recruiting. In those industries where a degree from a specific education is a formal prerequisite for practice (e.g., law, auditing), this expectation is only mentioned in passing. The grades obtained during education are described as a selection criterion in some industries (e.g., advertising, auditing, law, management consulting), but generally not as an indicator of knowledge obtained. Rather, grades are described as a proxy of the skills and attitudes of the candidates, such as ambition, the ability and willingness to learn and to work hard, and the ability to handle stress.

Overall, however, a formal knowledge base, acquired through an (academic) education is regarded as a basic requirement, but not particularly a selection criterion, as it is perceived as too generic to distinguish one candidate's competence and potential from others. In order to assess professional knowledge, other indicators are used. In some industries, such as advertising and architecture, work samples are viewed as important indicators of the knowledge the candidates possess. In others, emphasis is put on previous (work) experience as a way of assessing professional knowledge and the ability to apply such knowledge beyond an educational setting. Here, firms often seek specific knowledge, for example, being able to actively participate in public debate (communication consulting), having an understanding for a specific business sector/industry (IT consulting), or knowledge of the situation of the clients and of how they think and work (technical consulting).

The picture that emerges is that formal knowledge plays a rather limited role in the assessment of professional competence. The expectation that professionals have relevant academic education or work experience could be seen as more of a hygiene requirement. What is considered as "relevant" depends on the professional sector. In professions with a more well-defined knowledge base (e.g., law, auditing, architecture, technical consulting), relevant education background is rather well defined. In industries with a less clear-cut knowledge base (e.g., communication and management consulting), in contrast, what is considered relevant is broadly interpreted and may include a wide range of academic fields, which is in line with findings in previous research (Alvesson, 1993, 2001; Schön, 1983). In assessing the competence of professionals, organizations look for aspects beyond formal competence. Professional skills and attitudes are what are in focus here.

The Ambitious Team Player: Skills and Attitudes of the Generic Professional

In discussing the desired competence of a professional, respondents focused on the professionals' attitudes and to some extent their skills. As one of them emphasized, "Hire for attitude, train for skills." Taken together, the respondents produced a rather long list of different skills and attitudes considered necessary in their respective organizations and industries (see Table 2.2). However, the level of articulation of necessary skills and attitudes, as well as the specific skills and attitudes mentioned, differed across different professional sectors.

In terms of the extent to which necessary skills and attitudes are clearly elaborated, a pattern emerges that suggests the professional sectors with the least well-defined knowledge base produce the most elaborate and broadest conceptions of necessary skills and attitudes. Those sectors with a more well-defined knowledge base gave more sparse lists. Advertising, communication consulting, and management consulting all mentioned 6 or more (6 to 10) key skills, describing them with an elaborate list of over 17 keywords (17 to 27). The other sectors (architecture, auditing, IT consulting, law, technical consulting) mentioned both fewer skills (4) and described them with fewer keywords (12 or fewer; see Table 2.2). The latter sectors all have rather specific educational backgrounds. Only advertising, communication consulting, and management consulting are open to applicants from broad educational backgrounds. It thus seems that a lack of delimitation of the profession in terms of a well-defined formal knowledge base is compen-

TABLE 2.2 Skills and Attitudes Mentioned as Important in Recruitment in Different Professional Service Sectors

	Law	Technical Consulting	Architecture	Auditing	IT Consulting	Management Consulting	Advertising	Communication Consulting
Ambitious	• Ambitious • Wants to work hard	• Self-driven	• Curious • Alert • Interested • Takes on new knowledge and competence	• Driven	• Driven • Proactive • Not reactive • Wants to move forward	• Ambitious • Driven • Takes things on • Curious • Wants to perform well • Hungry for knowledge • Hungry to do a good job • Proactive • Takes own initiatives • Sells themselves	• Driven • Hungry • Rolls up one's sleeves • Works hard • Shows commitment	• Ambitious • Driven • Energetic • Energy giver
Team player	• Fits in • Can develop relations	• Fits into the group • Gets the client to feel heard • Gains client's trust	• Functions in a (the) team • Fits in	• Can cooperate with the client • Social competence	• Can cooperate • Fits in • Social competence	• Social competence • Empathy • Fit into the culture	• Ability to function on a team	• Team player • Social • Warm • Can work with people • Ability to create trust • Fits in
Analytical				• Analytical thinking	• Analytical, logical	• Analytical ability		• Analytical

(continued)

TABLE 2.2   Skills and Attitudes Mentioned as Important in Recruitment in Different Professional Service Sectors

	Law	Technical Consulting	Architecture	Auditing	IT Consulting	Management Consulting	Advertising	Communication Consulting
Smart			• Ability to learn	• Brilliance	• Ability to learn	• Smart	• Smart • Having a clue	
Self-confidence		• Ability to give quick answers without hesitating and questioning oneself			• Stand on your own two feet	• Stable perception of oneself	• Dare to enforce one's ideas • Dare to show who you are • Dare to show what you do • Trust oneself • Centered and stable in oneself • Not shy • Not afraid to be a go getter • No intrigue maker	• Strong • Radiates competence
Self-awareness	• Maturity	• Self-knowledge (be able to mention things one can do better)	• Not a skewed self-image • Receptive to feedback					• Aware of how other perceive them • Open with weaknesses

(continued)

TABLE 2.2 Skills and Attitudes Mentioned as Important in Recruitment in Different Professional Service Sectors

	Law	Technical Consulting	Architecture	Auditing	IT Consulting	Management Consulting	Advertising	Communication Consulting
Structured				• Thorough, but not too thorough			• Structured • Organized	• Structured • Good planner
Humble	• Unpretentious						• Humble • Down to earth	• Open with one's weaknesses • Dare to open up
Creative							• Creative • Does things that are different • Ability to come up with new things • Thinks in new ways	• Creative
Communicative				• Ease of communication • Verbal ability				• Write well • Stylistic ability

(continued)

TABLE 2.2 Skills and Attitudes Mentioned as Important in Recruitment in Different Professional Service Sectors

	Law	Technical Consulting	Architecture	Auditing	IT Consulting	Management Consulting	Advertising	Communication Consulting
Passionate					• Enthusiasm		• Loves the advertising assignment • Love what you do	
Flexible					• Propensity to change			• Flexible • Adaptable
Other			• Doesn't seem dull • Odd (if you can afford it)	• Someone you like the company of • Diversity of individuals		• Nice guy/girl		• Not a problem seeker, not problem oriented • A genuine person
Number of skills mentioned/ Categories of skills	6/4	6/4	11/5	10/7	12/7	17/6	26/8	25/11

sated by a more elaborate delimitation of the profession in terms of desired skills and attitudes of the professionals.

Overall, 12 different attitudes and skills were mentioned by the respondents: ambitious, team player, analytical, smart, self-confident, self-aware, structured, humble, creative, communicative, passionate, and flexible. Only two of these were mentioned in more than half of the sectors. "Ambitious" and "team player," in contrast, were mentioned in all the professional sectors studied. Four of the skills and attitudes were mentioned in half of the sectors: analytical, smart, self-confident, and self-aware. The rest of the skills/attitudes (being structured, humble, creative, communicative, passionate, flexible) were mentioned more sporadically and may thus be viewed as more industry specific (Table 2.2).

The wide proliferation of "ambitious" and "team player" across the different professional sectors (these two personal characteristics were also described most vividly) indicates the existence of a generic professional subjectivity that is sought for in all professional service sectors (and possibly beyond these). "Ambition" comprises an internal drive to perform, to take initiative, and to be proactive (rather than reactive). Within management consulting, this was described as follows:

> More generally you want to feel that the person is hungry for knowledge and hungry to do a good job so that you don't have to feel that this is a person you need to delegate tasks to all the time, else they do nothing. That they are proactive in selling themselves. (Management consulting)

"Ambition" is described as an enabler of hard work and long hours, which are sometimes necessary, but also as a way of ensuring that the professional contributes to the organization and its (economic) value creation. In an ambiguous, project-based work structure, where economic value is created by individuals charging their time to clients, the companies seek professionals who will take the initiative and responsibility of ensuring that most of their time will be billable to their clients.

The second characteristic sought among professionals in all sectors was a "team player" attitude. This referred to general "social skills" that enable collaboration both with colleagues and with the clients. Moreover, collaboration was also emphasized in relation to the need to build trust.

Being a team player also had a second meaning, which relates it to a specific firm through a focus on "fitting in." While this ability also entails general social skills, it also implies a more specific fit of the candidate with the central values and attitudes of a specific firm or even work-group, in other words, the ability to become a part of the social community:

> We don't hire anybody we think seems dull, because they should also fit in with who we are so that they can become a part of the group. (Architecture)

LEEDS METROPOLITAN UNIVERSITY LIBRARY

Taken together, these two skills/attitudes represent what may be described as the characteristics of the *generic professional.* What is noteworthy is that these skills/attitudes are far from those skills and attitudes that have been attributed to professionals in previous research, such as loyalty to the profession, altruistic service to the client, self-regulation, and civility (Cooper et al., 1996). In contrast to the previously portrayed subjectivity—an individualistic expert with strong needs for autonomy and a loyalty to the profession and the knowledge domain (Løwendahl, 2005)—the generic professional constructed across the different service sectors included here is a collaborating, hard-working, and self-motivated cog in the money-making machinery of the professional services firm. This finding is in line with the claimed reorientation of professional service firms from a focus on professional norms and values towards a more commercial orientation (Cooper et al., 1996).

Industry Specific Skills and Attitudes

Beyond "ambition" and "team worker," professional skills and attitudes were more local than global. Four additional skills/attitudes were mentioned in half of the sectors studied: analytical, smart, self-confident, and self-aware. Analytical skills entailed "the ability to draw conclusions—to solve a logical problem, or establish a reasoning that leads to a conclusion about what is good or bad" (Management Consulting). This skill/attitude is partly linked to "smartness," in three out of the four sectors in which analytical ability is mentioned, the respondents also mention smartness in terms of general aptitude, the ability to learn, or plainly "being smart." Both "analytical skills" and "smartness" are mentioned as criteria only in the "business service" industries (auditing, IT consulting, management consulting). In communication consulting only "analytical skills" was mentioned, and in advertising only "smart" was noted. Architecture, law, and technical consulting, being more "technical" professional sectors, did not mention either analytical skills or smartness, although there is no reason to believe that the tasks performed in these sectors are less analytical or require less smartness than the other industry sectors. Instead, the importance of these criteria in a subset of organizations may be understood in relation to their signaling effect in the labor market. All the organizations that emphasized either "analytical" or "smart" recruit heavily from business schools. Here analytical ability and "smartness" are highly valued skills defining the elite among students, and in order to be perceived as an attractive employer these central attitudes/skills need to be reproduced (see, for example, Armbrüster, 2006).

Together, "self-confidence" and "self-awareness" were mentioned as important in all but one industry (auditing) and only briefly in law. "Self-confidence" was mentioned in five industries and "self-awareness" in four. Only in technical consulting and communication consulting both of these characteristics were mentioned. "Self-confidence" and "self-awareness," as described by the interviewees, both reflect the candidate's relation to him or herself. "Self-confidence" is more externally directed, also including how a person presents her or himself to others, both within and outside of the company. A self-confident person is described as someone who "radiates competence" and who can "give quick answers without hesitating." "Self-confidence" is thus conceptualized as the result of a person having a solid knowledge base and being able to show and act upon that knowledge. It is also noteworthy that "self-confidence" is emphasized as important in those industries (advertising, communication consulting, management consulting, IT-consulting, technical consulting) that are not among the classic professions. A possible interpretation of this pattern is that the lack of clear definitions of the knowledge base and professional norms needs to be compensated for by professionals who are self-confident and can act in ways that suggest they have a solid knowledge base for their advice.

"Self-awareness," as opposed to self-confidence, is internally directed and often given to mean that "you need to be aware of your weaknesses" and able to take feedback both from clients and from colleagues. Self-awareness is thus also connected to the need to be a "team player," in other words, to get along with others and not get offended by criticism. Self-awareness was mostly mentioned in the more established professions with, for example, architecture firms stressing that professionals should "not have a skewed self-image" and law firms stressing the need for "mature" individuals. In these instances, the well-defined and structured knowledge base may create grounds for highly specialized and technical expert subjectivity, making individuals insensitive to the feedback of others.

Additional skills/attitudes are "structured," "creative," "communicative," "passionate," and "flexible," which are mentioned in one to three sectors. The limited mentioning of aspects such as "communicative" and "flexible" is noteworthy, as communication skills have especially been pointed out as a key competence in professional services (Alvesson, 2001; Clark, 1995).

Professional Competence: A Balancing Act

When looking closer at the emphasized personal attitudes and skills in the different sectors, a pattern of paradoxes and contradictions among different skills/attitudes emerges. Three key tensions can be identified: between being ambitious versus being a team player, between being self-confident versus being humble, and between being well-structured versus being creative. These aspects of competence are generally mentioned together, and the tension between them is typically acknowledged among the respondents.

A first tension is constructed between personal drive and ambition and team work. A strong personal drive is argued to not necessarily be compatible with team work and a team spirit, as personal ambition may get in the way of collaboration both in internal work and in work with the client:

> We are a bunch of stars here, but we also need to function as a team when we are out there to do a job and meet the client. (Advertising)

A second tension is that between self-confidence, an ability to act confidently and convincingly in a complex and ambiguous world, and being humble, open to external input, others' opinions, and learning based on these outside factors:

> You must be a consultant, you must be perceptive and dare to push the ideas you believe in. (Advertising)

> Does the person radiate competence? And is the person still open enough with his or her weaknesses? (Communication consulting)

A third tension is that between order and structure on the one hand and creativity and chaos on the other hand. Again, these two aspects are presented as in need of balancing:

> You cannot be a creative genius and totally unstructured. (Advertising)

> At the same time you should not be too thorough either. It's a balancing act. You must not spend your time on small errors because if you do you go in the wrong direction. Instead you need to be able to let go a little. (Auditing)

These comments suggest that professional competence may go beyond possessing some defined set of knowledge, skills and attitudes but that it also—and maybe most importantly—entails the ability to enact these knowledge, skills and attitudes in a productive way in the specific situation. Such more dynamic and situated conceptualizations of professional competence are, however, mainly lacking among the interviewees in this study. The current study thus indicates that conceptualizations of professional competence reproduce a rater technical objectivist approach to knowledge (Schön, 1983), which is in line with how knowledge is constructed in the classical professions—as something that is well defined and may serve as the basis for regulating entry to the profession. Skills and attitudes seem to have replaced formal knowledge as the key aspects of professional competence—even if they are treated in the same objectivist way as formal knowledge.

CONCLUSIONS

This chapter examined the nature of professional competence in professional services firms as constructed by professionals in relation to recruitment. While previous studies have assumed large similarities between different professional service sectors in terms of key competencies, the current study focused on a comparison of constructions of competence in eight professional service sectors. Based on the findings, a number of conclusions can be drawn.

First, the kind of formal competence highlighted as a defining characteristic of the professions is found to be of limited importance in the overall assessment of professional competence. It is mentioned as a hygiene factor, but not as a factor predicting success in the performance of professional services. This observation is in line with previous research that has underlined the limitations of formal professional knowledge as a basis for professional performance (e.g., Alvesson, 2001; Schön, 1983).

Second, instead of formal competence, specific skills and attitudes are found to be key aspects of professional competence. This is true in all professional sectors studied, but our findings indicate that the image of necessary skills and attitudes for successful professional performance was more elaborate and multifaceted in sectors such as advertising and communication consulting, in which the formal knowledge base was more unclear and which attracted employees with a broad range of educational backgrounds.

Third, a number of different key skills/attitudes were identified; however, only two of these emerged across all the professional service sectors, indicating the existence of a generic professional service subjectivity sought by these firms. This subjectivity may be summarized as "an ambitious team worker," with both a strong drive, directing large amounts of energy towards the fulfillment of organizational (rather than professional) goals, and an ability and willingness to do so in interaction with colleagues and representatives of the client organization. These two key skills/attitudes are in stark contrast with classical professional values, including commitment to the profession as well as strong needs for autonomy (Løwendahl, 2005). They are more in line with a commercial professional orientation that has been argued to be emerging across several professional fields for some time (Cooper et al., 1996). The identification of "ambition" and a "team worker" mindset as the key skills/attitudes in professional work contribute to the literature, as they have only been identified to a limited extent in previous research (e.g., Alvesson, 2001). The skill most often mentioned in previous research concerns communication and persuasion skills. These are, however, found only in a small subset of the professional service sectors studied here.

Finally, the current study points at the prevalence of "balancing acts" in the promotion of professional competence. While our study identifies a number of key attitudes and skills, it is also striking that respondents highlight not only the availability of these skills/attitudes but also the need and ability to balance opposing skills and attitudes, such as individual ambition and teamwork or creativity and structure. This observation is in line with a more "knowing" based understanding of professional competence, which has been acknowledged in research for some time (cf. Hicks et al., 2009; Sandberg & Pinnington, 2009; Schön, 1983). However, conceptualizations of professional competence in professional service firms seem to maintain a more technical and objectivist conceptualization of professional knowledge.

There are, of course, some limitations of the current study that should be pointed out. The current findings are based on interviews regarding assessment criteria in recruitment situations. While this information provides a good overview of the professional competence needed to enter the organization, and thus the overall competencies needed to succeed as a professional, other competence assessments, for example, in relation to promotion or compensation decisions, may point to additional aspects of professional competence. Future studies may thus focus on competence assessment and the criteria used in situations other than recruitment. Furthermore, the focus on interviews in the current study may confine the findings to explicit and official criteria used in judging professional competence. A closer, observation based study of recruitment situations may reveal additional selection criteria as well as provide additional insights into the nature and judgment of the criteria identified in this chapter.

REFERENCES

Abbott, A. (1988). *The system of professions.* Chicago, IL: University of Chicago Press.

Alvesson, M. (1993). Organizations as rhetoric: Knowledge-intensive firms and the struggle with ambiguity. *Journal of Management Studies, 30*(6), 997–1015.

Alvesson, M. (1995). *Management of knowledge intensive companies* (D. Canter, Trans.). Berlin, Germany: de Gruyter.

Alvesson, M. (2001). Knowledge work: Ambiguity, image and identity. *Human Relations, 54*(7), 863–886.

Alvesson, M. (2002). 'Up-or-out' versus 'fun-and-profit': A study of personnel concepts and HR themes in two IT/management consulting firms. Institute of Economic Research Working Paper Series, University of Lund.

Alvesson, M. (2004). *Knowledge work and knowledge-intensive firms.* Oxford, England: Oxford University Press.

Alvesson, M. & Kärreman, D. (2007). Unraveling HRM: Identity, ceremony and control in a management consulting firm. *Organization Science, 18*(4), 711–723.

Armbrüster, T. (2006). *The economics and sociology of management consulting.* Cambridge, England: Cambridge University Press.

Berglund, J. & Werr, A. (2000). The invincible character of management consulting rhetorics. *Organization, 7*(4), 633–655.

Bloomfield, B. P. & Danieli, A. (1995). The role of management consultants in the development of information technology: The indissoluble nature of socio-political and technical skills. *Journal of Management Studies, 32*(1), 23–46.

Clark, T. (1995). *Managing consultants.* Buckingham, England: Open University Press.

Cooper, D. J., Hinings, B., Greenwood, R., & Brown, J. L. (1996). Sedimentation and transformation in organization change: The case of Canadian law firms. *Organization Studies, 17*(4), 623–647.

Covaleski, M. A., Dirsmith, M. W., Heian, J. B., & Samuel, S. (1998). The calculated and the avowed: Techniques of discipline and struggles over identity in big six public accounting firms. *Administrative Science Quarterly, 43*(2), 293–328.

Czarniawska, B. (1990). Merchants of meaning: Management consulting in the Swedish public sector. In B. A. Turner (Ed.), *Organizational Symbolism* (pp. 139–150). Berlin, Germany: Walter de Gruyter.

Furusten, S. & Werr, A. (Eds.). (2005). *Dealing with confidence: The construction of need and trust in management advisory services.* Copenhagen, Denmark: Copenhagen Business School Press.

Grey, C. (1998). On being a professional in a 'big six' firm. *Accounting, Organizations and Society, 23*(5/6), 569–587.

Hargadon, A. B. (1998). Firms as knowledge brokers: Lessons in pursuing continuous innovation. *California Management Review, 40*(3), 209–227.

Hicks, J., Nair, P., & Wilderom, C. (2009). What if we shifted the basis of consulting from knowledge to knowing? *Management Learning, 40*(3), 289–310.

Jones, M. (2003). The expert system: Constructing expertise in an IT/management consultancy. *Information and Organization, 13*, 257–284.

Løwendahl, B. R. (2005). *Strategic management of professional service firms* (3rd ed.). Copenhagen, Denmark: Copenhagen Business School Press.

McKenna, C. D. (2006). *The world's newest profession: Management consulting in the twentieth century.* Cambridge, England: Cambridge University Press.

Morris, T. & Empson, L. (1998). Organisation and expertise: An exploration of knowledge bases and the management of accounting and consulting firms. *Accounting, Organizations and Society, 23*(5-6), 609–624.

Sandberg, J. & Pinnington, A. H. (2009). Professional competence as ways of being: An existential ontological perspective. *Journal of Management Studies, 46*(7), 1138–1170.

Schön, D. (1983). *The reflective practitioner: How professionals Ttink in action.* Aldershot, England: Avebury.

Starbuck, W. H. (1992). Learning by knowledge-intensive firms. *Journal of Management Studies, 26*(6), 713–740.

Sturdy, A. (1997). The consultancy process: An insecure business. *Journal of Management Studies, 34*(3), 389–413.

Werr, A. (1999). *The language of change: The roles of methods in the work of management consultants.* Stockholm, Sweden: Stockholm School of Economics.

Werr, A., Stjernberg, T., & Docherty, P. (1997). The functions of methods of change in management consulting. *Journal of Organizational Change Management, 10*(4), 288–307.

Visscher, K. (2006). Capturing the competence of management consulting work. *Journal of Workplace Learning, 18*(4), 248–260.

Von Nordenflycht, A. (2010). What is a professional service firm? Toward a theory and taxonomy of knowledge-intensive firms. *Academy of Management Review, 35*(1), 155–174.

CHAPTER 3

INFORMAL CLIENT RELATIONSHIP DEVELOPMENT BY CONSULTANTS

The Star Players and the Naturals

Yvette Taminiau, Liselore Berghman, and Petra den Besten

Initiating and maintaining informal client contact forms a crucial part of the daily routine of a consultant. Yet, while partners, directors, and senior managers of consultancy organizations devote a lot of time to informal contact with clients, thus far little research has been conducted to determine the specific role of such informal contact. This explorative study, based on in-depth interviews with 125 European consultants, sheds light on the function and value of informal relationships with clients, revealing the tensions and paradoxes that consultants encounter as they engage in such informal contact. The metaphors *game* and *art* provide a framework on which to arrange the five paradoxes identified in the study.

Exploring the Professional Identity of Management Consultants, pages 51–71
Copyright © 2013 by Information Age Publishing
All rights of reproduction in any form reserved.

The chapter begins with a discussion of existing theories on the topic of consultant–client relationships. The next section describes the study methodology, followed by the interview findings and the analysis. The chapter concludes with reflections on the study, drawing out our main conclusions as well as relevant points of discussion.

THE CONSULTANT–CLIENT RELATIONSHIP

The relationship between a consultant and a client can be examined from a number of perspectives. For example, a clear divide can be distinguished between studies, based on the position and intensity of control within a consultant–client relationship. Werr and Styhre (2002) differentiate between a critical perspective and a functional perspective on the consultant–client relationship. According to the critical perspective, control rests with the consultant in this relationship, since the client is subject to the rhetorical skills of the consultant and the impression he or she thereby creates. The consultant is described as a "manipulator of symbols in order to fashion valuable impressions" (Werr & Styhre, 2002, p. 46). The functional perspective, in contrast, attributes the control to the *client*, as he or she is after all the consumer of the service and therefore the one to decide who will be called in to provide that service and at what moment the service is no longer required. In this perspective, the client is far from a naïve victim of the consultant's persuasive sales techniques (as suggested in the critical perspective). Instead, the client is seen as a competent consumer who is very aware of his or her personal needs and desires. The more recent literature on consultancy services supports this shift from the consultant's role as a powerful expert (*outsider role*) to a more procedural and collaborative role (*insider role*) (Sturdy, Handley, Clark, & Fincham, 2009; Sturdy, Werr, & Buono, 2009; Sturdy, 2011; Sturdy & Wright, 2011). Today, the responsibilities of consultants are to a large extent shaped by their objective to develop a relationship with their clients. This change is largely due to the fact that clients are more highly educated than before, as they often have an MBA or even previous experience as a consultant themselves (Sturdy, 2011). Also, an increase in competition on the consultancy market has resulted in more balanced relationships between consultants and clients.

In this context, Nikolova, Reihlen, and Schlapfner (2009) raise the notion of a *social learning model* in which the interaction between the consultant and the client is seen as a participative learning process in which both parties contribute equally. Nikolova et al. (2009) offer a clear representation of the complexity of the consultant–client relationship. They emphasize the equality of the role of the client to that of the consultant. They pose that the consultant–client relationship is a symbolic system of interaction, characterized by rhetorical, linguistic games in the form of success stories and metaphors. Fincham's (1999) study of consultancy processes emphasizes the interaction between the consultant and the client in the context of a consultancy project as well. This work suggested that consultancy processes do not involve a "necessary structure" and that the consultant–client relationship is continually subject to change, thus creating a multiplicity of configurations. Richter and Niewiem (2009) capture the nature of this relationship as "open-ended, repeated interactions that go beyond the usual professional contact, trust, loyalty, blurred boundaries" (p. 279).

Research by Glückler and Ambrüster (2003) indicates that most consultancy assignments are submitted to consultants with whom the client has had a good, personal experience in the past. Czerniawska (2007) states that without a good relationship, a consultant will not be able to do the job well—and without doing a good job, the consultant will not be able to establish a good relationship. Therefore, the ability to "read" the client's needs and desires is crucial for a consultant in order to recognize needs that should or could be met. Maister (2005) argues that the consultant should strive to cultivate the relationship to the point of an emotional duet. Much like "real life," qualities such as reliability, authenticity, openness, attentiveness, empathy, and compassion are considered valuable features.

The interaction between the consultant and the client appears to be at the center of every effort to define critical success factors. As Nikolova et al. (2009) argue, "Successful consultancy projects demand an unremitting social process of negotiating mutual expectations and developing shared conditions and identities" (p. 296). Fullerton and West (1996) argue that unsuccessful relationships between consultants and clients are often the result of diverging opinions on that which makes a relationship truly effective. Therefore, an interpersonal "fit" between the consultant and the client proves to be an essential prerequisite for success in a consultancy process (Appelbaum & Steed, 2005; Fullerton & West, 1996). Caluwé and Stoppelenburg (2002, p. 8) propose a number of success factors with regard to consultancy assignments, including a mutual understanding of expectations concerning the allocation of time to specific elements of the process, good teamwork, trust, and a clear division of roles. Richter and Niewiem (2009) confirm that trust plays an important role in a successful relationship between a consultant and a client. In their conclusion, they state that the significance of a true bond of trust goes far beyond the mere commercial exchange of clearly delineated services between organizations. Consultant–client relationships cause existing boundaries between the consultant's organization and the client's organization to blur, producing a collective sense of responsibility (Richter & Niewiem, 2009). As such, the psychological and social dimensions of a consultant–client relationship are essential to a successful consultancy process (Schein, 2006).

Informality and Client Contact

Enduring business relations can be strengthened by informal activities like dinners or social events. Sturdy, Schwarz, and Spicer (2006) state that informal activities can be a way for the consultancy to gain the trust of the client. It can also bring about an alternative (often more efficient) way of exchanging information (Taminiau, Smit, & de Lange, 2009). Informal contact between a consultant and a client can lead to a foundation of trust that will contribute significantly to the relationship between both parties. Morand (1995) describes two social *modes* as well as mode-specific categories of behavioral and contextual attributes. Informality is described as "casual, spontaneous, rather impromptu forms of social interaction and behavior" (Morand, 1995, p. 831). Formality is seen as: "more rigid and deliberate, impersonal conduct, as well as environments that encourage such conduct" (Morand, 1995, p. 831). Although the term "informal relationships" is regularly used to indicate friendly relations, Morand (1995) argues that contrary to friendships, informal contact can well be associated with the aims of the organization. *Behavioral informality* can be instrumental in creating more organic, innovative organizations (Morand, 1995). In addition, informality can strengthen the mutual understanding between the consultant and the client. Shared cultural values form the basis for a successful relationship (Mohe, 2008).

Recognizing the proper attitude and approach within a consultant–client relationship—finding the role that will allow the consultant to do a job in the best possible way—can cause a lot of tension on the part of the consultant. Whittle (2006) shows that the activities that are essential for a consultant to do a job well contain many paradoxical elements. For example, the consultant needs to offer solutions, while at the same time rendering him or herself indispensable by calling attention to new problems. The consultant is considered to be a critical and independent observer, yet he or she is also often seen as a friend. Essentially, there are myriad paradoxical dilemmas that consultants are faced with during their daily activities. Switching between roles and having to meet varying client expectations at different times can invoke paradoxes and areas of tension in numerous ways (Kaarst-Brown, 1999; Kakabadse & Louchart, 2006; Kitay & Wright, 2004; Sturdy et al., 2006; Whittle, 2006). The consultant is already confronted with such paradoxes at the first onset of informal client contact.

Summarizing, the literature clearly shows a shift in consultant–client relationships from a rather detached and content-driven relationship to a more balanced, relationship-driven one (assuming that the expertise of the consultant is at the same high level in both cases). This shift creates added insecurity in the consultant, as the relationship is often open-ended in nature and develops differently depending on the clients and on the situations that present themselves. Prior research indicates that informality and informal settings are conducive to furthering business relations and to a more efficient exchange of knowledge. Nevertheless, little research has been done so far on the interface between these two topics. A similar lack of attention applies to the paradoxes and the areas of tension that can become apparent in the course of informal client contact. This is a subject that is very deserving of attention, however, since the dividing line between the success and failure in a consultant–client relationship can be very fine—as research by Appelbaum and Steed (2005) points out. This study thus focuses on the following research questions: What are the motives for consultants to initiate and maintain informal client contact? How do consultant–client relationships work? Which paradoxes are faced in informal consultant–client relationships and within informal settings?

METHODOLOGY

This explorative study is qualitative in nature, providing insight into the informal interactions that take place between a consultant and a client. As discussed above, although the interest in this topic is growing, there has not been much development of theories with regard to the subject (Sturdy et al., 2006). Although informal client contact forms a crucial part of the daily routine of consultants, the activities related to such contact, as well as their consequences, are difficult to translate into causal connections and critical success factors. Thus it seems appropriate to use a qualitative research approach, which may serve as a platform for developing further theories in this area.

Through interviews with consultants from seven European countries, the study intends to establish an outline of the way in which consultants interpret, approach, and implement informal client contact. It does not aim to verify existing theories by testing them against the interviews. Instead, this study's goal is to *contribute* to the limited knowledge regarding informal client contact in the consultancy sector. A well-founded theoretical approach seemed the most appropriate for acquiring knowledge and developing a theory.

This study is a part of a larger, international study in eleven countries, consisting of 250 interviews.[1] This specific part is based on a selection of 125 interviews with consultants in seven European countries (Germany, France, Italy, the Netherlands, the United Kingdom, Sweden and Switzerland, see Table 3.1). We employed a standardized interview protocol. For the purpose of this study, a fixed questionnaire addressed the following six topics: (1) setting the scene; (2) what; (3) when and where; (4) why; (5) types; and (6) success and "never do's."

TABLE 3.1   Summary of the Dataset

Country	N	Size of organization
United Kingdom	15	Small: 7 Medium: 0 Large: 8
The Netherlands	20	Small: 0 Medium: 0 Large: 20
France	19	Small: 2 Medium: 5 Large: 12
Germany	16	Small: 3 Medium: 3 Large: 10
Italy	21	Small: 8 Medium: 2 Large: 11
Sweden	19	Small: 5 Medium: 8 Large: 6
Switzerland	15	Small: 1 Medium: 1 Large: 13

The 125 consultant respondents—88 men and 37 women—were active in a consultancy organization in one of the seven aforementioned European countries. The respondents stemmed from different hierarchic levels within their organizations, ranging from junior level to upper management. The interviews with junior-level consultants proved to contain less useful information than the interviews with higher-level consultants. For that reason, only three junior level transcripts were included in the dataset. The consultants worked in small (50 staff members), medium (50 to 100 staff members), and large (100 staff members) consultancy organizations. The names of the organization are withheld for privacy reasons. The professional services provided by these organizations vary from strategic management, financial services, and human resource management, to financial management, communication, and IT.

Respondents were recruited using a "snowball sampling" technique. Initial contacts were for the most part made through existing networks of the researchers. The interviews took place over a period of six months during the first part of 2009. The study involved a single measurement of the consultants' perceptions by means of semi-structured interviews that took an average of 60 minutes to conclude. All interviews were recorded and transcribed, and then submitted to the consultant in question for approval before including them in the dataset. The interviews were conducted in either English or Dutch. English proved to be the most suitable interviewing language, as it is the language most widely used within European business life.

The interview questions were formulated according to the concepts that appear in literature on client contact in the consultancy sector. The themes addressed in the interviews are closely connected to the project's central theme—the nature and significance of informal client contact. The transcripts were analyzed using an interpretative approach, which involved organizing and reducing the data in such a manner that patterns could be recognized regarding human activities and their implications (Berg, 2001). Such an inductive approach made it possible to use the data as a starting point for exploring informal client contact in the consultancy sector. At the same time, a deductive approach was employed, as the theoretical framework proposed themes that could be of import as well. Strauss (1987) proposes that analytical induction through a combination of encoding and analysis can lead to an improved view on reality.

The collected data have subsequently been carefully encoded, analyzed, and re-analyzed, as is the common procedure in qualitative research. We employed open encoding using the qualitative data analysis program atlas-ti. Each step in the process of data-analysis was based on existing qualitative encoding techniques. The step-by-step plans by Berg (2001) were used. During the analysis, a logbook was kept, consisting of memos in atlas-ti. These memos contained remarks, motives, and (un)certainties regarding the process. Based on the encoding, the data were then categorized according to setting, motives, and the function of informal client contact.

FINDINGS

This section provides a brief overview of the informal activities that we encountered most frequently in the dataset. Subsequently, the analysis examines the motives for, and functions of, informal client contact. Finally, the five paradoxes that emerged from the analysis will be examined more fully.

Background: The Setting and the Function

The majority of the consultants defined informal client contact as the interaction that transpires outside of the formal business context, although some of the respondents pointed out that it is possible to engage in informal contact *at the office*. The type of informal client contact that is most frequently entered into is the business lunch, as it takes place during normal working hours. Even if some consultants have no objections to meeting their clients in the evening or on the weekend (because they hold the opinion that such is part of the job of a consultant), the general inclination among consultants is to limit their meetings to regular working hours. Consequently, a business dinner is considered to be more informal than a business lunch, because it happens during the consultant's private time. Other examples that were offered of informal meetings outside of working hours included playing golf, attending sports events, and visiting exhibitions. Also, topical events and conferences that involve informal activities are deemed traditional venues for establishing informal contact. The consultants stressed the fact that working in the consultancy sector entails routinely working long hours, making it inevitable that informal client contact will also occur in the consultant's private time. The length of a particular project also affects the degree to which consultants are favorably disposed to meeting outside of working hours, as the relationships that are established in the course of long-term projects are often of a more personal nature.

We found many similarities among consultants with respect to their motives for establishing and maintaining informal client contact. The main reasons for consultants to engage in informal client contact consist of building relationships, acquiring future assignments, creating trust, gathering information, and solving problems. Creating a bond of mutual trust was considered to be the principal motive. Informal client contact may consist of one-on-one interaction, but it can also include networking on a somewhat larger scale and thus generating company recognition and awareness. As a close relationship develops between the consultant and the client, they become more well-disposed towards each other; the client will grant (new) projects to the consultant, while the consultant will "try just a bit harder" than they may do for other clients. Moreover, this reciprocity of trust will not only help consultants to secure new and/or subsequent assignments, it will also facilitate in obtaining important information that will make it easier for the consultant to understand and solve problems that may arise. In turn, this dynamic reinforces the bond of trust as far as content is concerned. Trust seems to derive from both informal contact and expertise. Expertise alone will not be sufficient for a consultancy firm to distinguish itself from other firms. In that regard, consultants refer to informal client contact and bonds of mutual trust as intangible competitive advantages. However, informal relationships can also lead to tensions and uncertainties for the consultants.

The Five Paradoxes

This section explores five principal areas of tension. We use the term "paradox" (i.e., apparent contradiction) in order to describe these areas of tension. The five paradoxes are: (1) formalizing the informal; (2) the insider or outsider role; (3) blurring boundaries between the professional and the personal; (4) creating a demand without making a sale; and (5) adapting while maintaining authenticity.

Formalizing the Informal

"Formalizing the informal" certainly sounds like a paradox. The consultant faces the challenge of finding a proper way of combining personal and professional elements so that he or she may achieve his or her goals. This is done through mirroring as well as by matching the right consultant to a specific client. At the higher hierarchic levels in particular (partners), informal client contact constitutes a well-considered strategy in which the organization's image is carefully managed.

> It is always prepared. You have an objective, after all: something you want to talk about during the lunch. You have to know very well what it is that you want to talk about. You focus on a few points and prepare these before the lunch. (French consultant)

At the same time, informal client contact needs to take place in the most natural way possible. The *chemistry* between two people is both indefinable and intangible. Consequently, informal client contact is in fact so abstract that it is difficult to extrapolate generalities from specific social situations.

> We don't have a specific methodology: you just do things like that. (Swedish consultant)

The consultant must find a balance between *planning* informal client contact and allowing it to run its natural course. If he or she fails to do so, the informal contact will lose its strength and effectiveness.

Insider or Outsider role?

A second paradox that the consultant encounters lies in the fact that he or she is at once an *insider* and an *outsider*. On the one hand, informal contact generates a sense of unity, a "we-feeling." The consultant needs to bridge any gap between himself or herself and the client, while simultaneously remaining aware of both the existence and the necessity of that gap. The consultant continually switches between these roles, the boundaries of which are often unclear and changing.

> The informal contact, the saying of *we* instead of *me* and *you*, will help you to implement the solution that you have come up with in the company. (German consultant)

> You know what to expect. You see each other as "hey, they're just people too, and relaxed ones to boot." This lessens the "us versus them" feeling and makes it possible to just work together very comfortably. (British consultant)

The best way for a consultant to determine the motives of the client is to reveal some of his or her own personal life to that client. If the consultant becomes too personal, however, this will harm his or her effectiveness as well as the client's perception of the consultant's competence.

> There is a difference between what is personal and private, and what is business. (Swedish consultant)

> You can never, or rarely, step fully and truly outside your professional role. You are always in that role because that's part of the game. (Swedish consultant)

Ultimately, the *precise* combination of personal and professional elements depends a great deal on the personalities of the consultant and the client, the amount of time that they have know each other, the setting, and their respective positions within the organization.

Blurring Boundaries between the Professional and the Personal

The third paradox is also related to the balance between business and private matters. Although it can be difficult to distinguish between the professional and the personal, two types of consultant–client relationships can clearly be distinguished: a *personal* business relation versus a *professional* business relation. The professional business relation remains businesslike at all times. Informal moments are rare and conversation topics are limited to the projects at hand. A professional business relation may be just as successful as a personal business relation in generating and/or continuing assignments. After all, some clients simply do not feel the need for informal contact. The consultants who were interviewed in the course of this study pointed out that it should be clear to both parties involved at which stage in the relationship they find themselves: personal/informal or formal/professional.

> It depends on the relationship you have with them. With some you have a quite close relationship and with others you stay more on a business level. (Swiss consultant)

In the case of a personal business relationship (the most common in our dataset), it is the personal "click" that is strived for. Therefore, personal matters can become a topic of conversation.

> You always need to be connected to the people who can provide you with business. That's why you have to establish a very close relationship. But you never

forget that it is business, not private life. Even if it seems to others as if you are friends sometimes: you're not, it's business. (French consultant)

Many respondents stated that they make a clear distinction between their business lives and their private lives.

It is very hard to manage the mix between an informal and a formal relationship. If you are too formal, the relationship is very cold and everything. But if you become too informal, then it is not always easy to go back to a professional setting. (Italian consultant)

Separating the professional from the personal can be quite paradoxical, especially when it is hard to differentiate between them. Significantly, the consultants noted that it is even difficult to define what constitutes a working day.

The question is—when does your working day start and when does it end?... I think the line between private life and business life is very blurry. (Swiss consultant)

During the interviews, the consultants had trouble establishing the times at which they engaged in informal client contact (*during* or *outside* of working hours). They also found it difficult to produce an unequivocal description of the mix between the personal and the professional.

Creating a Demand without Making a Sale

The fourth paradox that the consultant is confronted with during informal client contact is the fact that he or she is expected to create a demand, but is not supposed to do so by "selling" their organization or their services. However contradictory, the consultant must essentially sell without selling (i.e., no "hard" selling). The consultant will therefore attempt to create a "click" between himself or herself and the client, which will result in creating a demand on the part of the client without having to resort to active sales techniques. As one of the consultants noted, "The best way to sell something is to let people ask for it" (French consultant). Creating a demand for the services you offer is considered an indication of success by the majority of the consultants. It is regarded as one of the added values of informal contact.

One of our colleagues is always pushing his business cards. I never give out business cards just like that. I wait until the client asks me if I have a business card. But I do maneuver my client, or potential client, into a position in which they will need my business card. As in: Did you know this? No, I didn't know that. Perhaps this information would be useful for you then? Oh yes...

do you have a business card? Only then do I give it. That's pulling instead of pushing. (Swedish consultant)

This game of "pulling, instead of pushing" (Swedish consultant) requires a great ability on the part of the consultant to thoroughly appreciate the needs of the client and to adapt to these needs. This dynamic results in a fifth area of tension—adapting while maintaining authenticity.

Adapting while Maintaining Authenticity

The final paradox that the consultant needs to contend with is when he or she needs to adapt to the client while maintaining his or her authenticity. The consultant needs to mirror the client, yet remain himself or herself. In order to do so, the following characteristics are essential to a consultant: the ability to truly listen, sincerity, transparency, and the ability to move easily between formal and informal roles. In addition, the consultant needs to be aware of the specific needs and desires of the client, so that the informal contact can be tuned to those needs and desires as much as possible.

> If everybody sings . . . you have to sing as well. (German consultant)

> If you are with a king, be a king. If you are with a farmer, be a farmer. Because you are the one who has to adapt to the level of your client. (Italian consultant)

The respondents indicated that it is of the essence to remain faithful to one's own values, traits and personality in a flexible, straightforward manner. The consultant should not do anything for the sole purpose of pleasing the client.

> It's important that you show that you are your own person, that you have your own character traits. People respect and admire you if you set your own standards. If you don't, they might think that you are just aiming to please. (German consultant)

The value of a consultant–client relationship to the project increases with the degree to which the consultant is able to create a sense of equality and reciprocity in his or her relationship with the client, thus establishing mutual expectations.

> Informal contact only works if it's driven by both sides. It's a bit of give and take. (Swiss consultant)

The process of becoming acquainted and growing to understand each other plays an important role in this as well. Both the client and the consultant need to disclose themselves to a certain extent in order to come to a concordant collaboration. There is, of course, always the possibility that a relationship between a consultant and a client is not as successful as hoped. In such cases, as explained by one of the respondents, the client should be transferred to a colleague: "try to find out who is the best match for a client" (Swiss consultant). The consultants explain that consultancy is *human* interaction, and after all, it is always possible that two people simply don't suit each other.

In summary, the paradoxes mentioned above certainly pose an enormous challenge to consultants. The consultant wants to know what it is that drives the client in order to create a demand that matches the client's specific needs and desires. At the same time, he or she wants to keep his or her distance from the client and keep clear boundaries between the professional and the personal, despite the ambiguity of these boundaries. While the consultant must disclose himself or herself to the client so as to determine the motives of the client, the consultant should not become too personal, since that could infringe on his or her effectiveness as well as the client's perception of his or her competence.

The Game and the Art

Is it possible to strategically plan a relationship, or is developing a relationship much too abstract to do so? Many of the consultants that were interviewed in the course of this study used the phrase "*that depends*" in response to this question. The consultants explained that a consultant–client relationship consists of many unique social situations and interactions that are difficult to "exactly put a finger on." Still, consultants in all of the different countries that were a part of this study do seem to have found ways of developing effective consultant–client relationships (such as creating a demand instead of "pushing"). In order to gain a better insight into the five paradoxes and the ways in which the consultants act in response to these, the analysis explores two metaphorical approaches to informal client contact—as a *game* and as an *art*.

The Game

If a consultant wishes to develop an effective consultant–client relationship, it is of the utmost importance that he or she becomes familiar with the client—who is this individual and what does he or she want or need? The consultant needs to obtain information regarding the client, the client's organization, and their branch of business, for example on the Internet, in newspapers, or through one-on-one exchanges. All gathered information is committed to memory in one way or another. One consultant memorizes everything by heart, while another records the information in files or documents. This client information not only enables the consultant to do his or her job with regard to content, it also helps him or her establish or maintain a personal relationship with the client. This information allows the consultant to be considerate towards the client, thus evoking a feeling of importance in him or her. Larger organizations may have well-structured systems that can be consulted for *leads* on clients. However, most of the respondents think it too much work to input information into such systems and do not actively use them.

Creating trust between the consultant and the client is always the principal goal. Underlying the desire to create such trust is often a well thought-out strategy with the intention of attaining a "click" between the consultant and the client. Nothing is left to chance. Some of the consultants we interviewed suggested that informal client contact should always be engaged in with a purpose and a plan, so that time will not be wasted—either the time of the consultant or the time of the client. Some also called it *deliberately constructing an image* and defining the organization's position within the market. Generally, the responses that were offered by the consultants evoke the image of informal client contact as a game—a game that can only be won if the consultant manages to create a demand for his or her services.

> Informal situations need to be well prepared. (Italian consultant)

> The further away from the office, the better. The contact starts at the office. After that, I try to keep moving them farther and farther away. Typically, it will be something like this: client's desk—client's meeting room—meeting room in a different part of the building—coffee at the office—lunch at the office— meeting room in my building—lunch outside the office—dinner outside the office—sports or charity event. (British consultant)

Although the use of a game metaphor may create the impression that the consultant is manipulating the client, consultants are highly aware of their reliance on the client.

> Part of the chemistry you can achieve by listening. (Swiss consultant)

> Make sure that you are the first one to move the stakes as far as the subjects go that you talk about. Make it personal. Find out as much as you can about their private life as soon as they seem to be comfortable discussing that. It's also important that you really listen to your client, and that you serve their interests only, not yours. That generates trust and you will reap the harvest of that trust later on in the relationship. Personally, I think that it is important to get them away from their office as soon as possible. Developing a relationship requires a different setting than that of the office. (British consultant)

It is remarkable that many of the consultants mentioned that creating a demand is "just part of the game." They were unable, however, to specify the rules of that game, other than that the consultant should "pull" instead of "push." This latter view reflects a different sentiment, that informal client contact is more of an "art"—based on emotion and intuition, without clearly defined rules.

The Art

A number of consultants described informal client contact first and foremost as *chemistry*, an unspecified art form running a natural course and lacking set rules. They also explained informal client contact by calling it "the normal interaction between people." The consultant knows day-to-day things about the client, just as in private life people know day-to-day things about others. The interaction is natural.

> I just go with the flow, every situation is different. (British consultant)

> The higher you are in the organization the more general you must start. You talk for example about the results of the G20; you should be able to have an opinion on that. It has to concern their company; there is no way you can start talking about UFOs to them. After that, you can get deeper in matters of short-term business if it has meaning, or about personal things. But in that case there are no rules because it depends on the mood you are in, the relationship with the guy, and the amount of alcohol you consumed (laughs). (French consultant)

The main advantage of allowing informal contact to run a natural course is that the consultant will have to make less of an effort in the long-term to acquire new assignments—they will be inevitably granted to him or her.

> The time spent on submitting quotes is disproportional to the time you need to develop your relationships. I've often had the experience that jobs were simply granted to me, without even having to quote an estimate, just handed to me. (Dutch consultant)

Some of the consultants felt skeptical about colleagues who work very systematically (by memorizing or recording informal information). They wonder whether such a structural approach could be a sign of insufficient skills or talent in the area of informal client contact.

> Yes the most structured people are the least good at building the best relationships. That's right. (British consultant)

Another way of looking at the socially talented could be the *naturals*. They do not employ or need a premeditated strategy. Instead, they possess a natural talent for interacting with a client.

Overall, is it clear that consultants have different views about informal client contact. The *star player* emphasizes the necessary preparation and importance of a good strategy. The *natural,* in contrast, relies on his or her relationship with the client running a spontaneous and natural course. In the final portion of the chapter, the relationship these two visions have with each other are explored, focusing on those consultants who make use of elements from both approaches.

DISCUSSION AND CONCLUSION

This study is based on the premise that a sound, personal bond of trust is an essential part of the relationship between the consultant and the client. This view reflects those of existing empirical studies on consultant–client relationships, which pose that an informal, personal and close relationship with a client may contribute significantly to the success of a consultancy project (Czerniawska, 2007; Maister, 2005; Sturdy et al., 2006). Expertise alone does not suffice to develop a consultant–client relationship on an interpersonal level (Nikolova et al., 2009; Richter & Niewiem, 2009). Informal contact in the form of establishing and expanding relationships and networks plays an important role within the formal business context, as Sturdy and associates (2006) have established. In particular those consultants who are active at the highest hierarchical levels tend to be very skilled at moving from a professional to an informal setting (Kanter, 1977). It is at these higher levels that many informal activities take place, in which clear points of contact with the client are sought after. Ultimately, it is the goal of the consultant to develop a sustained relationship with the client through which he or she may gain the most insight possible into the client organization (Kitay & Wright, 2004). Although the majority of the interviewed consultants strive for a personal relationship, many of them emphasize that this relationship should not become a true friendship.

The study's main contribution is drawn from the paradoxes that the consultant is frequently faced with in the course of his or her interactions with the client (Whittle, 2006). Sturdy et al. (2006) have argued that it can become increasingly difficult to delineate the boundaries between the insider and the outsider roles of the consultant. The line between the professional and the personal is even thinner in informal settings than it already is in other situations. This blurring of the boundaries confronts the consultant with areas of tension and contradiction. The consultants who were interviewed in the course of this study tried to keep their work and their private life separate but found it difficult to determine where that boundary actually lies. The consultant is expected to develop a personal relationship, but it should not become too personal, since this would harm his or her professionalism. The exact balance between these roles appears to depend on both the persons involved and the specific situation. As the relationship between the consultant and the client becomes more personal, the boundary between the professional and the personal may become more unclear—with regard to which Richter and Niewiem (2009) spoke of "blurred boundaries," "open-endedness," and "interactions that go beyond the usual professional contact" (p. 279).

According to Fullerton and West (1996), an interpersonal "fit" between the consultant and the client is a critical success factor in a consultancy project. As suggested by many of the comments in our study, finding the right match between a consultant and a client proves to be an important strategy for achieving such a successful *fit*. Long-term personal relationships are of importance because many new projects ensue from previous projects—the so-called *repeat business*. The consultant knows that the client prefers to work with consultants with whom he or she has already established a bond of trust (Richter & Niewiem, 2009). The consultant is also aware of the fact that personal experience plays an important role in choosing a consultant, as Glückler and Ambrüster (2003) have indicated. The consultant is successful when he or she adopts a flexible attitude towards the needs and desires of the client, and at the same time remains himself or herself. Sincerity and authenticity are crucial elements of success within informal client contact.

Consultant–client relationships have been described and categorized before in literature—for example, the functional versus the critical perspective (Werr & Styhre, 2002) and the social interaction model by Nikolova et al. (2009, p. 290). Based on this study, we can add a classification by *views* to these prior categorizations. During our research, we encountered two types of consultants, each of whom have a specific view on informal client contact: the tactical consultant and the natural. Tactical consultants play a game according to a premeditated strategy, while the naturals, those socially talented artists, do not adhere to set rules, relying more fully on intuition during informal contact. Table 3.2 places the underlying paradoxes on a continuum, contrasting the game view with the art view.

TABLE 3.2 Game Versus Art

Game vs. Art

1	Formal/planning ⟷ Spontaneous/no rules
2	Outsider ⟷ Insider
3	Professional ⟷ Personal
4	Focus on business ⟷ Focus creating a demand
5	Adapt ⟷ Remain authentic

Those consultants with a more strategic and structured view of interactions with the client will more often take the acquisition of assignments into account and will adapt to the client to a considerable degree, even if they simultaneously keep an appropriate professional distance. Their method symbolizes an instrumental approach to social relationships. In contrast, there are those consultants that employ a more flexible and more spontaneous approach—the so-called *naturals*. They are more inclined to blend the professional and the personal and tend to remain themselves while doing so. They are conscious of the fact that a sustained relationship both takes time and needs to run its natural course.

It is difficult to ascertain how the *star players* (the tactical consultants) relate to the *naturals*. It is possible that the naturals have played the game often enough that in the end they can rely entirely on their instincts and interactive client skills as they have been developed and fine-tuned over the years. This group has completely internalized the social interaction with clients. When asked about the way informal client interaction works, they typically respond that there are no rules. After some prodding, they may admit that there are implicit rules, but that they cannot specify what they are. It is also possible that an informal conversation with a client starts in a structured manner but veers off in its own direction after a while and as such loses much of the initial structure. A similar transformation from structured to more flexible is also possible within the course of a relationship.

Most consultants move between the two extremes. They make use of a lightly structured approach and attempt to learn as much information as possible with regard to the client by heart in order to come across as sincere and interested as possible. It is not unlikely that some consultants, the true *naturals*, have an advantage over other consultants due to their background and the social capital that they have built on further over the years (Adler & Kwon, 2002; Bourdieu, 1995; Nahapiet & Ghoshal, 1998). A (prior) membership of a (student) association or a business society, or participating in valued extracurricular activities (hockey or rowing club) can also have an effect on the "talents" of the consultants in relation to informal contacts (Heemskerk, 2007). In fact, the more exclusive, the better (Bourdieu, 1979). It is therefore very feasible that the *naturals* began their careers as planners. On the other hand, it is equally possible that, over the years, a *natural* becomes increasingly aware of his or her talent in the area of informal client contact, and will begin to develop methods and models to both further expand his or her client relationships and transfer that knowledge to less experienced colleagues. Follow-up research could shed more light on the relation between the naturals and the star players.

Another interesting topic for follow-up research would be to examine the client's perspective on informal contact with the consultant, thus creating an overall picture of informal consultant–client relationships. Other methods of investigation could be used (such as observation) in order to include non-verbal communication in the analysis. The effect of training on the success and the content of informal client contact could also be a fascinating subject for follow-up research. The content of such training could be examined to determine whether the Anglo-American business model has a dominant position in the subject matter and as such influences informal client contact on a global scale (Boussebaa, 2009). Finally, it would be very interesting if follow-up research would focus not on the *similarities* between consultants from different countries, but on the cultural *differences* that could play a role in informal settings (Beugelsdijk, Koen, & Noorderhaven, 2006). The paradoxes uncovered in this phase of our research point to a number of intriguing dynamics underlying our understanding of consultant–client relationships.

NOTES

1. The interviews were conducted by eight graduate students (two in the Netherlands) from the Master's program "Business Management: Strategy & Organization" at the Free University (VU) in Amsterdam. Each of these students carried out individual interviews in different European countries. In addition to the countries mentioned here, interviews were held in Belgium, Spain, the United States and Canada. However, these countries were added to the study at a later stage. Therefore, they are not included in the analysis as described in the chapter.

REFERENCES

Adler P., & Kwon, S. (2002). Social capital: Prospects of a new concept. *Academy of Management Review*, 27(1), 17–40.

Appelbaum, S. H., & Steed, A. J. (2005). The critical success factors in the client-consultant relationship. *Journal of Management Development*, 24(1), 68–93.

Berg, B. L. (2001). *Qualitative research methods for the social sciences*. Boston, MA: Allyn and Bacon.

Beugelsdijk, S., Koen, C. I., & Noorderhaven, N. G. (2006). Organizational culture and relationship skills. *Organization Studies*, 27(6), 833–854.

Bourdieu, P. (1979). *La distinction, critique sociale du jugement [Distinction: A social critique of the judgment of taste]*. Paris: Minuit.

Bourdieu, P. (1995). The forms of capital. In J. G. Richardson (Ed.), *Handbook of theory and research for the sociologie of education* (pp. 241–258). New York, NY: Greenwood.

Boussebaa, M. (2009). Struggling to organize across national borders: The case of global resource management in professional service firms. *Human relations*, 62(6), 829–850.

Caluwé, L. de & Stoppelenburg, A. (2002). *Omgaan met externe adviseurs [deal with external consultants].* Retrieved from http://www.decaluwe.nl/articles/Omgaan-MetExterneAdviseurs.pdf

Czerniawska, F. (2007). *The trusted firm: How consulting firms build successful client relationships.* Chichester, England: Wiley.

Fincham, R. (1999). The consultant–client relationship: Critical perspectives on the management of organizational change. *Journal of management studies, 36*(3), 335–351.

Fullerton, J., & West, M. A. (1996). Consultant and client—Working together? *Journal of Managerial Psychology, 11*(6), 40–49.

Glückler, J., & Armbrüster, T. (2003). Bridging uncertainty in management consulting: The mechanisms of trust and networked reputation. *Organization Studies, 24*(2), 269–297.

Heemskerk, E. M. (2007). *Decline of the corporate community: Network of the Dutch business elite.* Amsterdam: Amsterdam University Press.

Kaarst-Brown, M. L. (1999). Five symbolic roles of the external consultant: Integrating change, power and symbolism. *Journal of Organizational Change, 12*(6), 540–561.

Kakabadse, N. K., & Louchart, E. (2006). Consultant's role: A qualitative inquiry from the consultant's perspective. *Journal of Management Development, 25*(5), 416–500.

Kanter, R. M. (1977). *Men and women of the corporation.* New York, NY: Basic Books.

Kitay, J., & Wright, C. (2004). Take the money and run? Organisational boundaries and consultants roles. *The Service Industries Journal, 24*(3), 1–18.

Maister, D. (2005). *Do you really want relationships?* Retrieved from http://www.david-maister.com/articles/2/80/index.html

Mohe, M. (2008). Bridging the cultural gap in management consulting research. *International Journal of Cross Cultural Management, 8*(1), 41–57.

Morand, D. A. (1995). The role of behavioral formality and informality in the enactment of bureaucratic versus organic organizations. *Academy of Management Review, 20*(4), 831–872.

Nahapiet, J., & Ghoshal, S. (1998). Social capital, intellectual capital, and the organizational advantage. *Academy of Management Review, 23*(1), 242–266.

Nikolova, N., Reihlen, M., & Schlapfner, J. F. (2009). Client-consultant interaction: Capturing social practices of professional service production. *Scandinavian Journal of Management, 25*(3), 289–298.

Richter, A., & Niewiem, S. (2009). Knowledge transfer permeable boundaries: An empirical study of clients' decisions to involve management consultants. *Scandinavian Journal of Management, 25*(3), 275–288.

Schein, E. H. (2006). Coaching and consultation revised: Are they the same? In M. Goldsmith & L. S. Lyons (Eds.), *Coaching for leadership: The practice of leadership coaching from the world's greatest coaches* (pp. 17–25). San Francisco, CA: Pfeiffer.

Strauss, A. (1987). *Qualitative analysis for social scientists.* New York, NY: Cambridge University Press.

Sturdy, A. (2011). Consultancy's consequences? A critical assessment of management consultancy's impact on management. *British Journal of Management, 22*(3), 517–530.

Sturdy, A., Handley, K., Clack, T., & Fincham, R. (2009). *Management consultancy boundary and knowledge in action.* Oxford, England: Oxford University Press.

Sturdy, A., Schwarz, M., & Spicer, A. (2006). Guess who's coming to dinner? Structures and uses of liminality in strategic management consultancy. *Human relations, 59*(7), 929–960.

Sturdy, A., Werr, A., & Buono, A. F. (2009). The client in management consultancy research: Mapping the territory. *Scandinavian Journal of Management, 25*(3), 247–252.

Sturdy, A. & Wright, C. (2011). The active client: The boundary-spanning roles of internal consultants as gatekeepers, brokers and partners of their external counterparts. *Management Learning, 42,* 485–503.

Taminiau, Y., Smit, W., & de Lange, A. (2009). Innovation in management consulting firms through informal knowledge sharing. *Journal of Knowledge Management, 13*(1), 42–55.

Werr, A., & Styhre, A. (2002). Management consultants—Friend or foe? *Studies of Management & Organization, 32*(4), 43–66.

Whittle, A. (2006). The paradoxical repertoires of management consultancy. *Journal of Organizational Change Management, 19*(4), 424–436.

SECTION II

CONSULTANTS AS AGENTS OF CHANGE

CHAPTER 4

CONCEPTUALIZING DEVELOPMENTAL SPACE FOR INNOVATING GROUPS

Karin Derksen, Léon de Caluwé, and Robert Jan Simons

According to several authors, organizations need to change and innovate rapidly (Drucker, 2001; Harrison & Kessels, 2004; Kessels, 2004; Senge et al., 1999; Wierdsma, 2007). Kessels (2004) and Gratton (2007) state that innovation requires new knowledge and new combinations of experience and knowledge. Most authors also focus on the process needed for innovation—cooperation among individuals in a group (see Gratton, 2007; Vroemen, 2009). Innovation requires new knowledge, or new combinations of knowledge, and a work environment in which individuals are able to collaborate.

This chapter focuses on the work environment of groups that is needed for innovation. We assume that a working environment should be stimulating and challenging in order to facilitate innovation. This premise is based on three insights. First, the idea of Coenders (2008) and Wenger (1998) that learning cannot be designed—it is not possible to force people to learn. It is possible, however, to design a stimulating environment that challenges and entices people to learn. Second, our idea is further endorsed by research showing that workers learn mainly in an informal way

Exploring the Professional Identity of Management Consultants, pages 75–98
Copyright © 2013 by Information Age Publishing
All rights of reproduction in any form reserved.

(Borghans, Golsteyn, & de Grip, 2007; Cross, 2007; Hager & Halliday, 2009; Ruijters, 2007). These authors claim that informal learning itself cannot be designed, but a stimulating and challenging environment to support informal learning can be. Last but not least, according to Arets and Heijnen (2008), in most cases, environmental factors, not a lack of competencies, cause performance problems.

Our study takes a model of Coenders (2008) as the point of departure. Coenders states that developmental space in groups is a condition for successful innovation. He describes developmental space as a social space created by the interaction in the group. Space is a dynamic notion, and it is related to what people do and do not do (Coenders, 2008). In many instances, management consultants (MCs), in a role as facilitators, support these groups as process consultants. When group members and MCs have insight into the dimensions of the developmental space, they may be able to improve it. We think, however, that the model is not complete yet and too complex for groups and MCs to provide them with that required insight. This premise thus raises a key research question concerning the type of developmental space model that groups and MCs can use to analyze (descriptive) and influence (prescriptive) that space.

As suggested above, in examining Coenders' (2008) model, we have determined that it is too complex and incomplete to be truly useful. Our goal is thus to build on that work to design a useful model of the developmental space, going through a step by step process that leads to what we refer to as model 3.0 of developmental space. In the Netherlands, the role of the designer is a common role for an MC. According to Plomp, Feteris, Pieters, and Tomic (1992), designing is creating solutions for "made problems" in a systematic way. As designing is a part of the MC's profession, this study, as developmental research, bridges research and practice (Derksen, 2011). When we speak of a facilitator, we mean an MC in the role of facilitator supporting groups as a process consultant.

The chapter begins by defining the three main concepts used in the research: innovation, group, and developmental space. Next, Coenders' (2008) model of developmental space, including its strengths and weaknesses, is explained, followed by a description of the research method and findings, including a new model of developmental space. The chapter ends with a discussion of the implications for how we think about innovation in group context.

KEY CONCEPTS

The three core concepts on which the research is based—innovation, group, and developmental space—are defined and discussed in this section.

Innovation

Innovation is conceptualized as developing a new product, process, or service for a problem in practice for which existing solutions are insufficient (Kessels, 2004). It refers to new knowledge or new combinations of existing knowledge, with the inclusion of the social process (Clegg, Kornberger, & Pitsis, 2005). It is both the outcome of the process and the process itself. The driving force behind an innovation is not always the same. Two considerations are highlighted: the roles of different stakeholders and the fact that innovation does not happen in a vacuum (Clegg et al., 2005). An influential school of thought on innovation comes from Mintzberg (2007). He places innovation and innovation strategies on a continuum from planned to emergent, and he relates this to organization types. Mintzberg (2007) describes the adhocracy type as "teams of experts working on projects to produce novel outputs, generally in highly dynamic settings" (p. 340). This kind of group is similar to the groups in our research.

According to Mintzberg, the suitable innovation strategy for the adhocracy is a learning process. For complex innovations, in which the direction and results cannot completely be foreseen, Boonstra (2004) also recommends a learning process. Gratton (2007) and Kessels (2004) confirm that these innovations can only be realized by creating new knowledge or by new combinations of knowledge and experience. Kahane (2010) also stresses that these kinds of practices for innovation are an ongoing process of taking steps. The paradox of innovation is that the new is already known and established, but disguised in new clothes, or if it is really new, it is unrecognizable and beyond the ken of our understanding (Clegg et al., 2005). Pascale (1999) introduced four new principles that can frame the innovation process: (1) equilibrium equals death: innovation pushes away from equilibrium (stability) and increases the necessary variety; (2) self-organization is important: it is a break with the past; (3) you need some foolishness to go in a foolish direction; and (4) innovation can be disturbed, but not directed. We build upon these principles.

Group

A group can be a project team, regular team, network or community of practice. The crucial aspect for our research is that the group is working on an innovation. The group size in our research varies from three to 20 persons. Diversity among group members is important for innovation (Gratton, 2007; Homan, 2005; Kahane, 2010; Wenger, McDermott, & Snyder, 2002). Yet, although diversity is valuable, it is also difficult to make diversity productive. Team members must learn from each other, by being curious about other's expertise, experiences, and knowledge and in this way create new knowledge. This dynamic depends upon an environment in which group members trust and respect each other. Edmondson (1999) showed that psychological safety in groups is related to their team learning and their effectiveness. As she argued, "Team psychological safety involves but goes beyond interpersonal trust; it describes a team climate characterized by interpersonal trust and mutual respect in which people are comfortable being themselves" (Edmondson, 1999, p. 354). Gratton (2007) and Kahane (2010) also stress the importance of trust and good relationships among group members. In that case, people can listen to one another with an open mind and can respect each other's ideas, in contrast to Janis' (1972) groupthink, which is counterproductive and can be harmful as Janis illustrates.

Developmental Space

The developmental space is a social and mental space arising from interaction among people (Coenders, 2008; Homan, 2005). In the developmental space, group members feel free to share their knowledge, experiences and ideas, and they feel invited to do so. In this space, group members are comfortable and challenged at the same time. Thrift (2006) speaks of a dynamic place concerned with movement, interactivity, and continuous birth. This space can vary from very limited to almost unlimited in nature. According to Coenders (2008), this space can be substantial and is makeable. Developmental space, however, is not absolute, as it is bound to a certain situation and moment.

The developmental space in our research is about the collectively experienced developmental space in the group. The group makes this developmental space itself; it is partially influenced by the environment of the group. A sponsor or other stakeholders outside the group can exert positive or negative influences on the space experienced by the group members. We first define this core concept according to Coenders (2008), redefining it based on our findings. The research and analysis support the argument that developmental space is needed in order to be able to innovate.

COENDERS' MODEL OF DEVELOPMENTAL SPACE

Coenders' (2008) model of developmental space consists of four dimensions—synchronicity, reflexivity, regulativity, and finality—that define the developmental space (see Figure 4.1). *Synchronicity* refers to the coincidence of people and ideas in the creating process. *Reflexivity* means developing from different perspectives and taking a "helicopter view." *Regulativity* is

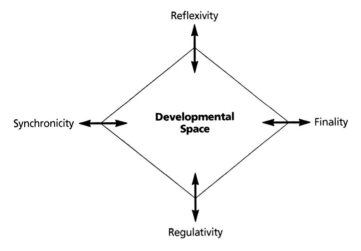

Figure 4.1 Coenders' model of developmental space (Coender, 2008, p. 140).

about communication and alignment. *Finality* means focusing on the result. According to Coenders (2008), the essence is finding a balance among these four dimensions. The model has two learning orientations—giving meaning and a revenue orientation—that are assumed to be naturally conflicting. Coenders (2008) typified his research as a theory-guided bricolage. He designed the model during four successive case studies (see Figure 4.2), which were situated in the service industry. Participants were highly educated professionals, and Coenders acted as a facilitator in the cases.

A few things in Coenders' (2008) research trigger further research. It is increasingly common for groups in organizations to work on innovation and for MCs to facilitate such groups. The idea that these groups need developmental space and that they create this space during interaction seems logical. The relative simplicity of the model, with only four dimensions, is appealing. It might provide an aid for groups to become aware of and to analyze and influence their developmental space. As such, Coenders' (2008) model seems promising, but the background of the concepts is complex, and the terminology is uncommon. To us, the model seems attractive but not easy to use, neither for analyzing nor for influencing the developmental space. Both the attraction and critique of the model forms the starting point for our research.

RESEARCH METHOD AND FINDINGS

Further development of a theoretical model is the main objective of this research, and it can best be characterized as developmental research

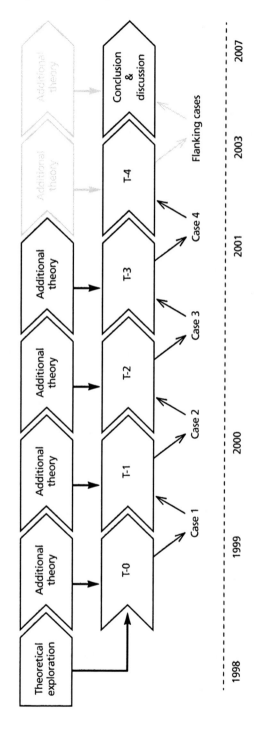

Figure 4.2 Coenders' research steps (Coender, 2008, p. 27).

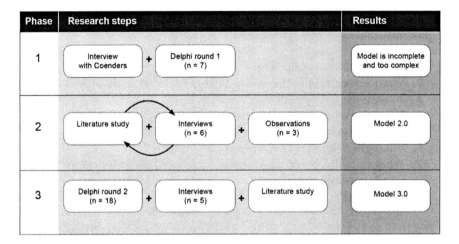

Phase	Research steps			Results
1	Interview with Coenders +	Delphi round 1 (n = 7)		Model is incomplete and too complex
2	Literature study +	Interviews (n = 6) +	Observations (n = 3)	Model 2.0
3	Delphi round 2 (n = 18) +	Interviews (n = 5) +	Literature study	Model 3.0

Figure 4.3 Research steps and results.

(Gravemeijer, 1998). According to Gravemeijer (1998), in developmental research, theory is developed gradually in an iterative and cumulative way. The theory grows out of the process of designing and testing rather than taking the shape of a formative evaluation: "Instead, developmental research is seen as a form of basic research that lays the foundation for the work of professional developers" (Gravemeijer, 1994, p. 277). According to Gravemeijer (1998), this is a part of theory-guided bricolage. A bricoleur uses as many materials as possible that happen to be available, combining different methods in the research (Denzin & Lincoln, 2000). Figure 4.3 captures our research process, delineating the steps taken in the project. For each phase, the research method and findings are described.

Phase 1: Coenders' Model

The research began with an interview with Coenders and a Delphi study with seven experienced facilitators of innovating groups. The interview with Coenders was open-ended, and the dimensions and concepts behind those dimensions were explored thoroughly. Questions such as "What do you mean?" and "What do you think of the applicability of the model?" were frequently asked, analyzing each of the concepts one by one. In the Delphi study, seven facilitators received an e-mail with the following instructions: "While answering the questions keep a group in mind that had, in your opinion, a lot of developmental space." Developmental space was defined for these facilitators as "A social space existing in the experience of individuals in a group (and the shared experience). This developmental space is needed to realize an innovation with each other in a group." The questions that were posed included:

1. What kind of a group is it?
2. What is your role in the group (group member, facilitator or other)?
3. What is the innovation they work on?
4. What does developmental space mean to you?
5. Which factors affect the developmental space?
6. What gives the idea of developmental space?
7. What does the group (and you as facilitator) do to influence this developmental space?

Three respondents answered as group members (self-managing groups) and four as facilitators of a group. The groups varied from a new management team working on becoming a team for organizational change to an innovating project team working as a think tank for inventing new hospital care concepts.

Evaluating Coenders' Model

Coenders' most important statement was "The model is not ready to use yet, but I was ready with it." He chose to use uncommon terminology because with common terms people easily think that they understand what is meant and give their own meaning. Coenders argued that this tendency and the absence of instruments may have inhibited the model's applicability. In the Delphi study, there were no differences between the answers given by respondents as group members and facilitators. The answers to questions 3 to 6 (see questions above) were applied to Coenders model, and the respondents' words and sentences (or parts of sentences) were classified into the dimensions of the model and its underlying concepts. All four dimensions of Coenders' model (parts of) were found, but not every concept was linked to every dimension. The distinction between the dimensions was not always clear. Thus, the four dimensions seem to be important, but that was not the case for all the concepts behind the dimensions. Based on the comments, interaction with the environment also seemed to be important and is missing in the model. None of the respondents used the terminology Coenders used for the dimensions. We concluded in this initial phase that the model was promising but too complex and incomplete.

Phase 2: Initial Redesign

Adjustments to Coenders' model began with "rapid prototyping" (Visscher-Voerman 1999), in which literature study and interviews were mingled. In addition to a second interview with Coenders, five researchers in related fields (e.g., knowledge productivity, networked learning, learning and power) were interviewed. In each of the interviews, a revised model was presented to the respondent, taking the previous interviews into account. The main questions were:

- What do you and do you not recognize in the model?
- From your research, what ideas can you give to improve it?
- Which elements do you recognize? Which ones would you not use?
- What literature can you recommend?

At the end of this phase, three groups in a government agency were observed to examine the redesigned model in practice. Every group consisted of six human resource management professionals who were innovating in their own work. Their innovation goal was to deliver better work with fewer people. The observations were written down in a scheme with the six dimensions: synchronizing, creating future, reflecting, organizing, communicating, and interacting with the environment. In the observations three additional questions were used:

- Which of the observations confirm the model?
- Which ones challenge it?
- What cannot be placed in the model?

Evaluating the Redesigned Model

The first change in the model was the addition of a new factor—*interaction with the environment*—and the extension of the dimension "creating future" by adding *value creation*. As part of our research process, the model was developed step by step, analyzing each interview and the recommended literature. The first interview was conducted with a cloud model (see Figure 4.4), as a result of phase one. In a cloud model, every text cloud is a representation of words that seem important and seem to be linked to each other. The bold words seem the most important. The advantage of starting with a cloud model is that it provides subjects with "room" for change because it is clear that it is not complete yet.

From this first model, a revised model 2.0 was developed step by step during the interview process (see Figure 4.5). The results of the observations of the three groups were as follows. Every group produced a solution within five minutes for a problem that has existed for years. After finding the solution, they started to plan how they would put it into practice. They hardly ever asked a question or looked at the problem or solution from a different perspective—they focused on creating future and organizing, but neglected reflecting, communicating, and the environment. The groups

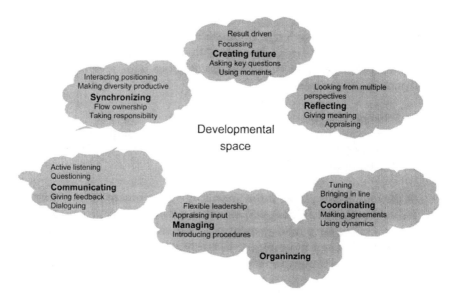

Figure 4.4 Cloud model of the developmental space.

recognized this when it was fed back to them. They confirmed that their results would have been better if they had reflected more, communicated better, and focused on the environment. As one group member noted, "In this way, we did not really come up with new ideas that might work." These three steps—the interviews, observations, and literature review—thus led to model 2.0 of the developmental space.

Phase 3: Second Redesign

The purpose of the third phase was to test and refine model 2.0. The research questions that guided this phase were:

- Are these the right dimensions of the developmental space for groups working on innovation?
- How clear and meaningful are the dimensions?
- What do colleagues think of the model?
- How does the model relate to similar models in the literature?

We executed a second Delphi study with 18 participants, five interviews and further literature review. In the Delphi study, the seven experts from the first round and 11 new experts participated. This time, we compared extremes (Brinkerhoff, 2002). We asked the respondents to "Answer all the

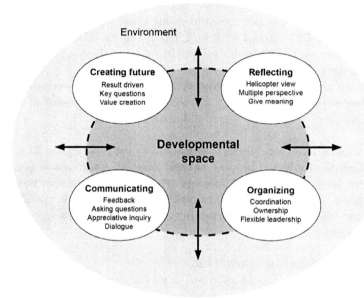

Figure 4.5 Model 2.0 of the developmental space.

questions twice"—with a group that was deemed to be successful in its innovation and another group that was seen as unsuccessful. This comparison resulted in 17 successful and 17 unsuccessful groups (n=34), as one respondent only answered for a successful group and another only answered for an unsuccessful group. The questions were:

- Describe the group and its assignment.
- Were you a group member or a facilitator?
- What do you recognize of the dimensions, creating future, reflecting, organizing, communicating and interaction with the environment?
- Which other dimensions do you think determine the developmental space?
- What do you think of this model?
- Are there other reactions you would like to give?

The answers to every dimension of the groups are categorized as: "+" for groups that paid attention to a dimension, with or without help of a facilitator, and "–" for groups that hardly paid attention to that dimension. Finally, "±" was given whenever a group was viewed as "in the middle." The following illustrates the way in which answers were scored for the *reflecting* dimension:

- Score +: "It was a continuous process of taking a step back, looking from multiple perspectives, and giving meaning together."
- Score −: "This did not work well. The group members did not tell and ask much. The leader was talking most of the time and not giving room to others."
- Score ±: "The group reflected well during coaching sessions when they were invited to reflect. But whenever daily tensions and emotions were at hand the group did not reflect at all."

The Delphi study was followed by interviews with five of the 18 respondents. They were selected because of their personal questions or questions that arose from their answers. Another trigger for an interview was when respondents asked intriguing questions, such as, "How is it possible that my unsuccessful group was far better in two of the five dimensions than my successful group?"

Evaluating the Redesigned Model (2.0)

All successful groups paid attention to all the dimensions. At the beginning, they often paid less attention to one or two dimensions, but with the help of a facilitator they were able to broaden their focus, focusing on all four dimensions. The unsuccessful groups had at least two dimensions that hardly received any attention (see Table 4.1). So the combination of the five dimensions of the model seems to be important.

Drawing on the interviews and feedback, a number of points were raised. First, the *communicating* dimension could be more precise, with such crucial points as asking questions, dialoguing, and appreciative inquiry. The impact of the *space given by a principal* was mentioned as a missing dimension. Although the facilitators commented mostly on the *reflecting* and *communicating* dimensions, they had diverse reactions to the model. Some facilitators reported that they would like to use the model immediately, while others were looking for an alternative purpose. Still others mentioned that, "At last there is a model that gives support and language to what I do in practice."

The five additional interviews were used to look more closely at the underlying dilemmas in the framework. For instance, the dimension *creating future* was paid attention to in both successful and unsuccessful groups (see Table 4.1). The difference is that the successful groups seemed to have a shared and realistic view of the future, whereas the unsuccessful groups often had a more fragmented and unrealistic view of the future. One important result from the interviews is that there is a need for better specifications of the dimensions. This Delphi study and interviews lead to the revised model 3.0 (see Figure 4.6).

The new model 3.0 was compared with three relevant similar theories—Gratton's (2007) "hot spots," Scharmer's (2007) "Theory U," and Kahane's

TABLE 4.1 Results of the Delphi Study 2

Respondent	1	2	3	4	5	6	7	8	9	10	11	12	13	14	15	16	17	18
Successful groups																		
Participant/Facilitator	F	P	F	P	F	F	P	F	F	P	F	P	F	P	F	F	F	P
Creating future	+	+	+	+	+	+	+	+	+	+	+	+	+	+	+	+	+	+
Reflecting	+	+	+	+	+	+	+	+	+	+	+	+	+	+	+	+	+	+
Organizing	+	+	+	+	+	+	+	+	+	+	+	+	+	+	+	+	+	+
Communicating	+	+	+	+	+	+	+	+	+	+	+	+	+	+	+	+	+	+
Interacting with environment	+	+	+	+	+	+	+	+	+	+	+	+	+	+	+	+	+	+
Unsuccessful groups																		
Participant/Facilitator	F	P	F	P	P	P	F		F	P	F	F	F	F	P	P	P	F
Creating future	±	+	±	−	+	−	−		+	+	+	−	±	+	+	+	+	±
Reflecting	−	−	+	−	−	−	±		−	−	±	−	−	−	±	−	+	−
Organizing	+	−	±	−	−	−	−		−	+	−	−	+	−	±	+	±	±
Communicating	+	−	±	−	−	−	−		−	−	+	−	−	−	−	−	±	−
Interacting with environment	+	+	−	−	−	+	−		−	−	−	−	−	±	±	−	−	−

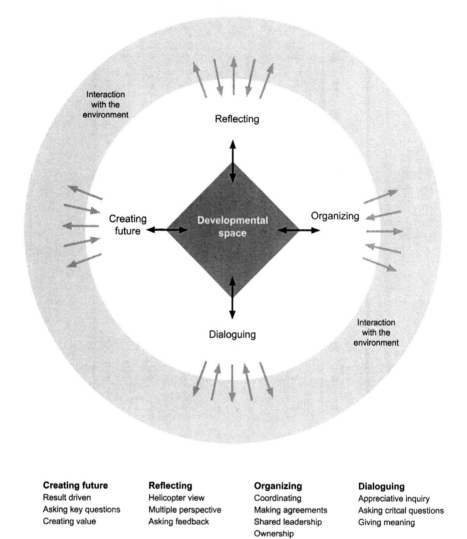

Creating future
Result driven
Asking key questions
Creating value

Reflecting
Helicopter view
Multiple perspective
Asking feedback

Organizing
Coordinating
Making agreements
Shared leadership
Ownership

Dialoguing
Appreciative inquiry
Asking critcal questions
Giving meaning

Figure 4.6   Model 3.0 of the developmental space.

(2010) "power and love." We used three headings for comparison: dimensions, results and principles. The four models all had the same starting point, that complex problems and innovations can best be realized collectively. Comparing the four models, it became clear that hot spots and power and love were close to the idea of developmental space. The process and principles of Theory U, in contrast, were further removed. A more precise comparison is provided in Table 4.2.

TABLE 4.2   Model of Developmental Space 3.0 Compared to Three Other Models

Developmental space 3.0	Hot spots	Power & love	Theory U
Dimensions of the developmental space compared			
Creating future	Catching goal; igniting purpose	Power	Co-creating
Organizing	Productive capacity; boundary spanning	Power	Co-creating and co-evolving
Dialoguing	Cooperation aimed thinking	Love	Co-initiating and co-sensing
Reflecting	Crossing borders; cooperative mindset	Love	Co-presencing
Interacting with environment	Crossing borders	Power and love	Co-sensing and co-evolving
Results compared			
Bigger chance on success in innovation	Flow	One step further; step by step	Emerging future
Principles compared			
Strive for balance	First attention for the relation, later for productivity	Strive for balance by reinforcing the weaker side	Steps that follow one another during time
The group creates	The group creates	The group creates	Facilitator can play an important role
Group arises naturally, or is put together	Group arises naturally, or is put together	Group arises naturally, or is put together	Group arises naturally, or put together.
No separate room to experiment	No separate room to experiment	"Container/Ba" (as room to experiment)	"Ba" (as room to experiment)

MODEL 3.0 OF DEVELOPMENTAL SPACE

The research steps led to model 3.0 of the developmental space as presented in Figure 4.5. The model consists of four dimensions: creating future, reflecting, organizing, and dialoguing. These dimensions emerge during interaction in the group; therefore, they are constructed as verbs. Groups that pay attention to all four dimensions create an environment that increases their chance to be successful in their innovation, as can be concluded from Table 4.1. This finding corresponds with the results of Coenders' (2008) study. Besides the four dimensions, there is one other factor influencing the developmental space—*interacting with the environment*. This factor differs from the other dimensions because it not only occurs within the group, but it also includes pressure from stakeholders, limitations from the sponsor, or conflicting political interests. To be successful, the group must interact with its environment. If the group fails to do this, it is almost impossible to create value. The model consists of two orientations, which Coenders (2008) already mentioned—revenue and meaning-giving orientation. The revenue orientation, with creating future and organizing, limits the space. The meaning-giving orientation, with reflecting and dialoguing, in contrast, stretches the space.

The Four Dimensions of Developmental Space

In the second Delphi study, it became clear that the dimensions needed more specific description. The descriptions given hereafter are based on (1) the outcomes of this research, including the literature study, (2) Coenders's (2008) earlier research, and (3) our definition of innovation.

Dialoguing

As Kessels, Boers, and Mostert (2002) state, a dialogue has three characteristics: (1) searching for reasons, views, beliefs and standards; (2) postponing solutions and decisions; and (3) being open to and appreciating the differences of others. Dialoguing is a space-creating way of communicating. It creates room for others to tell their stories, their motives, beliefs, and allows room for oneself, by postponing one's own opinions and judgments. In dialogue, groups create shared meaning, which is crucial for innovation (Bolhuis, 2009; Boonstra & de Caluwé, 2007; Boonstra & Smid, 2003; Homan, 2005). The starting point for the dialogue to innovate is looking for what there already is: in other words, appreciative inquiry (Cooperrider, Whitney, & Stavros, 2008). Dialoguing asks for vulnerability and learning behavior and is not common. Nowadays, discussion is more common. According to Bolhuis (2009), a high tolerance for uncertainty is related to dialogue.

Reflecting

A common description for reflection is coming to a halt and examining *why* something was started and *what* was intended (Kessels et al., 2002; Leijen, 2008; Schön, 1983). For the developmental space needed for innovation and thus creating knowledge, reflection is also about connecting theory and practice by judging concepts in practice (determinative judgment) and testing one's experience on concepts (reflective judgment). Joint re-flection is needed for making knowledge implicit and experience explicit (van Woerkom, 2004) and to decrease the chance of misconceptions and prejudice (Marsick & Watkins, 1990). Finally, it also means searching for alternatives. According to van Es (2008), this is crucial for innovation. It is not easy, because it asks for a process of deconstruction and construction, and not getting attached to results (Bolhuis & Simons, 1999; Coenders, 2008; Kahane, 2010).

Creating Future

Working on a complex innovation without clear direction and goal from the beginning still requires focus. This can be given by an inspiring opin-ion (Gratton, 2007) or an urgent and intriguing question (Verdonschot, 2009), or a described output result, leaving room for interpretation (Van-dendriessche & Clement, 2006). Tolerance of uncertainty (Bolhuis, 2009) may be crucial to the type of start a group prefers. It is crucial for the spon-sor and the group members to find just the right challenge (see Vermunt, 1996; Vygotsky, 1978). An innovation in organizations needs to be valuable for the organization, individuals, and/or the society. So the *creating future* dimension automatically leads to interaction with the environment, as the group needs to know what the environment is waiting for. Gratton (2007) and Wenger, McDermott, and Snyder (2002) make clear that group mem-bers will be more motivated when their work also creates value for them-selves, for instance, because the group members extend their own experi-ence and knowledge.

Organizing

Groups working on innovation want to realize a result within limited time and resources. This requires organizing the cooperation and starts with making agreements about who joins the group, who is doing what, when, in which way, and so on (Vroemen, 2009). Sometimes this leads to a project plan. According to Mintzberg (2007), in an adhocracy plans should be flexible and leading to strategic learning. Innovating groups tend to look like an adhocracy (Coenders, 2008) "teams of experts working on projects to produce novel outputs" (Mintzberg, 2007, p. 342). Organizing also re-quires leadership. For the developmental space, a leader should be able to pay attention to all the dimensions, in this framework, distributed leader-ship fits best. Taking the lead can be done by doing a proposal or giving a résumé. Schweigert (2007) writes: "followers freely choose their leaders . . . and a shift in consciousness among those gathered can quickly turn an of-ficial leader into a follower struggling to keep up" (p. 326). Finally, whoever takes the lead, the dimension of organizing is also about feeling responsible for, and taking ownership of, the intended innovation as a group member.

CONCLUSION

Reflecting on the descriptive part of the guiding research question—
"What is a useful model of developmental space for groups and MCs?"—it
appears that what we refer to as model 3.0 captures the essence of the
developmental space. This model still comes close to Coenders' model
with a number of modifications, notably (1) changed terminology into
more common language, (2) simplified interpretation of the dimensions
by bringing them back to their essence, and (3) an added focus on interaction with the environment.

Answering the Research Question

Based on this study, the model seems to be recognizable and understood
by many groups and MCs. We doubt, however, if the model as currently crafted is sufficient for groups and MCs in their facilitator roles to analyze the
developmental space. A question for further research thus focuses on the
type of instrument groups and MCs can use to help them analyze their developmental space. Analyzing the developmental space may imply measuring the dimensions, but this is problematic. For instance, in thinking about
dialoguing a number of questions emerge: when do you need to dialogue, at
what time in the process, how much dialogue is necessary, how does quality
vary across different dialogues, and so forth. It is also difficult to measure
because it concerns an experienced space. An experiment in groups, using
statements for every dimension on a five-point Likert scale, already shows
that individuals in a group value the dimensions differently. But when they
discuss their scores, they come up with the same examples to explain their
scores and subsequently easily reach a shared idea about the developmental
space of the group. Conducting an analysis in this way is especially appealing
for the *reflecting* and *dialoguing* dimensions. Analyzing the developmental
space as a group requires developmental space! Thus it could be that a truly
useful instrument should incorporate all the dimensions.

Moving beyond analysis per se, the second part of the research question
focuses on a model of developmental space that groups and facilitators can
use to influence their space. The current findings from the second Delphi
study imply that groups at least need to pay attention to all the dimensions
to be successful. This matches Coenders' (2008) argument that the four
dimensions need to be in balance. This dynamic seems similar to Kahane's
(2010) balance between "power and love," and de Caluwé and Vermaak's
(2003) position that innovating groups need to focus on the product and
process at the same time. Bringing the dimensions into balance is difficult.
People are used to thinking in contradictions or in choosing between alter-

natives, but here we have to avoid thinking in good or bad or in either/or terms. It is having both (Kahane, 2010; Quinn, 2005); too much of one side leads to a problem on the other side (see Ofman, 2001).

Balance also seems to indicate that one can measure the dimensions and the group needs a shared idea about the developmental space; the difficulty with both has already been discussed. Finally, it is difficult because looking at the dimensions separately contradicts the idea of balance, by means of which you look at the dimensions as a whole. The way a group handles the tensions among the dimensions may give a better insight into how they handle the balance. Yet, paying attention, at the same time, to the revenue and meaning giving orientations seems to be a dilemma. An articulated dilemma consists of two contradictory statements, each of which is defendable and good. Coping with dilemmas asks for recognizing the dilemma, considering the advantages and disadvantages of choosing one position, and then choosing actions for each context or case based on the considerations. The dilemma is always present and evident (see Hoebeke, 2004; de Caluwé, 2007).

Balance means the creation of tensions and variety in order to move. It is opposite to the term *equilibrium*, which implies a stable, non-moving state, in which every part fits into other parts like a puzzle (see Pascale, 1999). A fundamental dilemma of the developmental space is limiting (the revenue orientation) or amplifying (the meaning giving orientation) the space at the same time or reciprocally. Homan (2005) states that an unlimited space leads to uncertainty and losing one's way and the disappearance of change energy. On the other hand, too limited a space will frustrate the group and also lead to a low level of energy. It is a challenge to create the "optimal" space as a group or as an MC. Interesting questions for future research focus on how successful and unsuccessful groups cope with the dilemmas between the revenue and meaning-giving orientations, and the nature of the optimal developmental space for an innovating group.

Assessing Model 3.0 of Developmental Space

Reflecting and *dialoguing* seem to be similar concepts. Bolhuis (2009) stated that dialogue is needed for reflection. Still, for the developmental space, dialogue and reflection are distinguished, because they are both crucial for this space. Reflecting stands for *what*, looking from a distance and from multiple perspectives. Dialoguing gives more the *how*, the method for acting by asking questions in an appreciative, inquiring way. *Creating future* is also more about the *what*, a key question, opinion or result, and *organizing* is more the *how*, coordination and distributed leadership. Model 3.0, as Coenders' (2008) model, consists of four dimensions and two orientations. A question that lingers, however, is whether the model really consists of four dimensions or only of two. Drawing on the definition of dimension, "one of the parameters describing a space" (Dimension, n.d.), it does appear that there are four dimensions. The model, however, may not suggest the idea of two axes.

There are still a number of questions that remain unanswered, for example, how interaction with the environment could be embedded in the model. We think that the group also needs to balance the four dimensions in their interaction with the environment, and, as such, power and leadership probably play a role in such interaction. Thus, related questions concern the ways in which power and leadership inside and outside the group influence the developmental space, and the type of leadership that is supportive for developmental space. A final question for management consultants focuses on how MCs can facilitate groups in analyzing and influencing their developmental space.

Discussing the Methodology

Our methodology, developmental research as part of theory-guided bricolage, suits the goal—creating an applicable model of developmental space for innovating groups and MCs that is consistent with Coenders' (2008) earlier research. With a goal to innovate the model of developmental space, we need developmental space ourselves. Consistent with this, we used interviews and Delphi studies as knowledge-creating methods. This approach may have been stronger if we also used group interventions. Group members and facilitators who work on innovation play a key role in the research, because the model is meant to help them. In our research, participants were all highly educated and experienced facilitators. In Coenders' (2008) research, all participants were also highly educated. Next research steps could include less-educated group members, especially those who lack facilitating experience. In the second Delphi study, the questions were suggestive, such as "what do you recognize of the dimension … ?" This approach was chosen because we were looking for specific feedback on the redesigned model, and it seemed justifiable because of Coenders' methods in combination with our research steps. We tried to avoid any blind spots by also asking the respondents whether there are other dimensions that determined the developmental space, what they thought of the model, and whether there were other reactions they would like to give. This openness minimizes the risk of getting only desired answers.

In the second Delphi study, the respondents selected and compared successful and unsuccessful groups. They do this without specific criteria. Since it is their subjective opinion, by judging the developmental space of a group they are also, in effect, judging themselves. Interestingly, the answers given by facilitators for unsuccessful groups were a little more positive compared with the answers given by participants.

Implications for Management Consulting

The outcome of this study, in line with the study by Coenders (2008), makes it clear that MCs as facilitators of innovating groups should ensure that all four dimensions of the developmental space receive attention. This means that MCs should be able to recognize the dimensions during the process and help the group pay attention to all the dimensions. How much attention and at what moments exactly is still unanswered. In the cases studied, all the groups almost automatically pay attention to some of the dimensions—creating future and organizing—which could be inherent in our action-oriented organization culture (Quinn, 2005). The facilitators in the second Delphi study noted that they focused much of their attention to dialoguing and reflecting, activities in which MCs are generally skilled.

Organizations need to innovate rapidly nowadays. Innovation requires new knowledge, or new combinations of knowledge, and a work environment in which individuals are able to collaborate. This challenge requires a stimulating and challenging work environment. Groups make this work environment themselves through their interaction. We call it developmental space. Groups need this space to be successful in innovation. Our research resulted in an understandable model of developmental space for groups and management consultants.

Developmental space consists four dimensions: creating future, reflecting, organizing, and dialoguing. Our research and earlier research shows that groups are more successful in their innovation when they are able to pay attention to all those four dimensions. This is difficult, because these dimensions are partly diametrically opposite of each other. Thus, having an understandable model is not enough for groups and management consultants to analyze their developmental space and create that space in a goal-oriented way. Our next challenge, therefore, is developing instruments for analyzing and creating developmental space.

REFERENCES

Arets, J., & Heijnen, V. (2008). *Kostbaar misverstandVan training naar business improvement.* [Costly misunderstanding: From training to business improvement.] Den Haag, The Netherlands: Academic Service.

Bolhuis, S. (2009). *Leren en veranderen* [Learning and change] (3rd ed.). Bussum, The Netherlands: Coutinho.

Bolhuis, S. M., & Simons, P. R. J. (1999). *Leren en werken* [Learning and working]. Deventer, The Netherlands: Kluwer.

Boonstra, J. J. (2004). *Dynamics of organizational change and learning.* Chichester, West Sussex: John Wiley & Sons.

Boonstra, J., & de Caluwé, L. (2007). *Intervening and changing: Looking for meanings in interactions.* Chichester, West Sussex: John Wiley & Sons.

Boonstra, J. J., & Smid, G. A. (2003). Nieuwe eisen aan leiders [New requirements for leaders]. *Tijdschrift Voor Management Development, 11*(3), 21–24.

Borghans, L., Golsteyn, B., & de Grip, A. (2007). Wat leert onderzoek ons over informeel leren? [What does research learn us about informal learning?]. *Handboek Effectief Opleiden, 44/65*(8.6-1), 1–20.

Brinkerhoff, R. O. (2002). *The success case method: Find out quickly what's working and what's not.* San Francisco, CA: Berrett-Koehler.

Clegg, S., Kornberger, M., & Pitsis, T. (2005). *Managing and organizations: An introduction to theory and practice.* London, England: Sage.

Coenders, M. (2008). *Leerarchitectuur. Een exploratief onderzoek naar de relatie tussen ruimte en leren in werksituaties en het ontwerpen voor leren dichtbij de praktijk* [Learning architecture: An explorative research for the relation between space and learning in work situations and the design of learning near practice]. Delft, The Netherlands: Eburon.

Cooperrider, D. L., Whitney, D., & Stavros, J. M. (2008). *Appreciative inquiry handbook for leaders of change,* 2nd ed. San Francisco, CA: Berrett-Koehler.

Cross, J. (2007). *Informal learning: Rediscovering the natural pathways that inspire innovation and performance.* San Francisco, CA: Pfeiffer.

de Caluwé, L. (2007). Using simulation gaming for change of organizations and for change of corporate culture. In W. Kriz (Ed.), *Planspiele für die Organisationsentwicklung [Games for Organizational Development]* (pp. 41–62). Berlin: Wissenschaftlicher Verlag.

de Caluwé, L., & Vermaak, H.. (2003). *Learning to change: A handbook for the organizational change agent.* Thousand Oaks, CA: Sage.

Denzin, N. K., & Lincoln, Y. S. (2000). *Handbook of qualitative research.* London, England: Sage.

Derksen, K. (2011). Interactie praktijk en wetenschap [Interaction between practice and science]. *Tijdschrift voor Ontwikkeling in Organisaties [Journal for Developing Organizations], 1,* 58–64.

Dimension. (n.d.). In *Encyclo online encyclopedie.* Retrieved from http://www.encyclo.nl/begrip/dimensie

Drucker, P. (2001). A century of social transformation: Emergence of knowledge society. In P. F. Drucker (Ed.), *The essential Drucker* (pp. 299–320). New York, NY: Harper Business.

Edmondson, A. (1999). Psychological safety and learning behavior in work teams. *Administrative Science Quarterly, 44*(2), 350–383.

Gratton, L. (2007). *Hot spots: Why some teams, workplaces and organizations buzz with energy—And others don't.* San Francisco, CA: Berrett-Koehler.

Gravemeijer, K. 1(994). Educational development and developmental research in mathematics education. *Journal for Research in Mathematics Education, 25*(5), 443–471.

Gravemeijer, K. (1998). Developmental research as a research method. In A. Sier-pinska & J. Kilpatrick (Eds.), *Mathematic education as a research domain: A search for identity* (pp. 277–298). Dordrecht, The Netherlands: Kluwer Academic.

Hager, P., & Halliday, J. (2009). *Recovering informal learning: Wisdom, judgment and community*. Dordrecht, The Netherlands: Springer.

Harrison, R., & Kessels, J. (2004). *Human resource development in a knowledge economy: An organizational view*. New York, NY: Palgrave MacMillan.

Hoebeke, L. (2004). Dilemmas and paradoxes in organizing change processes: A critical reflection. In J. Boonstra (Ed.), *Dynamics of organizational change and learning* (pp. 149–171). Chichester, West Sussex: John Wiley & Sons.

Homan, T. (2005). *Organisatiedynamica. Theorie en praktijk van organisatieverandering* [Organization dynamics: Theory and practice of organizational change]. The Hague, The Netherlands: SDU.

Janis, I. L. (1972). *Victims of groupthink: A psychological study of foreign-policy decisions and fiascoes*. Boston, MA: Houghton Mifflin.

Kahane, A. (2010). *Power and love: A theory and practice of social change*. San Francisco, CA: Berrett-Koehler.

Kessels, J. W. M. (2004). The knowledge revolution and the knowledge economy: The challenge for HRD. In J. Woodall, M. Lee, & J. Stewart (Eds.), *New frontiers in HRD*, (pp. 165–179). London, England: Routledge.

Kessels, J., Boers, E., & Mostert, P. (2002). *Vrije ruimte. Filosoferen in organisaties*. [Free space: Philosophize in organizations]. Amsterdam, The Netherlands: Boom.

Leijen, Ä. (2008). *The reflective dancer: ICT support for practical training*. Unpublished PhD dissertation, Utrecht University.

Marsick, V. J., & Watkins, K. E. (1990). *Informal and incidental learning at the workplace*. London, England: Routledge.

Mintzberg, H. (2007). *Tracking strategies: Toward a general theory*. New York, NY: Oxford University Press.

Ofman, D. D. (2001). *Core qualities: A gateway to human resources*. Schiedam, The Netherlands: Scriptum.

Pascale, R. (1999). Surfing the edge of chaos. *Sloan Management Review, 40*(3) 83–94.

Plomp, T., Feteris, A., Pieters, J. M., & Tomic, W. (1992). *Ontwerpen van onderwijs en training* [Designing education and training]. Heerlen, The Netherlands: Lemma.

Quinn, R. E. (2005). *Building the bridge as you walk on it: A guide for leading change*. (Trans. L. Belt). The Hague, The Netherlands: Academic Service.

Ruijters, M. (2007). 'Goh, het lijkt net werk. . .' Het organiseren van informeel leren ['Gosh, it looks just like work.' Organizing informal learning]. *Leren in Organisaties [Learning in Organizations], 12*, 14–18.

Scharmer, C. O. (2007). *Theory U: Leading from the future as it emerges: The social technology of presencing*. Cambridge: Society for Organizational Learning.

Schön, D. (1983). *The reflective practitioner*. New York, NY: Basic Books.

Schweigert, F. J. (2007). Learning to lead: Strengthening the practice of community leadership. *Leadership, 3*, 325–342.

Senge, P., Kleiner, A., Roberts, C., Ross, R., Roth, G., & Smith, B. (1999). *The dance of change: The challenges to sustaining momentum in learning organizations*. New York, NY: Doubleday.

Thrift, N. (2006, October). *Re-animating the place of thought: Transformations of spatial and temporal description in the twenty-first century.* Paper presented at the DIME conference for Communities of Practice, Durham, United Kingdom.

van Es, R. (2008). *Veranderdiagnose. De onderstroom organiseren* [Change diagnoses. To organize the undercurrent]. Deventer, The Netherlands: Kluwer.

van Woerkom, M. (2004). The concept of critical reflection and its implications for human resource development. *Developing Human Resources, 6*(2), 178–192.

Vandendriessche, F., & Clement, J. (2006). *Leidinggeven zonder bevelen. De outputmanager. Een praktijkboek over leidinggeven vanuit visie* [Managing without demands. The output manager. A practical guide about managing out of vision.]. Tielt, Belgium: Lannoo.

Verdonschot, S. (2009). *Learning to innovate. A series of studies to explore and enable learning in innovation practices.* Unpublished PhD dissertation, Twente University, Enschede, Netherlands.

Vermunt, J. D. (1996). Metacognitive, cognitive and affective aspects of learning styles and strategies: A phenomenographic analysis. *Higher Education, 31,* 25–50.

Visscher-Voerman, J. I. A. (1999). *Design approaches in training and education: A reconstructive study.* Unpublished PhD dissertation, Twente University, Enschede, Netherlands.

Vroemen, M. (2009). *Team op vleugels. Gids voor geïnspireerd samenwerken* [Team on wings: Guide for inspired cooperation]. Deventer, The Netherlands: Kluwer.

Vygotsky, L. S. (1978). *Mind in society: The development of higher psychological processes.* Cambridge, MA: Harvard University Press.

Wenger, E. (1998). *Communities of practice: Learning, meaning and identity.* Cambridge, UK: Cambridge University Press.

Wenger, E., McDermott, R., & Snyder, W. M. (2002). *Cultivating communities of practice.* Boston, MA: Harvard Business School Press.

Wierdsma, A. (2007). A methodology for increasing collective competence: A context for co-creative change. In J. Boonstra & L. de Caluwé (Eds.), *Intervening and changing: Looking for meanings in interactions* (pp. 243–260). Chichester, West Sussex: John Wiley & Sons.

CHAPTER 5

MANAGERS' PERCEPTIONS OF ORGANIZATIONAL CHANGE SKILLS

Within their Own Organization and Those Sought from Management Consultants

Karen Somerville and Dawn-Marie Turner

Continuous change has become the norm for many organizations (By, 2005; Hoag, Ritschard, & Cooper, 2002; Rossi, 2006). Often organizational change originates from environmental factors such as new government legislation, globalization, new technologies, customer preferences, and industry and competitive factors (Cawsey, Descza, & Ingols, 2012). Several researchers (e.g., Beer & Nohria, 2000; Higgs & Rowland, 2000; Hirschhorn, 2002; Knodel, 2004; Sirkin, Keenan, & Jackson, 2005) have noted that the majority of change initiatives fail. Various reasons have been cited for these failures, including the absence of change management competence (Griffith, 2002).

Exploring the Professional Identity of Management Consultants, pages 99–118
Copyright © 2013 by Information Age Publishing
All rights of reproduction in any form reserved.

The requirement for organizational change skills is a global issue as organizations are facing significant challenges in managing and leading change initiatives, yet, surprisingly, the literature provides little information about what specific change management and change leadership skills are necessary for successful organizational change (Somerville & Whelan-Berry, 2009). Research relating to appropriate skills and competencies of the effective change manager is quite limited (Nikolaou, Gouras, Vakola, & Bourantas, 2007). Further, the literature pays relatively little attention to the identification of specific organizational change skills. For example, while Cawsey et al. (2012) agree that leading through change is a "necessary skill for all managers," in their chapter entitled "Becoming a Master Change Agent" they identified only three types of organizational change skills: interpersonal, communication, and political skills.

A study by Somerville and Whelan-Berry (2009) included a literature review that identified specific organizational change skills. This literature review identified 11 groups of organizational change skills: managing the change process, resistance and conflict, coalitions and networks, vision, resources, communication, interpersonal and social, change leadership, power and politics, internal and external environment, and trust. A brief description of these 11 groups of organizational change skills is provided in Table 5.1.

Given the relatively limited literature that identifies and discusses specific organizational change skills, this study was undertaken. In addition to seeking a managerial perspective on key skills related to organizational change, the question of the role of management consultants in leading and managing organizational change initiatives was also included in this study. While organizations hire management consultants as they need the consultants' resources (MacDonald & Simpson, 2001), it is unclear whether organizations rely on their own employees to lead and manage change initiatives, or if these are primarily the roles of management consultants. Consultants are hired by organizations for a variety of reasons including providing expertise not available in-house, validating internally developed approaches and acting as a "coach" to internal personnel who do most of the work (Gable, 2007). If management consultants are playing a significant role in leading and managing change initiatives, what skills do they bring?

This study has five main research objectives, to:

1. identify what role(s) management consultants play related to organizational change initiatives;
2. identify what specific organizational change skills are sought from management consultants;
3. identify what organizational change skills already exist within organizations and to compare and contrast these with those skills sought from management consultants;

TABLE 5.1 Summary of Change Skill Topics in the Literature

Change Skill Topics	Brief Description	Frequency in the Literature	Literature Sources
Managing the Change Process	This is a broad range of skills that concern the steps in the change process. These include knowing what needs to be changed, convincing people of the need for change, developing comprehensive plans, and implementing policies and procedures to embed the changes within the organization.	12	Shanley, 2006; Buchanan & Boddy, 1992; Moss Kanter, 2000; Zaccaro & Banks, 2004; Woodward & Hendry, 2004; Williams & Williams, 2007; Harris & Cole, 2007; Rock & Donde, 2008a; Rock & Donde, 2008b; Hill, 2006; Bennis, 1993; Carnall, 2003
Resistance and Conflict	This is a subset of skills for managing the change process that includes effectively managing the resistance and conflict relating to the changes.	6	Buchanan & Boddy, 1992; Shanley, 2006; Harris & Cole, 2007; Munner, 2007; Burnes, 2000; Burke, 2002
Coalitions and Networks	This is a subset of skills for managing the change process that includes skills to build and manage effective coalitions and networks both within and outside of the organization relating to the change initiative.	4	Buchanan & Boddy, 1992; Moss Kanter, 2000; Carnall, 2003; Shanley, 2006
Vision	This is a subset of skills for managing the change process that includes developing a desirable, realistic vision for the change and translating the vision into workable strategic and tactical plans.	3	Buchanan & Boddy, 1992; Woodward & Hendry, 2004; Zaccaro & Banks, 2004
Resources	This is a subset of skills for managing the change process that includes ensuring adequate resources for the change initiative and related effective budgeting.	2	Williams & Williams, 2007; Harris & Cole, 2007
Communication	Effective communication skills include the ability to speak, write and listen, in change management communication about change visions, and their ongoing implementation are seen as important.	9	Buchanan & Boddy, 1992; Bennis, 1993; Moss Kanter, 2000; Zaccaro & Banks, 2004; Woodward & Hendry, 2004; Shanley, 2006; Williams & Williams, 2007; Munner, 2007; Bennis, 1993

(continued)

TABLE 5.1 Summary of Change Skill Topics in the Literature (continued)

Change Skill Topics	Brief Description	Frequency in the Literature	Literature Sources
Interpersonal and Social	This includes a broad range of interpersonal and social skills such as inspiring, motivating, influencing, identifying the concerns of others and treating people fairly, which become even more important during organizational change when individuals are asked to change their work, may resist change, and want to be heard in terms of any questions about change initiatives.	10	Buchanan & Boddy, 1992; Matthew, 2009; Kotter & Cohen, 2002; Zaccaro, 2002; Burke, 2002; Shanley, 2006; Woodward & Hendry, 2004; Zaccaro & Banks, 2004; Buchanan & Boddy, 1992; Harris & Cole, 2007
Change Leadership	These skills include self-confidence, emotional resilience in the times of setbacks and difficulties, and making difficult decisions, all of which are frequently required during organizational change.	6	Burke, 2002; Shanley, 2006; Woodward & Hendry, 2004: Hill, 2006; Burnes, 2000; Carnall, 2003
Power and Politics	These skills include negotiating effectively to gain support, and addressing power and political dynamics that can affect the implementation and resourcing of organizational change efforts.	3	Shanley, 2006; Buchanan & Boddy, 1992; Burke, 2002
Internal and External Environment	This topic relates to skills to analyze and understand the internal and external environmental factors and dynamics concerning the change initiative.	3	Shanley, 2006; Moss Kanter, 2000; Warrick, 2006
Trust	The ability to build and maintain trusting relationships is key to effectively managing organizational change.	2	Shanley, 2006; Bennis, 1993

Source: Somerville & Whelan-Berry, 2009, pp. 57–59.

4. determine if management consultants hired for organizational change initiatives tend to be hired from large consulting firms or smaller consulting firms; and
5. determine whether management consultants' involvement in organizational change initiatives is generally perceived as typically contributing in a positive way to the change initiative.

LITERATURE RELATED TO ORGANIZATIONAL CHANGE SKILLS

Given the lack of more recent literature concerning organizational change skills, the summary of the literature developed by Somerville and Whelan-Berry (2009) is used for this current study (see Table 5.1). As noted by Somerville and Whelan-Berry (2009), the literature emphasizes managing the organizational change process, interpersonal and social, and communication skills. However, it is not completely clear from the literature included in Table 5.1 which skills are most frequently used or are most important to effective organizational change. This study helps to address those questions.

METHODOLOGY

This section briefly discusses the study's sample, data collection process, and analysis.

Sample

Using a convenience sample, possible candidates were identified for interviews from a broad range of industries and different organizational sizes. These candidates were perceived to be knowledgeable about the nature of this research project. A letter of invitation was sent to potential candidates, and telephone calls were made as required. The invitation letter explained the nature of the study, the objectives of the research, the research team, and other pertinent information, including the expectation that each interview would take between 30 and 45 minutes and could be conducted on the telephone.

Data Collection

In total, 55 organizational leaders were invited to participate in this study. Forty-two leaders from Canada and the United States participated, representing a 76 percent response rate. A standardized interview guide was used to ensure consistency of questions between the two researchers. The majority of interviewees were provided with a copy of the general interview questions in advance of the interviews to expedite the interview process, exclusive of the interviewer prompts and the list of change skills found in the literature (Somerville & Whelan-Berry, 2009). The list of change skills was not provided in advance so that the change skills that could be identified by the interviewees without prompting could be determined. Interview responses were word processed into a document during the interview. All interviews except one were conducted by telephone. The other interview was conducted in person.

Data Analysis

Data from the interview documents were entered into SPSS for data analysis. A small amount of the data was analyzed manually given that it was qualitative in nature. The results of this manual data analysis concerns managers' perceptions of management consultants' contributions to organizational change, including examples, and is presented later in the results section (see Table 5.14).

RESULTS

Table 5.2 provides a summary of characteristics from our sample of 42 managers (30 men and 12 women). Twenty-two of those interviewed were from Canada, with the remaining 20 from the United States. The majority of the

TABLE 5.2 Characteristics of the Sample

	Male (n = 30)	Female (n = 12)
Corporate profiles:		
Percent in senior manager/executive roles	87%	67%
Percent in organizations of more than 500 employees	43%	58%
Number of direct reports	6 employees	5 employees
Number of indirect reports	37 employees	19 employees
Personal profiles:		
Location	20 – Canada	2 – Canada
	10 – United States	10 – United States
Percent with university degrees	80%	75%
Number of different employers	4	4
Years of work experience	27.8 years	30.5 years

interviewees were in senior management and/or executive roles and had university degrees. On average, those interviewed had had four different employers since starting full time work, with approximately 30 years of work experience. Table 5.3 provides a summary of the job function of the managers. Table 5.4 summarizes the industries represented by the managers. Table 5.5 provides a summary of the size of each of the organizations based on the number of employees in the organizations.

Table 5.6 provides the managers' perceptions of change in their organizations in the past five years, when considering four main indicators: whether there was introduction and/or abandonment of major service/product lines, whether there was a major restructuring of the organization, whether there were significant changes in staff numbers (up or down), and whether the organization had undergone a major transformation in work

TABLE 5.3   Job Functions of Respondents

Job Function	Frequency	Percent
Marketing and sales	8	19%
President/CEO	14	34%
Accounting and finance	3	7%
COO	2	5%
Human resources	4	10%
Production	2	4%
Mergers and acquisitions	2	4%
Information technology/information management	4	10%
Other administration/services	3	7%
Total	**42**	**100%**

TABLE 5.4   Industries Represented by Respondents

Industry	Frequency	Percent
Finance, insurance and real estate	9	21%
Public administration/Government	3	7%
Manufacturing	10	24%
Agriculture, forestry, mining, electricity, gas	4	10%
Health care	1	3%
Other services	4	10%
Transportation, construction	2	4%
Retail	3	7%
Other	6	14%
Total	**42**	**100%**

TABLE 5.5   Organization Size by Respondents

Number of employees in organization	Frequency	Percent
Fewer than 25 people	2	5%
25 to 100 people	8	19%
101 to 500 people	12	28%
501 to 5000 people	5	12%
More than 5,000	15	36%
Total	**42**	**100%**

TABLE 5.6   Managers' Perceptions of Change in their Own Organizations in the Past Five Years

Type of Change	Frequency Yes	% Yes	Frequency No	% No
Introduced and/or abandoned major service/product lines?	32	76%	10	24%
Undergone major restructuring?	29	69%	13	31%
Significant changes in staff numbers (up or down)?	26	62%	16	38%
Undergone a major transformation in work processes?	25	60%	17	40%

processes. The majority of managers indicated that their organizations had experienced all four of these types of changes in the past five years, indicating a high level of organizational change.

Managers were initially asked if they used management consultants, and 12 managers (twenty nine percent) indicated they did not use management consultants. Managers that indicated they used management consultants were asked about the role(s) management consultants play related to their organizational change initiatives. Table 5.7 summarizes the responses. The most frequently cited roles included working with C-Level executives, knowledge transfer, education and training, and project management.

Prior to the sharing of the organizational change skills identified in the literature (Somerville & Whelan-Berry, 2009) with the managers, managers were asked to identify organizational change skills they perceive existed in their own organizations and those organizational change skills sought by hiring management consultants. Table 5.8 summarizes the responses to these questions. The highlighted organizational change skills in this table represent the skills managers identified prior to being given the list of change skills but that align with the list of skills identified in the literature. The skills not highlighted in Table 5.8 were new organizational change skills identified by the managers that had not been previously identified in the article by Somerville and Whelan-Berry (2009).

TABLE 5.7   Managers' Perceptions of Roles Played by Management Consultants in Relation to Organizational Change Initiatives

Role Played by Management Consultants in Relation to Organizational Change Initiatives	Frequency	Percent
Work with C-Level executives	8	19%
Knowledge transfer, education and training	6	14%
Project management	4	10%
Organization structure/reorganization	3	7%
Assessment and benchmarking	3	7%
Identification of opportunities	3	7%
Communication	3	7%
Recommendations related to production	2	5%
Identification of best practices	2	5%
Strategic planning	2	5%
Diagnostics to identify problems	2	5%
Leadership roles	2	5%
Facilitation	2	5%
Construct HR manuals with employment practices	1	2%
Review employee skill sets	1	2%
Recruitment	1	2%
Develop methodologies	1	2%
Bring change tool kit to our organization	1	2%
Design the process of change	1	2%
IT implementation	1	2%
Gather data	1	2%
Mediation	1	2%
Ask difficult questions	1	2%
Provide industry pay scales and variable incentive plans	1	2%
Develop and communicate a vision	1	2%
Learning and development initiatives for the new organization	1	2%
Planning for the change	1	2%
Marketing	1	2%
Board governance	1	2%
Mentoring	1	2%
Extra arms and legs	1	2%

Thirty one percent of managers (13) did not identify any organizational change skills before they were provided with the list of organizational change skills. Of those skills from the Somerville and Whelan-Berry (2009) article, the organizational change skills most frequently identified by the managers were communication (for both skills in their own organization and sought from management consultants) and skills related to managing the change process (again, for both their own organization and sought from management consultants). Two organizational change skills that were

TABLE 5.8 Managers' Perceptions of Organizational Change Skills (without Change Skills List)

Organizational Change Skills	In own Organization (Frequency)	% (n = 42)	Sought from Management Consultants (Frequency)	% (n = 42)
None identified	13 participants	31%	13 participants	31%
Managing the change process	3	7%	14	33%
Resistance and conflict	1	2%	3	7%
Coalitions and networks	2	5%	—	—
Vision	1	2%	1	2%
Resources	1	2%	1	2%
Communication	11	26%	9	21%
Interpersonal and social	2	5%	—	—
Change leadership	3	7%	2	5%
Power and politics	—	—	2	5%
Internal and external environment	5	12%	2	5%
Trust	—	—	—	—
Project management	5	12%	4	10%
Training	5	12%	5	12%
Creative	—	—	2	5%
Challenging the status quo	—	—	1	2%
Culture change	—	—	1	2%
Organization design	—	—	1	2%
Facilitation	—	—	2	5%
Mentoring	1	2%	—	—
Other general management skills, such as recruiting, general planning	7	17%	1	2%

Notes: Some participants identified more than one skill, so percentages do not add to 100.
   Highlighted skills are from the literature summarized in the Somerville and Whelan-Berry (2009) article.

highlighted by managers before they were provided the list of 11 change skills that were *not* identified in the article by Somerville and Whelan-Berry (2009), were project management and training—again for both their own organization and skills sought from management consultants.

The organizational change skills summarized in the Somerville and Whelan-Berry (2009) article, as well as a brief description for each skill (see Table 5.1), were presented to the managers. Then managers were asked to respond with "yes," "no," or "somewhat" if they believed the change skills currently existed in their organization. Their responses are summarized in Table 5.9. It is interesting to note that once provided with a list of specific types of organizational change skills, with the exception of resistance and

TABLE 5.9 Managers' Perceptions of Organizational Change Skills Currently in their Own Organization—When Provided the Literature Summary of Change Skills

Organizational Change Skills (Somerville & Whelan-Berry, 2009)	Frequency Yes	% (n = 42)	Frequency Somewhat	% (n = 42)	Frequency No	% (n = 42)	Frequency Total
Managing the change process	24	57%	10	24%	8	19%	42 (100%)
Resistance and conflict	17	41%	9	21%	16	38%	42 (100%)
Coalitions and networks	25	60%	11	26%	6	14%	42 (100%)
Vision	30	72%	9	21%	3	7%	42 (100%)
Resources	26	62%	8	19%	8	19%	42 (100%)
Communication	29	69%	8	19%	5	12%	42 (100%)
Interpersonal and social	22	52%	12	29%	8	19%	42 (100%)
Change leadership	29	69%	6	14%	8	19%	42 (100%)
Power and politics	22	52%	10	24%	7	17%	42 (100%)
Internal and external environment	22	52%	11	26%	10	24%	42 (100%)
Trust	29	69%	6	14%	9	22%	42 (100%)

conflict management, the majority of respondents responded "yes" regarding whether the skills currently exist in their organization.

Next, using the summary of organizational change skills from Somerville and Whelan-Berry (2009), managers were asked about their perceptions of change skills sought from management consultants. The responses are found in Table 5.10. Skills concerning managing the change process were most frequently cited.

Following the identification of the change skills both within their organization and sought from management consultants, managers were asked to rate the importance of each of the 11 categories of change skills. This was done using a Likert scale of one to seven, with one as "unimportant" and seven "very important." The results are summarized in Table 5.11. It is interesting to note that all 11 categories of change skills were rated as important, even though the majority of change skills were not identified by managers before they were provided with the 11 categories.

Managers were also asked about the size of management consulting firms used for organizational change initiatives (see Table 5.12). Overall, 10 organizations (24%) use large consulting firms, 17 organizations (40%) use small consulting firms, three organizations (7%) use both large and small consulting firms, and 12 organizations (29%) do not use consulting firms for their organizational change initiatives.

Finally, those managers whose organizations use management consultants for organizational change initiatives were asked if they perceive management consultants' contributions as generally positive. These results are summarized in Table 5.13. Twenty-seven managers (90 percent) responded "yes," two managers (7 percent) were unsure, and one manager (3 percent) indicated "no."

The 27 managers who stated they use management consultants and that management consultants contributed positively to their change initiative were asked to describe the contribution that was made. An analysis of these descriptions identified three broad categories of contribution. The first category is labeled *experience* and relates to the consultants' ability to bring knowledge and experience from other organizations and engagements to assist with the manager's current organizational change initiative. The second category, *process*, reflects the consultants' understanding, knowledge and use of process. This is not limited to just the change process but also included strategic planning and other organizational processes. Finally consultants contribute by simply being an *additional resource* to the organization. Table 5.14 shows the number of responses in each category and provides examples of the comments used to identify and support the category. Two respondents did not provide a description or elaborate on the positive contribution of management consultants. It should be noted that some responses were identified as fitting into two categories.

TABLE 5.10 Managers' Perceptions of Organizational Change Skills Sought From Management Consultants—When provided the Literature Summary of Change Skills

Organizational Change Skills (Somerville & Whelan-Berry, 2009)	Frequency Yes	% (n = 42)	Frequency Somewhat	% (n = 42)	Frequency No	% (n = 42)	Frequency Total
Managing the change process	25	60%	3	7%	14	33%	42 (100%)
Resistance and conflict	17	40%	0	—	25	60%	42 (100%)
Coalitions and networks	5	12%	3	7%	34	81%	42 (100%)
Vision	17	40%	4	10%	21	50%	42 (100%)
Resources	16	38%	3	7%	23	55%	42 (100%)
Communication	17	40%	2	5%	23	55%	42 (100%)
Interpersonal and social	6	14%	2	5%	34	81%	42 (100%)
Change leadership	18	43%	1	2%	23	55%	42 (100%)
Power and politics	6	14%	1	2%	35	84%	42 (100%)
Internal and external environment	21	50%	3	7%	18	43%	42 (100%)
Trust	10	24%	4	9%	28	67%	42 (100%)

TABLE 5.11   Managers' Perceptions of Importance of Organizational Change Skills

Organizational Change Skills identified in Literature	Importance: 1–7	Standard Deviation
Managing the change process	6.29	.81
Resistance and conflict	5.31	1.21
Coalitions and networks	4.45	1.25
Vision	6.17	.96
Resources	5.52	1.13
Communication	6.24	.79
Interpersonal and social	5.38	1.46
Change leadership	5.91	1.14
Power and politics	5.00	1.41
Internal and external environment	4.95	1.32
Trust	6.23	1.01

TABLE 5.12   Managers' Perceptions of the Size of Management Consulting Firms for Organizational Change Initiatives

Number of employees in organization	Consulting Firms				
	Large Firms (%)	Small Firms (%)	Both Large and Small Firms (%)	Don't Use Consultants (%)	Total (%)
Fewer than 25 people	1 (2%)	— (—%)	— (—%)	1 (2%)	2 (4%)
25 to 100 people	— (—%)	5 (12%)	— (—%)	3 (7%)	8 (19%)
100 to 500 people	— (—%)	5 (12%)	1 (2%)	6 (14%)	12 (28%)
501 to 5000 people	2 (5%)	3 (7%)	— (—%)	— (—%)	5 (12%)
More than 5,000	7 (17%)	4 (10%)	2 (5%)	2 (5%)	15 (37%)
Total	10 (24%)	17 (40%)	3 (7%)	12 (29%)	42 (100%)

TABLE 5.13   Managers' Perceptions Regarding Whether Management Consultants' Contributions are Generally Positive

Consultants' Contributions Positive?	Frequency	Percent
Yes	27	90%
Unsure	2	7%
No	1	3%
Total	30	100%

Note: This table sums to 30 rather than 42, as 12 organizations did not use management consultants.

TABLE 5.14 Managers' Perceptions of Management Consultants' Contribution to Organizational Change Initiatives

Response Category	Number of Responses	Examples of Comments
Experience	10	"...bring a broader perspective" "...push us to do things might be uncomfortable otherwise" "...helped expand and helped people grow" "...bringing experience to the table"
Process	11	"...just making sure certain processes are done correctly" "...if we follow their counsel can mitigate the negative consequences..." "...making sure certain processes are done right"
Resource	4	"...basically move a project forward that we wouldn't have time to do" "...he works with us to use our own kind of stuff. He talks like we talk..."
No elaboration	2	
Total	27	

DISCUSSION

This research addresses a gap in the literature by highlighting managers' perceptions relating to five research questions concerning organizational change skills and management consultants. This section includes a discussion relating to these five research questions and conclusions.

The Role(s) Management Consultants Play in Organizational Change Initiatives

As noted in Table 5.7, the most frequently cited roles for management consultants include working with C-Level executives, knowledge transfer, education and training, and project management. In addition to these areas, there are a further 28 specific roles identified. Given the broad range of different types of organizational change initiatives undertaken by organizations, this lengthy list of roles for management consultants is not surprising.

Specific Organizational Change Skills Sought from Management Consultants

First the results will be presented relating to when the interviewer did *not* provide the managers with the list of change skills from the literature organizational. As a follow-up, responses when managers were provided with the list of specific organizational change skills by the interviewer will be discussed.

The responses by managers *without* the list of change skills are presented in Table 5.8. Thirteen managers (31 percent) did not identify any specific organizational change skills that are sought from management consultants. The most frequent response (14 managers, 33 percent) by those who did identify specific organizational change skill sought from management consultants were skills relating to managing the change process. The second most frequent response (9 managers, 21 percent) was communication skills. The frequency of additional skills cited dropped off significantly for the remaining skills identified.

These responses from managers *with* the list of change skills are summarized Table 5.10. As noted previously, managers were read the list of Somerville and Whelan-Berry's (2009) 11 categories of organizational change skills. The majority of respondents highlighted two types of change skills that were definitely sought from management consultants: managing the change process and change leadership. When the "somewhat" responses are added to those who responded "yes," the majority of respondents also include internal and external environment.

The differences between managers' responses with and without the list of change skills suggest that even though they have the skills in their organization, managers may not realize the broad range of skills required for successful organizational change and/or are not actively thinking about the specific skills needed when seeking help from management consultants. Some of the respondents commented on the large number of skills on the list.

It is also interesting to note that without the list, the majority of managers highlighted communication skills; however, when specifically prompted for communication skills, the majority of managers did not include communication skills. The unprompted response appeared more related to the development of communication strategies, plans, and tools while the skills definition from the literature (that was provided during the interview) was directed at specific communications skills such as speaking, writing and listening. Table 5.9 identified that 69 percent of the managers believe they have these communication skills in their own organization. Therefore, these results suggest that while broad communication support such as planning, strategy development, and new tools or techniques are sought from management consultants, the specific skills related to listening, speaking and writing are not.

Organizational Change Skills: Skills Existing within Organizations versus Skills Sought from Management Consultants

Again, the results will be initially presented when the interviewer did *not* provide the managers with the list of specific organizational change skills. Then the results when managers were read the list of specific organizational change skills by the interviewer will be discussed. As summarized in Table 5.8, without the list of change skills, 31 percent (13 managers) of those interviewed did not identify any specific organizational changes skills within their own organizations or those sought from management consultants. Fourteen (33 percent) of the managers identified managing the change process as a skill sought from management consultants, which was the most frequently sought skill from management consultants. The second most frequent response regarding organizational change skills sought from management consultants was communication skills (9 managers, 21 percent). The frequency of additional skills sought from management consultants dropped off significantly for the remaining skills identified.

When presented with the list of change skills (see Table 5.9), the majority of respondents indicated that ten of the 11 categories of skills are currently represented in their own organizations. Further, the majority of the respondents indicated that even though they believe they have skills related to managing the change process and change leadership in their organization, they also seek these skills from management consultants. This could be because they are seeking to understand current best practices for these skills and perceive management consultants to have these best practice skills. Other explanations could be that they are seeking to validate internally developed approaches (Gable, 2007) and/or are requesting consultants to act as coaches for less experienced internal resources (Gable, 2007). The only category where the majority of respondents did not perceive the skills to be in their own organization was resistance and conflict skills (17 managers, 40 percent). Since the majority of respondents in this study did not have a background in human resources, they may seek the expertise of an outside consultant to assist with the management of resistance and conflict. Doyle (2002) identified the need for managers to develop the softer, behavioral skills in change management.

It is interesting to note the differences in responses with and without the list of change skills provided by the interviewers. These finding are similar to the second research objective (skills sought from management consultants) discussed in the previous section. The results suggest that managers may not realize the broad range of skills that are required for successful organization change and/or are not actively thinking about skills within their organization when it comes to their organizational change initiatives. Although not directly studied in this research, the relationship between managers' perception of organizational change skills and success of organizational change needs to be considered. Doyle (2002) found that the responsibility for introducing and leading change was shifting from a stand-alone role to being integrated into managers' operational and professional roles. The Doyle (2002) study also identified that many of these leaders were "change agent novices" and lacked the skill to successfully lead change.

Managers were asked to rate the importance of each of the 11 organizational change skill categories regardless of whether they were sought from outside consultants or were found internally. The results are summarized in Table 5.11. A seven point Likert scale with one being "not important" and seven being "very important" was used to rank each category. Managers identified all 11 categories as important. Mean scores were calculated for each category. Coalitions and networks scored the lowest at 4.45 with a standard deviation of 1.25. Managing the change process received the highest ranking at 6.29 with a standard deviation of .81. This result for skills relating to managing the change process was not surprising since the majority of respondents identified it as a skill both within the organization and sought from management consultants.

The 11 categories of organizational change skills identified by Somerville & Whelan-Berry (2009) have not been previously empirically tested for validity with practitioners. These results suggest that the 11 categories of organizational change skills used for this research are appropriate, based on the managers' responses in this study.

Management Consultants and Organizational Change Initiatives: Large versus Small Consultancies

As indicated in Table 5.12, 29 percent (12 managers) of the managers stated that they do not use management consultants at all. Large organizations with more than 5,000 employees use a combination of both large and small consulting firms, often depending on the type of change initiative underway. These results also suggest that organizations with fewer than 5,000 employees tend not to use large consulting firms. The most frequent reasons given by these organizations for not using large consulting firms were the perceived cost of large consulting firms (five responses), and the perception that large firms insist on using their own methodologies, rather than tailoring their approach to the client (seven responses). Organizations with more than 500 employees use both large and small consulting firms. Some of the reasons identified by managers for hiring larger consulting firms include their world class methodologies and the capacity found in large consulting firms. All nine managers who indicated that they do not use consultants indicated that they do not hire management consultants as they have the necessary skills within their own organization.

Perceptions of Management Consultant Involvement in Organizational Change

The vast majority of managers from organizations that use management consultants (27 or 90 percent) perceive that management consultants' contributions are generally positive (see Table 5.13).

CONCLUSION

This exploratory research was an initial step to focus on organizational change skills both within an organization and those sought from management consultants. As such, interviews were drawn from a relatively small North American sample. Future research needs to increase the sample size and expand the breadth and depth of understanding of managers' perceptions of the skills needed for successful organizational change. Questions that could be addressed in future research include: Do managers from different industries perceive organizational change skills differently? Is there a difference between the perception of skills in an organization and the use of management consultants in other countries? How do these perceptions influence the success of organizational change?

Given that continuous change has become the norm for many organizations (e.g., Hoag et al., 2002), change skills are necessary for all managers (Cawsey et al., 2012). These results suggest that the 11 categories of organizational change skills used in this research provide an appropriate focus for managers in planning and implementing their organizational change initiatives. As well, these results suggest that organizations may not realize the broad range of organizational change skills required for successful change. As such they may not be ensuring that individuals assigned to their various change initiatives have the required skills to successfully lead and implement the change. If managers did recognize the broad range of organizational change skills required, and ensure that adequate and appropriate resources are assigned to organizational change initiatives, it could have important positive results for organizations and their employees, for example, by increasing the success rates of change initiatives. As noted by Kotter (2008), "a 70 percent failure rate [for change] is an *enormous* drag on a company, a government, an economy, or a society. Investors are obviously hurt, but the pain goes in all directions: to employees, customers, our families" (p. 13).

We agree with Kotter and hope that this empirical study will contribute to the theory and practice concerning organizational change skills.

REFERENCES

Beer, M., & Nohria, N. (2000). *Breaking the code of change.* Boston, MA: Harvard Business School Press.

By, R. (2005). Organizational change management: A critical review. *Journal of Change Management, 5*(4), 369–380.

Cawsey, T., Deszca, G., & Ingols, C. (2012). *Organizational change: An action-oriented toolkit,* 2nd ed. Thousand Oaks, CA: Sage Publications, Inc.

Doyle, M. (2002). From change novice to change expert: Issues of learning, development and support. *Personnel Review, 31*(4), 465–481.

Gable, J. (2007). Eight tips for working with a consultant. *Information Management Journal, 41*(4), 42–48.

Griffith, J. (2002). Why change management fails. *Journal of Change Management, 2*(4), 297–304.

Higgs, M., & Rowland, D. (2000). Building change leadership capability: The quest for change competence. *Journal of Change Management, 1*(2), 116–130.

Hirschhorn, L. (2002). Campaigning for change. *Harvard Business Review, 80*(7), 98–104.

Hoag, B., Ritschard, H., & Cooper, C. (2002). Obstacles to effective organizational change: The underlying reasons. *Leadership & Organization Development Journal, 23*(1), 6–15.

Knodel, T. (2004). Preparing the organizational "soil" for measurable and sustainable change: Business value management and project governance. *Journal of Change Management, 4*(1), 45–62.

Kotter, J. (2008). *A sense of urgency.* Boston, MA: Harvard Business Press.

Macdonald, S., & Simpson, M. (2001). Learning from management consultants: The lesson for management researchers. *Prometheus, 19*(2), 117–133.

Nikolaou, I., Gouras, A., Vakola, M., & Bourantas, D. (2007). Selecting change agents: Exploring traits and skills in a simulated environment. *Journal of Change Management, 7*(3-4), 291–313.

Rossi, J. (2006). Organizational change on the rise. *Training & Development, 60*(1), 15.

Sirkin, H., Keenan, P., & Jackson, A. (2005). The hard side of change management. *Harvard Business Review,* October, 109–118.

Somerville, K., & Whelan-Berry, K. (2009). Organizational change skills: A study of the literature and education available form American and Canadian MBA programs. *The International Journal of Knowledge, Culture & Change Management, 9*(10), 55–65.

CHAPTER 6

STRUGGLING TO CHALLENGE AN INFORMAL FIELD ORDER

Professional Associations as Standard Setters

Susanna Alexius and Frida Pemer

The management consulting industry can be characterized as an "unbounded profession" with fuzzy borders (Alexius, 2007; Glückler & Armbrüster, 2003). Despite attempts to define subfields within management consultancy, such as PR consultancy, HR consultancy, IT consultancy, and so forth, it is not easy to determine what management consultancy is and is not. This lack of a clear definition creates opportunities for consultants to adapt to their clients' changing needs and add on new services, which may be valuable both for them and their clients (Kipping, 2002). But it also causes confusion in client organizations regarding what can be expected from consultants and how to evaluate their services (Alexius & Furusten, 2005; Clark, 1995; Näslund & Pemer, 2012; Pemer, 2008). Moreover, it creates a market with very low entry barriers and fierce competition among the consultancy firms (Løwendahl, 2005).

Exploring the Professional Identity of Management Consultants, pages 119–138
Copyright © 2013 by Information Age Publishing
All rights of reproduction in any form reserved.
119

Looking at these circumstances, one could easily believe that an increased formalization of the consulting industry would be welcomed by both clients and consultants. There are clear functional reasons for consultants, such as ambitions to increase the status of the consultancy firms, to reduce competition, and to stimulate market demand for consultancy services (Beaverstock, Faulconbridge, & Hall, 2010; Evetts, 2003; Grob & Kieser, 2006; McKenna, 2006; Werr & Pemer, 2007). Besides that kind of functional reasons for professionalization, there are also institutional reasons to expect an increasing formalization, as our modern society is characterized by an increasing number of rules (Brunsson & Jacobsson, 2000). But, in fact, to this day management consultants are much less regulated than other professionals (Alexius, 2007; O'Mahoney, 2010). A significant difference between management consultants and individuals performing traditional and "bounded" professions such as medicine, law, or accounting is the lack of an abstract expert system for management consulting (Abbot, 1988; Beaverstock et al., 2010; Furusten, 2003; Giddens, 1990; Glückler & Armbrüster, 2003). In most countries there is no state regulation restricting the choice of consulting methods applied, and anyone can call him/herself a management consultant since the title lacks legal protection (Kyrö, 1995, for an account of the Austrian exception see Grob & Kieser, 2006). The state regulation that does exist, often in the form of public procurement acts, aims at regulating the *clients* and their selection process, the use, and purchasing of consulting services, and not the consultants (Roodhoft & Van den Abbeele, 2006; Schiele & McCue, 2006).

The order of the management consultancy field continues to be based largely on informal alternatives to regulation such as mutual adjustment, shared norms and values, a common background building confidence and trust, personal friendships and informal networks (Furusten & Werr, 2005; Pemer, 2008) as well as brand building, word-of-mouth testimonials, prior personal experience and time- and resource-consuming risky trial employment (Freidson, 1994). In this chapter we refer to these alternatives to formal field regulation as the *informal field order.*

Studies have found that on a discursive level many consultants openly ignore existing professional field regulation, they belittle its problem solving capacity, and above all they suggest alternative informal solutions to traditional regulatory problems (e.g., Alexius, 2007; Furusten, 2003; Furusten & Werr, 2005; Rydmark, 2004). Professionalization via formal regulation is perceived by many as "unnatural interference" with the consultants' private businesses, something that is greatly opposed to the "free market," which in turn is described as the "natural state" in this field. Contrary to the typical marketing slogans of modern standard setters, many consultants associate professional standardization with inertia, inefficiency, and old-fashioned bureaucracy (Alexius, 2005, 2007). This opinion is found among the clients as well. As empirical studies have shown, many managers oppose the idea of regulating their use of consulting services and either criticize the attempts to standardize overtly or turn into a maverick in buying behavior (Lindberg & Furusten, 2005; Werr & Pemer, 2007). For instance, the Swedish law of public procurement, the Public Procurement Act (PPA), has been widely opposed and is evaded by consultants and clients alike (Lindberg & Furusten, 2005).

In spite of the well established informal alternatives and the regulatory resistance described above, there have been a number of attempts to formalize the consulting field (Beaverstock et al., 2010; Grob & Kieser, 2006; McKenna, 2006). However, as research has already shown, these attempts have generally not been very successful (Alexius, 2007; Grob & Kieser, 2006; Kipping & Saint-Martin, 2005; McKenna, 2006). But despite difficulties, the struggle continues.

In this chapter, we set out to explore the strategies that are used by professional associations when attempting to set and promote standards for management consultancy. We use a broad definition of management consultancy, including consultancies working in the areas of strategy, business, information, PR, advertising, education, staffing, and human resources. The study was conducted as an extensive longitudinal field study of seven Swedish professional associations in the consulting field and their attempts to increase their own authority and their industry's professionalism and status by setting various types of formal professional standards. By studying what motives they had, what challenges they met, and, ultimately, what strategies they used when attempting to introduce professional standards in the field, we aim to contribute to the literature on standardization and professionalization processes by highlighting the institutional influence of the established field order.

The chapter is structured as follows. Following a short introduction to the role of professional associations in standardization and professionalization processes, we then describe our research design and present our analysis and findings. The chapter ends with a concluding discussion, in which contributions and implications for future research and for practitioners are discussed.

PROFESSIONAL ASSOCIATIONS' ROLE
IN PROFESSIONALIZATION PROCESSES

One type of actor that often plays an important role in the professionalization processes is the professional association (Greenwood, Suddaby, & Hinings, 2002). By defining a certain area of expertise and often by introducing formal regulation such as certifications, ethical standards, and sanctions for members, professional associations may contribute to a professionalization process (Karseth & Nerland, 2007; Kipping & Saint-Martin, 2005). Professional associations typically apply various strategies to reach their goals. Formal means such as professional standards are often used, and, in addition, professional associations may function as arenas for interaction and negotiation where members can present themselves to each other and to potential clients, and where the content of the services and activities provided within the profession are defined (Greenwood et al., 2002).

Despite their potentially important role in professionalization processes, professional associations have been given relatively little attention in the literature and just a few empirical studies have been performed (Greenwood et al., 2002; Karseth & Nerland, 2007; McKenna, 2006). We do not know enough about what professionalization activities professional associations undertake and how these activities are combined with their simultaneous attempts to establish themselves as legitimate and attractive organizations for their members.

The history of professional associations in the consulting industry is rather long and has been characterized by struggles for legitimacy—both for the associations themselves and for the consulting industry in general (Kipping & Saint-Martin, 2005; McKenna, 2006). Today there exist professional associations both on the international and local levels. The international associations such as FEACO and ICMCI function as meta-organizations (organizations having other organizations rather than individuals as their members—in this case having the national associations as their members, see Ahrne & Brunsson, 2008), so there is a hierarchy of associations supporting their members with structure, knowledge, and legitimacy. The ambition of these organizations is to improve the status and legitimacy of the consulting profession. This is done by creating standards and certifications and by providing a platform for network activities where the members can meet, learn, and share ideas and experiences (e.g., www.icmci.org; www.feaco. org). The rationale behind these attempts to regulate and professionalize consultants and their work is that it may create a more transparent market for the clients, give the certified consultancies higher status, and build a body of expertise that is specific for the management consulting field (Kipping & Saint-Martin, 2005).

However, as Kubr (1996) has shown, fewer than fifty per cent of the world's management consultants are members of any professional association, and in Sweden fewer than ten percent of the Swedish management consultants are members of any professional association (Alexius, 2007; Furusten, 2003). Similar findings have also been reported in the German context, where of the approximately 14,400 consultancy firms that existed in Germany in 2002 only 0.4 percent were members of the dominating association BDU. These member firms employed about 20 percent of German consultants and represented a market share of 26 percent (Grob & Kieser, 2006) One explanation for these comparatively low levels of membership is that many professional consultancy associations have had difficulties recruiting larger and well established consultancy firms as members as they have used their own brand for signaling exclusiveness and expertise (McKenna, 2006) and that the consultancies in general—large and small—have cherished their freedom to adapt the content of their services to their clients' needs (Kipping, 2002; Alexius, 2007). Many professional associations thus face the challenge of convincing existing and potential members of their legitimacy, attractiveness, and value (Alexius, 2007; Grob & Kieser, 2006).

As Hood (1986) pointed out, industry self-regulation—in other words, rule setting initiated by industry representatives themselves rather than by governments or other legislative bodies outside the industry—may have many advantages (see also Haufler, 2001). It ensures that rules can be set, interpreted, and followed by those closest to action. It makes certain that the spirit of the rules is enforced and that adaptation may be rapid and efficient. But self-enforcement also has its limits. For one thing, rule setters can only be expected to enforce self-regulation that is broadly in line with the interests of the group in general (see also Tamm Hallström and Boström, 2010, pp. 140–162 for a similar argument). Based on our field study of the seven professional associations and their ambiguous identity as standard setters, we elaborate on Hood's (1986) idea to explore what it may be like to balance the identity of the controlling standard setter and the identity of the loyal industry representative in a field where standards and other formal regulation are met with much skepticism and resistance (Alexius, 2007; Pemer, 2008).

Standards as a Means of Professionalization

As many scholars have pointed out, the emergence of the so called knowledge and service society has increased the demands for organizations to become more professional (e.g., Evetts, 2003). Laws, standards, control mechanisms, and sanctions are all formal means of professionalization. In the consulting industry, however, state regulation is scarce (with the PPA as exception) and softer types of industry self-regulation such as standards are launched as alternatives (Alexius, 2007). Standards can take on different forms such as accreditations, codes of conduct, delineated areas of expertise, rankings, and so on. A shared characteristic for them is that, in contrast to laws and state regulations, they are voluntary, meaning that organizations are relatively free to choose whether to follow them (Ahrne & Brunsson, 2004; Brunsson & Jacobsson, 2000; Mörth, 2004).

Since standard followers are not required to become formal members of the standard setter's organization, the lack of regulatory monopoly puts pressure on standard setters to convince potential standard followers of the value and legitimacy of their standards and of their own rule setting authority (Tamm Hallström & Boström, 2010; de Vries, 2001). How easy or difficult it will be to convince potential standard followers of the value and legitimacy of standards depends on the degree of *institutional pressure* for standardization in a certain context, in other words, the degree to which taken-for-granted (institutionalized) norms reflect rule following as appropriate (Brunsson, 2000; Meyer & Rowan, 1977; DiMaggio & Powell, 1983). In many fields skeptical potential standard followers have a hard time finding legitimate reasons and strategies to avoid standard following, due to the institutional pressure to conform to such taken-for-granted norms of rule following (Ahrne & Brunsson, 2004) Besides handling urgent messages of risk and responsibility, they may, for example, find it useful to question standards based on scientific and technological expertise (Jacobsson, 2000).

But there are exceptions, and although standardization is often portrayed as a success story, standard setters may face a number of challenging obstacles to their efforts to set and launch formally voluntary rules. In this chapter, we bring forth findings from one such exception, a field where there rather seems to be institutional pressure *against* standardization—the consulting industry. As mentioned above, this industry is characterized as one with fuzzy borders and in a state of continuous change—both in the type of services provided and the type of actors involved. Moreover, it has a strong informal field order, where mutual adjustment, shared norms, and relationships play an important role in the shaping of the industry (see Ahrne, Brunsson, & Tamm Hallström, 2007). As will be shown in the analysis below, this informal field order came to affect the attempts of the professional associations in a way that was not entirely expected by them.

RESEARCH DESIGN

This chapter is based on a still ongoing longitudinal field study on professional associations and their attempts for professionalization in the Swedish management consultancy field. The data presented here was collected mainly between 2000 and 2007. Several qualitative techniques and materials were combined, interviews and documentary studies being the most important.

A pilot empirical part of the study started out in 2000–2001, aiming to map various regulatory activities and initiatives in and around the Swedish management consultancy field, mainly using documentary studies of websites, consultancy magazines, and so on. A selection of non-mandatory professional associations was then made based on a listing of consultancy subfields in the annual Swedish consultancy magazine Konsultguiden (the Consultancy Guide), which had been covered in the pilot study. Nine pro-

TABLE 6.1 Overview of the Seven Studied Professional Associations

Professional Association	Type of Consultancy	Foundation Year
Bemanningsföretagen (previously SPUR)	Staff agencies	1996
HRK	Human resources	1989
PRECIS	Public relations	1992
SAMC	Management consulting	1989
SMIF	Market information	1990
SRF	Advertising	1996
UF	Education	1992

fessional associations targeting consultants—although not all of them exclusively consultants—were first selected for comparison (see Alexius, 2005 for empirical details). Out of these nine (see Table 6.1), the following seven were found to act as standard setters: Bemanningsföretagen (The Swedish Association of Staff-Agencies), HRK (The Swedish Association of Human Resource consultants), PRECIS (The Association of Public Relations Consultancies in Sweden), SAMC (The Swedish Association of Management consultants), SMIF (The Swedish Association of Market Information consultants), SRF (The Associations of Swedish practitioners in advertising), and UF (The Association of Education consultancies in Sweden).

An interview study was conducted in 2004–2005 when one or two semi-structured interviews were made with one or a few representatives—usually the chairman and/or the CEO/president—for each of these seven professional associations studied in this chapter. The aim of these interviews was to find out more about the professional associations' motives for introducing standards, what challenges, if any, were faced, and what strategies were applied. Documentary studies continued, following the developments of the organizations' websites, the websites of their members, as well as various rule documents. Among the rule documents, both rules internal to the associations (directives) and their professional standards such as certifications, ethical standards, rankings, price competitions, and so on were analyzed. A second follow-up telephone interview round was conducted in 2007, and a third is planned for 2012.

STANDARD SETTING IN SEVEN PROFESSIONAL ASSOCIATIONS

In this section, we first describe the motives behind the professional associations' standardization attempts and continue by describing the challenges they faced and, ultimately, the strategies used to handle these challenges.

Standardization Motives

According to classic notions of self-regulation, membership associations and standards are created following threats of public regulation after attention to industry scandals: the industry is organized as a reactive response to a legitimacy crisis (Haufler, 2001; Nordström, 2004). However, in this study, there was only one clear case of such a development: the founding of SPUR, Bemanningsföretagens' predecessor. In 1993, a new Swedish law made it legal to set up private businesses recruiting and hiring temporary staff. In 1997, a public investigation on the Swedish staffing industry was presented (SOU 1997:58), suggesting self-regulation, and recommending the Swedish state to give a membership association a chance to show whether the industry could self-regulate and discipline any misconduct. Before long the SPUR association launched its own certification procedure (see also Ahrne, Brunsson, & Garsten, 2000). Association representatives explained that in this situation, self-regulation was seen as "the better of two evils", in other words, the general perception was that if there *had* to be formal regulation, the industry preferred self-certification instead of state certification. However, in time the staffing industry came to appreciate its self-regulation. When the Swedish law of public procurement (PPA) was enforced, the SPUR certification became a prerequisite for the majority of the deals with public customers. This development substantially increased the number of applicants for SPUR membership and certification.

Even when there was no direct state threat to regulate the profession, as was the case in the other six consultancy subfields studied, there could be general public legislation affecting the consulting business, such as the PPA. Many consultants and clients complained about PPA being complicated and ill suited for consulting services (see also Lindberg & Furusten, 2005). As a formal protest, all of the studied associations were found to have written their own guidelines for the procurement of consultancy services. These standards were introduced on the associations' websites in terms of "a welcome free-of-charge help" to clients (see for instance www.uf.a.org and www.precis.se).

Lobbying against unwanted public regulation such as the PPA was found among the standardization motives. UF, for example, was founded with the specific purpose to lobby for a change of public regulation. Their members thought it was discriminating. It was thought too risky for an individual firm to question public rules on its own, but according to the UF president, the UF members liked the idea of a formal "third party" organization giving voice to their concerns. Summing up thus far, both Bemanningsföretagen and UF were found to have been fairly successful in creating a demand for their professional standards and certifications by referring either proactively or reactively to unwanted public regulation.

In the other five associations in this study, the professional standards were introduced as a means to gain a higher professional status when facing increasing competition from a growing number of firms entering the expanding Swedish consulting field in the late 1980s to mid 1990s. As suggested by Ahrne and Brunsson (2008), existing networks had been natural starting points. HRK, SAMC and UF all started off as CEO clubs in the sense that they were initiated by a respected senior consultant or researcher in his or her personal network of senior colleges at other firms. PRECIS and SMIF can be added to this group as well, as they came about after a subgroup of the other groups decided to break out from a broader association.

In these cases standards were thought of as a means to differentiate a "qualified" subgroup from the rest. As a typical case, HRK was initiated and founded by a researcher in his personal network in 1989, at a time when the whole Swedish consultancy field was expanding quickly. HRK founders saw the many start ups in the Swedish HRM consulting industry as a potential threat to their market positions. In this situation they regarded their membership and the professional HRK standards as a means to differentiate themselves from this threat of the new competitors. Members hoped the HRK logo would signal exclusiveness and high quality, values they hoped would ensure or improve their current price levels and market shares. Summing up, the motives behind the attempts to introduce standards were twofold: a first motive was to avoid unwanted state regulation, and a second motive was to increase the status of the professional associations. As we will see below, however, these attempts did not succeed completely.

The Standards

Founding a professional association did not prove to be difficult, even in a rule skeptic field like the Swedish consulting field. And when browsing the official presentations at the associations' websites, standardizing consultancy work looked to be a fairy uncomplicated task as well—at least judging by the ample supply. Out of the seven associations offering professional standards and/or certifications, two of them (PRECIS and SAMC) had versions of their own, having a meta-meta-standard of the international association (ICCO and FEACO respectively) in their subfield as a point of reference. Another three of the associations (Bemanningsföretagen, HRK and UF) had developed standards all on their own. Just one of the seven associations—SRF—was found to simply refer to an existing meta-meta standard: All SRF members were required to follow the international ICC standards for advertising (SRF is a member of ICC) although SRF also organizes several popular creative price competitions that theoretically can be seen as open standards or rankings. Out of the seven associations studied, SMIF was the strictest, requiring members to adapt to *both* the ethical standards and professional guidelines of the international marketing association ESOMAR and of ICC, the International Chambers of Commerce (as SMIF was a member of both organizations) *and* to SMIF's own version of these standards called "the common terms." All in all, standard supply looked sufficient. But to learn more about the dynamics of standardization in the field, we decided to follow these initiatives over time.

Standardization Challenges

Our initial findings, which were based on a surface snapshot of the consultancy standardization, revealed nothing out of the ordinary. Standards seemed to be motivated and launched even in this informally ordered field, albeit more often motivated by a changing market situation and increased competition than by a threat of public regulation. However, when we decided to dig deeper and interview association representatives as they had embarked on their maiden voyages to the world of standards, an obstacle surfaced, and we realized that our initial findings had to be modified.

As Hood (1986) notes, if self-regulatory membership organizations are made up out of "nothing," risks are high they will be discredited or ignored. A serious challenge for the professional associations in our study was just that: to show whether membership and standard following actually added anything to the members' bottom line. In the consultancy field clients very rarely mention association membership and standard following as mandatory criteria for business, and consultants who choose to remain outside or to leave the associations usually do quite well for themselves—sometimes even better than members and followers (Kipping & Saint-Martin, 2005; Rydmark, 2004). Many association representatives complained to us that convincing consultants to join a professional association and to adopt professional standards was indeed a tough task since in this field standards were perceived not as soft but as quite *hard* in comparison to the established informal order of the field. Nobody seemed to care much for most of the professional standards. We found little demand for the formal self-regulation but much talk about "softer" already established alternatives such as a common culture and professional norms, networks, mutual adjustment, and personal confidence.

As is the case in many modern associations (Ahrne & Brunsson, 2008), another common struggle was striking: the balance between statements of similarity and difference among the members. A classic line of division is concerned with size. Typically, there were major differences between the large and the small members concerning work methods and organization. While the larger members had a philosophy inspired by large scale production of services and an organization at least partly institutionalized, made up of standardized building blocks (compare Brunsson & Sahlin-Andersson, 2000), the small members often emphasized heavily the individual uniqueness of their services (see also Furusten & Bäcklund, 2000). As found by Witz (1992), small- and medium-sized consultancies may view associations as valuable when attempting to build a reputation and increase their competitiveness (Grob & Kieser, 2006).

In our study, however, some of the representatives of the larger and rather independent member firms complained that they were not interested in paying for the certification of smaller competitors. We found that in the struggle to deal with such complaints and to balance statements of similarity and difference, standards were altered—the associations typically exchanged a strict paragraph for a more flexible wording or removed the controversial paragraph altogether. The following quote from the SMIF president illustrates a typical reflection some years after promoting a professional consultancy standard:

> The purpose of the standard was to become more similar in our basic services. But if we all do the same, clients won't know what the different firms stand for. Members don't like the thought of being anonymous and neutral.

To open up for increasing competition, in other words, increasing differences among its member firms, SMIF decided to remove certain paragraphs from its original standard formulation. For example, there used to be a paragraph stating how and when to bill clients. SMIF removed this rule and left it up to each firm to decide on a payment policy. There also used to be a rule requiring all SMIF members to go through an ISO certification. This initiative originally came from EFAMRO, the European association for marketing firms, of which SMIF is a member. However, this rule was later removed from the SMIF policy as members became increasingly dissatisfied with the certification procedure and its results. The individual members wanted the freedom to choose any documented quality system they preferred. And finally, the whole paragraph requesting a documented quality system was removed from the SMIF policy. The exact same scenario happened in PRECIS as well.

In conclusion, things may have looked promising at the start, but as time passed, in several cases it became clear that the "exclusive branding" of the rule logo had started to signal not high status, but a *lower* market status and an inability to apply the popular informal alternatives to formal rules. As Ahrne and Brunsson (2004, 2008) suggest, meta-organizations such as our seven professional associations risk becoming organizations for the weak—in this case, organizations for consultants who have not (yet) created sufficient regulatory alternatives. As the HRK president told us:

> If perhaps you are new to the consulting business and you haven't had the time to develop a network, then membership and standards may be important. I think they can create a dimension of certainty. Clients can be safe knowing there has been an inspection of the tools and methods used by this firm.

Furthermore, their inability to motivate the market value of their standards seemed to make the organizations anxious to apply their own carefully crafted inclusion and exclusion systems. Following the reasoning of Hood (1986), the sanctioning mechanisms (reminders, warnings, and expulsions) were thought to be inefficient when punishing any but the worst violations. The association representatives all said they had not experienced a single expulsion due to rule breaking. The few expulsions that had taken place were all caused by financial difficulties, typically members facing bankruptcy.

In summary, the professional associations faced several challenges. A major challenge was to convince the members that the standard actually would be value adding for them and that it would fulfill members' wishes for being both similar and different from each other. Another challenge was to protect the standard itself from becoming associated with lower status rather than with exclusivity. As will be illustrated in the next section, the professional associations soon found themselves swinging like line rope dancers, trying to balance their two identities—that of the controlling rule setter and that of the loyal industry representative.

Strategies

How did the professional associations handle these challenges? We found that neither special rights for large members nor mergers nor international anchoring proved to be sufficient to do the trick to convince the rule skeptic consultants of the benefits of standard following (see also Alexius, 2005). Rather, we found that three other strategies were applied, which will be discussed in more detail below: starting a service firm, returning to the CEO club, and standardizing others.

Starting a Service Firm

A first strategy was to diminish the traditional self-regulation identity and to put more effort into commercial sales of various services. A clear cut example of this strategy was seen at SRF. The SRF members were still required to follow the international ICC standards for advertising, but SRF's core activities gradually shifted to focus more on service provision than standardization. SRF offered members judicial advice, industry statistics, current research, courses, workshops, and good deals on insurances, hotel rooms and car rentals (www.reklam.se). Certain services were not covered by the "service fee" though. For such additional services members were offered a "discounted SRF member fee." Among the more popular additional services were the three creative competitions arranged annually by SRF: *AEA* (Advertising Effectiveness Awards), *Coredesign,* and *Guldägget* (the Golden Egg, a prestigious and well known Swedish advertisement competition).

Returning to the CEO Club

A second strategy adopted by some of the associations in this study (SMIF, HRK and SAMC) was to focus more on the individuals representing the member firms. This strategy was described by the association representatives as a sign of failure. They also made jokes about it being a smart and successful way to finance a CEO club. However, typically, this strategy was linked to the standardization struggles:

> This may be what has happened somewhere in the midst of our problems, SMIF has become a CEO club for mutual admiration. The common employees at the member firms rarely ever notice SMIF.

The HRK president said she noticed reluctance from members to be associated with the association when interacting with their clients. What member representatives liked and appreciated most was meetings where they could discuss their jobs as CEOs. This view was expressed most by member representatives of smaller firms who did not have access to other such arenas. When listing the benefits of membership on HRK's website, "access to a network of high competence within the HR arena" came out on top and "access to a quality logo" on the very bottom of the list. In an interview the HRK president made the following statement:

> I think the members need the association a lot more than the clients do. It is a question of belonging, of knowing you are part of something... a network.

When studying SAMC and its strategies for attracting and keeping members, the ambiguous identity of the association was obvious. SAMC had ethical and professional standards as well as formal rules and requirements, which signaled exclusiveness. But instead of expressing the exclusiveness of membership, the association presented itself as a "platform" for informal networking and a "club" where individual representatives, typically CEOs from various consultancy firms, could meet to exchange ideas and socialize. In an interview, the SAMC chairman said he believed this informal networking approach to be the reason why SAMC had not yet ceased to exist. When taking a closer look at the SAMC standard, we found its texts common sense like and vague in character. When asking the chairman to comment on the importance of the standard, he simply said:

It is not too bad after all, nothing out of the ordinary really... I think it pretty much reflect current practice.

SAMC's focus on "voluntary," "fun," and "casual" activities for senior consultants—such as breakfast seminars—made SAMC look more like yet another informal network for individual consultants than a formal standard setter. As the chairman put it:

The association has become a platform to meet and discuss with other CEOs. I think this is what makes our members stay.

Standardizing Others

A third strategy used to cope with the standardization challenges in this informally ordered field was noticed when looking more closely at the actual rule formulations of the professional standards and codes of conducts. It then became obvious to us that one of the more successful standard setters in the field, PRECIS, used their standard in a proactive and rather hypocritical way: as a cost efficient, trendy marketing initiative and as a legitimate means to standardize *others*, preferably clients and future employees. This strategy was first noticed in the following statement by a PRECIS representative:

We want to show that we are a number of serious firms in this market... but the real purpose is of course to show how PR can be useful to business.

From the start in 1990, PRECIS's members decided to follow the ethical standard of the international PR association ICCO. But in 2001, when the standard was up for discussion at a PRECIS meeting, members criticized it for being too shallow and common sense like. PRECIS therefore decided to develop its own standard, which was launched in the following year (2002). PRECIS's members complained that their environment did not know enough about the benefits of PR consulting. They noticed that in certain client circles it was still taboo to spend money on PR. The association therefore came to view the making of its own standard as a chance to legitimately influence common norms about the PR firms and to make PR more attractive among clients and future employees:

We see the rules as a means to strengthen our professional identity, as a chance to make PR consulting honorable and useful.

First of all, PRECIS wanted to define PR as something different from politics, journalism, and advertisement. There was an important strategic reason behind this move. In politics and journalism, the norm is for the professional to propagate his or her *personal* views. Even advertising firms rarely take on the accounts of competing clients. However, this was exactly what the PRECIS firms wanted to do. The PRECIS standard therefore clearly stated that a PR consultant above all had a professional *business* interest. This formulation was meant to indicate that he or she could propagate any views clients may have, keeping his or her personal opinions aside. This new formulation was created to make it legitimate for PR consultants to handle competing client accounts. The focus of PRECIS's "self-regulation" was thus clearly aimed at changing the attitudes and behavior of *others*. The PRECIS standard also opened up the field for value based pricing of PR consulting services, a rather controversial pricing method that will be further described in the next section.

Summing up, the field study showed that the professional associations' attempts to introduce standards were met with skepticism and challenges. To cope with these challenges, three different strategies were tried out: starting a service firm, returning to the CEO club, and standardizing others. The three strategies had a common denominator: a partial reconfiguration of the standard and/or the association identity.

CONCLUDING DISCUSSION

If we wish to understand professionalization processes, we must not only look for success stories but also explore fields where professionalization attempts have been challenged and have been confronted with resistance. In this chapter we have contributed to this end with an empirical comparative study of seven professional associations in the Swedish management consultancy field (broadly defined) and their role as actors of professionalization, focusing specifically their role as standard setters.

As for the motives behind the professional standardization, we have found that only two out of these seven associations—the professional associations Bemanningsföretagen and UF—were motivated in their professional standardization by referring either proactively (UF) or reactively (Bemanningsföretagen) to unwanted public regulation. In five cases—the professional associations HRK, PRECIS, SAMC, SMIF and SRF—professional standards were introduced as a means to differentiate and gain a higher status facing a threat of increasing competition at a time when the field expanded rapidly, clearly a professionalization motive.

Along the same lines, we found that the greatest challenge to the associations in their role as standard setters was related to the balancing act described in the introduction as typical of self-regulators (e.g., Haufler, 2001; Hood, 1986; Tamm Hallström & Boström, 2010). Creating demand for the standards proved to be a difficult task. The associations had difficulties communicating the market value of standard following and portrayed ambivalence when faced with skepticism and resistance from potential standard followers and members. A uniformity critique from consultants and managers wishing to be different from others also had to be handled in most cases. Such struggles often meant standards were eventually dismantled. A strict paragraph was replaced by a more flexible wording, or controversial parts of the standard were simply removed, as in the case of SMIF. Similarly, in another study of a pricing standard for value based pricing introduced by a consulting firm (Alexius & Furusten, 2005), an "appendix approach" was introduced as an innovative means to tailor make the standard for "unique" projects, thus granting adopters maximum flexibility. This is not the typical purpose of standardization.

Facing skepticism and resistance, the professional associations reprioritized their standard setting ambitions and even "hid" them behind more attractive informal initiatives and offers. As suggested by Brunsson (2000), the institutional pressure against standardization and other forms of formal regulation in this field seemed to have forced (or perhaps tempted) standard setters back onto the beaten track.

In line with the reasoning above, we also found that the professional associations in our study used "soft" rather than hard arguments to win legitimacy for their regulatory aspirations (e.g., Boström & Garsten, 2008). By using arguments such as increasing competitiveness, coordination, transparency, learning, and support, they could draw on a larger discourse on standardization (see e.g., Brunsson, 2000) and portray their activities as "softer" than public regulation and other directives. Time will tell. We suspect that in the informal consultancy field such arguments may in fact weaken the professional associations' regulatory authority and make them even more vulnerable to competition from already established informal ordering mechanisms. Instead of sticking to and standing up for stringent professional standards, they showed a remarkable rule setting ambivalence—emphasizing breakfast seminars and good insurance deals rather than, for instance, ethical standards—an ambivalence that is likely to damage their already frail authority as rule setters even further and to help sustain the existing informal field order. The only association in our study that seemed to thrive and to gather eager rule followers in this rule skeptical field was PRECIS, the professional association whose standards were found to be addressed not to consultants, but to their clients—in other words, paradoxically a "self-regulation of others," as standards were in fact modified to focus on clients as the actual rule followers (Alexius, 2005).

We have a last reflection on the work on identity of the associations. It seems to us that in order for their bureaucratic aspirations not to meet an early death, the associations had to draw on either of the two dominating ordering logics present in their context; that of the market and/or that of the clan (Ouchi, 1980). In most cases, the standard setting identity seemed uncomfortable for the professional associations. They therefore struggled to change their profile. When searching for a suiting identity for their associations, the choice seemed to fall on either the client/seller identity— referring to the familiar market logic and relation between seller and buyer—or on the colleague identity or even "circle of friends"—referring to the established informal clan order featuring individuals' networking. The bureaucratic aspirations of the associations in our study were thus generally toned down, and in their place the identities of the *service provider* (SRF and the client firms) or the *CEO club* (for example, HRK and SAMC) were preferred. As an illustration, when SRF found consultants reluctant to join a formal association and to pay for standard following, SRF chose to focus on the consultants' market orientation. And sure enough, SRF found consultants more inclined to sign a "service agreement" with a "service partner" offering judicial advice, industry statistics, current research, courses, workshops, good deals on insurance, hotel rooms, and car rentals, and competitive price competitions.

Summing up, the results indicate that the dominating informal field order in the consulting industry influences and puts a strain on attempts to formalize the field. Standard setting became a high risk project for the professional associations, a balancing act that could cause them a loss of legitimacy and members. Facing this threat, the attempts for professionalization were adjusted to fit the norms of the informal field order. The associations were found to be strongly influenced by the institutional pressure against rule following that existed in the sector.

There are theoretical and practical implications of these findings. Firstly, the findings add to our understanding of why attempts to standardize are not always successful. When discussing the influence and pressures to adjust to the existing field order, which is informal in this case, we have highlighted the importance of an institutional perspective when scrutinizing the outcomes of standardization attempts. Secondly, by demonstrating how professional consultancy associations struggle to balance their perceived need for professionalization and their need for legitimacy, we have shed light on an actor that may play a vital role in the professionalization processes, but has so far gained little attention in the literature (Greenwood et al., 2002). More research is needed, however, to explore these avenues further.

REFERENCES

Abbot, A. (1988). *The systems of professions.* Chicago, IL: University of Chicago Press.

Ahrne, G., Brunsson, N., & Garsten, C. (2000). Standardizing through organization. In N. Brunsson & B. Jacobsson (Eds.), *A world of standards* (pp. 50–66). Oxford: Oxford University Press.

Ahrne, G., Brunsson, N., & Tamm Hallström, K. (2007). Organizing organizations. *Organization, 14*(5), 619–624

Ahrne, G., & Brunsson, N. (Eds). (2004). *Regelexplosionen* [The rule-explosion]. Stockholm: EFI.

Ahrne, G., & Brunsson, N. (2008). *Meta-organizations.* Cheltenham: Edward Elgar.

Alexius, S. (2005, June). *Self-organizing others: Meta-organizational Strategies in the Swedish consulting-field.* Paper presented at the 21st EGOS Colloquium, Berlin.

Alexius, S. (2007). *Regelmotståndarna—om konsten att undkomma regler* [Rule-resisters—on the art of escaping rules]. Unpublished doctoral dissertation, Stockholm EFI, Stockholm, Sweden.

Alexius, S., & Furusten, S. (2005). Dealing with values. In S. Furusten & A. Werr (Eds.), *Dealing with confidence: The construction of need and trust in management advisory services* (pp. 201–216). Copenhagen: Copenhagen Business Press.

Beaverstock, J. V., Faulconbridge, J. R., & Hall, S. J. (2010). Professionalization, legitimization and the creation of executive search markets in Europe. *Journal of Economic Geography, 10*(6), 825–843.

Boström, M., & Garsten, C. (2008). Organizing for accountability. In M. Boström & C. Garsten, *Organizing transnational accountability* (pp. 1–26). Cheltenham: Edward Elgar.

Brunsson, N. (2000). Standardization and fashion trends. In N. Brunsson & J. Bengtsson (Eds.), *A world of standards* (pp. 151–168). Oxford: Oxford University Press.

Brunsson, N., & Jacobsson, B. (2000). Following standards. In N. Brunsson & B. Jacobsson (Eds)., *A world of standards* (pp. 127–137). Oxford: Oxford University Press

Brunsson, N., & Sahlin-Andersson, K. (2000). Constructing organizations: The example of public sector reform. *Organizational Studies, 21*(4), 721–746.

Clark, T. (1995). *Managing consultants. Consultancy as the management of impressions.* Buckingham: Open University Press.

De Vries, H. J. (2001, September). *Standardisation—outline of a field of research.* Paper presented at 3rd Interdisciplinary Workshop on Standardization Research, Department of Standardization, Delft, Universität des Bunderwehr.

DiMaggio, P. J., & Powell, W. (1983). The iron cage revisited: Institutional isomophism and collective rationality in organizational fields. *American Sociological Review, 48*, 147–160.

Evetts, J. (2003). The sociological analysis of professionalism. *International Sociology, 18*(2), 395–415.

Freidson, E. (1994) *Professionalism reborn: Theory, prophecy and policy.* Cambridge: Polity Press.

Furusten, S. (2003). *God managementkonsultation—reglerad expertis eller improviserat artisteri?* [Good management consultancy—regulated expertise or improvising artists?]. Lund: Studentlitteratur.

Furusten, S., & Bäcklund, J. (2000). Koncentration och differentiering på marknaden för managementkonsultation i Sverige [Concentration and differentiation on the market for management consulting services in Sweden]. *Nordiske Organisasjonsstudier, 2*(1), 60–83.

Furusten, S., & Werr, A. (2005). *Dealing with confidence—The construction of need and trust in management advisory services*. Copenhagen: Copenhagen Business School.

Giddens, A. (1990). *The consequences of modernity*. Stanford, CA: Stanford University Press.

Glückler, J., & Armbrüster, T. (2003). Bridging uncertainty in management consulting: The mechanisms of trust and networked reputation. *Organization Studies, 24*(2), 269–297.

Greenwood, R., Suddaby, R., & Hinings, C. R. (2002). Theorizing change: The role of professional associations in the transformation of institutionalized fields. *The Academy of Management Journal, 45*(1), 58–80.

Grob, C., & Kieser, A. (2006). Are consultants moving towards professionalization? *Research in the Sociology of Organizations, 24*, 69–100.

Haufler, V. (2001). *A public role for the private sector: Industry self-regulation in a global economy*. Washington DC: Carnegie Endowment for International Peace.

Hood, C. (1986). *Administrative analysis—an introduction to rules, enforcement and organizations*. Brighton: Wheatsheaf Books.

Jacobsson, B. (2000). Standardization and expert knowledge. In N. Brunsson & B. Jacobsson (Eds.), *A world of standards* (pp. 40–49). Oxford: Oxford University Press.

Karseth, B., & Nerland, M. (2007). Building professionalism in a knowledge society: examining discourses of knowledge in four professional associations. *Journal of Education and Work, 20*(4), 335–355.

Kipping, M. (2002). Trapped in their wave: The evolution of management consultants. In R. Fincham & T. Clark (Eds.), *Critical consulting* (pp. 28–49). Oxford: Blackwell

Kipping, M., & Saint-Martin, D. (2005). Between regulation, promotion and consumption: Government and management consultancy in Great Britain. *Business History, 47*(3), 449–465.

Kubr, M. (1996). *Management consulting: A guide to the profession*. Geneva: ILO.

Kyrö, P. (1995). *The management consulting industry described by using the concept of "profession."* Unpublished doctoral dissertation, University of Helsinki, Helsinki.

Lindberg, K., & Furusten, S. (2005). Breaking laws—making deals: Procurement of management consultants in the public sector. In S. Furusten & A. Werr (Eds.), *Dealing with confidence—the construction of need and trust in management advisory services* (pp. 169–183). Copenhagen: Copenhagen Business School Press.

Løwendahl, B. (2005). *Strategic management of professional service firms*. Copenhagen: Copenhagen Business School Press.

McKenna, C. D. (2006). *The world's newest profession. Management consulting in the twentieth century*. Cambridge: Cambridge University Press.

Meyer, J., & Rowan, B. (1977). Institutionalized organizations: formal structure as myth and ceremony. *American Journal of Sociology, 83*, 340–363.

Mörth, U. (2004). *Soft law in governance and regulation—an interdisciplinary analysis*. Cheltenham: Edward Elgar.

Nordström, A. (2004). Reglerare, reglerade och regelskapande processer [Rule-setters, rule-followers and rule-creating processes]. In G. Ahrne & N. Brunsson (Eds.), *Regelexplosionen* [The rule-explosion] (pp. 9–43). Stockholm: EFI.

Näslund, L., & Pemer, F. (2012). The appropriated language: Dominant stories as a source of organizational inertia. *Human Relations, 65*(1), 89–110.

O'Mahoney, J. (2010). *Management Consultancy.* Oxford: Oxford University Press.

Ouchi, W. G. (1980). Markets, bureaucracies and clans. *Administrative Science Quarterly, 25,* 129–179.

Pemer, F. (2008). *Framgång eller fiasko? En studie av hur konsultprojekt värderas i klientorganisationer* [Failure or Success? A study of how consulting projects are evaluated in client organizations]. Unpublished doctoral dissertation, Stockholm EFI, Stockholm, Sweden.

Roodhoft, F., & Van den Abbeele, A. (2006). Public procurement of consulting services: Evidence and comparison with private companies. *International Journal of Public Sector Management, 19*(5), 490–512.

Rydmark, S. (2004). Hur man undviker regler—fallet managementkonsulterna [Avoiding rules—the case of management consulting]. In G. Ahrne & N. Brunsson (Eds.), *Regelexplosionen* [The rule-explosion] (pp. 66–98). Stockholm: EFI.

Schiele, J. J., & McCue, C. P. (2006). Professional service acquisition in public sector procurement. *International Journal of Operations & Production Management, 11,* 14–27.

SOU 1997:58 Privat arbetsförmedling och personaluthyrning? [Swedish Public Investigation 1997:58 Private employment agencies and staffing?]

Tamm Hallström, K & Boström, M. (2010). *Transnational multi-stakeholder standardization: Organizing fragile non-State authority.* Cheltenham: Edward Elgar.

Werr, A., & Pemer, F. (2007). Purchasing management consulting services—From management autonomy to purchasing involvement. *Journal of Purchasing and Supply Management, 13,* 98–112.

Witz, A. (1992). *Professions and patriarchy.* London: Routledge.

SECTION III

ACQUIRING AND DISSEMINATING CONSULTING SKILLS

CHAPTER 7

PROFESSIONALIZING PRACTICES IN ADVISORY WORK

Presenting a Conceptual Approach to Study the Relations among Institutionalization, Reflective Learning, and Quality in Consultancy

Sonja van der Arend, Bertien Broekhans, and Sebastiaan Meijer

In the open and loosely demarcated occupational field of consulting, the roles and identities of those doing advisory work are under continual adaptation and negotiation. Many of the efforts to adapt or negotiate what consultants do may be defined as efforts to professionalize the trade—they are geared at enhancing the quality of advisory work. In this chapter, we propose a conceptual approach to professionalization and the quality of consulting. We operate from the premise that professionalization is an ongoing, multifaceted process in the interactions and relations among con-

Exploring the Professional Identity of Management Consultants, pages 141–162
Copyright © 2013 by Information Age Publishing
All rights of reproduction in any form reserved.
141

sultants as a profession and between consultants and their clients—governments, the public and other individuals and organizations they meet in their work. Together, these actors develop institutions, such as shared rules, habits, identities, routines, and norms, while individually they reflect on the way institutions are put into practice—both to improve the effectiveness and the quality of their work. However, higher quality is not guaranteed in this process, as professionalization efforts may have unexpected and counterproductive consequences—such as market distortions or arrogant behavior towards clients. Hence, it is necessary to study the effects of professionalizing activities in practice.

This chapter discusses a variety of research streams related to consultancy to illustrate how our conceptual framework may help to combine information from different sources and angles into a coherent perspective on changes in the professional roles and identities of consultants.

CONSULTANTS AS PROFESSIONALS

Is the consultant someone you call when a difficult task requires knowledge that is not available in the organization—or simply someone wearing fancy clothes and driving an expensive car, who runs in and out of organizations, indifferent to what he or she leaves behind? These are just two of a range of popular frames on consultants, and, as with all generalizations, there is a piece of truth in each of them.

In both frames, consultancy is imbued with a high social status, be it of a different kind. Even though the daily working life of consultants may be a lot less glamorous, the question is how consultancy has achieved this status, and even more important, how it manages to keep it. Apart from the educational background of most consultants, there is a variety of forces that may help or hinder the professional quality of both the individual consultant and the branch as a whole. For instance, consultants compete for tenders on both price and quality. This seems a paradox: a lower price would lead to lower quality, as a balance between quality and costs is not as linear as in, for instance, products or physical services. After all, who wants poor advice? The issue here is that the quality of the work of a consultant is hard to judge a priori for the client (Akerlof, 1970). Moreover, too many tenders won for a low price with poor quality will damage the image of the group as a whole. So, consultants compete for business and the associated profits, and thus collectively produce an image of their profession.

In this chapter, we seek to conceptualize the relations between professionalism and the quality of consultancy work. We do not claim that the consulting trade aspires to or will ever gain the status of a full profession in the classical sense. Still, professionalism as a goal certainly influences the direction in which consultancy is heading. As the quality of advisory work is not guaranteed, it is necessary to study the actual effects of professionalizing efforts in practice in order to develop an understanding of which efforts work, when, and how. In this chapter, we propose a conceptual approach to the professionalization and quality of consulting that may be used to conduct research that may generate such understanding. We discuss a broad variety of research publications on consultancy to illustrate how our conceptual framework may help to combine information from different sources and angles into a coherent perspective on changes in the professional roles and identities of consultants.

Rooted in the sociology of professions and theories on learning and reflection, this conceptual approach allows for the distinction and combination of a range of perspectives, sites and data on consultants' activities, roles, and identities. In exploring the practices and activities of consultants, we received help from a group of students in a co-taught seminar "Consultants as Professionals" in the Consultancy curriculum at Delft University of Technology (September 2010–January 2011). The students surveyed literature and documents and did short interviews to get an impression of what consultants are really doing when they try to enhance their skills and their trade. The results were laid down in a collaborative book (Broekhans, Van der Arend, & Meijer, 2011). This chapter presents our joint findings.

HOW CONSULTANTS PROFESSIONALIZE THEIR OCCUPATION AND THEIR WORK

With regard to the development of consultancy as a profession, the first question is if we should think about consultants as a group or as individuals. Both perspectives have been elaborated theoretically. Sociologists study professionalism as a characteristic shared by a group. In education sciences and related fields such as coaching, professionalism is an individual quality. The central tenet of this chapter is that both approaches should be combined to be able to grasp the empirical dynamics and actual effects of professionalization in practice. Before the interaction between the individual and the collective attempts to professionalize can be discussed, this section will introduce the two main perspectives on professionalization.

Consultants as a Group

The original sociology of the professions focused on those occupations that would possess the traits of a "true profession," such as a mandatory academic education and a sanctioning system (MacDonald, 1995). This model of the profession, typically exemplified by medicine and law, is of little use to our cause, as it is an ideal-typical and static representation of how professions form and maintain themselves. Much more helpful is the more recent "interactionist" tradition in the sociology of the professions—as developed since the 1970s—in which the focus is on professionalization as a process. This tradition identifies the *institutionalization* of daily practices into rules, standards, and customs as the driving mechanism of group formation among people doing similar work (MacDonald, 1995). In this vein, we argue that it is irrelevant to determine if consultancy meets, will ever meet, or should meet the terms of a "true" profession. Rather, it allows us to recognize that the formation of a profession is an ongoing, multifaceted process that is situated in the interactions and relations between consultants and with clients, governments, the public, and other people and parties they meet in their work. Such interactions and relations breed shared rules, habits, identities, routines, and norms for the execution of advisory work. This is what we call "professionalization on the collective level."

Consultants as Individuals

Whether they are part of a group or not, individuals doing advisory work on a daily basis are not just applying collective rules and regulations. Nor are they thoughtlessly improvising their way through subsequent project assignments. Their professional identity as consultants hinges on the way in which they themselves do their job. So, most practicing consultants will try to understand what they are doing in order to do it better in the future. Apart from giving advice, their job consists of observing their actions and rethinking their implications for solutions, actions, and strategies in the near future. Deliberating on their activities can help professionals in making informed decisions, and observing and interpreting (the effects of) their practices in particular contexts. They can learn how to plan activities and even to act against the mainstream when necessary. In short, we see that what we call "professionalization on the individual level" is driven by learning through *reflection* (Argyris, 1991; Schön, 1983). Like collective professionalization, this is an ongoing, multifaceted process, taking place in the relations and interactions between consultants and others.

Each collective and individual effort to professionalize consultancy expresses the desire to "make things better" and may create some stability in the relations between consultants and others. Nevertheless, the goals pursued may differ or collide, desired outcomes are not guaranteed, and roles, relations, and identities of consultants will most probably never be fixed—all the more because, besides these efforts, there are many other factors that change or stabilize institutions and methods of consulting, for the good and for the bad. Just think how the textbook example of professionalism—the medical order—is forever busy with establishing the institutions that separate medical practice from quackery, and with reflecting on what it means in concrete cases to act as a good doctor.

CONTEXTS OF PROFESSIONALIZATION

Based on sociological theories of professionalization (Eliot, 2001; MacDonald, 1995; Mok, 1989), we distinguish three fields, or contexts, in which the two ongoing, multifaceted processes of professionalization are taking place (Van der Arend, 2007). Like other highly skilled workers, consultants can be seen to institutionalize their trade and reflect on their work in these three fields. Although they do contain real buildings and events to go to, each of these fields as a whole is rather abstract. The first field is the market where consultants offer, sell, and perform their services. This is the context in which consultants "form" their practices: where they organize their daily advisory activities—what they do—and where they individually reflect on these practices and collectively institutionalize them. The second field is the field of science, research, and education. This is where consultants develop their knowledge: where they each develop their knowledge and their skills to be better consultants individually, and where they collectively institutionalize what a professional consultant knows.

The last field is the least concrete of the three. It may be called ethics or the public interest, and it includes places and events such as conversations with complaining clients, major cases of fraud, and public debates, for example, on the number of consultants hired by government. This field is where consultants take care of legitimation, in other words, where they account that what they do is valid and right. Individual professionalization in this field means that consultants reflect on their motivations, values, and the effects of their actions to learn how to better guard, integrate, and promote these values in their work.[1] Collective professionalization happens when motivations, values, and ways of accounting become established in professional standards and other institutions.

In the three succeeding sections below, we will elaborate on the professionalization of consultancy in these three fields. We will discuss examples of individual and collective professionalization from relevant publications and from our own studies. In the last two sections of the chapter, these examples and discussions will serve to draw some tentative conclusions on the intricate relations between professionalization and quality in advisory work.

The Formation of Practice: How Consultants Seek to Enhance What They Do

The first field of professionalization is the market. Studies indicate that the market for advice is ever on the rise: the amount of consultants increases (Curnov & Reuvid, 2003; De Sonnaville, 2003; McKenna, 2006; Nooteboom, Zwart, & Bijmolt, 1990), as does their influence in politics, business, governance, and society (Czerniawska, 1999; Ernst & Kieser, 2002). Lahusen (2002) gives two explanations for the growth of consultancy in the public sector: an increasing demand for information and monitoring in policy making, and a cultural change in politics, where arguments are increasingly supported with research and reports. Similar developments would back the growth of consultancy in the private sector (Sturdy, 1997, 2002).

The key to enhancing advisory work in a growing market is distinction: being discernible and visible as a group and as an individual between other service providers. Hence, specialization of consultancy is an important collective concern of consultants (Czerniawska, 2002, 2005). The better their work is distinguished as a specific service, the better clients will be able to find them and the more they will be willing to pay for their services. Specialization as a group may bring the further advantage that individual consultants obtain some protection from market fluctuations, for example, because they can share work among them. Specialization involves having a shared name for the service and its providers. Institutions of specialization include specific routines, procedures, methods, textbooks, tools, instruments, dress codes, and other rules and regularities.

A second type of collective institutionalization on the market is internal specialization: manifest distinctions among different types of consulting services. Internal specialization allows for consultants to develop a more in-depth understanding of a specific, limited line of work. Management consultancy, for instance, is not strictly defined, but it usually excludes advising on finance, IT, or engineering (Kubr, 2002). Generally on a market, the issues, problems, and questions for advice, and the solutions and services offered tend to get more detailed over time. Today, the market for consulting services offers a plethora of topics, tasks, and problems to be advised on (Grossmann, 2011; Keeble & Schwalbach, 1995). An adequate level of internal specialization would theoretically generate an efficient market; too much specialization would make the market less transparent for clients. Perhaps that is why some companies feel inclined to label and categorize different types of consulting.

Individually, consultants themselves make the difference in their daily activities. Like other knowledge workers, consultants desire a high degree of autonomy in the management of their tasks (De Bruijn, 2010; Donnelly, 2009; Mintzberg, 1983). Ideally, the ability and experience of professional consultants to manage and enhance their performance by themselves would be the key source of joy and pride in their work (Jansen, Van den Brink, & Kole, 2009). In reality, consultants may use their autonomy to aim for all sorts of objectives, such as: delivery in accordance with the order, making a good profit, doing good, working comfortably, making a career, becoming a partner, balancing work and personal life, and so on. Whatever the goal, professional autonomy implies making choices and evaluating whether the choices made have been effective (Donnelly, 2011), which in turn requires reflection. Only by reflecting in and on action (Schön, 1983) can consultants direct their activities, solve problems effectively, and try to improve their performance.

Autonomy does not imply absolute freedom; in the formation of their own practice, consultants incessantly interact with clients, principals, fellows, colleagues, competitors, managers, family, neighbors, and many others. In all these relations they seek and acquire certain roles and identities as advisors (Styhre, Olilla, Wikmalm, & Roth, 2010). With these roles and identities, they contribute to the image of their organizations and companies (Alvesson & Robertson, 2006) and the branch as a whole. Even reflection is not something always done alone. It is said to work better when done with colleagues, fellows, a senior or a coach: inter-vision, supervision, coaching (Groen, 2008; Oliver, 2005).

Our investigations in the Dutch market suggest that although many types of consultants are active there, the boundaries among them and around the entire branch are not clearly institutionalized at all. Only some variants show clear signs of distinction, for instance, a group of advisors on "Quality, Working Conditions, and Environment" who are sharply demarcated within the otherwise rather unstructured branch of environmental consultancy. Such demarcated specializations can often be explained by the existence and requirements from legal provisions, and national and international standards, for example, ISO (Broekhans et al., 2011). We expect to find similar patterns in other branches of consulting. The result is a dual image of institutionalization: some consultants are highly specialized and deliver strictly defined services, but consultancy as a whole is hardly demarcated as a separate segment. The Dutch consultancy sector can be characterized as an open profession, in which some groups of specialists form (more or less) closed markets.

The open character of the sector implies that the burden of distinction is largely put on the shoulders of individual consultants and their firms. This could explain why many consultants decorate themselves with big cars, fancy clothes, and slick talk (Clark, 2004; Kam, 2004; Tzioti, 2010). This typical "exclusive" way of presenting seems to be developing into a largely unquestioned custom for large sections of the consulting branch, as it appeared difficult to have consultants reflect on this phenomenon in our interviews.

The interviewees said to not aspire to an exclusive image themselves, yet they use all sorts of other words to positively distinguish themselves from other consultants, such as "special knowledge," "unique processes," and "authenticity." Furthermore, the interviews indicate that internal consultants—those advising within their employing organization—feel less need to distinguish themselves than external consultants, who give advice to other organizations (Broekhans et al., 2011).

Knowledge Development: How Consultants Seek to Enhance What They Know

A second way for consultants to excel compared to others is through knowledge, training, and education. Institutions in this field will constitute what a consultant is expected to know and apply. Textbooks, curricula, trainings, scientific journals, degrees, and certificates are examples of such institutions.

But as far as we know, the final curriculum to become a consultant is yet to be designed. Many universities and especially their business schools offer courses and curricula to at least train aspects important to become a consultant. However, consultants also need knowledge about the object and the subject of advice. Management consultancy requires both knowledge of management and organization studies and knowledge about the profession(al) of management to be advised. And above all, a consultant needs educational and communicative skills. A professional consultant succeeds in balancing the different knowledge and skills (Reihlen & Nikolova, 2010; Sturdy, Clark, Handley, & Fincham, 2009). Although they are much sought after for their analytical competences, graduates are often confronted with a lack of empirical knowledge and experience. Clearly, although academic knowledge is of use in advisory work, one needs more types of knowledge to become a professional consultant (Buono, 2002; Mieg, 2008).

But these other types of knowledge that professional consultants use to formulate good advice—besides their domain knowledge—are often less clear to point out (Grossmann, 2011; Janes, 2011). They are defined as educational and communicative skills, management skills, creativity, reasoning skills, common sense, or "tacit knowledge" (Bouwmeester, 2008; De Bruijn, 2010). "Tacit knowledge of a professional is the source of his professionalism . . . [But] professional intuition can deceive. There are a number of errors typical of professionals who rely on their tacit knowledge" (De Bruijn, 2010, p. 34). Consultants make intensive use of such "non-substantive" knowledge in their daily work. But rather than explicating this type of knowledge verbally, they implicitly show they possess it when they actually use it. Tacit knowledge becomes evident only in the form of the skills consultants profess when they do their job (Hicks, Nair, & Wilderom, 2009).

Consequentially, professionals have to maintain and develop their skills based on tacit knowledge in everyday practice. Usually, professionals, most probably including consultants, do not even realize that they do this; it just happens (De Bruijn, 2010, p. 10). This is somewhat ironic, as the essence of consulting is to help others to learn to do things differently, change organizations, implement new techniques, and so on. Although some consultants use standardized concepts, models, and proven techniques (e.g., balanced score card, lean manufacturing)—in essence choosing secure ways of working and knowledge—every application and resulting advice must still be tailor-made, putting pressure on the general applicability of knowledge.

Moreover, for consultants each contract is unique, based on their existing knowledge and the need for new knowledge, and the client organization can learn from the advice they give. One would think that these very features make consultants good at learning. Reality often proves the contrary, according to Chris Argyris (1991), who claims that many consultants are just doing so much to learn for themselves. Precisely the organizations and people who are convinced that the success of their work depends on "learning," often do not know how they themselves learn and should learn. They make every effort to help others continually improve their work, but that is also the obstacle to think about how they can improve their own work.

This assessment does not imply that consultants do not aspire to knowledge development. Literature and interviews show that they think learning is extremely important. The favorite modes of knowledge development among our students and the consultants they interviewed were all kinds of learning-on-the-job, such as cooperation between junior and senior consultants, tutorships, and juniors coaching seniors.

Legitimation: How Consultants Seek to Enhance What They Value

The third form of professionalization efforts takes place in the area of ethics and the public interest. Here, consultants reflect on the moral aspects and consequences of their work and develop institutions that foster and regulate legitimation (or moral justification) (Mok, 1989; Von Weltzien, Høivik & Føllesdal, 1995). Eventually, such activities determine what consultants are accepted to do and supposed to abstain from.

The key institution of legitimation is the professional association (Czerniawska & May, 2004). Traditionally, founding a professional association is the formal way to organize the quality and trustworthiness of the profession as a collective; it is the precondition to establishing such institutions as professional codes of behavior, certificates, accreditations, and disciplinary rules. A professional association represents the members of a profession in the public debate and in contact with government. Through their professional association, a group of service providers is better placed to convince the general public that their job has an important value for society, in other words, should be seen as a profession. Based on such legitimacy, government may allow the group special privileges, such as a monopoly for a specific service or a compulsory academic education before entry in the profession. Another mechanism of institutionalization is certification (Kubr, 2002). A well known example in consultancy is the Certified Management Consultant (CMC) certificate as awarded by the Institutional Council of Management Consulting institutes (ICMCI) and its members (the national professional bodies of management consultancy).

Such professional institutions regulating the ethics of consultancy gained great significance after a host of public scandals—most notably the Enron affair, which has seriously undermined the credibility and reputation of the Arthur Andersen consulting company (Broekhans et al., 2011; Chaney & Philipich, 2002). This affair and also many other, smaller events have provoked strong political and public pleas for regulation of the contracting of consultants and the outsourcing of crucial expertise in public organizations (Alvesson & Johansson, 2002; Glückler & Armbrüster, 2003; Grijzen, 2010; Groenlinks, 2001).

Still, however, most branches in consultancy are not strictly organized through legitimizing institutions. But also without a professional association, consultants develop shared attitudes, norms, and thoughts about what is and is not acceptable. Even such "light" or "soft" institutions—think of unwritten rules and cultural practices—have a disciplining and evaluative function, which may turn out to be more effective in practice than written rules. The disadvantage of written rules is that they do not guarantee moral behavior, but typically depend on official controls and punishments to be actually implemented by consultants in their daily work. In contrast, unwritten rules and cultural practices work through shared beliefs and are reinforced by direct social control.

While consultancy is to some degree regulated through formal and informal institutions, these are not always maintained in practice. In their daily work consultants find themselves in stressful settings with multiple—often contradictory—interests and many uncertainties. Their activities may have significant impacts on their clients, the managers, and employees involved, and on the stakeholders and environment of these clients. In such settings, stringent norms may cause conflicts: short-term objectives such as deadlines obstruct the production of the best advice, and choices made can have unforeseen and unwelcome consequences. From literature and interviews we have learned that consultants assume that moral behavior contributes to professional charisma, trustworthiness, and reputation. Constituted in literature, the claim is that honest behavior will contribute to the company's profit (Broekhans et al., 2011; Maister, 2005; Treviño & Nelson, 1999). Therewith, individual consultancy firms also have a responsibility for the sector and profession of consultancy as demonstrated by the drop of share prices due to the Enron scandal.

Literature and most of the interviewed consultants in Broekhans and associates' (2011) study confirm that the actions and decisions of individual consultants in delicate situations are more decisive than the institutionalization of general codes and norms. That is, for professionalization in the field of ethics, individual reflection is more important than collective institutions. Like practices and knowledge, moral behavior can be socialized and improved by rethinking choices and decisions that are made consciously and unconsciously. Through reflection, professionals will contemplate their own motives, values, norms, and pitfalls. Awareness and understanding of their personal behavior enables consultants to be of service to society and to foster their personal development and integrity (Maister, 2005; Martin, 2000). Moreover, reflection contributes to the transparency that is demanded of a consultant who is confronted with a complaint, claim, or lawsuit. Only if they are aware of their motives and values can consultants explain their actions and choices and account for them to clients and wider audiences.

A CONCEPTUAL FRAMEWORK OF PROFESSIONALIZATION IN CONSULTANCY

This chapter proposes a conceptual approach to professionalization and the quality of consulting. The previous sections showed that professionalization is an ongoing, multifaceted process in the interactions and relations among consultants and clients, governments, the public and other actors they meet in their work. They develop institutions, such as shared rules, habits, identities, routines, and norms, and individually reflect on the way institutions are put into practice. Constituted in literature from the sociology of professions, management studies, and education related sciences, we distinguish three forms of professionalization, each working on the individual and the collective level: the formation of practices, the development of knowledge, and legitimation. These concepts are brought together in the framework in Table 7.1.

This framework serves to combine information from very different sources and angles into a coherent perspective on changes in the professional roles and identities of consultants. Our joint investigation only made

TABLE 7.1 Conceptual Framework: Forms and Levels of Professionalization

Levels of Professionalization:	Forms of Professionalization:		
	Practice Formation	Knowledge Development	Legitimation
Individual: reflecting on ...	what one does as a consultant	what one knows and is able to do as a consultant	what one ought (not) do as a consultant
Collective: institutionalizing ...	what consultants do	what consultants know and are able to	what consultants are expected/entitled to

an exploration of professionalizing activities of consultancy. This section will summarize what we have learned.

Thus far, the different forms of professionalizing efforts of consultants have been studied from different theoretical perspectives, but the scientific literature about consultancy does not cover all sides of the multifaceted practices of consultancy. Many publications intend to describe professional experiences, and most of them lack a critical, interpretive, and reflective outlook on advisory practices (Clark & Fincham, 2002). Moreover, we observed some trends (Broekhans et al., 2011):

- In literature, particular advisory issues, techniques, and skills attract a great deal of attention (Boonstra & De Caluwé, 2007; Fincham & Evans, 1999; Hale, 2006; Rasiel, 1999).
- Among scholars, management consulting seems far more popular than other branches of consultancy (Buono, 2011; Clark & Fincham, 2002; Czerniawska, 2002; Czerniawska & May, 2004; Sturdy et al., 2009).
- We have hardly found any literature about the difference between professionals in consultancy and "amateurs," "laymen," "moonlighters," and so forth.
- Although many themes in the framework on professionalization are covered in literature, the professionalization of Dutch (management) consultancy has hardly been studied (with exception of De Sonnaville, 2003, 2005; Hellema & Marsman, 1997).
- Although research is done on aspects of professionalization—like reflection, ethics, authority, knowledge management—in consultancy, the mutual dependencies among those aspects remain underexposed. Only when we integrate the collective and individual level, can we understand and assess to what extent professionalization efforts lead to quality enhancement. What exactly are the qualities that

consultants are working on, while organizing practices, developing and managing knowledge, and implementing and discussing values?

THE PURSUIT OF QUALITY IN CONSULTANCY WORK

We claim that quality in consultancy is not definite, but is continuously reproduced, interpreted, and constructed in the daily ongoing, relational activities of consultants. The conceptual contribution of this chapter is the framework that centralizes and combines multiple perspectives on professionalization in consultancy. Many scholars—more than we could refer to in this chapter—add valuable insights into aspects of professionalization and show how to study these aspects. Remarkably, however, the interrelation between reflection and institutionalization is hardly ever studied or discussed at all. The framework presented here shows that this is an omission, as the improvement of consultancy work is a product of the continuous interaction of the simultaneous development of institutions and the active reflection on institutions in everyday practices and activities. Furthermore, as professionalization may take different forms, the concept of quality in consultancy work is in need of refinement. In this section we will first discuss how to understand the interrelations between professionalization on the collective and the individual level. Second, the concept of quality of consultancy work will be elaborated using the distinctions among practice formation, knowledge development, and legitimation. Lastly, we will briefly go into some of the complexities of enhancing the quality of consultancy work by connecting institutionalization and reflection.

Quality, then, typically arises from the interface between individual and collective professionalization. To explain it in a metaphor: collective and individual professionalization are related like the uploading and downloading of open source programs (collectively constructed software, e.g., Linux). Institutionalization in a young, open, unstructured profession is like building the rules of the open source program in development. Everyone can contribute to the step by step improvement of the joint product through small adjustments. And then the contributors and others can download the entire (beta) program and apply it in practice. In doing so they will adjust their daily working practices to the new program—they learn how to use it and as such it may improve their work and their results. But they will also observe how the program functions in practice, what works, and what does not. These experiences are then used to further develop and rewrite the program. Transferred to professionalization of consulting, this relation between collective rule-making and individual reflection would be a very productive interaction.

Next, the concept of quality is to be refined using the distinction among the three forms of professionalization that we drew from the sociology of the professions: practice formation, knowledge development, and legitimation. Following this distinction, professionalization efforts linking the individual and collective level—the uploading and downloading of professional rules—revolve around three aspects of professional performance: quality in practice on the market of services; quality in knowledge in the field of research, science, and education; and quality in legitimation in terms of the public interest. With regard to quality in practice, we have seen that the adequacy of both the level of external and internal specialization and of the amount of professional autonomy are measured in terms of efficacy. Ideally then, a good interrelation between the collective and individual formation of practice would lead to effective consulting. Likewise, well-combined institutionalization and reflection on knowledge development generates well-informed (or intelligent, competent) consulting, while the adequate uploading and downloading of rules for legitimation would make for reliable consulting. In all three cases, a good interrelation does not only result in the enhancement of the efficacy, competence, or trustworthiness of particular consultants themselves. Also, and perhaps more importantly, a good interrelation means that the institutions needed to judge and adjust the efficacy, knowledge, and legitimacy of consulting work are in the right place and well-understood, by consultants as well as by their clients, "victims," and publics.

As we have seen above, however, some lessons are hard to upload, such as tacit knowledge and implicit behavior. And the examples on legitimation in particular show that also the downloading is not just simple application, but it revolves around the interpretation of rules in specific situations and involves the possibility to not follow but to adapt or ignore them. Interpretation will have an individual touch in the particular situations and projects in which consultants find themselves. Quality, therefore, resides in an open interaction between concrete experience and general rules: institutions that help to understand practice but not so severely that they dictate behavior. A veritable professional knows the rules, but also himself and his practice. Only by "anchoring" the rules in practice can they be made applicable. Vice versa, developing practices can change the (interpretation of) rules over time.

Our framework emphasizes the need to investigate the complex interactions between processes of reflection and institutionalization. It shows that representations of quality as the simple application of rules or as the natural result of good intentions should be distrusted and problematized. The relation between the uploading and downloading of rules may be hard to investigate and may have been neglected as a result. Not only reflections and institutions may often be hidden and implicit, but also the translation from individual reflections towards collective institutions (uploading) and vice versa (downloading) is neither linear nor unproblematic and is often ambiguous. Institutions are interpreted in individual reflections and will be expressed through actions. Individuals reflect on their actions and strategies in unique settings. How do they share and learn from experiences to make them useful for future actions? Individual reflections and experiences may contribute to professionalization if consultants manage to diffuse experiences and are able to transform their reflections and lessons learned to future situations, actions, and practices. However, not the experience of only one individual, but of many, will gradually change institutions over time.

To be able to understand, assess and manage professionalization of consultancy—in other words, the uploading and downloading of reflections and institutions—we should first be interested in how individual reflections and experiences travel and diffuse among consultants, clients, and others (diffusion and transformation among individuals) and how they may scale up (translation from the individual to the institutional level) to shared re-interpretations of institutions and possibly to new institutions. The key problem is that the interaction and interrelationship between institutional development and reflective learning by no means guarantees quality. Consultants should not only strive for institutionalization, but also investigate how institutions perform and thus what quality means for their profession. To conclude this chapter, we sketch some issues with regard to the development of consultancy as a profession that raised our interest and may lead to questions for further investigation.

A BALANCING ACT

Over time, consultants jointly develop more and more specific ideas, routines, and rules about what they know, do, and value. Thus, they position consultancy as a profession and demarcate themselves as a group of professionals. They offer particular services and create a demand for those services. Institutions may help to differentiate them from lay people, moon lighters, bunglers, and amateurs and exclude those from market competition. Professionalism is the set of habits that would characterize individuals who are called professional consultants (e.g., expertise, working full-time, getting paid). In its other sense, professionalism is not an individual habit, but a culture of a collective. Institutions may contribute to professional autonomy, attractive salaries, privileges, and status (MacDonald, 1995). Individual consultants reflecting on their daily practices and activities co-produce the meaning of institutions and the development of professional practices, knowledge, and values. The development of knowledge contributes to competence; the formation of practices aims at effectiveness; and the operationalization of professional values realizes reliability.

Consultants who are recognized as professionals hardly need additional proof or arguments to convince clients of their expertise, competences, or integrity. But the demarcation of professionalism also comes with restrictions. Institutionalization, by definition, restricts professionals in their freedom to act, because they are supposed to carry out the generic rules, procedures, agreements of their trade. But acting like a professional also includes that a professional should be able to assess when to deviate from these rules under extraordinary circumstances. Reflection on such situations and daily practices should prevent consultants from over-institutionalization. Then, reflection not only contributes to individual learning, but also serves to readjust superseded or contra-productive institutions.

Above, we observed that consultancy is not that much institutionalized and that consultants say they are (or at least should be) reflective practitioners. We should be interested in what that teaches us about the current and apparent balance between institutional and reflexive mechanisms of professionalization of consultancy. Understanding the precarious balance between institutionalization and reflexivity might, for example, explain whether every professional can become a successful consultant, or not.

The Influence of Market Mechanisms

Market forces in the industry influence the development of institutions in consultancy, both positively and negatively. From our exploratory study of consultancy as a profession (Broekhans et al., 2011), examples were found in which market forces and professionalization strengthened the commitment to quality; a good reputation or profound expertise would add to both profitability and quality of consultancy. Thanks to the functioning of such economic principles, the consultancy sector owns an adequate level of specialization as a form of professionalism. In other cases, market forces and the quest for quality are clearly contradictory movements, illustrated by the well-known accounting scandals. In line with economic theory (North, 1990; Williamson, 2000), it may be expected that openness of the consultancy market has a major impact on the contribution of professionalization to the quality of professional advice. A market can only be properly selected if quality information about that market is open, accessible, and available. Strong institutions, lock-in, and other observed phenomena can cause market failure. As far as the authors have been able to ascertain, the investigation of such mechanisms in the consulting industry is still relatively new, marked by Thomas Armbrüster (2006). Based on the experiences gained in the educational research project that led to this chapter, the authors argue that the interaction between market mechanisms and the institutionalization of the quality of consultancy work deserves more attention.

The Professional Culture of Legitimacy

To guarantee the quality of advisory work, individual consultants are expected to act in all conscience upon collective institutions. In-depth reflections enable individual consultants to choose quality and professional conduct, even when—despite working institutions—this leads to a loss of profit. In all this, continuous comparative assessments between short and long-term profit play a role. The more consultants focus on the continuity of their business, the more they will tend to act professionally. Culture, and specifically the long-term orientation (Hofstede & Hofstede, 2005), plays an important role in determining what is "legitimate" behavior in a specific society. Most often, the uploading and downloading of institutions and reflections—and the further professionalization of consultancy—is just a matter of course. But sometimes much effort, energy, and control are needed to protect the legitimacy of the profession against short term economic interests. At first sight, these last attempts only seem to succeed eventually when seeking effective, competent, and reliable consultancy work can be streamlined somewhat with economic sanctions or if unprofessional behavior is sufficiently stringently controlled. But we found that consultancy is not strictly regulated by codes of conduct and branch organizations. That raises questions about what mechanisms shape the professional culture of legitimacy among consultants, what standards are at work, and how they are enforced.

The Market of Scale

All literature confirms that the development and management of consultants' knowledge is core to the profession and the quality of advice. Obviously, small consultancy firms deal differently with this challenge than their larger competitors. The so-called schools of some larger Dutch consultancies—such as Berenschot Academy, McKinsey Euro Academy, Royal Haskoning Academy, Accenture Academy for SAP—are examples of collective knowledge that are beyond the spending power of small businesses but very beneficial to large corporations. The network externality (Economides, 1996) of establishing and operating an academy is in fact large. This means that an increase in the number of like-trained consultants increases the added value of a single participant and consequentially adds to the quality of advisory work and the reputation of firms and the profession. The network externality here can be explained mainly from reduced transaction costs for internal coordination and the search for knowledge partners. Small and independent consultants will be more dependent on the open market for education. On the other hand, many self-employed consultants report that they took more responsibility for their knowledge from the moment they left their former employers to become independent. In short, small and large businesses have divergent interests in the balance between individual and collective professionalization. Hence, they strive for different types of practical, knowledge-related and ethical institutions, for example, in large firms or industry-wide trade associations. This draws our attention to another side of professionalization: it is not only a commitment to quality, but also an arena for competition between different business types in the consultancy sector. The outcomes of such competitions may seriously affect the reputations of different types of consultants.

CONCLUSION

In this chapter we observed that the development of consultancy in the Netherlands has resulted in some traditional institutions such as standardized training and education, professional associations, codes of conduct, and performance indicators but that these are loosely coupled and implemented on a voluntary basis. The result is that the quality of performance is to be produced by deeply reflective consultants and consultancy firms. Institutions are seen to contribute to leveled performance, but they could hence also hamper quality improvement of advisory work with individual consultants.

Ongoing specialization in the market of advisory work will contribute to the efficacy of advice. But it may cause perverse, Enron-like effects as well, if the sector ignores critique and peer assessment. Reflection should contribute to a balance between profit maximization and professional behavior. Institutions may guide their actions, but eventually individual consultants will have to cope with dilemmas and challenges with this regard in their everyday projects. From research and literature, we hardly know how these actions acquire their meaning, what coping strategies consultants use, and what the implications are for consultancy institutions, practices, and professionalization. Future research should integrate the studies and insights in the different isolated cells of our framework.

NOTE

1. Note that these values may range from the well-being of the poor in developing countries, to helping businesses to increase their profits, or becoming the best(paid) consultant in town.

REFERENCES

Akerlof, G. (1970). The market for 'lemons.' *Quarterly Journal of Economics, 84,* 488–500.

Alvesson, M. & Johansson, A. (2002). Professionalism and politics in management consultancy work. In T. Clark & R. Fincham (Eds.), *Critical consulting: New perspectives on the management advice industry* (pp. 228–246). Oxford: Blackwell Publishers.

Alvesson, M. & Robertson, M. (2006). The best and the brightest: the construction, significance and effects of elite identities in consulting firms. *Organization, 13*(2), 195.

Argyris, C. (1991). Teaching smart people how to learn. *Reflections, 4*(2), 4–15.

Armbrüster, T. (2006). *The economics and sociology of management consulting.*Cambridge: Cambridge University Press.

Boonstra, J. J. & De Caluwé, L. (2007). *Intervening and changing: looking for meaning in interactions.* Chicester: Wiley-Interscience.

Bouwmeester, O. (2008). *Advice as Argument: Economic deliberation in management consulting and academic contract research.* Amsterdam: VU University.

Broekhans, B., Van der Arend, S., & Meijer, S. (2011). *Consultants as professionals—de kwaliteit van advieswerk als opgave* [quality of advisory work as an assignment]. Delft: TUDelft.

Buono, A. F. (2011). *Changing paradigm of consulting: Adjusting to the fast-paced world.* Charlotte, NC: Information Age Publishers.

Buono, A. F. (Ed.). (2002). *Developing knowledge and value in management consulting* (Vol. 2). Charlotte, NC: Information Age Publishers.

Chaney, P. K. & Philipich, K. L. (2002). Shredded reputation: The cost of audit failure. *Journal of Accounting Research, 40*(4), 1221–1245.

Clark, T. (2004). Management fashion as collective action. In A. F. Buono (Ed.), *Creative consulting: Innovative perspectives on management consulting* (pp. 3–25). Charlotte, NC: Information Age Publishers.

Clark, T. & Fincham, R. (2002). *Critical consulting: New perspectives on the management advice industry.* Oxford: Blackwell Publishers.

Curnov, B. & Reuvid, J. (Eds.). (2003). *The international guide to management consultancy: The evolution, practice and structure of management consultancy worldwide.* London: Kogan Page Limited.

Czerniawska, F. (1999). *Management consultancy in the 21st century.* West Lafayette, IN: Purdue University.

Czerniawska, F. (2002). *Management Consultancy: What next?* (Vol. 4). Basingstoke: Palgrave Macmillan.

Czerniawska, F. (2005). The new business consulting landscape. *Consulting to Management, 16*(4), 3.

Czerniawska, F. & May, P. (2004). *Management consulting in practice: Award-winning international case studies.* London: Kogan Page Limited.

De Bruijn, H. (2010). *Managing professionals.* London: Routledge.

De Sonnaville, H. (2003). Developments in management consultancy: From stagnation to evaporation or condensation? In B. Curnov & J. Reuvid (Eds.), *The international guide to management consultancy: The evolution, practice and struc-*

ture of management consultancy worldwide (pp. 121–133). London: Kogan Page Limited.

De Sonnaville, H. (2005). *Retorische aspecten van professionaliseren: een zoektocht naar beroepsvorming bij organisatieadviseurs* [Rhetoric aspects of professionalizing: A search into shaping the profession in management consultants]. Amsterdam: Univerity of Amsterdam.

Donnelly, R. (2009). The knowledge economy and the restructuring of employment: The case of consultants. *Work, Employment & Society, 23*(2), 323.

Donnelly, R. (2011). The coalescence between synergies and conflicts of interest in a top consultancy firm: An analysis of the implications for consultants' attitudes and behaviours. *Human Resource Management Journal, 21*(1), 60–73.

Economides, N. (1996). The economics of networks. *International Journal of Industrial Organisation, 13,* 673–699.

Eliot, F. (2001). *Professionalism: The third logic—on the practice of knowledge.* Chicago, IL: University of Chicago Press.

Ernst, B. & Kieser, A. (2002). In search of explanations for the consulting explosion. In K.Sahlin-Andersson & L.Engwall (Eds.), *The expansion of management knowledge* (pp. 47–72). Stanford, CA: Stanford Business Press.

Fincham, R. & Evans, M. (1999). The consultants' offensive: Reengineering–from fad to technique. *New Technology, Work and Employment, 14*(1), 32–44.

Glückler, J. & Armbrüster, T. (2003). Bridging uncertainty in management consulting: The mechanisms of trust and networked reputation. *Organization Studies, 24,* 269–297.

Grijzen, J. (2010). *Outsourcing planning: What do consultants do in a regional spatial planning in the Netherlands.* Amsterdam: Vossiupers UvA.

Groen, M. (2008). Professionele situaties en relaties. *Effectief handelen door reflectie- bekwamer worden als professional* [Being effective by reflection—becoming more proficient as a professional] (pp. 57–74). Groningen/Houten: Wolters-Noordhof.

Groenlinks, W. B. (2001). *De staatsgreep van de zesde macht? De opkomst van externe adviseurs bij de overheid* [Fighting for office by the sixth power? The rise of external consultants in public administration] Utrecht: Groen Links Party.

Grossmann, R. (2011). Delineating the paradigm shift. In A. F. Buono (Ed.), *Changing paradigm of consulting: Adjusting to the fast-paced world* (pp. 3–17). Charlotte, NC: Information Age Publishers.

Hale, J. A. (2006). *The performance consultant's fieldbook: Tools and techniques for improving organizations and people.* San Fransisco, CA: Pfeiffer & Co.

Hellema, H. J. P. & Marsman, J. H. (1997). *De organisatie-adviseur: opkomst en groei van een nieuw vak in Nederland, 1920–1960* [The management consultant: the rise and growth of a new discipline in The Netherlands]. Amsterdam: Boom Koninklijke Uitgevers.

Hicks, J., Nair, P., & Wilderom, C. (2009). What if we shifted the basis of consulting from knowledge to knowing? *Management Learning, 40*(3), 289.

Hofstede, G. & Hofstede, G. J. (2005). *Cultures and organisations: Software of the mind.* New York, NY: McGraw-Hill.

Janes, A. (2011). Developing expertise and social standing in professional consulting. In A. Buono (Ed.), *Changing paradigm of consulting: Adjusting to the fast-paced world* (pp. 309–327). Charlotte, NC: Information Age Publishing.

Jansen, T., Van den Brink, G., & Kole, J. (Eds.). (2009). *Beroepstrots—Een ongekende kracht* [Pride in the profession—An unknown force]. Amsterdam: Boom/SUN.

Kam, J. (2004). Selling professionalism? Image making in the management consulting industry. In A. F. Buono (Ed.), *Creative consulting: Innovative perspectives on management consulting* (pp. 27–50). Charlotte, NC: Information Age Publishers.

Keeble, D. & Schwalbach, J. (1995). *Management consultancy in Europe.* Cambridge: University of Cambridge.

Kubr, M. (2002). *Management consulting: A guide to the profession.* Geneva: International Labour Office.

Lahusen, C. (2002). Commercial consultancies in the European Union: the shape and structure of professional interest intermediation. *Journal of European Public Policy, 9*(5), 695–714.

MacDonald, K. M. (1995). *The sociology of the professions.* Thousand Oaks, CA: Sage.

Maister, D. (2005). Professionalism in consulting. In L. Greiner & F. Poulfelt (Eds.), *Handbook of management consulting: The contemporary consultant* (pp. 23–34). Mason, OH: Thomson South-Western.

Martin, M. (2000). *Meaningful work: Rethinking professional ethics.* Oxford: Oxford University Press.

McKenna, C. (2006). *The world's newest profession.* Cambridge: Cambridge University Press.

Mieg, H. (2008). Professionalisation and professional identities of environmental experts: The case of Switzerland. *Journal of Integrative Environmental Sciences, 5*(1), 41–51.

Mintzberg, H. (1983). *Structure in fives: Designing effective organizations.* Englewood Cliffs, NJ: Prentice-Hall.

Mok, A. (1989). *In het zweet uws aanschijns . . . Een inleiding in de arbeidssociologie* [Blood, sweat and tears . . . An introduction into work sociology]. Houten: Stenfert Kroese.

Nooteboom, B., Zwart, P., & Bijmolt, T. (1990). *Vraagstukken in de advisering aan middelgrote en kleine bedrijven* [Dilemmas in advising small and medium-sized enterprises]. Tilburg, Netherlands: Open Access publications from Tilburg University.

North, D. (1990). *Institutions, institutional change and economic performance.* Cambridge: Cambridge University Press.

Oliver, C. (2005). *Reflexive inquiry: A framework for consultancy practice.* London: Karnac Books.

Rasiel, E. (1999). *The McKinsey way: Using the techniques of the world's top strategic consultants to help you and your business.* Columbus, OH: McGraw-Hill Companies.

Reihlen, M. & Nikolova, N. (2010). Knowledge production in consulting teams. *Scandinavian Journal of Management, 26,* 179–189.

Schön, D. A. (1983). *The reflective practitioner: How professionals think in action.* Jackson, TN: Basic Books.

Sturdy, A. (1997). The consultancy process: An insecure business? *Journal of Management Studies, 34*(3), 389–413.

Sturdy, A. (2002). Front-line diffusion: The production and negotiation of knowledge through training interactions. In T. Clark & R. Fincham (Eds.), *Critical consulting: New perspectives on the management advice industry* (pp. 130–151). Oxford: Blackwell Publishers.

Sturdy, A., Clark, T., Handley, K., & Fincham, R. (2009). *Management consultancy: Boundaries and knowledge in action.* Oxford: Oxford University Press.

Styhre, A., Olilla, S., Wikmalm, L., & Roth, J. (2010). Expert or speaking-partner? Shifting roles and identities in consulting work. *Leadership & Organization Development Journal, 31*(2), 159–175.

Treviño, L. K. & Nelson, K. A. (1999). *Managing business ethics: Straight talk about how to do it right.* New York, NY: John Wiley.

Tzioti, S. (2010). *Let me give you a piece of advice: Empirical papers about advice taking in marketing.* Rotterdam: Erasmus University.

Van der Arend, S. (2007). *Pleitbezorgers, procesmanagers en participanten: Interactief beleid en de rolverdeling tussen overheid en burgers in de Nederlandse democratie* [Advocates, process managers and participants: interactive policy and the division of roles between government and civilians in the Dutch democracy]. Delft: Eburon.

Von Weltzien Høivik, H. & Føllesdal, A. (1995). *Ethics and consultancy: European perspectives.* Dordrecht: Kluwer Academic Publishers.

Williamson, O. E. (2000). The new institutional economics: Taking stock, looking ahead. *Journal of Economic Literature, 38*(3), 595–613.

CHAPTER 8

TEACHING CONSULTING TO ACADEMICS

Reflections on Professionals Supporting an Academic Teaching Program

Sebastiaan Meijer, Geert Roovers, Tanja Verheij, and Ivo Wenzler

The recruitment of new talent for consultancy firms confronts these firms with a gap between the academic traditions taught in university and the professional attitude or identity required for a consultant to work in a professional firm (Kerr, 2001). This chapter reflects on an initiative to bridge this traditional gap. In 2010, Delft University of Technology developed a minor in consultancy. In this minor a combination has been made between a traditional academic course and a course that involved practicing senior consultants supervising and evaluating small groups of students in real-world consultancy practices.

The senior consultants supervised the students on two assignments. First, ten weeks were spent on formulating advice on a real problem of a real client. Each senior consultant supervised two groups of four to six students.

Exploring the Professional Identity of Management Consultants, pages 163–172
Copyright © 2013 by Information Age Publishing
All rights of reproduction in any form reserved.

All the groups had weekly meetings with the university teacher to discuss progress reports and potential academic input. The second assignment was the simulation of an acquisition of a consultancy trajectory in a tender format. The senior consultants acted as the stand-in clients for real tenders they participated in themselves.

This chapter reflects on the process of supervision of the senior consultants and their influence on the resulting student-completed documents. The central question focuses on how the supervision, which was done by both the consultants and the academics, contributed to the learning outcomes of the students. In examining how professionals learn, Argyris (1991) emphasizes the positive value that comes from consultants reflecting upon their work and confronting each other with their findings. Our case is different because the students are not yet by any means professionals. It could be seen as a professional learning community (PLC) in which the students had taken up temporarily. With respect to these PLCs, Stoll and associates (Stoll, Bolam, McMahon, Wallace, & Thomas, 2006) specifically point to the importance of collaboration and networks around a learning institute. TU Delft involved senior consultants from its network to form a joint team of academics and professionals. This example fits what Hargreaves (2000) calls the current postmodern age of professionalism in teaching—major attention is paid to the (self) learning of professionals, to teacher professionalism, and to the transfer of practical skills and tacit knowledge from experienced to young workers. This chapter contributes to the literature by examining the dynamics that occur where the learners are not yet professional, but academic students without work experience in consulting. This situation is different from the transfer of tacit knowledge in the worker domain, as it is not only about the tacit knowledge of doing the job, but also providing the contextual setting to raise the conceptual level of understanding of theoretically taught contents.

The chapter is structured as follows. First we describe the learning goals and the way they have been arranged in the course structure. This delineation positions the place where senior professionals can contribute. The discussion then describes qualitatively the learning that took place, which we use to identify the differences between the academic and professional supervisors. The chapter ends with conclusions on success factors for learning in this setting.

LEARNING GOALS AND CURRICULUM DESIGN

The minor curriculum had been designed after the observation that external consultancy functions have an increasingly important role in the future work setting of engineers. The number of young engineers that start in a consultancy firm or in an engineering firm in an advisory role is growing, and the graduates who don't take such a job will be confronted with external advisors visiting their future employer. Delft University of Technology educates engineers in a range of fields from electrical and civil engineering to architecture and policy science for the technological domain. From an educational perspective, a need to provide more background on consultancy to interested students in the engineering studies had been apparent for some years already. In early 2010 the decision was made to build a minor curriculum in consultancy.

The minor consists of 30 ECTS points (equivalent to approximately half a year fulltime study load), organized in one block so that students can be completely immersed in the topic of the minor. The target audience consists of third year BSc students. In the first year 24 students participated in the program, from eight different studies.

To define the learning goals, we followed the popular categorization scheme for types of objectives (taxonomy of objectives for the cognitive domain) set up by Benjamin Bloom (Bloom, Engelhart, Furst, Hill, & Krathwohl, 1956) in *Taxonomy of Education Objectives*, which includes the following levels:

- *Knowledge:* Primarily concerned with students' ability to memorize or recall certain specific facts.
- *Comprehension:* Usually involves the ability to interpret, paraphrase, and extrapolate, thus demonstrating students' basic understanding of ideas that they did not originate.
- *Application:* Includes activities in which the student applies concepts and principles to new and/or practical situations.
- *Analysis:* Concerned with breaking down a piece of information into its constituent parts, differentiating, and denoting.
- *Synthesis:* Involves the blending of elements and parts to form a whole. Students should be able to create a structural pattern that was not previously present.
- *Evaluation:* At this highest level, students might judge the value of a work, the logical consistency of written data, or the adequacy of someone else's conclusions.

Based on these levels, we formulated the following learning goals. After a successful completion of the minor, the student:

1. Knows and can paraphrase the 30 most used models in management consultancy, their application, and limitations. (Knowledge)
2. Can comprehend the different roles of consultants in organizations. (Comprehension)

3. Can apply different methods of working in technical consultancy. (Application)
4. Can analyze the complexity of the power relations in and around an organization. (Analysis)
5. Can apply the most used tools, skills, and instruments for consultants. (Application)
6. Can evaluate the quality of a presentation and report. (Evaluation)
7. Can synthesize theory on professionalization in public and private sector consultancy. (Synthesis)

For the theoretical foundations the minor builds upon four courses, and for the application of the knowledge on the two assignments described above. The four courses are taught by the academic staff, with the addition of some consultants for guest lectures.

The Consultant as Analyst

The use of models in different contexts requires insight into the generic applicability of these models and their constraints. The balance between generic models and specific solutions is further complicated by the incomplete or even contested information available. In this course, five ways of analyzing the problem were discussed, being:

1. The 30 most used management models
2. Multi-agent simulation
3. Serious gaming/gaming simulation
4. Societal cost-benefit analysis
5. Taxonomy of analytical models.

Consultants in Multi-Actor Settings

Both within and around a client organization, power relations, interests, and relations among stakeholders have a major influence on the work of a consultant. This includes media, the general audience, and sometimes shareholders. Guided by literature and exemplary cases, this course shows the specific options and constraints of the political minefield that an external expert has to handle.

Tools, Skills, and Techniques for Consultants

In addition to the domain-specific knowledge of a consultant, each student has to master a range of tools, skills, and techniques to collect information, facilitate group processes, and present reports and outcomes. In this course a range of tools, skills, and techniques are taught and practiced in role-play and other exercises.

Consultants as Professionals

The growing role of consultants in the public sector raises questions about quality insurance and transparency. In the private sector there is a tendency to make the consultant (partially) responsible for the achievement of a result or an improvement. These developments push consultants to safeguard their professionalism both individually and as a group. In this course, theory on quality management, ethics, and professionalizing are reviewed, and we have a look on its practical implementation in various firms.

INVOLVEMENT OF CONSULTANCY FIRMS

For this minor, we found three consultancy firms willing to contribute. Consultants of these firms were involved in four different ways:

1. The supervision of student teams in the first group assignment. This involved an advisory process in the medium- to small-scale business domain. Each of the student teams had three meetings with the senior consultant assigned to them.
2. The supervision of student teams tendering for a fictitious client. The senior consultants had two meetings with each team and were present at the presentations of the proposals of the students. Each senior consultant was assigned two student groups who had to compete for his tender, in which he enacted the role of the client. The tender was a real one that the consultant had worked on himself in real life.
3. Each firm gave access to consultants to be interviewed for the course on the topics of professionalization and quality insurance.
4. On occasional request, we had guest lectures of the senior consultants in the courses mentioned above on selected topics.

REFLECTING ON THE LEARNING

Through the four courses, students learned the seven learning goals up to a level of application in the Bloom (Bloom et al., 1956) hierarchy of learning levels. The evaluation was done by the traditional university examination techniques like a written exam (for the course The Consultant as an Analyst), essays (for the course Consultants in Multi-Actor Settings), and portfolios combined with oral exams (for the Tools and Professionals courses). It goes beyond the scope of this chapter to go into the learning results of each of these courses. Our hypothesis here is that the involvement of real senior consultants helps to increase the level of learning. This means that learning goals 1, 2, 3, and 5 can be obtained through the academic staff, but that learning goals 4, 6, and 7 require further investigation here.

The four authors of this chapter who were involved as consultants reflected upon their contribution to the learning on four topics: the planning process, understanding the client expectations, the development of a solution, and their own role in this. In this we follow the perspective as taken by Akerlind (2004) who used a phenomenographic perspective on academics' ways of experiencing or understanding being a university teacher. Here we put the consultants in the role of experiencing and understanding their role as teachers.

Observations on the Process of Planning their Work

All senior consultants noted the very linear process that the students had in mind when starting out with the assignments. From the analysis to the advice, they built in limited room for iteration and continuous engagement with the client. As one of these individuals noted, Engineering students. They are trained to find a solution, for every problem. One problem, one solution, until the Minor Consultancy.

Reflecting on the group work, the consultants noted that during their first meetings with the student groups there was an interesting dynamic in how different roles and responsibilities within the teams were assumed or assigned. It was an emergent, almost organic process, very unlike the reality of most consulting teams. In reality the roles and responsibilities are the result of specific competencies team members need to bring to the team and/or hierarchical relationships within the teams.

Observations on the Process of Understanding Client Expectations

The students had a strong inclination to take the written document provided by the client as the main source of understanding what the client wanted, instead of using it only as one source for structuring their questions to the client, which is what a professional consultant would do. The students had an expectation that the client not only knew exactly what he needed but that he was able to express it clearly and unambiguously in the briefing he provided, resulting initially in a limited challenge on the definition of the need as well as the definition of the expected outcome of the advice (what should be the result of their work). In an early meeting with the client, which the senior consultants had to suggest and encourage in their role as advisors, the students confessed that they had difficulties in focusing only on the questions and not already discussing the solution. This is also a common issue with many real-life consultants who think that they know better what the client wants than the client. Another interesting observation is that it appears that just by assuming the role of consultant there was a shift in student attitude, towards a slightly arrogant "you have a problem and I have a solution" orientation.

The senior consultants noted that in the case of one assignment with two principals, the students had problems understanding that two principals can make two perceptions of a problem. Most problems in the minor had many stakeholders as well, each with their own perception of the problem, and many different interests. As one of the consultants asked rhetorically,

> So, engineer students, for which problem are you going to find a solution? And what about the rest, dear? Learn about multi-issuing!

The senior consultants had to confront the students on their assumptions about data: if you measure right, the data is right. In practice this is not the case with different stakeholders, with different problems and different views. Data is contested, methods are contested, system-boundaries are contested. "*So what now, engineer students?*" The senior consultants made the students find out that rational instruments, like economic and environmental assessments, aren't always useful to solve a problem, or to make a right decision. Besides, what is "right," in a multi-stakeholder environment?

Observations on the Process of Developing the Solution

One of the key success factors when helping clients with their performance challenges or opportunities is making a clear distinction between the solutions to the perceived problems or opportunities and the questions that need to be answered in order to come to the right set of actions addressing the problems or opportunities. All student teams had some difficulties in the beginning in making this distinction, not realizing that the solution is the responsibility of the client. Their role mainly lies in ensuring that a right set of questions are being addressed and answered, to ensure that the proposed solution is specific, measurable, actionable, and can be resourced. The senior consultants had to confront the students with these insights. In the beginning the teams were also not focusing on the value of their advice to the client—what will each of the proposed actions deliver, what is the "size of the prize" of these actions, what are the choices the client has (in terms of required effort and the implementation speed), and what is the rationale behind these choices.

Major attention of the senior consultants went into the art of questioning, in other words, to teach students to postpone their professional judgment, and to search first for the question behind the question. What does your principal really need? To find out what not yet can be seen. Only the art of questioning makes an engineer a consultant. And that is what the students found out.

Some Observations on the Scholarly Role as a Senior Consultant

The senior consultants all expressed that it was a very nice experience in doing what they do every day at Accenture, Oranjewoud or Berenschot (the consultancy firms involved) , but then for an audience that is yet starting to learn about the challenges of being a management consultant. Their major difficulty was in preventing themselves from taking over the process or dominating it through their experience, thus preventing the students from learning by doing instead of by just repeating what they told them that needs to be done. At the actual client engagement, the senior consultants would intervene much more quickly, since there is often no room for an unguided learning process. Another challenge was in trying to engage the whole team of students, and not only the few proactive members of the team. In the actual consulting setting the structure of the team would be quickly adjusted to ensure that all the competencies required are on board, and that there is a clear agreement on who is responsible for what. The dynamics would be less free flowing and more structured.

It was nice to observe that students were genuinely eager to learn and that all of the suggestions, either on what they should be doing or on how they should be doing it, were taken seriously and executed to the extent that the students were able to and regarding the short time they had and the lack of experience in such settings. The senior consultants found it pleasant to see that the students were able to switch quickly in the way that they interacted with them, depending on the role they took. Due to the limitation in the students' access to the real client (during the proposal work) the seniors were role-playing the client in addition to being their advisor on how to approach the client and the problem at hand.

CONCLUSIONS AND DISCUSSION

The reflections show that the senior consultants added context and knowledge to the consultancy minor in ways that cannot be taught from theory. The academic teachers gave the students background and theories to actually start working, to *apply* and partially to *analyze* problems in the consultancy domain. The senior consultants were able to provide guidance to the students to bring the level of the learning towards *synthesis*, where students could create new advice and creative solutions, useful for real clients. It should be noted that for one out of the six student teams, the actual advice led to a presentation for the governmental board working on the water recreation topic, and that their advice was accepted and is now in preparation for implementation. The learning level *evaluation* of the quality of the advice proved present at the final symposium that ended the minor. Here the students were judged on a poster presentation in which they defend and evaluate a statement on a topic in consultancy. Out of the 24 students, 22 successfully defended their topic at the *evaluation* level. Every student was scored by a team of professionals and academics on the live defense of a poster in an oral face-to-face defense. Each member of the evaluation team went through the Bloom taxonomy to see whether every level up to the evaluation level was present, and how. For each student the scores were discussed and then graded.

Our empirical findings and reflections can provide food for thought for the field of research on mentoring of professionals over students. The medical sector has put considerable efforts into evaluating this type of learning, though it still suffers with perceived barriers found on an organizational level. In medicine, the master-associate-junior system as known from the guilds is still in place, but major efforts have been put into putting together protocols for the interaction between doctors (the "masters") and their students, assigning both responsibilities and dues. Motivation for development is found on an individual level and often related to the notion of teaching as a "private business" (Stenfors-Hayes, Weurlander, Dahlgren, & Hult, 2010). Bringing in professionals to the classroom to co-teach may overcome some of these barriers.

REFERENCES

Akerlind, G. S. (2004). A new dimension to understanding university teaching. *Teaching in Higher Education, 9*(3), 363–375.

Argyris, C. (1991). Teaching smart people how to learn. *Harvard Business Review*, (May-June), 99–109.

Bloom, B. S., Engelhart, M. D., Furst, E. J., Hill, W. H., & Krathwohl, D. R. (1956).

Taxonomy of educational objectives: The classification of educational goals. Handbook 1: Cognitive domain. New York, NY: David McKay.

Hargreaves, A. (2000). Four ages of professionalism and professional learning. *Teachers and Teaching: History and Practice, 6*(2), 151–182.

Kerr, C. (2001). *The uses of the university.* Cambridge, MA: Harvard University Press.

Stenfors-Hayes, T., Weurlander, M., Dahlgren, L. O., & Hult, H. (2010). Medical teachers' professional development—perceived barriers and opportunities. *Teaching in Higher Education, 15*(4), 399–408.

Stoll, L., Bolam, R., McMahon, A., Wallace, M., & Thomas, S. (2006). Professional learning communities: A review of the literature. *Journal of Educational Change, 7,* 221–258.

CHAPTER 9

SKILL ACQUISITION OF EXECUTIVE COACHES

A Journey Toward Mastery

John L. Bennett and Kelly D. B. Rogers

Executive coaching continues to increase in popularity, and the body of knowledge that informs the practice continues to grow. Yet, with more than 40,000 people identifying themselves as coaches (Hamlin, Ellinger & Beattie, 2009) and hundreds of coaching, training, and education organizations focused on developing coaches, the skill development of coaches remains more an art than a science (Sherpa Coaching, 2011). A review of the literature reveals that while international dialogue and research on coaching continues to expand, there is no agreement on the definition of executive coaching (Brotman, Liberi & Wasylyshyn, 2000; Grant, 2003; Kilburg, 1996), the qualities one needs to be an executive coach (Crane, 1998; de Haan, 2008b; Dotlich & Cairo, 1999; Fitzgerald & Berger, 2002; Freas, 2000; Hargrove, 1995; Hurd, 2003; Kampa-Kokesch & Anderson, 2001; O'Neill, 2007; Zeus & Skiffington, 2001), or the standards for coaching programs that prepare coaches for practice (Graduate School Alliance for Executive

Exploring the Professional Identity of Management Consultants, pages 173–201
Copyright © 2013 by Information Age Publishing
All rights of reproduction in any form reserved. **173**

Coaching, n.d.; Sherpa Coaching, 2011; Worldwide Association of Business Coaches, n.d.).

There is also a need to increase the foundation of empirical research and a shared body of knowledge in order to cultivate the field of coaching practitioners (Bennett, 2006; Grant, 2003; Kampa-Kokesch & Anderson; 2001; Kilburg, 1996; Lane, Stelter & Rostron, 2010; Laske, 2004; Laske, Stober & Edwards, 2003). As Orlinsky and Ronnestad (2005), in their study of the development of psychotherapists, assert:

> All modern therapeutic approaches are based on the notion, variously expressed, that self-understanding contributes importantly to professional effectiveness, rational self-management, and personal well-being. To facilitate that self-understanding, we rely individually on our supervisors, our colleagues, and our own psychotherapists; but we also need to understand ourselves collectively, as a profession (or, more accurately, as a set of related professions) ... the only real path to reliable collective self-knowledge is through systematic empirical research. (p. 4)

It is through this work in particular, and this type of inward examination, that coaches will ultimately be able to know how practitioners develop individually and collectively.

Popular author Daniel Pink (2009) writes about certain elements of mastery being essential to the learner. A learner must have a particular mindset that values learning goals over end performance goals. A learner must have tenacity, as the journey is often lined with obstacles. A learner must also hold the idea that mastery is impossible to realize fully. In the process of mastering an area of discipline, the expert is always learning, and as Pink argues, the joy is in the quest. The studied and applied research of Anders Ericsson, Krampe, and Tesch-Römer (1993), made popular by Malcolm Gladwell (2008), contends that a person needs to devote 10,000 hours of practice in order to achieve expertise in an area of discipline. If a person is so motivated, has such tenacity, enjoys learning, and devotes the time and energy, then logically one would want and need to understand the skills, methods, and theories—as well as qualified teachers—of the identified discipline of mastery.

The Dreyfus (2004; Dreyfus & Dreyfus, 1980, 1986) model of skill acquisition offers a useful framework for understanding the differences between the novice and the expert as a progression through five levels of proficiency. As Benner (1984/2001, 2004, 2010) has found, the Dreyfus model was generalizable to the field of nursing, suggesting broad application possibilities. The studies of Benner and her colleagues, as well as Orlinsky and Ronnestad (2005), became the inspiration for the current research that will address the question: What, if any, distinguishable characteristic differences are there in the advanced beginners' and experts' descriptions of similar executive coaching experiences? The original focus of the research reported in this chapter was based on the comparison of the novice coach with the expert coach; however, the question was altered to compare the advanced beginner with the expert due to the availability of research participants.

THE LITERATURE

The literature review addresses executive coaching, competency models and accrediting bodies in coaching, adult learning and skill acquisition, and staged-based skill acquisition.

Executive Coaching

Coaching can provide business leaders the developmental skills and support needed to fully optimize their potential and to positively impact their organizations. However, there is a need to clarify what executive coaching is, whether or not it is a valid profession, how it relates to consulting, and what qualities make a "good coach." There is no universal understanding of what coaching is (Brotman et al., 2000; Grant, 2003; Kilburg, 1996). Moreover, there are a sufficient number of descriptive qualifiers that provide specificity to the variants, such as "executive" or "life" when applied to coaching, that there is even further ambiguity (Hamlin et al., 2009).

Hamlin, Ellinger, and Beattie (2009) collected 36 definitions of coaching and sorted them by type descriptor. The content of the definitions were examined with attention to intentions/purposes, processes, and key words. This chapter draws on the synthesized definition of executive coaching created from their meta-analysis:

> Executive coaching is a process that primarily (but not exclusively) takes place within a one-to-one helping and facilitative relationship between a coach and an executive (or manager) that enables the executive (or manager) to achieve personal-, job- or organizational-related goals with an intention to improve organizational performance. (Hamlin et al., 2009, p. 18)

Skills and Abilities of Executive Coaches

Identifying the qualities of a skilled coach practitioner is a precursor to becoming one, educating one, or even hiring one. Although much has been written on the processes, techniques, and models to help executive coaches find ongoing success (Bush, 2004; Crane, 1998; Dotlich & Cairo, 1999; Fitzgerald & Berger, 2002; Hargrove, 1995; Kilburg, 1996, 2000;

Laske, 2004; O'Neill, 2007; Zeus & Skiffington, 2001), the skills and abilities that a successful coach should possess remain ambiguous.

There are, of course, some commonly held ideas about what makes a skilled coach, but as is true for defining the practice, there are no widely agreed upon qualifications. A review of the literature related to coaching skills and competencies reveals several skills that are generally accepted as necessary for the skilled practitioner. These skills include the ability to:

- *Give feedback* (Crane, 1998; Hargrove, 1995; Kampa-Kokesch & Anderson, 2001);
- *Be present and listen actively* (Crane, 1998; O'Neill, 2007);
- *Build trusting relationships* (de Haan, 2008a, 2008b; Kampa-Kokesch & Anderson, 2001; O'Neill, 2007; Zeus & Skiffington, 2001);
- *Understand the context and culture of executives* (Kampa-Kokesch & Anderson, 2001; Zeus & Skiffington, 2001);
- *Be aware of business/management goals/impacts* (Dotlich & Cairo, 1999; Freas, 2000; Kampa-Kokesch & Anderson, 2001; O'Neill, 2007; Zeus & Skiffington, 2001);
- *Create a commitment for change* (Crane, 1998; de Haan, 2008b; Dotlich & Cairo, 1999; Hargrove, 1995; Hurd, 2003);
- *Foster self-awareness/reflection* (de Haan, 2008a, 2008b; Dotlich & Cairo, 1999; Hurd, 2003; Zeus & Skiffington, 2001);
- *Act on intuition with courage* (de Haan, 2008b; Hargrove, 1995); and
- *Be a reflective practitioner* (Fitzgerald & Berger, 2002; Hargrove, 1995).

Hargrove (1995) asserts that "a coach is something that you 'be'" (p. 39). Therefore, "the first question to ask, then, is not 'What do I do?' but 'how do I 'be'" (p. 39). Hargrove identifies the coach as being who one *is*, as opposed to an approach or model that one must follow step by step. Developing "being" shifts the dynamics with a client. The awareness of self, confidence, and focus allows a coaching engagement to be what it needs to be for the client. Masterful coaching, as Hargrove (1995) defines it, becomes a transformational experience for a client, with the coach holding the space and a presence that allows the transformation to manifest as an effortless next step of evolution.

Competency Models and Accrediting Bodies

Competency models serve as an anchor in the field of coaching and provide us with a common language of minimum criteria. For the purposes of reviewing the research on coaching, competency is defined as the knowledge, skills, attitudes, and behaviors that differentiate levels of effectiveness

(Auerbach, 2005). The body of research on coaching shows evidence of chosen characteristics or competencies of expert coaching, which include components of self-awareness/self-management, listening, promoting action, and demonstrating intuition (see Brotman et al., 2000; Guthrie & Alexander, 2000; Hargrove, 1995; Whitworth, Kimsey-House, Kimsey-House, & Sandahl, 2007). However, expert coaches, professional coaching associations, scholars, and the business community do not have one central governing body, oath of conduct, or even a shared set of competencies for executive coaching.

According to the global 2011 Executive Coaching Survey (Sherpa Coaching, 2011), 400 coach training schools have been identified, accredited by sixteen different trade associations. The need for collaboration among training organizations is evident.

Adult Learning and Skill Acquisition

To be a good coach, one must have acquired key skills and abilities. Since skills and abilities are learned and developed through various methods, adult learning and skill development will be familiar to good coaches on their journeys of growth, as well as part of their knowledge base in providing quality care for their clients.

Primary models for designing and evaluating learning are rooted in Bloom's Taxonomy of Learning Objectives (Bloom, Engelhart, Furst, Hill, & Krathwohl, 1956) and Howell's (1982) conscious competence model. Bloom's education model that focuses on learners mastering subjects and being conscious of personal development was a direct rebuttal to the transactional fact-sharing from teacher to learner that was the dominant educational model for centuries. What is now known as "Bloom's Taxonomy," with three domains—*cognitive, affective,* and *psychomotor,* or more commonly known as *think, feel* and *do*—is used for classifying educational goals and objectives (Krathwhol, 2002). A key premise of Bloom's Taxonomy is that mastery must be achieved at each level of a domain before advancing to the next.

Awareness emerges in Bloom's model as a major factor in skill acquisition. Awareness may also be used, in part, to describe a learner's level of consciousness. Krathwhol's (2002) further development of Bloom's Psychomotor Domain begins with a level of imitation and advances to a level described as naturalization. Once a learner achieves the level of naturalization, he has become automated, in a sense, and the activity is subconscious (often referred to as an "unconscious" state in the literature). Such progression of repeating a process before gaining precision and achieving mastery can be compared with Howell's (1982) conscious competence model.

Howell (1982) describes a sequence of learning in which the learner starts in an *unconscious incompetent* state, wherein the individual may be unaware or unconcerned about the skill; progresses to *conscious incompetence*, wherein the individual becomes aware of the skill lacking and gains an understanding of improving the skill; advances to a *conscious competence*, wherein the learner is now demonstrating the knowledge needed and can perform reliably; and finally reaches an *unconscious competence*, wherein the learner is now performing the skill as a second nature or intuitively.

Taylor (2007) offers a fifth stage, naming it "reflective competency." Taylor asserts that this fifth stage is being conscious of unconscious incompetence. By continually challenging oneself in the fifth stage with self-study and peer review, evolved learners cycle back through the stage of unconscious incompetence where new enlightenment reveals something else they did not know. One might align this thinking with the adage: "the more I learn, the less I know." Therefore, with the addition of the fifth stage, Howell's model becomes much more cyclical and dynamic.

Johns (2009) describes a reflective practitioner as "someone who lives reflection as a way of being," with reflection defined as "awareness of self within the moment, having a clear mind so as to be open to possibility of that moment" (p. 3–4). An *effective* practitioner must have acquired knowledge, but a *reflective* practitioner understands that no two experiences are alike and therefore one cannot simply rely on learned paradigms. Knowing and applying evidence-based practices and theoretical models are essential to contextualize the human situation, but are inadequate without the practitioner's intuitive response (Johns, 2009). Through reflection, practitioners develop their intuitive processes. Through reflection, practitioners become conscious of their competencies and incompetencies, thereby creating further enlightenment (Taylor, 2007).

The Dreyfus Model of Skill Acquisition

To be a good coach, one must understand the elements of adult development—a lifelong process. Stuart Dreyfus (2004a, 2004b) and Hubert Dreyfus (Dreyfus & Dreyfus, 1980, 1986, 2004) developed a model of skill acquisition based on situated performance and experiential learning. Hunt and Weintraub (2007) identify the Dreyfus model of skill acquisition as "one of the most 'user-friendly' developmental frameworks" (p. 40).

The five stages of the Dreyfus model are identified as novice, advanced beginner, competent, proficient, and expert. The developmental model describes the stages through which an individual must progress to achieve mastery of a particular skill, advancing from abstract principles needed in a novice stage to a more intuitive, less self-conscious state in an expert stage (Benner, 2001; Dreyfus, 2004; Dreyfus & Dreyfus, 1980; Hunt & Weintraub, 2007).

The Dreyfus model distinguishes the skill acquisition of learning theory in an instructional setting from the context-dependent decisions and choices one makes in lived experience (Dreyfus & Dreyfus, 1980, 1986, 2004). Dreyfus and Dreyfus use learning the game of chess as an example of the applied model for intellectual skills and driving a car as an example of the applied model for physical skills. Their model has been used in a variety of disciplines, including nursing (Benner, 1984/2001), engineering (Vanderburg, 2004), teaching (Berliner, 2004), development of motor skills in sports (Moe, 2004), ski instruction, and treating anorexia nervosa (Duesund & Jespersen, 2004). Duesund and Jespersen (2004), in their work in treating anorexia nervosa with the Dreyfus model, offer two important insights: "1. A movement from reliance on abstract principles to use of past concrete experience, and 2. A passage from detached observer to involved performer in the situation" (p. 226). The distinctions noted by Duesund and Jesperson articulate the space between novice and expert. Applying this to coaching, one might assume that a novice coach is still observing and imitating experiences seen by more experienced coaches, whereas an expert coach is fully "being" in the moment with a client, as Hargrove (1995) describes the masterful coach.

Though it may seem that an emotional investment in the decision-making process at the point of moving from competent to proficient could give way to illogical choices, Benner's (1984/2001, 2004, 2010) study of clinical nurses shows otherwise.

Skill Acquisition in Clinical Nursing

Beginning in the mid-1980s, Benner (1984/2001, 2004, 2010) applied the Dreyfus model of skill acquisition in three different studies with nurses. Benner and her team conducted individual and small group narrative interviews and observed over 270 nursing students and clinical nurses from diverse disciplines and practices. Initially, Benner's (1984/2001) first study asked if there were "distinguishable, characteristic differences in the novice's and expert's descriptions of the same clinical incident" (p. 14). She wanted to know if differences could be attributed or understood and how such differences might be identified in the stages of the Dreyfus (Dreyfus & Dreyfus, 1980) model.

According to Benner (1984/2001), the nurses she studied displayed characteristic traits identified in the Dreyfus model: novice, advanced beginner, and so forth. At each level, characteristics, developmental stages, and learning needs of the clinicians were noted. As the nurse practitioner's expertise grew, there was a connection between the skill of involvement and the development of moral agency, or what Benner and Leonard (2005) define as "the ability to effect and influence situations" (p. 35). Additionally, some nurses would not go on to be expert nurses if they were unable to show capabilities with interpersonal skills and problem engagement, and if they had difficulty with understanding what she called "the ends of practice" (Benner, 2004, p. 198). Nurses who did not show a progressive development into a mastery-level skill set continued to rely on their logic and rationality, in contrast to an experiential, intuitive-based process. Moreover, Benner (2004) argued, "the most qualitatively distinct difference lies between the competent and proficient level, where the practitioner begins to read the situation" (p. 188). Benner's findings show that rational-technical skill in trained nurses must be accompanied by wise discernment and practice, and that experiential learning is key for continued development.

Coaching, like nursing, is a discipline that requires the practitioner be skilled in theory and practice (Benner, 1983). Coaching demands skillful judgment and decision making over time, as changes in the client and changes in the situation are ongoing. Using Benner's framework and the Dreyfus model as our foundation, the current research seeks to address what, if any, distinguishable characteristic differences there are in the advanced beginner's and expert's descriptions of similar executive coaching experiences. Our research into the skill acquisition of executive coaches explores the differences between advanced beginner and expert executive coaches, drawing out their experiences, practices, and the ways they interact and work with their clients.

METHODOLOGY

Building on the models of skill acquisition and expertise development, this qualitative, descriptive study involved 26 executive coaches with and without formal coaching credentials. Research participants were interviewed about their work with a client as the client made a shift in perspective or action. The research question and interview protocol was informed by Benner's (1984/2001, 2004) studies with clinical nurses. A pilot study was completed early in the project to test and improve the data collection processes. In particular, the focus was on the interview protocol, interview technique, and logistics. Although adjustments were made to refine the procedures, no significant changes were made, and the data collected from the pilot interview were used in the final analysis.

Study Participants

A total of 27 self-identified executive coaches based in the United States were recruited. Each participant completed a demographic questionnaire. Research participants were recruited using intentional convenience sampling, often referred to as snowball sampling (Marshall & Rossman, 2011; Miles & Huberman, 1994). The researchers' goal was to recruit participants who represented four categories: executive coaches with three or fewer years of coaching experience and did not hold a coaching credential from International Coach Federation (ICF) (International Coach Federation, n.d.), executive coaches who held an Accredited Certified Coach (ACC), executive coaches who held a Professional Certified Coach (PCC), and executive coaches who held Master Certified Coach (MCC) credentials from ICF (Henry, 1990; Marshall & Rossman, 2011). Participants were recruited and selected for participation based on the data provided on a participant data questionnaire. During the data collection phase, researchers learned that one participant did not meet the established criteria. Data from that interview were not used in the study. All participants ($n = 26$) granted their informed consent. Table 9.1 summarizes relevant participant demographics.

The researchers independently analyzed and sorted the 26 transcripts into the five stages of the Dreyfus (Dreyfus & Dreyfus, 1980, 2004) model. The two chapter authors then came together, compared the classifications of the research participants, and where classifications varied, arrived at consensus.

Data Collection

In addition to the demographic questionnaire completed by each participant, the researchers interviewed each of the 26 study participants (20 by one researcher; 6 by the other) using a semi-structured interview protocol (Creswell, 2007; McCracken, 1988; Weiss, 1994) as informed by the research interview model developed by Benner and Gordon (Benner, 2001). Data collected include explanations/stories of personal choices during a participant selected coaching experience in which the coach identified that the client made a shift in perspective or action. Participants were provided the first question and asked to consider it prior to the interview.

TABLE 9.1 Participant Gender and Level of ICF Credential

	No credential	ACC	PCC	MCC	Total
Male	1	2	1	1	5
Female	9	3	5	4	21
Total	**10**	**5**	**6**	**5**	**26**

Note: International Coach Federation (ICF)
      Associate Certified Coach (ACC)
      Professional Certified Coach (PCC)
      Master Certified Coach (MCC)

Interviews, lasting approximately 35 minutes, were digitally recorded and transcribed by a professional transcription service. Transcripts were reviewed by one of the researchers, compared to the recording, and edited before sending them to individual participants for verification. Prior to data analysis, each transcript was assigned a unique code in order to provide anonymity for the participants.

Study participants were offered the opportunity to review and revise their interview transcript prior to coding by the researchers. Bogdan and Biklen (1992) refer to this process as member checks with the participants, and it is intended to increase the credibility of the data collected. Of the 26 transcripts used in the study, four were revised by participants.

Data Analysis

Both researchers reviewed the transcripts to identify key themes in the text. Themes were compared and a total of 31 themes were identified and used for open coding purposes. Among the 31 themes, the five categories of mastery, identified by Dreyfus and Dreyfus (1980, 1986, 2004) and applied by Benner (1984/2001, 2004, 2010), were used to code the text. Researchers used ATLAS.ti software to code transcripts. A repetitive review and coding process occurred before coded texts were discussed and compared, producing approximately 85% consistency in coding. Differences were compared, discussed, and reconciled. Next, one researcher reviewed the coded text to identify key concepts associated with the selected text. The second researcher reviewed the codes and text to further refine the coding.

The researchers independently reviewed and coded the transcripts from the participants using the Dreyfus (Dreyfus & Dreyfus, 1980, 1986, 2004) model as a framework for categorizing participants in one of five levels of skill development (Novice, Advanced Beginner, Competent, Proficient, and Expert). Initial categorization using the Dreyfus (Dreyfus & Dreyfus, 1980, 1986, 2004) model by the two researchers was 75% consistent. Differences were resolved by discussing variations in coding and agreeing to a singular interpretation. As noted earlier, the original focus of the study was to look at characteristic differences between novice and expert coaches. However, it was determined that the sample did not include any coaches in the novice category. As a result, the researchers revised their focus to concentrate on 13 transcripts: seven advanced beginner and six expert coaches. Data from all other interview transcripts were removed from the data set for further analysis.

Using the coded transcripts, the researchers discussed and agreed to focus on 12 categories of data most closely related to the central research question. Transcript text associated with these codes was further reviewed and coded by each researcher, producing specific text supporting each category. This process allowed the researchers to conceptualize the data into findings through an inductive process. In addition, data were analyzed based on the deductive process using the Dreyfus (Dreyfus & Dreyfus, 1980, 1986, 2004) model (Denzin & Lincoln, 2003; Miles & Huberman, 1994; Neuendorf, 2002; Silverman, 2006; Wolcott, 1994).

Trustworthiness and Credibility

Several steps were taken to increase the trustworthiness and credibility of the research design and implementation (see Kirk & Miller, 1986). First, a pilot study was completed early in the project to test and improve the data collection processes. No significant changes to the protocol were required. Second, the authors used the same semi-structured interview guide. The protocol was reviewed and discussed prior to interviews being conducted. Third, the recordings of each interview were reviewed and discussed in order to enhance consistency of data collection. Fourth, the researchers independently coded the data. Finally, the researchers conducted independent and collaborative analysis of the data.

FINDINGS

The findings of the data analysis are presented in four sections. These findings are based on the semi-structured interviews with the coaches, wherein the coaches were asked to describe a time when they made a choice that created a significant shift for their client in a specific coaching session.

Study Participants

The researchers reviewed the interview transcripts and independently characterized the participants using the Dreyfus (Dreyfus & Dreyfus, 1980, 1986, 2004) model of skill development. Table 9.2 illustrates the consensus of this classification, along with the International Coach Federation (ICF) credential, if any, held by the participants.

Of the 26 participants, none presented consistent qualities of a novice coach. Therefore, the data comparison shifted from differences between novice and expert to differences between advanced beginner and expert (Dreyfus & Dreyfus, 1980, 1986, 2004). While classification resulted in some coaches falling into the stages of competent or proficient, these transcripts were set aside, as the scope of this particular study was concerned with characteristic differences between advanced beginner and expert coaches. Given

TABLE 9.2 Classification of Coaches with Dreyfus Model Stages and ICF Credentials

	No credential	ACC	PCC	MCC
Novice	0	0	0	0
Advanced Beginner	6	1	0	0
Competent	4	1	2	0
Proficient	0	2	4	0
Expert	0	0	1	5

Note: International Coach Federation (ICF)
   Associate Certified Coach (ACC)
   Professional Certified Coach (PCC)
   Master Certified Coach (MCC)

that distinction, the data that were the focus of the content analysis, as it relates to the research question, included seven interview transcripts from advanced beginner coaches and six interview transcripts from expert coaches.

The advanced beginner coach participants were comprised of six females and one male, aged 26 to 55 years old. All seven coaches had been coaching for less than three years, and two of the seven coaches had coached for less than one year. One of the seven coaches held an ICF Accredited Certified Coach (ACC) certification and received coach training through an ICF accredited coach training program. Six of the seven coaches received coach education at a graduate school and did not have ICF certification. Four of the seven coaches saw approximately one to five clients per year, while the other three saw approximately six to 12 clients per year.

The expert coach participant pool was comprised of four females and two males, aged 46 years and older. All six coaches had been coaching for a minimum of nine years. One coach had 13 to 20 years of coaching experience, and another had over 20 years of coaching experience. Six of the seven coaches held the ICF Master Certified Coach (MCC) certification, and one coach held the ICF Professional Certified Coach (PCC) certification. All six coaches received coach training through a dedicated program, and all six coaches held a graduate or advanced graduate degree (master or doctorate). Three of the six coaches worked with 13 to 20 clients per year; one worked with 21 to 30 clients per year; one worked with 31 to 40 clients per year; and one worked with more than 50 clients per year.

Advanced Beginner Coaches

There were six themes that emerged from the advanced beginner coaches: self-awareness, awareness of the coaching client, confidence, role of the coach, acquisition of coaching skills and abilities, and application of coaching skills and abilities. There was a clear consciousness on the part of the advanced beginner coaches, wherein they were able to readily recall thoughts and feelings of the specific coaching engagement and articulate what transpired in the interaction. In some situations, there was a complete retelling of the event with great detail from the perspective of the coach and the coach's perception of their client's perspective.

Self-Awareness

Self-awareness in the coaching engagement surfaced as one theme among the advanced beginners. Study participants expressed feelings of fear and discomfort, feelings of joy and validation, desires to help their clients, and moments of personal growth, like trusting themselves as coaches, as illustrated by the following quotations from participants:

007: I was allowing myself as a coach to probe, even if it got uncomfortable. Because what I was doing before, once I would start to feel her discomfort, I would back off. And what really helped was to keep going.

002: So, yes, for me I would say it was the feeling of it being okay to trust my gut, that there wasn't one perfect next thing to say.... the simplification for me was really around trusting myself. And letting go of being perfect.

Awareness of the Coaching Client

The advanced beginner coaches also showed awareness of their coaching clients. Coaches talked about clients coming into their own awareness and the satisfaction of being a part of the process. Coaches celebrated their own success and growth during moments of successful coaching sessions:

006: You know as a coach you're always assessing... you try to see it from your client's eyes... looking at the things that she may need to help her be successful.... and I didn't want it to be some way that I perceived it to be, but I wanted the client to see it for herself.

004: I was thrilled for her, and I was thrilled for me that I took the risk and challenged her and that it moved her forward. She was able to confront something, and so was I. So, it was very powerful.

Confidence

A range of levels of confidence were expressed by the study participants. While some coaches expressed moments of confidence in the coaching session, many others expressed feelings of angst, fear and doubt, for example:

003: My heart rate was high because I wasn't sure where this was going to go. I wasn't sure what epiphany she was or was not going to have... And then after there was some sense of relief. There was that sense of yeah! She did it!.. so it was validation that I learned something. I'm on the right path.

Role of the Coach

Another theme that emerged from the advanced beginner data was the consideration of the role of the coach. Participants questioned if they were choosing the best strategy and taking the right approach for their clients. In some instances, coaches discussed not knowing what action or line of questioning would be the best choice to make. Additionally, concerns and doubts about being in the role of a coach were evident among this group of respondents, as the following quotations illustrate:

> **001:** I was thinking, where am I going to go from here? Now that we've done this, how do I get to that next level?

> **003:** I'm a nurturer so I very much wanted to help her. So the hope that I had was that the relationship would work. I hoped that what I was doing was the right thing.

> **004:** . . . my job as a coach was to help her clarify this [issue], to make an observation that she was kind of struggling with prioritizing and working that out and that it was my job to challenge her a little bit, to stretch her a little bit, her skills, her thought process, to broaden it, and that's what I was there for.

Acquisition of Coaching Skills and Abilities

Advanced beginner coaches reported acquiring their skills and abilities in an array of different ways, including: training programs; graduate schools; previous work experience; feedback from clients, peers, and teachers; practice; reading/self-study; specialized training/assessments; mentors; and innateness.

> **001:** . . . I definitely learned by practice and from instructors and classmates.

> **007:** . . . I still do a lot of reading. I try to keep up with articles.

Application of Coaching Skills and Abilities

Research participants reported that they had a broad range of coaching skills and abilities, including: self-awareness, being confident, self-trust, relationship building/trust, communication, gut/intuition, active listening, observing, being present, empathy, compassion/caring, patience, client focus/goal focus, thought partner, holding client in high regard, reading people, being client-centered, forward momentum/movement to action, telling, asking open-ended questions, challenging, using exercises, and being analytical. As two of the subjects noted:

002: ...trusting my intuition helped...being fully present and active listening...the ability to build some rapport with him.

006: ...my ability to read people and part of that is through coaching, through experience, through life experience....

Expert Coaches

The same six themes emerged from the analysis of the expert coaches: self-awareness, awareness of the coaching client, confidence, role of the coach, acquisition of coaching skills and abilities, and application of coaching skills and abilities. While the themes from both the advanced beginner coaches and the expert coaches are the same, the behaviors and skills presented differently from one group to the other as we will describe in more detail later in the chapter. This group of expert coaches spoke of relying on past experience and what had worked well before in order to inform their current decisions—more specifically, the decisions they were discussing in the interview. The expert coaches in the sample often had difficulty isolating specific thoughts and feelings regarding the specific coaching event.

Self-Awareness

One theme that emerged from the expert coach data was self-awareness. Experts seemed focused on clients without becoming enmeshed in the clients' issues or emotions. As illustrated by the following quotes, expert coaches used their self-awareness to leverage opportunities of insight for their clients:

022: I'm usually pretty relaxed. But, I do remember almost taking on that tension. And I think that's probably where I remember thinking to myself, "Okay this has to stop; this has to break here because ... I'm not going to take this on for him."

025: It was a combination of, you know, a little apprehension, a little anxiety. You haven't led me astray before but the stakes are really high. I was aware that I was asking him to consider new approaches and the high stakes environment. But I also was aware of pulling not pushing.

Awareness of the Coaching Client

Another theme that was apparent among expert coaches was awareness of the client. Study participants talked about knowing the needs of their clients and being delighted by client successes. Being aware of one's client also seemed to allow for moments of confrontation or challenge in some circumstances. Coaches discussed recognizing patterns and strategies they employed in the coaching engagement.

023: I felt pretty confident that it was an okay strategy to take. I know this client. I know this client has a strong and assertive personality. I really wasn't terribly worried about her, or about my being too directive. There were times when I would ask a question or suggest something that we put a spotlight on something and [she could] say, "nah, I don't want to go there." Oh okay, that's fine.

023: I pay attention to patterns, and particularly patterns of sidestepping, in coaching clients, and if sidestepping seems to be apparent around a particular issue, and that issue is perhaps the lynchpin or avoiding that issue is perhaps standing in the way of resolving the issue the client says they want to resolve, then I tend to bring it up. I've had a couple of clients that I found that to not be particularly fruitful with, and I realize that maybe I have gauged, I've misjudged their readiness to address that particular point. Or addressing that particular point really opens up some deeply rooted can of worms that they're not able to address at this time.

Confidence

Confidence emerged as another theme in the data. Though apprehension was still described by some of the expert coaches, it did not seem to be a barrier for effective engagement with the coaching client. Research participants discussed using a wide repertoire of tools/experience and taking risks with their clients. A developed sense of self-trust and extensive knowledge base was evident among the expert coaches:

023: And it felt like a bit of a risk because clearly we were going to get into some very personal territory and she had set out very clear boundaries. I also thought, well, if she's going to work up a head of steam she might direct it at me. But, oh well, I've had people be mad at me before, you know. And I felt very strongly that unless I put it on the table to name that elephant in the room, we would tiptoe around it forever, and it would always be there, but just an obstacle that we would try to ignore.

024: I think it was just an acknowledgment in myself that I needed to intervene. It was time. And sometimes you have perfect timing and sometimes you don't.

Role of the Coach

Expert coaches described strategies and approaches that they used with their clients. Additionally, being present and holding the client's agenda surfaced as key elements in the role of the expert coach.

025: I knew the outcome that he wanted. He wanted this merger to be successful blending the two organizations. I understood as the coach and consultant what that would take.

022: I set it up with my clients that if there is ever anything that they don't feel comfortable with they can always say I don't feel comfortable with it. Or if they feel like the question or something that I ask them to do isn't appropriate that they would say that as well. And so I trust that they will and they trust me. And it's okay with me if they would say, "well that's the stupidest thing I ever heard of."

Acquisition of Coaching Skills and Abilities

Expert coaches reported acquiring their skills and abilities in the following ways: training programs; graduate schools; previous work/life experience; feedback from clients, peers and colleagues; practice; reading/self-study/research; specialized ongoing training; innateness; experimenting; being coached; reflecting; teaching others; and conferences.

021: I'm a professional certified coach and therefore I really have to renew my coaching credentials this fall, So, I went back and had to get some continuing education. The other part is after a coaching session, doing some reflection about what seemed to work and what didn't work in terms of my interactions.

023: I teach coaches. I train coaches...I offer graduate education, and I do mentoring and supervision, and I think every coach is a distinctive alchemical blend of formal training, certainly in both coaching and a variety of other fields...It's embedded, you know. It's in the bones. It's part of the cellular structure. And some of it is personality type. Some of it is my own life experiences and years of experience of trial and error with clients. I mean, I've learned a lot of what not to do as a coach.

Application of Coaching Skills and Abilities

The subjects in the expert category said they had the following coaching skills and abilities: self-awareness, being confident, being free, establishing rapport/relationship/trust with client, setting clear boundaries, using intuition/instinct, listening, observing, being present, being empathetic, getting clarity with client about focus/agenda, partnership, accepting not having the right answers, being objective/not judging, paying attention to what the client is feeling, paying attention to what the client is choosing to act on, seeing past the words/hearing past what is said, and, knowing the client. In addition, they noted recognizing patterns of behavior; validating clients; assessing clients and making decisions/actions; affirming growth and progress; being curious, open to what may come next; asking tough questions/confronting; asking clients to take risks; being willing to push and hold back; understanding of theory/systems/knowledge base; using past experiences, using metaphors, accessing others' expertise and resources, and using judgment and business acumen. As two of the subjects noted:

021: Well, it's the very thing that the client's experiencing, which is being present in the moment, paying attention to any kind of internal messages, their thoughts and feelings, recognizing them, what they are, choosing to act on them, and then phrasing it a way that the client can hear it. So the very thing that he experienced was the very thing that I was experiencing in terms of intervening in the moment. It's based on kind of a cognitive and intuitive perspective that this is an interesting piece of data... help him understand, there's a context to this experience. There's a deeper meaning to it in terms of evidence of his own growth and development. So what I experienced was a real mirror of what he experienced, and in that regard maybe it's modeling behavior for him.

023: Well, I think I can establish a strong trusting relationship and I can only do that kind of thing if there's a real trust and sense of safety, if the client feels safe. I have certain cognitive skills. You know, I'm very good at picking up patterns, particularly patterns and language and noticing both the implicit as well as the explicit. I'm good at putting pieces together and holding the macro picture as well as the micro. I think I can present challenging statements in a way that does not sound aggressive.

Comparison of Advanced Beginner and Expert Coaches

Table 9.3 captures the descriptive terminology for both groups of coaches in each of the six theme categories. Both advanced beginner coaches and expert coaches expressed high levels of self-awareness. An important distinction to note is the degree to which the expert coaches were able to use their own self-awareness in the moment of coaching to benefit the coaching experience for their client. In some cases, when the advanced beginner coaches experienced areas of new areas of growth during a coaching session, they would turn their energies toward processing their own awareness instead of

TABLE 9.3 Theme Comparison Between Advanced Beginner and Expert Coaches

Advanced Beginner	Categories	Expert
Self-focused	Self-awareness	Self-aware
Client-aware	Awareness of the Coaching Client	Client-focused
Hopeful	Confidence	Free
Explored	Role of the Coach	Known
Learning/Weaving	Acquisition of Coaching Skills and Abilities	Experimenting/Reflecting
Compassionate Thought Partner	Application of Coaching Skills and Abilities	Reflective Sage

holding the client's agenda. This distinction can be characterized in that the advanced beginner is *self-focused* and the expert is *self-aware*.

Awareness of the coaching client is foremost for both groups of coaches. Expert coaches presented a more client-centered re-telling of the coaching event and were able to articulate the client's needs and goals in a more succinct fashion. While advanced beginner coaches were conscious of holding the client agenda, as suggested above they were much more concerned about their personal performance and their own need to help than was the expert coach. One way to capture this distinction in the coach-client relationship is that advanced beginners tend be *client-aware* while experts are *client-focused*.

While both the advanced beginner coaches and expert coaches told of their fears and doubts, as well as their confidences and validations, distinctions can be seen. Advanced beginner coaches discussed their growing confidence in their own abilities and delight when their clients responded to their coaching approach. Advanced beginners did display more doubts and fears than did their expert coach counterparts. Doubts and fears were expressed from the group of expert coaches as well, though a sense of knowledge-based confidence was pervasive in their descriptions of coaching events. Advanced beginner coaches were *hopeful* of the confidence they were gaining, and the expert coaches acted *freely* with great confidence.

Advanced beginner coaches described choosing a particular coaching approach or technique, but they were not always cognizant of why they chose one approach over another. They relied on instinct, much like the expert coaches; however, they were uncomfortable with the ambiguity of what would happen next. Experts had a firm understanding of their role and used their resources, as well as being content with simply being present and holding the client's agenda. The role of the coach is still being *explored* by the advanced beginner and is *known* by the expert.

Inquiry prompted research participants to describe their coaching skills and abilities in their own words. The advanced beginner coaches and expert coaches self-identified similar skill sets, though the choice of descriptive language differs. Comparing the two lists of skills, the advanced beginner coach is seen as a *compassionate thought partner* and the expert coach as a *reflective sage*.

When research participants were asked about how they acquired their skills and abilities, both groups of respondents gave similar answers. One slight variation for advance beginner coaches is in the reference to mentors or mentor coaches. Expert coaches noted five areas that were unique to their group: experimenting, reflecting, being coached, teaching coaching, and attending conferences. One way of looking at the data is considering the advanced beginner *learning and weaving* the knowledge and experience together, and the expert is evolving by *experimenting and reflecting* on knowledge and experience gained to date.

In conclusion, the comparative findings between the advanced beginner coaches and the expert coaches show some similarities and some distinctive differences related to the six themes (self-awareness, awareness of the coaching client, confidence, role of the coach, acquisition of coaching skills and abilities, and application of coaching skills and abilities). Further examination of the findings, in combination with the literature, will be used to explore our main research question—what, if any, distinguishable characteristic differences exist between advanced beginners' and experts' descriptions of similar executive coaching experiences.

IMPLICATIONS

As supported by the research findings, there is a distinction between the advanced beginners' and experts' descriptions of similar executive coaching experiences. This section explores these differences within the context of the research on and practice of coaching.

The Dreyfus Model Applied to Coaching

As noted earlier, the Dreyfus model of adult skill acquisition (Dreyfus, 2004; Dreyfus & Dreyfus, 1980) can be applied to executive coaching. The developmental model describes the stages through which an individual must progress to achieve mastery of a particular skill—advancing from abstract principles needed in a novice stage to a more intuitive, less self-conscious state in an expert stage. As Benner (1984/2001, 2010) discovered among clinical nurses, the Dreyfus model describes situated practice capacities rather than trait or talents of the practitioners.

We conclude that the Dreyfus model is a useful framework for describing the knowledge and skills needed at the various stages of executive coaching as supported by the findings. As described in the Dreyfus model, the advanced beginner is dealing with context, beginning to understand the situation, gradually using more sophisticated rules, and making decisions with an analytical mind, considering the actions available (Benner, 2001; Dreyfus, 2004; Dreyfus & Dreyfus, 1980; Hunt & Weintraub, 2007). Our findings show advanced beginner coaches worked with several clients and client issues and applied a coaching conversation model with little or no assistance—yet they were frequently aware of its presence. They also applied basic coaching skills of listening and asking questions with ease and began to use different approaches, applied additional coaching skills (e.g., reframing, metaphors), and were cautious about taking risks.

Our findings show expert coaches operated in a fluid manner, generally knew what to do and how to do it, were naturally creative, took risks, did not view problems or challenges as obstacles, and applied knowledge and skills to situations in different ways as appropriate.

The Dreyfus model as a framework for describing the knowledge and skills needed at the various stages of executive coaching is helpful to understanding foundational differences between the advanced beginner coach and the expert coach. These differences highlight the practice of coaching skills and the insights gained from reflecting on coaching experience over time.

Self-Awareness and Client-Centered Focus Increase with Skill Level

The level of self-awareness increases for the coach as skill level increases from the advanced beginner to the expert. As the skill level of the coach increases from advanced beginner to expert, the focus of the coaching engagement shifts from a shared focus (on coach *and* client) to a client-centered focus. Therefore, the advanced beginner is self-focused and client-aware and the expert is self-aware and client-focused. The literature discusses coaching skills that are generally accepted as necessary for the skilled practitioner, which include the ability to foster self-awareness/reflection (de Haan, 2008a, 2008b; Dotlich & Cairo, 1999; Hurd, 2003; Zeus & Skiffington, 2001) and the ability to build trusting relationships (de Haan, 2008a, 2008b; Kampa-Kokesch & Anderson, 2001; O'Neill, 2007; Zeus & Skiffington, 2001). De Haan, Bertie, Day, and Sills published research in 2010 proposing a new client-centered model of executive coaching based on the client's perspective.

The findings of this research show that both advanced beginner coaches and expert coaches expressed high levels of self-awareness in the identified coaching session, as well as an awareness of the client. The expert coaches used their self-awareness to benefit the coaching experience for the client, even though they appeared at times to lack the consciousness of doing so. Expert coaches were able to remain focused on the client in the engagement, without consciously processing their own awareness in the session. The advanced beginner coaches were having moments of self-awareness, were conscious of their self-awareness, and analyzed how to use it within the coaching session.

Coaching Presence: Confidence and Coaching Role Clearer as Skill Level Increases

The level of confidence that a coach embodies and the understanding of the role of coach increases with skill level. Being able to act with courage on one's intuition is a necessary skill for coaching that surfaced in the literature (de Haan, 2008b; Hargrove, 1995). As discussed earlier, Hargrove identifies the coach as being who one *is*, as opposed to an approach or model that one must follow step by step. Such "being" requires the coach to have developed character and certain abilities that are possible with practice and reflection over time. The awareness of self, confidence, and focus allow a coaching engagement to be what it needs to be for the client. Masterful coaching, as Hargrove defines it, becomes a transformational experience for a client, with the coach holding the space and a presence that allows the transformation to manifest as an effortless next step of evolution.

Both the advanced beginners and experts described having doubts and fears, though as one would expect, the lack of confidence was more pervasive in the group of advanced beginners. Often struggling with the role of coach, the advanced beginners explored their role, showing a desire to help their clients to the fullest extent of their skills. Expert coaches understood their role as coach and discussed having a partnership with their clients. Some participants described the display of confidence as "freedom."

The level of confidence that a coach embodies and the understanding of the role of coach is helpful to understanding foundational differences between the advanced beginner coach and the expert coach.

Expert Coaches Seek Knowledge and Experience in Distinct Ways

Expert coaches seek knowledge and experience in distinct ways. The advanced beginner is still learning and weaving together the knowledge of coaching with experience. The expert continues to evolve by experimenting and reflecting on the coaching knowledge and experience.

Taylor's (2007) addition to Howell's (1982) conscious competence model captures the essence of the expert in mature practice in what he names as a fifth stage: "reflective competency." As Taylor describes it, this being conscious of unconscious incompetence allows the learner to cycle back through the learning stages. Johns (2009) describes a reflective practitioner as "someone who lives reflection as a way of being" (p. 3) One might conclude that this is the optimum posture for a maturing coach. It is through reflection that practitioners hone their intuitive skills, which is tied to self-awareness, which is tied to confidence and the liberation that comes with the Hargrove's (1995) sense of "being" a coach.

Similar Coaching Skills Present Differently

Similar coaching skills present differently when comparing the advanced beginner coach to the expert coach. Another way to consider this result is that the same skills, when used by coaches at different developmental levels, manifest characteristically different behavior from clients, which then result in different outcomes. The literature review related to coaching skills and competencies uncovered a variety of commonly held ideas about what makes a skilled coach (Crane, 1998; de Haan, 2008a, 2008b; Dotlich & Cairo, 1999; Fitzgerald & Berger, 2002; Freas, 2000; Hargrove, 1995; Hurd, 2003; Kampa-Kokesch & Anderson, 2001; O'Neill, 2007; Zeus & Skiffington, 2001). Practical and scholarly literature does not identify a universal set of credentials.

When research participants were asked to identify skills and abilities they use, advanced beginner and expert coaches self-identified similar skill sets, though the choice of descriptive language differs. So, as the literature supports, a variety of skills were identified by the coaches. The advanced beginner and expert subjects in the study identified more than 50 skills, which were be sorted into over 15 groups of like meanings. These groups of skills are ones that a coach practitioner, outside of this research participant base, could review and recognize as descriptive of any level of coach practitioner.

We conclude that while skill sets of various developmental levels of coaches are likely the same, there is a distinct difference in the way those skills are manifested in order to bring about positive client comportment and outcomes. In sum, the practice of coaching skills and the insights gained from reflecting on coaching experience over time are key elements in creating those differences between the advanced beginner and the expert coach.

The Practice ... Over Time

If one measure of coaching skills is the number of hours a coach has logged, then we could compare the number of coaching hours to understand an additional element of the differences between the advanced beginner coach and the expert coach. Additionally, if one measure of the insights gained from reflecting on coaching experience over time is the length of time available for reflection, then we could compare the number of years of experience coaching to understand an additional element of the differences between the advanced beginner coach and the expert coach.

Of the seven advanced beginner coaches, only one coach had an Accredited Certified Coach (ACC) certification with ICF, which requires a coach to have a minimum of 100 hours of coaching experience; the other six coaches do not hold a certification with ICF (ICF, n.d.). All seven have three years coaching experience or less. Of the six expert coaches, one coach has a Professional Certified Coach (PCC) certification with ICF, indicating a minimum of 750 hours of coaching experience, and five have a Master Certified Coach (MCC) certification with ICF indicating a minimum of 2,500 hours of coaching experience (ICF, n.d.). All six coaches have been coaching for a minimum of nine years. In summary, of the 26 executive coaches interviewed, the seven participants who were categorized as advanced beginners have fewer than three years of coaching experience and a median of 125 hours logged, whereas the six participants who were categorized as experts have more than nine years of coaching experience and no fewer than 750 hours logged.

In conclusion, there is a distinction between the advanced beginners' and experts' descriptions of similar executive coaching experiences. Acquiring the skills to achieve progress through the levels of development as a coach is dependent on the learner in combination with factors of knowledge and skill building, experiential learning, and reflective practice over time.

LIMITATIONS

The research provides a few steps on the journey toward mastery as it relates to distinguishable differences between advanced beginner and expert coaches. As with any study, it has its limitations. First, research participants were all residents of and coached in the United States. Global representation was not the focus of the research pool of participants. Second, of the 26 research participants, no one matched the characteristics of the novice category. In part, the absence of novice coaches could be explained by the accessibility of participants in the recruitment process. The least experienced coaches had completed at least one year of a graduate school coaching certificate. Third, some research participants knew one or both of the researchers personally. The relationship could have influenced the perception of the researchers as they interviewed the participants. The relationship could have influenced the self-representation of the research participant to the researcher. Finally, the coaches' stages of development were assessed on one self-reported critical coaching moment. The description of the coaching engagement may or may not have been fully representative of an individual coach, and it may not have been significant to the client. Some of these limitations provide opportunities for future research.

FUTURE RESEARCH

An exciting part of concluding a portion of research is that it generates further questions and topics for study. Several areas of future research surfaced during this project. First, what, if any, distinguishable characteristic differences are there between the other stages of development in coaches? Is there a distinction between the competent coach and the proficient coach in the coaching field as there was in the nursing field in the Benner studies? Second, there is an opportunity to recruit novice coaches to participate in a repeated study that expands the participant pool. Third, a study could be designed to compare coaches and clients, with the caveat of sharing a focus on a mutually agreed upon client shift. Fourth, what skills, knowledge, experience, and best practices are identified that help coaches progress from one level of development to the next, and what assessments and development plans could be designed for coaches at various stages of maturation? Finally, an investigative study could be designed to conduct a comparison of the professional coaching organizations' (WABC, ICF, EMCC, etc.) competency models with the list of skills/abilities these coaches used. The journey toward mastery in coaching is rich with possibilities for exploration.

CONCLUSION

The journey onward will continue through the journey inward. As individuals, we develop as coaches by honing our skills, testing our competencies, increasing our capabilities, putting theories into practice, and reflecting on our experiences. As a body of practitioners, we evolve through increasing the body of empirical research on ourselves collectively, as a group of related professionals (Orlinsky & Ronnestad, 2005). The intent of the current study is to contribute to the body of research supporting the development of coaches and the collective field of practitioners.

In order to know where we are going on this journey, we must first locate where we are, individually and collectively. When we understand that coaching competencies are used by practitioners according to their present level of capability (Laske, 2006), we must ask the questions about what makes our capabilities distinct from one another. By finding theoretical frameworks like the Dreyfus model, we are able to begin seeing how we are similar and different from one another in our quests to become experts. We can conclude from current research that the practice of coaching skills and the insights gained from reflecting on coaching experience over time are fundamental for progression from advanced beginner level to expert level. We predict that these same findings may be essential to coaches' maturation at all levels of development. We must, as Johns (2009) describes, be "someone who lives reflection as a way of being" (p. 3), open to each moment, at each level of development, on the journey toward mastery.

REFERENCES

Auerbach, J. E. (2005, November). *Inviting a dialogue about core coaching competencies.* Paper presented at the Coaching Research Symposium, San Jose, CA.

Benner, P. (1983, April). Uncovering the knowledge embedded in clinical practice. *The Journal of Nursing Scholarship, 15*(2), 36–41.

Benner, P. (2001). *From novice to expert: Excellence and power in clinical nursing practice* (Commemorative ed.). Upper Saddle River, NJ: Prentice Hall. (Original work published 1984)

Benner, P. (2004). Using the Dreyfus model of skill acquisition to describe and interpret skill acquisition and clinical judgment in nursing practice and education. *Bulletin of Science, Technology & Society, 24*(3), 188–199.

Benner, P. (2010). Experiential learning, skill acquisition and gaining clinical expertise. In K. Osborn, A. Watson & C. Wraa (Eds.), *Preparation for practice* (pp. 32–44). Upper Saddle River, NJ: Pearson Education.

Benner, P., & Leonard, V. W. (2005). Patient concerns and choices and clinical judgment in EBP. In B. Melnyk & E. Fineout-Overholt (Eds.), *Evidence-based practice in nursing and healthcare: A guide to best practices* (pp. 163–182). Philadelphia, PA: Lippincott.

Bennett, J. L. (2006). An agenda for coaching-related research: A challenge for researchers. *Consulting Psychology Journal: Practice and Research, 58*(4), 240–249.

Berliner, D. C. (2004). Describing the behavior and documenting the accomplishments of expert teachers. *Bulletin of Science, Technology & Society, 24*(3), 200–212.

Bloom, B. S., Engelhart, M. D., Furst, E. J., Hill, W. H., & Krathwohl, D. R. (1956). *Taxonomy of educational objectives: The classification of educational goals. Handbook 1: Cognitive domain.* New York, NY: David McKay.

Bogdan, R. C., & Biklen, S. (1992). *Qualitative research for education: An introduction to theory and methods.* Boston, MA: Allyn & Bacon.

Brotman, L. E., Liberi, W. P., & Wasylyshyn, K. M. (2000). Executive coaching: The need for standards of competence. *Consulting Psychology Journal: Practice and Research, 52,* 201–205.

Bush, M. W. (2004). *Client perceptions of effectiveness in executive coaching.* Unpublished doctoral dissertation, Pepperdine University, Los Angeles, CA.

Crane, T. G. (1998). *The heart of coaching: Using transformational coaching to create a high-performance culture.* San Diego, CA: FTA Press.

Creswell, J. W. (2007). *Qualitative inquiry & research design: Choosing among five approaches.* Thousand Oaks, CA: Sage.

de Haan, E. (2008a). I doubt therefore I coach. *Consulting Psychology Journal: Practice and Research, 60*(1), 91–105.

de Haan, E. (2008b). I struggle and emerge. *Consulting Psychology Journal: Practice and Research, 60*(1): 106–131.

de Haan, E., Bertie, C., Day, A., & Sills, C. (2010). Clients' critical moments of coaching: Toward a "client model" of executive coaching. *Academy of Management Learning & Education, 9*(4), 607–621.

Denzin, N. K., & Lincoln, Y. S. (2003). *Strategies of qualitative inquiry.* Thousand Oaks, CA: Sage.

Dotlich, D. L., & Cairo, P. C. (1999). *Action coaching: How to leverage individual performance for company success.* San Francisco, CA: Jossey-Bass.

Dreyfus, H. (2004). What could be more intelligible than everyday intelligibility? Reinterpreting division I of being and time in light of division II. *Bulletin of Science, Technology & Society, 24*(3), 265–274.

Dreyfus, H., & Dreyfus, S. (1980). *The five-stage model of the mental activities involved in directed skill acquisition.* Berkeley, CA: Operations Research Center, University of California.

Dreyfus, H. L., & Dreyfus, S. E. (1986). *Mind over machine: The power of human intuition and expertise in the era of the computer.* New York, NY: Free Press.

Dreyfus, H., & Dreyfus, S. (2004). The ethical implications of the five-stage skill-acquisition model. *Bulletin of Science, Technology & Society, 24*(3), 251–264.

Dreyfus, S. (2004a). The five-stage model of adult skill acquisition. *Bulletin of Science, Technology & Society, 24*(3), 177–181.

Dreyfus, S. (2004b). Totally model-free learned skillful coping. *Bulletin of Science, Technology & Society, 24*(3), 182–187.

Duesund, L., & Jespersen, E. (2004). Skill acquisition in ski instruction and the skill model's application to treating anorexia nervosa. *Bulletin of Science, Technology & Society, 24*(3), 225–233.

Ericsson, K. A., Krampe, R. T., & Tesch-Römer, C. (1993). The role of deliberate practice in the acquisition of expert performance. *Psychological Review, 100*(3), 363–406.

Fitzgerald, C., & Berger, J. G. (Eds.). (2002). *Executive coaching: Practices & perspectives.* Palo Alto, CA: Davies-Black Publishing.

Freas, A. M. (2000). Coaching executives for business results. In M. Goldsmith, L. Lyons, & A. Freas (Eds.), *Coaching for leadership: How the world's greatest coaches help leaders learn* (pp. 27–41). San Francisco, CA: Jossey-Bass.

Gladwell, M. (2008). *Outliers: The story of success.* Boston, MA: Little, Brown and Company.

Graduate School Alliance for Executive Coaching. (n.d.). Retrieved on April 3, 2011, from http://www.gsaec.org/

Grant, A. M. (2003, November). *Keeping up with the cheese! Research as a foundation for professional coaching of the future.* Paper presented at the Coaching Research Symposium, Denver, CO.

Guthrie, V. A., & Alexander, J. (2000). Process advising: An approach to coaching for development. In M. Goldsmith, L. Lyons, & A. Freas (Eds.), *Coaching for leadership: How the world's greatest coaches help leaders learn* (pp. 299–306). San Francisco, CA: Jossey-Bass.

Hamlin, R. G., Ellinger, A. D., & Beattie, R. S. (2009, February). Toward a profession of coaching? A definitional examination of "coaching," "organization development," and "human resource development." *International Journal of Evidence Based Coaching and Mentoring, 7*(1), 13–38.

Hargrove, R. (1995). *Masterful coaching: Extraordinary results by impacting people and the way they think and work together.* San Francisco, CA: Pfeiffer.

Henry, G. T. (1990). *Practical sampling.* Newbury Park, CA: Sage.

Howell, W. C. (1982). *Information processing and decision making.* Mahwah, NJ: Lawrence Erlbaum Associates.

Hunt, J. G., & Weintraub, J. R. (2007). *The coaching organization: A strategy for developing leaders.* Thousand Oaks, CA: Sage.

Hurd, J. L. (2003, November). *Learning for life: An investigation into the effect of organizational coaching on individual lives.* Paper presented at the Coaching Research Symposium, Denver, CO.

International Coach Federation. (n.d.). Retrieved on March 10, 2011, from http://www.coachfederation.org/

Johns, C. (2009). *Becoming a reflective practitioner,* 3rd ed. West Sussex: John Wiley & Sons.

Kampa-Kokesch, S., & Anderson, M. Z. (2001). Executive coaching: A comprehensive review of the literature. *Consulting Psychology Journal: Practice and Research, 53,* 205–226.

Kilburg, R. R. (1996). Toward a conceptual understanding and definition of executive coaching. *Consulting Psychology Journal: Practice and Research, 48,* 134–144.

Kilburg, R. R. (2000). Executive coaching: Developing managerial wisdom in a world of chaos.

Kirk, J., & M. L. Miller (1986). *Reliability and validity in qualitative research.* Beverly Hills, CA: Sage.

Krathwohl, D. R. (2002). A revision of Bloom's taxonomy: An overview. *Theory Into Practice, 41*(4), 212–218.

Lane, D. A., Stelter, R., & Rostron, S. S. (2010). The future of coaching as a profession. In E. Cox, T. Bachkirova & D. Clutterbuck (Eds.), *The complete handbook of coaching* (pp. 357–368). Thousand Oaks, CA: Sage.

Laske, O. (2004). Can evidence based coaching increase ROI? *International Journal of Evidence Based Coaching and Mentoring, 2*(2), 41–53.

Laske, O. E. (2006). From coach training to coach education. Teaching coaching within a comprehensively evidence based framework. *International Journal of Evidence Based Coaching and Mentoring, 4*(1), 45–57.

Laske, O., Stober, D., & Edwards, J. (2003). *What is, and why should we care about evidence based coaching?* International Coach Federation Research and Development Committee. [Whitepaper].

Marshall, C., & G. B. Rossman (2011). *Designing qualitative research.* Thousand Oaks, CA: Sage.

McCracken, G. (1988). *The long interview.* Thousand Oaks, CA: Sage.

Miles, M. B., & Huberman, A. M. (1994). *Qualitative data analysis: An expanded sourcebook.* Thousand Oaks, CA, Sage.

Moe, V. (2004). How to understand skill acquisition in sport. *Bulletin of Science, Technology & Society, 24*(3), 213–224.

Neuendorf, K. A. (2002). *The content analysis guidebook.* Thousand Oaks, CA: Sage Publications.

O'Neill, M. B. (2007). *Executive coaching with backbone and heart: A systems approach to engaging leaders with their challenges* (2nd ed.). San Francisco, CA: Jossey-Bass.

Orlinsky, D. E., & Ronnestad, M. H. (2005). *How psychotherapists develop: A study of therapeutic work and professional growth.* Washington, DC: American Psychological Association.

Pink, D. H. (2009). *Drive: The surprising truth about what motivates us.* New York, NY: Riverhead Books.

Sherpa Coaching. (2011). *Sherpa executive coaching survey 2011.* Retrieved from http://www.sherpacoaching.com/surveyfp.html

Silverman, D. (2006). *Interpreting qualitative data.* Thousand Oaks, CA: Sage.

Taylor, W. (2007). Conscious competence learning model discussion [Online forum content]. Retrieved from http://www.businessballs.com/consciouscompetencelearningmodel.htm

Vanderburg, W. (2004). The human skill-acquisition model of Stuart Dreyfus: Stemming the tide of confusing our humanity with machines. *Bulletin of Science, Technology & Society, 24*(3), 175–176.

Weiss, R. S. (1994). *Learning from strangers: The art and method of qualitative interview studies.* New York, NY: The Free Press.

Whitworth, L., Kimsey-House, K., Kimsey-House, H., & Sandahl, P. (2007). *Co-Active coaching: New skills for coaching people toward success in work and life* (2nd ed.). Mountain View, CA: Davies-Black.

Wolcott, H. F. (1994). *Transforming qualitative data: Description, analysis, and interpretation.* Thousand Oaks, CA: Sage.

Worldwide Association of Business Coaches. (n.d.). Retrieved on March 10, 2011, from http://www.wabccoaches.com/

Zeus, P., & Skiffington, S. (2001). *The complete guide to coaching at work.* Sydney, Australia: McGraw-Hill.

CHAPTER 10

CONSULTANT SELF-REFLECTING CAPABILITIES AND CLIENT EVALUATION

Elsbeth Reitsma

Reflection is viewed as an important activity that helps a professional learn and professionalize (Van den Berge, 2005). Drawing on the Dutch association of consultancy Ooa and several consultancy education programs, Kessener (2003) argues that "reflection is an obligation for consultants" (p. 28). It is especially important for quality of service—in short, reflection helps you to become a better consultant. Based on this argument, my underlying premise is that clients prefer consultants with a high level of self-reflecting capabilities, especially in contrast to those consultants with a low level of such ability.

A goal of the present research was to learn more about how consultants reflect. We asked eighteen consultants about their experiences with reflection during their assignments, focusing on the moments they reflect and their appreciation of their reflective activities. The three central research questions were:

1. Are there differences in the reflecting capabilities across consultants?
2. How and when do consultants reflect?

Exploring the Professional Identity of Management Consultants, pages 203–212
Copyright © 2013 by Information Age Publishing
All rights of reproduction in any form reserved.

3. Are consultants with high self-monitor ratings (i.e., high capability of reflection-in-action) more appreciated by their clients than consultants with low self-monitor ratings?

This chapter describes the conceptual framework utilized in the research and the study's methodology and results, concluding with reflections on the ramifications for consultants and their clients.

CONCEPTUAL FRAMEWORK

Reflection is found to be essential for learning by professionals (Argyris, 2000; Kessener, 2003; Kolb, 1984; Schön, 1990; Van den Berge, 2005). It concerns the consultant's thoughts on a complex case and the consultants own actions in working on the assignment. And it is more than just thinking. It is discovering new valuable perspectives on the case as well, enabling the consultant to delve into content, theory, methodology, self-reflection, and the underlying normative perspective (see Kessener, 2003). As an example, a theoretical model might be helpful to distinguish main and side issues, or methodical reflection could focus on the choices of roles, positions, methods, and interventions. It is also possible to examine one's own feelings about patterns and one's own beliefs. Reflection can also be used to compare our own actions with the professional values and standards of the field, such as the Ooa's (Orde van Organisatiekundigen, 2010) Body of Knowledge and Skills.

In this study, the focus is on self-reflection as one of the important possibilities of reflection. Van den Berge (2005) defines reflection as "a self-assessment of the way in which a person shall respond to a situation" (p. 24). This ability includes exploring positive or negative emotions as well as exploring underlying assumptions or beliefs that influence responding. Another characteristic of reflection is that it is often context-specific, as the context also determines the options for solution.

The timing of reflection is also a distinguishing characteristic (Van den Berge, 2005; Kessener, 2003; Schön, 1990). *Anticipatory reflection,* for example, occurs prior to a situation, dealing with an idea about a possible situation and someone's own characteristic response (e.g., an if…then scenario). *Reflection in action* (sometimes referred to as active reflection or self-monitoring, occurs during the situation, where the consultant starts an action and at the same time has a certain detachment in his or her own response to the situation. The consultant examines and reconsiders his or her own action. *Retrospective reflection* (or reflection on action) is the most common form of reflection, looking back on what has happened. Finally, *reflection on reflection in action* is when the consultant also reflects on the reflection process itself. This capability, according to Schön (1990, pp. 12-17) serves two functions: enabling the individual to examine the (1) quality of the ongoing learning process, involving routines and non-functional patterns, and (2) accessibility of the learning process for others, specifically in training situations.

Thus far the discussion has focused on self-reflection in the context of learning and professionalization. There is also a social psychological perspective on reflection that provides additional insights. The main question concerns the extent to which an individual possesses a reflective ability by nature, drawing out the underlying motives and intent. The social psychological perspective places reflection explicitly in relation to the social environment, thus to others. Snyder (1979, 1987) introduces the concept of "self-monitoring," a social psychological construct that concerns the extent to which people differ in the way they can and do observe and control their expressive behavior and self-presentation. Individuals who score high on self-monitoring are thought to regulate their expressive self-presentation for the sake of desired public appearances, and are thus highly responsive to social and interpersonal cues of situation-appropriate performances. Individuals low in self-monitoring, in contrast, are thought to lack either the ability or the motivation to regulate their expressive self-presentations. Their expressive behaviors, instead, are thought to functionally reflect their own enduring and momentary inner states, including their attitudes, traits, and feelings. One could say that they are "true to their selves" (Barrick, Parks, & Mount, 2005).

Although there is ample discussion of the concept of self-monitoring in the literature, scholars do not always agree about its role. However, there is consensus on the fact that there are individual differences in the extent of self-monitoring. Although researchers have not reached consensus about the reasons, characteristics, and motivations of high and low self-monitors, they do agree that people differ in the degree to which they monitor their own behavior and that of others and, based on that insight, change their self-presentation (Briggs & Cheek, 1988; Ickes, Holloway, Stinson, & Hoodenpyle, 2006).

Research on self-monitoring has used multi-item self-report measures to identify people as high and low on this trait. The most frequently used instruments are the 25-item, true–false, original self-monitoring scale and an 18-item refinement of this measure (Snyder, 1979; Gangestad & Snyder, 2000).

Drawing on these insights, a measure was developed to capture the extent of a consultant's reflection. *Self-monitoring* is defined as the extent to which a consultant can and will observe, adjust, and control his or her expressive behavior and self-presentation. *Reflection in action* is described as when consultants start an action and at the same time detach their own response to the situation to examine and reconsider their own action. Although reflection in action and self-monitoring come from different perspectives, their meaning is very similar. Therefore this study uses Snyder's (1979, 1987) self-monitoring test to assess the consultant's extent of self-monitoring, providing us, in essence, with a self-report on the consultant's self-reflection capabilities during interaction in general.

Focusing on the timing of the reflection, we can relate self-reflection to the interaction process between the client and the consultant, distinguishing four categories of the consultant's reflective activities:

1. self-reflection *before* the interaction between consultant and client;
2. self-reflection *during* the interaction (reflection in action or self-monitoring);
3. self-reflection *after* the interaction (reflection on action); and
4. reflection as a *process of continuous learning* about the interaction between consultant and client (reflection on reflection-in-action).

RESEARCH STRATEGY

This chapter focuses on how and when consultants reflect and how self-reflecting capabilities of the consultant affect the evaluation of a client. The issue of self-reflecting or self-monitoring is part of a larger qualitative research project on the interaction between consultants and clients, as a way to improve our knowledge of how consultants are evaluated by their clients (de Caluwé & Reitsma, 2010; Reitsma & de Caluwé, 2009). Emphasis in this chapter is placed on relevant issues in self-reflection.

Research Population and Research Setting

The study focuses on twelve management consultants who are involved in an educational program with a large Dutch management consultancy firm and six management consultants who participated in a postgraduate training program of one of the Dutch postgraduate business schools for management consultants. Both programs are very similar. The consultants participated voluntarily in the research and were informed about the purpose and method of the researchers. The consultants received the results and feedback by the researchers after the sessions. The consultants' ages were between 25 and 55; 13 of them were male, and five were female. Six consultants had between one and five years of work experience, while four respondents had between six and ten years, and eight consultants reported more than ten years of work experience. All the consultants were educated in science or social science at the polytechnic or university level.

As part of both programs, the consultants go through a standardized, simulated consulting process with clients in a fictional company. The fictional company has a management team consisting of four managers: the director (CEO), the head of production, the head of finance or the head of the personnel department, and the head of marketing. Since the managers in the simulation were senior consultants in their own daily lives, they were very familiar with their roles in the simulation—the situations were very close to their real lives.

In the simulation, the fictional company had experienced a lot of bad results in recent times and required outside help in order to survive. There were also a number of problems and difficulties in cooperation within the management team. The consulting process was in the stage of diagnosis with interviews, feedback to the client, and developing a proposal for action.

Data Collection

Some weeks before the interaction with the client, we asked the consultants to fill in Snyder's self-monitoring questionnaire. During the interaction between the client(s) and consultants, the conversations were audio- and video-taped and observed by two researchers. The texts were carefully reproduced in a transcription, as verbally articulated by the involved clients and consultants. After the interaction, clients were asked for their evaluation of the quality of the consulting process and each consultant's individual behavior. These outcomes were recorded in an interview report.

Some weeks after the client-consultant interaction, the consultant was interviewed about his or her experiences and afterthoughts. In this interview, we also explored how and when the consultant reflected, discussed Snyder's questionnaire, and recorded all outcomes in a case-report.

Data Processing

The transcripts of the interaction sessions between consultant and client, along with the interviews, were analyzed with the qualitative analysis tool ATLAS.ti. As part of the analysis process, a codebook was developed by two researchers. The codes have different origins. Some of the codes are based on theory (see the discussion on the conceptual framework), which provides the opportunity to link theoretical insights to the empirical data. Other codes were self-created in that they emerged from the data. The next step was coding the data. To ensure the reliability of the coding process, two researchers individually coded the same parts of text, comparing their choices for each part of text. The discussion led to a final choice for the use of a code for a particular portion of the text. Additionally, a third research-er overlooked the process and periodically studied the results.

We expected to see differences in the evaluation of the interactions, which were seen through the eyes of the client. In order to be able to ex-plore these differences, we developed a special way of measuring by means of a "yardstick." The position on the yardstick was marked by the client's feedback about: 1) the consulting process, in terms of the interaction be-tween the client and the consultant; and 2) the consultant's behavior, assess-ing his or her strengths and weaknesses. The yardstick had three categories:

- *Positive evaluation*: the client's perception about the consulting pro-cess and the consultant's behavior were mainly positive.
- *Moderate evaluation*: the client's perception about the consultant and the consulting process contained both positive and negative ele-ments.
- *Negative evaluation*: the client's perception was mainly negative about the consulting process and the consultant's behavior.

Examining the 18 consultants in the study using this "yardstick," seven cases were evaluated by the client as positive, five were moderate, and six were characterized as negative.

RESULTS

The research results are presented in terms of the central questions dis-cussed in the introduction to the chapter: (1) the consultants' ratings on the self-monitoring scale and their experience with reflection; (2) the mo-ments when the consultants usually reflect and the difference between high and low self-monitors; and (3) the extent to which clients prefer consul-tants with a high level of self-reflecting capabilities.

Rating of Self-Monitoring

Based on Snyder's self-monitoring test, seven respondents had a low lev-el, and 11 respondents had a high level of self-reflecting capabilities during interaction with their clients.

Examining what the consultants reported about their experiences with reflection, low self-monitors found it difficult to create a concrete picture about reflection in action. These individuals felt or were told that they were insufficient in reflecting. Although they were aware about the need for re-flection, they found it hard to put into practice. Some of these individuals said that they have asked colleagues with a high level of self-monitoring to facilitate the social interaction in the assignment. As low self-monitors noted:

> It's hard to get a picture about myself.

> I'm not so hyper-sensitive. I like to have a story in mind. Sometimes I appear as arrogant. I have learned that I can be right but I need an agreement at that point as well.

High self-monitors, in contrast, do have a concrete picture about the moments and the ways they reflect. Yet, despite this clarity, they don't always experience their reflective capacities as functional and useful. Many of these respondents felt that it was a "pitfall" to focus on one's own thoughts, as it could cause neglect of the (inter)action with the client. In fact, high monitors could be extremely negative and critical about their own actions:

> I'm in my own head and miss the conversation.

> There is also a drawback to self-monitoring. You're always thinking on several levels.

> When I'm busy it turns in puzzling my head off.

Relating these outcomes to our first research question (examining whether there were differences in the reflecting capabilities across consultants), we can conclude that in our research population there were differences across the consultants. High self-monitors reflected frequently, but it may be a drawback when refection prevents (inter)action. The low self-monitors found it hard to put reflection into practice.

When Do Consultants Reflect?

We asked our eighteen respondents when they reflect. Most consultants reflect at multiple points: ten consultants reflect before interaction, fourteen consultants during interaction, fifteen consultants after interaction, and six consultants told us that they reflect with others in the context of learning and developing. Combining these moments of reflection with the evaluation by the client, the differences between the consultants become clear (Table 10.1).

Consultants with positive evaluations from their clients tend to practice reflection in more than one of the four categories—before, during, and after the interaction, and with others (reflection on reflection in action). Most of them combine reflection during the interaction with reflection before and

TABLE 10.1 Moment of Reflection with Client Evaluation

Evaluation Moment of Reflection	Positive (N = 7)	Moderate (N = 5)	Negative (N = 6)	Total (N = 18)
Before	5	1	4	10
During	7	3	4	14
Afterwards	6	5	4	15
With others	5	-	1	6

after the interaction, and they ask for feedback of others as well. Consultants with moderate evaluations from their clients mostly reflect after the interaction, and none of them reported asking for feedback of others.

High Self-monitor—Positive Client Evaluation?

An outcome of the study indicates that all consultants evaluated positively by the client have high levels of self-reflecting capabilities. Moderately evaluated consultants have lower levels of self-reflecting capabilities. Nevertheless our assumption that clients would prefer consultants with a high level of self-reflecting capabilities was not supported, as some of the consultants with high levels of self-reflecting capabilities were evaluated negatively. These consultants, however, were able to explain what went wrong immediately after the client-consultant interaction. They mentioned their own perceived shortcomings, such as "I tend to react immediately, which is my pitfall," "I could not stick to my role," and "I asked mainly closed questions." They also pointed to the context of the interaction, for example, "It was an unusual experience for me to work with someone I hardly knew."

Interestingly, a high score for level of self-reflection was not always appreciated by the consultants. As their comments suggest, they sometimes experienced themselves as being too critical and noticed that too much self-reflection could distract attention from interacting with their client, making them less effective in the engagement—in essence they felt that they could miss an essential point in the conversation or miss the dynamics. It seems that the clients might also miss the full attention of the consultant, as the consultant might be working intensively but mainly in his or her "own head." The consultants labeled their high reflecting capability as both a strength and a weakness. They tried to handle the drawback of "being in their own head" by focusing on the here and now, for instance, by speaking out their thoughts instead of keeping them to themselves.

CONCLUSIONS AND REFLECTION

In this study we focused on consultants' self-reflecting capabilities. As a conclusion we answer in short the questions addressed in this study. First, are there differences in the reflecting capabilities between consultants? According to the outcomes of Snyder's self-monitoring test, the study points to differences between the consultants. Despite education programs for consultants that attach great importance to reflection, especially reflection-in-action and reflection on reflection-in-action, some of our consultants are less aware of this type of reflection. Among our eighteen respondents, seven consultants have a low level of self-monitoring, and eleven consultants have a high level of self-monitoring.

Second, how and when do consultants reflect? Most consultants use a variety of approaches to reflection. Reflection during and after interaction are most mentioned; reflection with others, however, is less mentioned. Consultants who were evaluated positively by their clients combined the most types of reflection; all of them reflect during interaction, and most of them reflect (learn) with others as well.

Third, are consultants with high self-monitor ratings (high capability of reflection-in-action) more appreciated by their clients than consultants with low self-monitor ratings? Based on this research, it is unclear, although we found that all consultants who were evaluated positively by the client had high levels of self-reflecting capabilities. Moderately evaluated consultants had lower levels of self-reflecting capabilities. Nevertheless our assumption that clients would prefer consultants with a high level of self-reflecting capabilities was not supported, as some consultants with high levels of self-reflecting capabilities were negatively evaluated by their clients. As noted earlier, however, in contrast to moderately evaluated consultants, these consultants were able to explain what went wrong immediately after the client-consultant interaction.

While the present study provides us with some insight into the role of self-reflection in consulting effectiveness, there are some limitations of this research and its outcomes. First, the sample is relatively small. The results of the research should also be seen as a general indication of reflection activities among consultants. Further research is necessary to do more robust assessment about these initial findings. Second, the consultant's reflection capabilities were measured by Snyder's (1979) self-monitoring test. Although such self-monitoring is considered one of the most important skills in reflecting, it is only one part of the range of reflection opportunities.

Despite these limitations, it appears that self-reflection is an important tool of the consultant to work on the quality of the client-consultant interaction. Such self-reflection is not automatically done effectively, however;

training on quality and effectiveness deserves adequate attention in the professional development of the consultant.

REFERENCES

Argyris, C. (2000). *Managementadvies, toegevoegde waarde voor uw organisatie?* [Flawed advice and the management trap: How managers can know when they're getting good advice and when they're not]. Zaltbommel: Thema.

Barrick, M., Parks, L., & Mount, M. (2005). Self-monitoring as a moderator of the relationship between personality traits and performance. *Personnel Psychology, 58*(3), 745–767.

Briggs, S. R., & Cheek, J. M. (1988). On the nature of self-monitoring: Problems with assessment, problems with validity. *Journal of Personality and Social Psychology, 54,* 663–678.

de Caluwé, L., & Reitsma. E. (2010). *Leren adviseren, het belang van echt vakmanschap.* [Learning consultancy: The importance of real craftsmanship]. Amsterdam: Mediawerf.

Gangestad, S., & Snyder, M. (2000). Self-monitoring: Appraisal and reappraisal. *Psychological Bulletin, 126*(4), 530–555.

Ickes, W., Holloway, R., Stinson, L., & Hoodenpyle, T. (2006). Self-monitoring in social interaction: The centrality of self-affect. *Journal of Personality, 74*(3), 659–684.

Kessener, B. (2003). Reflecteren, meer dan evalueren. [Reflection is more than evaluation]. *Management Consultant Magazine, 5,* 28–31.

Kolb, D. A. (1984). *Experimental learning: Experience as the source of learning and development.* Englewood Cliffs, NJ: Prentice Hall.

Orde van Organisatiekundigen. (2010). *Body of knowledge and skills* (BoKS), version 3.0. http://www.ooa.nl/de-boks (09-21-2011)

Reitsma, E., & de Caluwé, L. (2009, June). *Qualifications of management consultants: What makes management consultants effective in interaction with their clients?* Paper presented at the Management Consulting Division, Academy of Management, 5th International Conference, Vienna.

Schön, D. A. (1990). Handelend leren, zoeken naar een andere epistemologie van de professionele praktijk [Learning in action: Searching for another epistemology of professional practice]. *Filosofie in bedrijf* [Philosophy in business], *2*(1), 12–17.

Snyder, M. (1979). Self-monitoring processes. In L. Berkowitz (Ed.), *Advances in experimental social psychology* (pp. 85–128). New York, NY: Academic Press

Snyder, M. (1987). *Public appearances/private realities: The psychology of self-monitoring.* New York, NY: Freeman.

Van den Berge, A. (2005). Reflectie: wat is dat? [What is reflection?] *Leren in ontwikkeling* [Learn in development], *4,* 24–27.

CHAPTER 11

FAR AWAY, SO CLOSE?

An Attempt to Cross-Fertilize Consulting and Academic Worlds—Experiences of an OD World Summit

András Gelei, Balázs Heidrich and Gergely Németh[1]

This chapter intends to capture the emotional work and thoughts of an organizing team at the first Organizational Development World Summit (ODWS), compare the intended goals of the summit with the achievements, and analyze the divergences. The ODWS (Organizational Development World Summit—Dialogue & Action) was held in Budapest in August, 2010.

The four main goals of ODWS were:

- To co-create a new world of organizations and communities (by fostering) dialogue and action (main title);
- To encourage cross-fertilization—among different fields, schools, and approaches;
- To have a significant global and social impact; and
- To give a special focus to non-conventional organizations.

Exploring the Professional Identity of Management Consultants, pages 213–240
Copyright © 2013 by Information Age Publishing
All rights of reproduction in any form reserved.

This international event was intended to be an unprecedented world summit of numerous professions, OD-related associations, and their members—who ordinarily belong to different communities of practice and, as a result, might be keen to identify themselves with a specific tradition or approach. The theme of the conference aimed at being significant not only for those specializing in OD but to all engaged in the current and future challenges of organizations and organizing; interested in studying, building and/or changing organizations and communities; or putting the social-societal consequences of organizing into focus. The aim was to invite everybody who works with organizations and organizational change, learning, and development: from representatives of the academic world to those from organizations consulting to and developing individuals, teams, organizations, communities, and even larger systems.

A huge diversity of OD consultancy firms as well as non-profit organizations like associations and institutions focusing on social issues and on the development of human systems were represented. As a special feature, founders and leaders of "non-conventional organizations" pioneering new ways of organizing were also invited. For more information on the summit, see the conference website: http://www.odworldsummit.org.

Throughout our project work, which lasted for more than two years, the so-called "academic team," which was responsible for the academic track of the summit, faced several emotional stages ranging from enthusiasm through to total disappointment. Being rather self-reflective, an ongoing self-analysis became just as important as the organizing work itself. As the learning points after the summit were still needed to be identified for us, we continued our work with a retrospective orientation. However this chapter aims at a wider perspective than simply the self-reflection of a project team. The two main research questions we want to address in this chapter are the following:

1. Was cross-fertilization among different fields, and, especially, between the so-called practice and academia really achieved at the summit on the one hand and during the organizing process on the other? And why or why not?
2. What is the current status of "theory" and "practice" in the work and thinking of OD practice and practitioners, and why?

Initially we had relied on there being a common ground for these different yet interlinked groups (practitioners and academics), so a particular motivation for us was to attract a group of participants—mainly, but not only, academics—from around the world, whose main focus, we thought, was in line with the central theme of the summit. After all, what is cross-fertilization all about? We did not consider this project a "mission impossible" since for decades the two worlds of professionals were quite overlapping and they often built on each other's results. But our hopes for an intense cross-fertilization soon faded away: although as organizers we approached almost 50 different academic associations and contacted 21 universities worldwide (mainly those that are known for their link to organization change and development), we hardly received any feedback. Eventually the presence of OD and change scholars at the ODWS was very, very limited. This is in sharp contrast to the whole summit, with almost 400 participants from some 50 countries, and with almost 100 different professional sessions.

Reflecting on this experience in this chapter we will discuss the relationship between OD theory and OD practice, whether through ODWS theory and practice came any closer, why or why not, and what is at stake. We will also look into the possibility of starting a (renewed) dialogue between academia and consultancy practice and explore what the true obstacles to overcome are.

THEORY VERSUS PRACTICE, RIGOR VERSUS RELEVANCE

For decades now, there has been much debate on the so-called "rigor-relevance" issue in the organization and management literature. The topic has at least three components: (1) whether existing academic research has any use for practicing managers and members in actual organizations or not, (2) whether organization and management studies should have practical "relevance" or only satisfy scientific criteria ("rigor"), and (3) whether rigor and relevance could be achieved at the same time or not. On a general level, obviously, the rigor-relevance debate touches upon the relationship between theorizing about management and organizing versus doing those in practice.

There seems to be a consensus over the first question in that the specialized, theory and methodology-driven academic approach has for long diverted from providing "useful knowledge" for actual managerial practice. In their landmark article, Astley and Zammuto (1992) view organizational science and practice "... as interdependent, yet semiautonomous, domains which engage in their own specialized forms of discourse or language games" (p. 443).

Based on the second part of the question a "problematizing" and a "non-problematizing" view can be discerned. The contributors to the classic book on "Doing Research that is Useful for Theory and Practice" (Lawler, Mohrman, Mohrman, Ledford, Cummings, & Associates, 1985), like Ed Lawler, Chris Argyris, Andrew Pettigrew or Warren Bennis, consider it a fundamental problem that knowledge produced in organization and management research is not accessible to, and not usable for, the real business decision maker and therefore, will have no impact on shaping the reality of organizations and the practice of management. It seems to us that for the vast majority of publications on the rigor-relevance divergence the "problematizing view" is common sense (see also Wilkerson, 1999). But apparently not common sense for all, as Astley and Zammuto (1992) claim that organization science and managerial practice are obviously, and also ideally, different in nature as they are different "language games" (worldviews, paradigms) with their respective communities and audiences, subcultures and norms, socialization procedures and institutionalized practices, methodologies, and quality criteria. It's not only that scholars and managers approach and deal with organizational issues quite differently, but what they define as an "issue" itself is totally different in nature. While managers deal with concrete problems and try order to solve them, academics should, instead of providing direct administrative solutions or methods, elaborate generalized and abstract constructs, models, and theories out of the concreteness of organizational reality. It is not the direct instrumental help (like applied research) but the more indirect, conceptual, linguistic and symbolic insight for which organization studies can be still useful for managers: in shaping their worldview, and in providing linguistic-rhetorical constructs (as reference points and communication tools) for finding words and foundations for managerial intentions (Astley & Zammuto, 1992).

The third part of the initial question refers to whether rigor and relevance are antithetical or not. Obviously, this question is linked to the "problematizing" view. Since we are socialized both in academia and in organization development practice, in line with Lawler et al. (1985) and many others, we think that theory and practice, and thus rigor and relevance, can and should be combined. But we also agree with Astley and Zammuto (1992) that the best way to do that is not through providing direct solutions (expert consulting, see Schein, 1992), nor is pure applied research our ideal. Instead, we argue for the various modes of experiential learning and action research (Reason & Bradbury, 2001) as the prime forms of integrating theory and practice on a high level. We assert that good organization and management science should, in any of the numerous possible ways, be embedded in real life practice, and managerial practice should, in some way, be based on well-founded (theoretical) knowledge and on (self-)reflection. Without idealizing academia and knowing that far too many academics and publications deviate from these criteria, some characteristics of *quality academic work* can be identified: (1) a stance that is, to a certain extent, *uncommitted, distant, contemplative and self-reflective*; that (2) does not take "it" for granted unless it is *cautiously and consciously studied*; that (3) aims at securing and examining the *validity or truth-value* of anything that represents itself as "knowledge;" and (4) for that to happen, it builds on *sound pre-existing knowledge* and *well-founded methodology*.

In this chapter we focus on the role, role-concept, the breadth, and the depth of perspectives applied by organizational consultants, especially OD consultants. Where do they stand in the rigor-relevance dimension? Should they be "agents of relevance" close to managerial practice? Or rather, should they be "representatives of rigor" and serve as "extended arms" of organizational and management science to real life organizational change? Are they "mediators" or themselves "instruments" of knowledge? Or are they "translators of knowledge," but if so, in which direction? And how well do they perform?

CONSULTANTS AS INTERMEDIARIES: OD CONSULTANTS AS (ORIGINALLY) MUCH MORE

In the scholarly articles on the rigor-relevance issue, the role of organizational consultant is often discussed just as a side topic. Consultants are the ones who translate knowledge between academia and practice (and not in the other direction): "... [for academics] backroom analysis is needed before the message can be 'translated' for transmission to practitioners, possibly *via intermediaries such as educators and textbooks*" (Beech, MacIntosh, & MacLean, 2010, p. 1350, our emphasis). In a similar vein, Astley and Zammuto (1992) devote little attention to consultants' "intermediary" or "translator" role; instead, they discuss the role of leading business periodicals: "Concepts from the academic sphere filter into lay discourse through consultants, books and magazines, executive education, and business school curricula. Consider, for instance, leading business periodicals...." (p. 453). This shallow handling is most surprising given that many who belong to the academic community of management and organization studies do take on the consultant role from time to time, as it is well represented in their biographies.

In this chapter we try to make sense of our experiences of the OD World Summit 2010; thus our main focus is on organization development consultants and OD consultancy. This is partly explained by the fact that the vast majority of the summit participants were OD consultants, and the authors are themselves fulltime or part-time OD consultants. Our other, equally important reason is that organization development, being a unique tradition of managing organizational change, an idiosyncratic approach to facilitating change and a unique attitude to organizational consultancy, used to have (and should have) a special relationship towards the rigor-relevance issue. The idiosyncrasy of OD in relation to "rigor vs. relevance" is based on its history and has been with OD since its very conception in the U.S. and the U.K.

OD as a Field of "Praxis"

The word "praxis," having ancient Greek origins, signifies the insepa-
rable relationship between theory and practice. In true praxis, on the one
hand, all practice is reflective practice (Schön, 1983), a constant cyclic process of experiential learning (Kolb, 1984). On the other hand, praxis links
action to theory: "Praxis—creating social change while developing a use-
able theory of knowledge from our practice" (Gordon, 2001, p. 317); or as
a business school's website phrases it: "praxis is 'practice informed by theory and theory informed by direct practice'" (Praxis Business School, n.d.).

Organization development (OD) is *not only a practice* of intervention,
change and consultancy, as it is *not solely an intervention theory or methodology*.
It is both at the same time, at least originally: a *constant reflexive relationship*
between theory and practice, and thus, between rigor and relevance. According to Cummings and Worley (1993) organization development is a
field of applied behavioral science focused on understanding and managing organizational change: a field of social and managerial action and a
field of scientific inquiry—and therefore, by definition, "praxis."

In its broadest sense,

> organizational development is a long-term effort, led and supported by top
> management, to improve an organization's visioning, empowerment, learn-
> ing, and problem-solving processes, through an ongoing, collaborative man-
> agement of organizational culture—with special emphasis on the culture of
> intact work team configurations—utilizing the consultant-facilitator role and
> the theory and technology of applied behavioral science, including action
> research. (French & Bell, 1995, p. 28)

Although organization development is not a single methodology but a
collection of several approaches and methods, there is quite a consistent
change philosophy and attitude that underlie the different approaches.
(see Cummings & Worley, 1993; French & Bell, 1995; Neilsen, 1984). These
can be summarized as the following (based on Gelei, 2002): (1) the purpose is to solve current organizational problems and to develop the organization in the long run, (2) a complex and systemic approach that focuses
on changing complex organizational systems, (3) mainly a process-oriented
intervention or process-consulting (Schein, 1992), inasmuch as the interventionist would not solve problems directly but enable organizational actors to solve their own problems and learn that, (4) a participative change
approach with the involvement of a wide range of organizational stakeholders in the change process, and (5), a value-based approach with a special
focus on linking human and organizational goals.

The abovementioned principles of OD are ensured by its foundation
in, and orientation towards, "action research" being a collaborative, self-

reflective and cyclic process of inquiry, learning and change, in which organizational members become co-researchers. The phases of most action research are: collective data gathering → feedback on the results → joint interpretation of data → action planning → action implementation → collective data-gathering → . . .[2]

To sum up, organization development is definitely not a "hammer-nail" view nor a "quick fix type" of intervention. Moreover, OD consultancy for us is qualitatively much more than just being an "intermediary" or "translator" of academic knowledge into practice. Instead, in our view, *OD is a field of praxis, and is itself knowledge*: a (1) broad and deep collection of collective insights gained from experimenting, experiencing and (self-) reflective practices; (2) a well-founded methodology for collaboratively researching organizations together with the local participants (3) a practicable mode of intervention and action that leads to change and development of systems; and (4) a theory building process through observing, reflecting on, learning from and generalizing upon the actual lived experiences within organizations.

The Original OD Authority Figures

For many decades the two worlds in OD, that of the consultants and of the academics, have been quite overlapping, and the key figures were scholars and practitioners themselves, building on each others' results. Although OD is an "applied behavioral science" (French & Bell, 1995), these people and many more were and still are doing far more than applied research. Let us think of some of the past and present OD authorities: among them, Kurt Lewin, Eric Trist, Chris Argyris, Donald Schön and Edgar Schein from the first and second generations, or David Kolb, Marvin Weisbord, William Torbert, Peter Senge, David Cooperrider, William Pasmore or Ron Fry from the later generations. They are all excellent examples of a real "cross-fertilization" between theory and practice, and also, of maintaining a good balance between academia and consulting.

What was/is distinctive in them? It is not that mostly they were linked in some ways to academia. Without romanticizing their contributions, the following criteria apply to the main OD authorities.

Social Scientists Dealing with Real Life Problems

This point has several facets: stemming from their deep and broad education in diverse scientific disciplines, these people are not embedded into only one specific tradition or approach. And their fluency in both theory and practice is well-illustrated by their publication records, reaching both academic and practitioner audiences.[3] But the main issue here is that they are not bound by the discipline; instead, they are problem-focused and trans-disciplinary: they start from the real life problem, use their broad disciplinary knowledge to approach the issue in a complex way, and team up with experts representing other fields. And, by involving the real life stakeholders, they carry out action research that results in lasting change and development.

Creators of Organizational Theory, Action Research Methodology and Intervention Praxis

For a first illustration let's consider the work of Chris Argyris, who is an organizational interventionist (Edmondson, 1996), an originator of the action research tradition called "action science" (Argyris, Putnam & Smith, 1985) and a theorist of organizational learning (e.g., Argyris & Schön, 1978, 1996). And the essence and principles of how to create "double-loop organizational learning" are always the same: creating valid information, establishing free and informed choice, and building internal commitment of members to these choices (Argyris, 1977). That is, the "Argyrisian way" of organizational learning (theory), organizational intervention (OD), and action research (empirical research) are not only well-integrated, they are different sides of the same coin. The same goes for Edgar Schein in connecting theory, intervention, and research: for him, shared basic assumptions underlying organizational culture (theory) (Schein, 1992) can only be deciphered via his so-called "clinical perspective to fieldwork" (research) (Schein, 1987a). But clinical research is in fact very much alike to "process consultation" (intervention) (Schein, 1987b). Process consultation and clinical research too are about fostering the organization's capacity to reveal its own culture, to solve its own problems, and to learn about itself (action learning).

A Well-Founded and Complex Approach to Organization Change and Development

The above points have an immensely important consequence: when the originators of OD were/are dealing with complex organizations issues and problems at hand, even though they would disagree in the actual remedy and in the best intervention practice (cf. Edmondson, 1996; Glassmann & Lundberg, 1988), they would all approach the situation with *enough complexity*. Since their approaches are complex and well-founded both theoretically and empirically, the danger of being one-sided and reductionist is minimized. Similarly, and stemming from the very nature of their "theories of change and intervention," there is no risk that they would be superficial in dealing with complex organizational dynamics.

A Capacity for Theoretical Reflection, Self-reflection and Dialogue

We suggest that the original key figures of OD were/are capable of reflecting on their own approaches and on themselves. Reflecting on their own approaches means more than only theoretical reflection (like testing their concepts, models, and intervention theories against existing academic knowledge). That could still be too discipline-bound and self-justifying. Instead, many of them have the capacity to link their own assumptions to the philosophy of science and to sociological paradigms (cf. Burrell & Morgan, 1979). For example, the Habermasian roots of action science are explicitly named (Argyris et al., 1985), while appreciative inquiry is explicitly based on social constructionist philosophy (Cooperrider & Srivastva, 1987). So the originators of OD have an idea of where they stand, what they represent, and what (explicit and tacit) assumptions lie behind their approaches (about organizational reality, society, human nature, change and development). Moreover, stemming from the mainly self-reflective, action learning-based character of their suggested interventions, we suppose that they themselves should be self-reflective in their roles and practices and as persons too.

To sum up, what we find is that OD was conceived and is maintained by influential figures who would qualify as *theoretically well-informed self-reflective OD practitioner-scientists*. For us this is qualitatively different from the "management guru" approach. As Kofman and Senge (1993) put it: "The problem with 'seven step methods to success,' 'keys to successful organizations,' and similar 'how-tos' is that, ultimately, they aren't very practical. Life is too complex and effective action too contextual. Real learning—the development of new capabilities—occurs over time, in a continuous cycle of theoretical action and practical conceptualization" (p. 7). If practiced well and constantly, this *educated and (self-) reflective* stance should lead us to a capacity to distance ourselves from own convictions—to be aware of own basic assumptions, be able to question, test, and refine own approaches, and also, to engage into genuine dialogue with others.

The fact that a continued dialogue and cooperation among likeminded scholars in the late Center for Organizational Learning (COL) seem to have proven difficult (see Edmondson, 1996) does warn us. And still, we believe that OD has no other way than to keep being a theoretically well-founded praxis that is continually self-reflective and open for dialogue

THEORETICAL BASES OF A WELL-FOUNDED AND SELF-REFLECTIVE OD PRAXIS

We suggest that OD consultancy should be *intervention praxis*: a constant, lively, and reflexive relationship between the theory of organizational change and the practice of OD. And OD practitioners should be, or should aim to become *theoretically well-informed reflective practitioners*, regardless of whether they are based in a consulting firm or at a university. Only through that capacity will *OD practitioners* be able (1) to have a broad and complex enough perspective to handle equally complex organizational issues; (2) to reflect upon their own favored approach(es) and methods by surfacing, testing and questioning own underlying assumptions or those implicitly encoded in "their" approaches, hence avoiding being "blinded by the method;" and (3) to be available for creative thinking about these approaches and methods. They also must be able to engage in true dialogue (1) with other colleagues representing different approaches; (2) with academia and theory in order to learn about relevant, sound, old or new, yet empirically grounded findings; and (3) with the client-system, managers and other organizational stakeholders in order to have a real sense of what they really face, need, and are ready (or not yet ready) to take responsibility for in making change happen.

Quite similarly, only through that attitude will *OD scholars* be able to gain real life, experience-based insights that can lead to deeper understandings of organizational change, solid (new or refined) theories and concepts, and improved action research methodologies.

We suggest that *OD as an intervention praxis* would result in OD consultants as well as scholars becoming more able to satisfy their role-requirements, and OD could again take on a more esteemed role in understanding and facilitating complex organizational change that lasts.

Theories that would substantiate OD as intervention praxis are manifold. The following discussion is oriented towards an *OD consultant* (and not to the OD scholar); thus we will argue for an extended perspective, in which doing, experimentation and experiencing is extended by theorizing and reflecting.[4] We believe though that the following discussion is valid for organizational consultancy in general too, inasmuch as the consultant's aim should be to make an accurate sense of organizational situations and build adequate interventions on that insight.

Experiential Learning: Gaining Insight from Experience, Self-Reflection and Theory

Kolb's (1984) well-known experiential learning theory has, as one of its main messages, put special focus on learning from the concrete experience that the learner encounters. Experiential learning has become a special buzz-word in especially OD-type interventions and training.

But probably many who espouse this model do not know that the experiential learning cycle (see Figure 11.1) underlines that practice and theory, action, and reflection should go hand in hand. Moreover, "reflective obser-

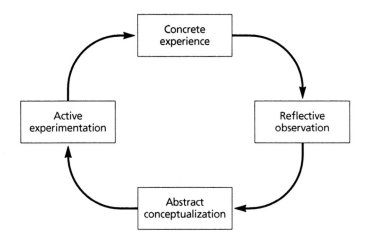

Figure 11.1 Kolb's experiential learning cycle (Kolb, 1984).

vation" is followed by "abstract conceptualization," that is, by the development or the use of generalized knowledge, like theories and concepts. This is why Kolb's idea of experiential learning is so very different from learning by doing, in which reflective and theoretical work is deemed unnecessary.

In order to have good insight and elaborate knowledge of what has happened and what needs to be learned from a given experience, one should be able to link experience to theory. But in case we are limited in our perspective by our "single best" theories and "best practice" methodologies, then abstract conceptualization, and thus the whole learning cycle, will be a closed, self-justifying system. One-sidedness will most prominently limit the self-reflective capacity of the consultant when evaluating the success of his or her chosen intervention, stemming from the fact that most best practice type methodologies also provide their own indicators to measure success. In this case no real learning will happen, as there will be no space for surprise and unexpectedness, no room for understanding encountered situations in new ways, and no ambition to look for alternative interventions.

In opposition to this, if the consultant is open in approach and deep in personal and theoretical reflection, then following the experiential learning cycle will enable him or her to gain new insight as well as learn and develop in the role (and as a person).

Breadth and Depth of the Consultant's Perspective

Taking Gareth Morgan's "Images of Organization," we could consider applying diverse "images of (OD) consulting" too. As Morgan (1986) says:

...we can enhance our ability to organize and solve organizational problems by understanding the link between theory and practice and by appreciating Kurt Lewin's famous dictum that "there is nothing so practical as a good theory." People who learn to read situations from different (theoretical) points of view have an advantage over those committed to a fixed position—for they are better able to recognize the limitations of a perspective. They can see how situations and problems can be framed and reframed in different ways, allowing new kinds of solutions to emerge. (p. 337)

Many consultants, at least in OD consultancy, use several approaches and methodologies in an eclectic way. Although this can be dangerous too, we see that as an advantage over a one methodology approach for all situations. The key is that we should use our intervention methodologies like metaphors—as "possible ways" rather than "the ways" of change and development. If our attitude towards our favored change theories and methodologies is a *metaphorical* one, then still being dedicated, we will nevertheless be able to (1) acknowledge the weaknesses of our approach, (2) know that there are possible and equal other ways, (3) read the organizational situation more attentively and search for other perspectives, (4) keep a healthy distance from the approach and method, be open to test their validity, and even (5) be willing to learn about the basic assumptions underlying any given approach and methodology.

We maintain it is not enough to learn methodologies only on a "how to do" level, even if we are trained in many approaches. Knowing methodologies and being able to use them well would imply knowing also about their explicit and, mainly, implicit assumptions. There are at least two types of assumptions underlying any intervention theory: (1) those that relate directly to its idea of organizational change, and (2) those that relate more indirectly to its assumptions about organizational reality (ontology), knowing (epistemology), social order, and human nature.

Just to give an illustration for the first, Edmondson (1996) used the following criteria to compare the explicit and implicit assumptions behind the different approaches of Edgar Schein, Chris Argyris, and Peter Senge: the primary source of ineffectiveness in organizations, kinds of data needed to be gathered, diagnostic output, next steps after diagnosis, research tradition, intervention strategy, temperament underlying the intervention, and the core challenge and gap of the given approach.

Proceeding to the second type, to the even deeper assumptions underneath any change theory and methodology, we should refer to Burrell and Morgan's (1979) "Sociological Paradigms and Organizational Analysis" that is based on the philosophy of science and social theory. The authors show that any approach to organization and organizational change is fundamentally paradigmatic and implies answers, mostly implicitly, to questions like: What is organizational reality (and what is not)?; What counts as a "relevant" problem (and what does not)?; What counts as a desirable organizational purpose (and what does not)?; What is our ideal organization (and what do we exclude)?; With what purpose to lead (and what is excluded)?; What is "good intervention" (and what is not)?; What is considered relevant methodology (and what is not)?; How should we measure success (and how not to)?; and Whose interests count (and whose do not)? For us, a well-founded and self-reflective OD praxis would imply both breadth and depth of perspective on the consultant's side.

Making Good Sense: "Reading" Organizational Reality Well

The complexity of organizational situations requires that organizational consultants, similar to decision makers, make not only sense but a "truthful sense" of organizational reality. The theory of sense-making is philosophical hermeneutics: the "philosophy and art of understanding" (Grondin, 2002; see also Gadamer, 1975/2004). One of its starting questions is: "How can we make sense of a text?" The difficulty lies in the fact that in every text and sentence, in the background there is the "author" and the context somehow being expressed, but mainly unexpressed. In no way is an author capable of expressing herself one hundred percent. No one is. The same goes for an oral discussion: for a full explication, in order tell *all of what we mean*, we would need to include the whole story in every word and sentence as a background. Eventually, we should always tell the whole story of ourselves. Because that's obviously not possible, we are constantly " ... in a search for the [right] language in order to express what lies on our hearts" (Grondin, 2002, p. 169, translated by the authors). Understanding ("verstehen") is the attitude and approach to get further than the first-level meaning, towards a "full" meaning of what is trying to be expressed. The listener or reader, being an interpreter herself, should try to infer from what's being presented, all that is not. To make it even more complex meaning is not individually created but rather is a socially constructed (linguistic-cultural) phenomenon. That applies not only to written or oral expressions, but to actions and interactions, and to social systems like organizations too.

Consultancy is about interpreting: to understand what is there in the organization and what is needed to be done. Organizational phenomena like words, actions and interactions (e.g., the main client's expectations), artifacts (like an organizational chart, procedures, the physical space), and certainly the presented "problem-situation" are to be interpreted. Organizational consultants have a special responsibility, since their understandings can have a significant impact on people's lives. When presented by the "story" of a problem-situation, consultants should try to have insight into the hidden realms (intentions, motivations, interaction patterns) too, and place the story in a broader context of the organization's history and culture. That is, the consultant, being an interpreter of the organization-as-a-text should read the organization as well as possible.

Faithful interpretation requires carefulness, sensitivity, a capacity to distinguish (a "good taste," which is close to sound moral judgment), deepness, and complexity. These attitude characteristics will help the consultant arrive at a *valid interpretation* of the situation, close to the truth of it. Strange as it may sound, from a hermeneutic perspective we can talk about the "truth" of the situation: this can never be grasped fully, but usually we have less difficulty recognizing "nonsense" interpretations (Gadamer, 1975/2004).

Faithfulness in interpretation also requires self-interpretation. Like every interpreter, consultants are themselves meaning creators. Whether we know it or not, and independently from our will, meaning is enabled by and attached on the basis of *our* "meaning horizon." "The horizon is the range of vision that includes everything that can be seen from a particular vantage point. Applying this to the thinking mind, we speak of narrowness of horizon, of the possible expansion of horizon, of the opening up of new horizons, and so forth ... A person who has an horizon knows the relative significance of everything *within this horizon...*" (Gadamer, 1975/2004, p. 301, emphasis added).

OD consultants, much more than other organizational actors, should be aware of their own horizons (e.g., basic assumptions, language, schema, knowledge, favored approaches). Moreover, they should be more receptive and faithful to the enfolding meaning of the situation, to what the situation "is telling," rather than to those selective, many times even limited, perspectives that their approaches imply. But for that to happen, they should be well aware of the underlying assumptions (e.g., about reality, ideal organizing, change, development, human nature etc.) that are encoded in those favored approaches.

To sum up, the sense that is made by the consultant of the presented problem is very much dependent on (1) his or her self-reflective capacity on his or her own horizon; (2) the level of his/her depth, good taste, discernment, and wholeness in reading complex organizational situations well; and (3) a willingness and capacity to get involved in a real dialogue with the situation by blending his or her own assumptions with those of the presenting situation. But in the dialogue they are advised to let the situation "talk for itself" as much as possible, rather than force unique situations into methodological straitjackets. Of course, the attitude suggested here is significantly different from applying pre-packaged or best-practice solutions, and even, from doing methodology-driven OD consultancy.

Dialogue or Cross-fertilization: Among Theory and Practice; Among Approaches

The concept of dialogue is well known, at least since it has been popularized by Senge (1990) and his colleagues (Senge, Kleiner, Roberts, Ross & Smith, 1994). They refer to Bohm and distinguish dialogue from discussion, by defining dialogue as "... meaning passing or moving through ... a free flow of meaning between people, in the sense of a stream that flows between two banks" (Bohm, 1965, quoted by Senge, 1990, p. 40). In dialogue "a new kind of mind begins to come into being which is based on the development of a common meaning ..." This is achieved when "individuals suspend their assumptions but they communicate their assumption freely. The result is a free exploration that brings to the surface the full depth of people's experience and thought, and yet can move beyond their individual views ... [so] ... individuals gain insights that simply could not be achieved individually" (Senge, 1990, p. 241).

It is not our aim to discuss the issues related to dialogue in detail (for a recent and extensive elaboration on the co-production and qualities of dialogue see Beech et al., 2010). Instead, we would like to show how much the capacity for real dialogue is related to the previous points: to OD consultants' self-reflexivity and openness, to the breadth and depth of our perspective, and to being more faithful to the presented problem than to our favored approaches.

In conversation, and especially in dialogues, regarded as "meaningful" conversations, we seek to understand and to be understood as properly as possible: to understand "the meaning." Whenever we truly aim for a dialogue—in general circumstances or, more specifically, between diverse intervention theories and methodologies, or between academia and practice—we try to create a common language that will result in a shared view of reality and enable common action (Blaikie, 1995). Shared reality does not necessary mean identical reality, that we should agree in everything, but at least we know in what we agree and in what we disagree and why, based on what assumptions. Knowing that, we can let the disagreements remain. In a dialogue we should balance advocacy with inquiry (Argyris & Schön, 1996; Senge et al., 1994) and with this attitude be open not only to what is said, but also to why things are said. This process should eventually lead to an understanding not only of explicit actions or expressions but, and most importantly, of one's own as well as others' fundamental assumptions.

In hermeneutic terms, dialogue is always a "fusion of horizons." As Blaikie (1995), referring to Gadamer, puts it,

> ... hermeneutics is about bridging the gap between our familiar world and the meaning that resides in an alien world ... collision with another horizon

can make the interpreter aware of his/her own deep-seated assumptions, of his/her own prejudices or horizon of meaning, of which s/he may have remained unaware; taken-for-granted assumptions can be brought to critical self-consciousness and genuine understanding can become possible. (p. 64)

Translating that to OD consultancy, this can only happen if, on the side of the consultant, there is (1) openness to reflect on one's own assumptions and oneself, and (2) a capacity to become conscious, either as a preliminary knowledge or as a dialogically constructed insight, about the assumptions underlying one's own methodologies. Or, to put it differently, if the approaches and methodologies that we apply are consciously chosen *orientations,* applied in a *metaphorical sense,* that is still open and can be influenced or even enriched. As we are not imprisoned by our languages (Grondin, 2002) and frames of minds, we should not be imprisoned by our theories, approaches, and methodologies either. But if there is a feeling and language of superiority on the side of any participants, as Beech et al. (2010) found in academic-practitioner exchanges, then dialogue is impeded. The same will happen if the influence is only one directional (as opposed to being mutual), when for example "ready-made" concepts or "cook-book" methodologies are sold to organizations as if organizational consultancy was a pre-structured didactic situation (Czarniawska & Joerges, 1996).

EXPERIENCES OF THE ORGANIZATION DEVELOPMENT WORLD SUMMIT (THE ODWS 2010)

In the following we will first move to more practical terrains and share some of what we experienced before and at the event of the Organization Development World Summit. Although these concrete episodes were in fact the triggers of our continued reflection (and self-reflection) processes, and so the inspirations to write this chapter, here they are better seen and handled only as illustrations, or embodiments, of our general theme, the "theory-practice" issue in organization development. In line with that, the short accounts will then be followed by a discussion part.

Disturbing Observations from the Conference

The Academic Track of ODWS: A "Deserted Territory"
We have already shared how ineffective we were in attracting OD scholars and academic institutions to ODWS. We equally failed to attract an audience to our academic track from among the conference participants. The average size of the audience was five plus the presenter and the two conve-

nors (out of more than 350 participants). The academic sessions that had fewest participants were those that were held by presenters from an academic context, and the best-attended session was that by a Peruvian senior consultant, who summarized what he had learned during his professional career. In contrast, the two presenters who were used to an academic environment felt like they were strangers and were looked at as such. These are just three further illustrations of how distant academia and practice were at ODWS, even in the so-called "academic track."

The Absence of Theoretical or Self-reflection: The Case of Appreciative Inquiry (AI) at the Conference

Appreciative inquiry (AI) is a relatively new approach and methodology in OD. Without going into a detailed account, AI focuses on "organization as a mystery to be embraced," that is, on "the best of what is and what could be" (Cooperrider & Whitney, 1999, p. 23). This is in sharp contrast to more traditional OD, which underlines the need to identify and analyze organizational problems and their causes, as a precondition to work out valid solutions and thus develop the organization in the long term (in AI terms the latter approach considers the organization "a problem to be solved"). Appreciative inquiry believes in the generative nature of language (Bushe, 2005) and therefore uses a positive language. The theoretical, even philosophical foundations of AI are well elaborated and reflected upon by the creators of the approach. Cooperrider and Srivastva (1987) refer mainly to "social constructionism," and in fact, to a quite radically relativist version of it outlined by Gergen, according to which (organization) reality is basically a linguistic construction. Of course, there is nothing wrong with AI in general; it definitely has a generative power, and the founding parents of the approach and many followers do have the theoretical insight and the self-reflective capacity to know what AI stands for, on what bases, and upon which underlying assumptions.

But how should we understand its overall stardom, even faith-like character at the ODWS? The sessions given on AI attracted huge audiences. Persons whom we have known for a long time and who, if they were aware, would never accept a social constructionist view of organizational reality, became quite zealous. Do these practitioners know what it is they commit themselves to? Will they be able to apply AI in an adequate way, matched with the needs of the actual situation? Or is AI an approach that would fit all circumstances?

We do not think so. But at the ODWS it was often presented as if it were. Throughout the conference we noted some alarming signs. First, at the panel discussion of the so-called inspirational leaders representing diverse approaches (like Future Search, AI, Gestalt, TA, etc.) a question from the audience challenged the participants to share the drawbacks of their approaches. The well-known representative of AI reacted something like this: "If 'drawback' is in your vocabulary, you will see drawbacks. Well, it's not in my vocabulary." Without reflecting on the truth-value of the statement, we clearly see how self-referential this argument was!

The other instance relates to a real life case-work session, an important element in the conference design. Here the charismatic AI representative from the U.S. fully hit the target and beat the imagined competition easily, but not through creatively adapting AI to the Hungarian company's special circumstances. Just the contrary, by presenting all that we know of AI, developed in a North-American context, as if it was applicable in an unmodified way. The question is whether an approach, based on underlying assumptions that fit the U.S., will fit without any modification a (Central-Eastern) European context? Are the famed representatives of the approach—of any approach not just AI—ready to work against exporting a North-American culture through OD (Amado, Faucheaux, & Laurent, 1991)? These experts did not seem to.

A Failed Dialogue: Panel Discussion among the Inspirational Leaders

The panel discussion among the diverse approaches was a key event at the summit. As it was expressed, at least allegedly, the representatives of these approaches were very supportive towards each other and claimed that their approaches were deeply rooted in all other approaches present (and especially on Gestalt). However, being in the organizing team of the conference we could obtain some insider information surrounding the panel discussion. It turned out that it had been extremely hard to persuade the inspirational leaders not to withdraw from the discussion at the very last moment, because there was much anger and envy among them, stemming from past, unprocessed events. Given that, we assert that the dialogue was more pretended than deep-seated.

The Academic Team: Experiencing Ourselves as a Subculture

We are aware that all that has been observed (and not) at ODWS, and how it is interpreted is a product of our subjectivity. But there is no way of escaping from subjectivity, and even if there were, we shouldn't. What we should escape from is being biased. Here we refer to Kvale (1996), who distinguishes between "biased subjectivity," which is self-fulfilling, and "perspectival subjectivity," which is based on critical self-reflection. To follow the latter, in the course of preparing this chapter we decided to reflect upon and constantly share among ourselves our lived experiences of ODWS (our thoughts, feelings and known prejudices), and eventually, to make sense of the academic team as a subculture.

If cultures in organizations imitate the culture of the society to which they belong, then it seems reasonable to assume that organizational cultures, even project organizations of a world summit, do not consist of a single homogenous culture but rather of multiple subcultures. According to Cohen (1955), subcultures are likely to form among members who interact often and who face similar problems, providing them with opportunities to exchange concerns about the existing culture and, through interaction, build relationships. When individuals work together on a task, subcultures may also form as values may become specific to the task on which the group is focused (Trice & Beyer, 1993). As with the development of subcultures in society, organizational subcultures can be said to exist when members of a certain work group develop and adopt common norms and values that may not be in line with the dominant culture. Boisnier and Chatman (2002) refer to the work of Berscheid (1985): "Like-minded individuals are attracted to subcultures in each of these cases for the same reasons: The well-supported similarity-attraction paradigm suggests that individuals would prefer to be around others with similar attitudes, including perceptions of the organization and their jobs" (p. 16). It is not only dissatisfaction but any shared belief or value that could bring together a subculture provided that there is also frequent interaction.

What is also important from the academic team's point of view is that Schein points to the possibility of the co-existence of subcultures and a dominant culture when dealing with pivotal and peripheral values (Schein, 1992). Pivotal values are central to an organization's functioning; members are required to adopt and adhere to the behavioral norms derived from these values and are typically rejected from the organization if they do not (Chatman, 1991; O'Reilly & Chatman, 1996). Peripheral values are desirable but are not believed by members to be essential to an organization's functioning. Members are encouraged to accept peripheral values, but can reject them and still function fully as members.

With Schein's work in mind, subcultures could be seen to exist that maintain the pivotal values but only some or a few of the peripheral values. In this way, the subcultures not only cannot be viewed as a counterculture—the academic team had never thought of itself as such—but should not affect the organization's function. According to Boisnier and Chatman (2002), the "members' degree of conformity to peripheral norms can vary considerably." Thus it could be claimed that subcultures may vary in the extent they are related to the dominant organizational culture.

Using these claims of Schein's and Martin's multi-perspective approach, the following map could be a potential outcome of mapping an organizational culture:

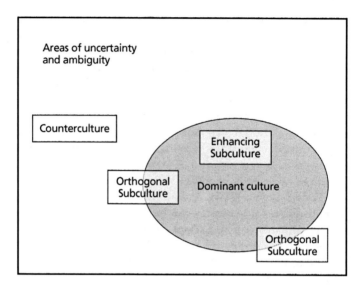

Figure 11.2 A multi-perspective model of organizational culture (adapted from Heidrich & Chandler, 2010).

As the organizing process went on and meetings were held with the design team of the overall summit, there was a growing sense within the academic team of being a somewhat orthogonal subculture in the larger organization of ODWS 2010. The pivotal values seemed to be coherent with that of the other sessions and organizing teams; however the peripheral values proved to be rather different. During the organizing process, within the academic team we often shared these differences of peripheral values, causing motivational conflicts at the individual and team level, and we often considered giving up the organizing work of the academic session.

DISCUSSION

For an interpretation of these experiences at the ODWS we provide a first-level analysis, but then, by reflecting on our theoretical bases, we attempt to dig deeper.

First-Level Analysis: Actors, Interests, Tendencies

On a pragmatic level, the financial crises hit the ODWS too, and the number of participants on the whole was much lower than originally expected. Adding to that, the participation fee ($900 USD), set according to practitioner-oriented conferences, was at least double of that of most academic conferences. Of course, academics in most countries can get their conference visits subsidized, but the World Summit, being the first of its kind and thus not having a pre-existing reputation, proved to be unattractive for "pure" academics. And still, we as organizers of the academic track had expected to attract many more participants to our session, certainly those participants who, like ourselves, are concerned bridging the gap between theory and practice.

In this retrospective analysis we attribute the low academic interest partly to the increasing divergence, even gap, between academia and practice. Although the studied phenomena (i.e., organizations and organizing, managers and managing, change and changing) are still the same, there is an increasing differentiation and specialization, both in academia and in intervention practice, that results in growing isolation. Clients, funding, measures of quality, favored terminologies, accepted approaches and methodologies, and, eventually, the socially constructed identity of an academic is increasingly different from that of an OD practitioner. Moreover, we suspect that the relationship between scholars and practitioners is too often characterized by non-awareness and negligence, or feelings of superiority (Beech et al., 2010) combined with envy, on both sides.

In academia, there is the strong pressure to publish or perish, and in that strong competition institutional (as well as individual) ranking is based mainly on academic publishing and impact factor. The academic way of using language is quite different than the language of practice: the concepts and constructs are embedded in a specialized academic community of practice, and meaning is derived from referencing related publications. Academic language is quite different from, or even antithetical to, the language (and the skill) of handling real life organizational issues. Although many doctoral students eventually end up in practice, a good PhD training "shall not" focus on practical managerial knowledge and skills, especially because quality of research in the traditional positivist sense is linked to rigorous research and "rigor" is defined per se against relevance. Although qualitative research has achieved a good status (especially in Europe), action research, the tradition that is directly linked to "praxis" is still rarely part of doctoral programs: it is considered too complicated, long and thus risky, and not even scientific in the mainly positivist academic culture. University-based action research programs are just being closed down in the U.S., U.K., and Australia. In teaching, despite the fact that real life business experience is a huge advantage at business schools, it is our experience that most of the management educators have an expert or expert consultant attitude rather than that of a facilitator or action researcher.

In consultancy practice, as the pace of working and competition on the market has increased radically, there seems to be a strong urge for simple quick-fix methodologies and solutions. It is not about understanding the nature of interventions but hitting the target. It is all right as long as this goes for the clients, but consultants, and especially OD consultants, should in no way become racing problem-solvers themselves. Then, how will they understand the organization, the different clients and the presented problems, and how will they teach the client-system to become better learners themselves? Eventually, how will they do organization development consultancy? The original and key OD figures ("Founding Parents" as labeled at the ODWS) are old or have passed away. Their students, the direct followers ("Inspirational Leaders" in ODWS terms), on the other hand, seem to be somewhat more oriented towards creating their own labels and fame (and business success). They have moved further away from academia. It is a danger that their advocated approaches become beliefs and they themselves (have) become the new priests. As we have indicated, this attitude might end up very far from the eagerness of academia to test validity and truth-value.

As we see it, the vast majority of today's OD practitioners are "users": they are socialized in certain intervention methodologies, and they train themselves to become even better in applying the specific approach or method.[5] Their approach is vastly pragmatic, which is good help in talking to the clients. Yet, if some clients buy solutions just as an escape from their own part in the often hard work of real deep-seated change, then OD consultancy will not do what it should. And, if this pure pragmatism on the consultant's side is mounted by a non-sophisticated, even too naïve approach towards the most intricate and most important dilemmas of the interventionist—for example, change vs. power, influence vs. oppression, communication vs. domination—then these consultants, and eventually OD, will be abused and become representatives of given ideologies and ideological control.

As to the *dialogue among diverse OD approaches* (at ODWS: "cross-fertilization"), we see the danger of at least two types of errors: (1) when, with some creativity and deep-level knowledge, certain OD approaches and methods could be blended creatively so that to handle complex organizational issues best, yet they are kept separate in different camps, the effectiveness of organizational intervention is artificially reduced; or (2) when there is a far too easy and superficial merging of diverse OD traditions and change methodologies that results in a chaotic (rather than a complex) intervention. "The messy history of OB & D" (Dent, 2002) indicates that dialogue among key OD figures and cross-fertilization among approaches was inevitable for OD to occur, but this development was created by individuals and groups who were fully dedicated to OD as a praxis (as opposed to pure practice).

Deeper Analysis: Is a "Well-Founded and Self-Reflective OD Praxis" Possible?

In this part we will briefly reflect on what's been suggested as (theoretical) bases for an ideal OD praxis. If the answer to the question posed is positive, what difficulties do we need to overcome?

The Difficulty of Being Inside (Acting) and Outside (Reflecting) at the Same Time

Acting entails immersing oneself into the here and now of the situation, physically, mentally, and emotionally. Reflecting, on the other hand, requires keeping a distance from the actual experience and a high level of self-consciousness. Having the capacity to "look below the surface" and critically reflect needs distance too. Distancing is more a characteristic of the academic world, while immersion is of practice. We even assert that academics in many cases are *overly distant, reserved*—physically, mentally and emotionally—and *critical*, whereas consultants, similarly to managers, can easily become *too close and absorbed* by the situation.

Praxis would be "both and": a reflective practitioner should be able to reflect on his/her own action, and even reflect on his or her action while acting (Schön, 1983). That requires finding the appropriate distance: an attitude that is fully committed yet fully conscious and open at the same time—to have control, while letting ambiguity remain. We think this attitude would help in making good sense of organizational situations, and also in encounters with (the representatives of) other approaches and methodologies. But it is very difficult, and we are not trained for this in our schools and workplaces.

The Difficulty of Leaving "Home Territory" in a Dialogue

From a Jesuit monk[6] we learned what might be the essence of dialogue: the capacity of fully leaving "home territory," letting the control (of the ego) go, making ourselves so open that we become equally vulnerable, and with that attitude, being able to "meet the other deeply" and genuinely understand him/her. Being non-judgmental and balancing advocacy with inquiry is ultimately based on this. For us this is also about finding the right distance, and about managing boundaries, internally and externally. If we set boundaries that are permeable, we will be able to remain open for new influences and still keep our boundaries and ourselves as a whole. But again, this is easier said than done.

The Difficulty of Questioning and Disapproving Our Approaches and Ourselves

Lack of self-reflection, no honest feedback from others, downplaying the value of empirical studies that do not support our interventions, feeling superior, denying, projecting, scape-goating—these mostly unconscious behaviors and dynamics are too familiar to us. Yet they oppose the mode of inquiry that is needed for a well-founded and self-reflective OD praxis.

Suggested Ways of Moving Ahead

Based on what has been articulated, we believe the professional development (train-the-trainer) programs are the first intervention points, because often these programs socialize *OD practitioners* into organization development and OD consultancy. We suggest that the theoretical grounding of these programs be strengthened, for example, with courses on organization theory, philosophy of science, as well as theories of social-organizational change. This should be done by instructors with a strong theoretical base and a capacity for doing organization praxis: to move from theoretical abstraction via methodology to practical niceties and vice versa, and to combine it with high levels of self-reflection. For them, instructors and mentors, OD in no way should be only about certain approaches and methods, especially not a faith in given best practices. Instead, it should be an intervention theory and methodology based (also) on empirically validated data. Ideally, in their OD practice, and in their teaching too, experiential learning and action research approaches should dominate. We also suggest that these mentors themselves should be involved in action research interventions together with other likeminded scholars and practitioners. As a result, we expect that students of OD will eventually become more self-reflective and well-prepared professionally and even ethically more responsive.

For those who pursue *an academic career in OD and change* we would emphasize, as a starting point, the inevitability of encountering managers and other organizational members regularly, and testing their knowledge in real life circumstances. It should include a combination of doing qualitative research, applied OD interventions, action research studies and self-reflection-based experiential learning courses, all with a focus on real life organizational (and societal) problems, and a collaborative inquiry approach. We think that a priori approaches, theories, models and concepts should be handled as orientations that serve to discover reality anew (as opposed to a reductionist approach of being themselves truth). We also suggest that academic researchers should *team up* with practitioners and work mutually for "generative dialogic encounters" (Beech et al., 2010). This, we believe, will lead to a co-production of knowledge based on both shared practice and shared reflection-on-action. Learning from each other will be most fruitful if "process knowledge" (the ways to approach issues, and the underlying assumptions) are also shared.

As a *general attitude* we believe we ourselves should practice and live with the paradox of being inside and outside, the tension of theory and practice, acting and reflecting, being committed and being distant, and to learn that from lived experience. Maneuvering on the boundary or moving "in and out" can be *practiced* for example in mixed teams, in double roles (being both a scholar and a consultant), by visiting both practitioner and academic events regularly. It can be *deeply experienced* in doing action research in whatever roles, and can be *radically enhanced* in, for example, personal development and therapy, in contemplative practices, or at so-called Tavistock (Group Relations) conferences. These forms of learning work well (1) because they provide enough time and space, the necessary emotional containment as well as the intensity of experience so that the learner could broaden and deepen his/her own meaning horizon; (2) because they themselves are a combination of deep insight and sincere action; and (3) because they radically enhance the self-reflective and self-understanding capacity of the actors and therefore their capacity to become open, and thus question and test their own practices, including the taken-for-granted assumptions.

Redefining theory and practice in OD as essentially "close," even inevitable to each other rather than keeping them "far away," is, we believe, the way forward for organization development—a way to enhance OD as a practice, as an intervention theory, and as a significant field of organizational change. Certainly, that shift would require a move more in line with the very traditions of OD than with its current developments.

NOTES

1. The authors' contribution to the text, and thus their responsibility, is distributed as follows: András Gelei: 70%, Balázs Heidrich: 20%, Gergely Németh: 10%.
2. Action research in current OD refers primarily to solving local problems and to the cyclic process of diagnosis and action. However, as originally meant by Kurt Lewin, in action research the experiences collected on the local level should be used to improve general theoretical knowledge as well, and vice versa. Action research in this original sense thus inherently refers to "praxis" (see Eden & Huxham, 1996).
3. To be fair to today's academics and consultants, disciplinary specialization at the times of their entry to the field was not as deep as it is now.
4. If, however, an "OD scholar" was in our focus, a move in the other direction should be theoretically examined.
5. See for example the current craze of executive coaching, the fact that most if not all OD consultants are, or would like to become, identified as a "coach."
6. Personal discussion with Péter Mustó SJ (2010).

REFERENCES

Amado, G., Faucheaux, C., & Laurent, A. (1991). Organizational change and cultural realities: Franco-American contrasts. *International Studies of Management and Organization, 3,* 62–95.

Argyris, C. (1977). Double-loop learning in organizations. *Harvard Business Review,* (September-October), 115–125.

Argyris, C., Putnam, R., & Smith, D. M. (1985). *Action science: Concepts, methods, and skills for research and intervention.* San Francisco, CA: Jossey-Bass.

Argyris, C., & Schön, D. A. (1978). *Organizational learning: A theory of action perspective.* Reading, Ma.: Addison-Wesley.

Argyris, C., & Schön, D .A. (1996). *Organizational learning II: Theory, method, practice.* Reading, MA: Addison-Wesley.

Astley, W. G., & Zammuto, R. F. (1992). Organization science, managers, and language games. *Organization Science, 3*(4), 443–460.

Beech, N., MacIntosh, R., & MacLean, D. (2010). Dialogues between academics and practitioners: the role of generative dialogic encounters. *Organization Studies, 31*(9), 1341–1367.

Berscheid, E. (1985). Interpersonal attraction. In G. Lindzey & E. Aronson (Eds.), *Handbook of social psychology* (3rd ed., pp. 413–484). New York, NY: Random House.

Blaikie, N. (1995). *Approaches to social enquiry.* Cambridge, UK: Polity Press.

Boisnier, A., & Chatman, J. (2002). Cultures and subcultures in dynamic organizations. In E. Mannix & R. Petersen (Eds.), *The dynamic organization* (pp. 87–114). Mahwah, NJ: Lawrence Erlbaum Associates.

Burrell, G., & Morgan, G. (1979). *Sociological paradigms and organizational analysis.* London: Heinemann Educational Books.

Bushe, G. (2005). Five theories of change embedded in appreciative inquiry. In D. Cooperrider, P. Sorensen, T. Yeager & D. Whitney (Eds.), *Appreciative inquiry: Foundations in positive organization development* (pp. 121–132). Champaign, IL: Stipes.

Chatman, J. A. (1991). Matching people and organizations: Selection and socialization in public accounting firms. *Administrative Science Quarterly, 36,* 459–484.

Cooperrider, D. L., & Srivastva, S. (1987). Appreciative inquiry in organizational life. In W. Pasmore & R. Woodman (Eds.), *Research in organization change and development* (Vol. 1, pp. 129–169). Greenwich, CT: JAI Press.

Cooperrider, D. L., & Whitney, D. (1999). *Collaborating for change: Appreciative inquiry.* San Francisco, CA: Berrett-Koehler Publishers.

Cohen, A. K. (1955). *Delinquent boys: The culture of the gang.* Glencoe. IL: Free Press

Cummings, T. G., & Worley, C. G. (1993). *Organization development and change* (5th ed.), St. Paul, MN: West Publishing Company.

Czarniawska, B., & Joerges, B. (1996). Travels of ideas. In B. Czarniawska & G. Sevón (Eds.), *Translating organizational change* (pp. 13–48). Berlin: Walter de Gruyter

Dent, E. B. (2002). The messy history of OB&D: How three strands came to be seen as one rope. *Management Decision, 40,* 266–280.

Eden, C., & Huxham C. (1996). Action research for management research. *British Journal of Management, 7,* 75–86.

Edmondson, A. (1996). Three faces of Eden: The persistence of competing theories and multiple diagnoses in organizational intervention research. *Human Relations, 49,* 571–596.

French, W. L., & Bell, C. H., Jr. (1995). *Organization development* (5th ed.) Englewood Cliffs, NJ: Prentice Hall.

Gadamer, H. -G. (2004). *Truth and method* (2nd ed., Trans. J. Weinsheimer & D. G. Marshall). New York, NY: Continuum. (Original work published 1975).

Gelei. A. (2002). *An interpretative approach to organizational learning: The case of organization development.* Unpublished doctoral dissertation, Corvinus University of Budapest, Budapest, Hungary.

Glassmann, A. M., & Lundberg, C. C. (1988). In search of the right consultant: An OD fable. *Group & Organization Management, 13,* 5–18.

Gordon, G. B. (2001). Transforming lives: Towards bicultural competence. In P. Reason & H. Bradbury (Eds.), *Handbook of action research: Participative inquiry and practice.* Thousand Oaks, CA: Sage Publications.

Grondin, J. (2002). *Bevezetés a filozófiai hermeneutikába.* Budapest, Hungary: Osiris Kiadó [original: *Einführung in die philosophische Hermeneutik* [Introduction to philosophical hermeneutics]. (2001)]. Darmstadt, Germany: Wissenschaftliche Buchgesellschaft]

Heidrich, B., & Chandler, N. (2010, October). *Mapping uncharted territory: Identifying organisational subcultures and their orientations in a post-merger higher educational institution.* Paper presented at the National and Regional Economics VIII. Conference, Technical University of Košice, Faculty of Economics, Slovakia.

Kofman, F., & Senge, P. M. (1993). Communities of commitment: The heart of learning organizations. *Organizational Dynamics, 22,* 5–23.

Kolb, D. (1984). *Experiential learning.* Englewood Cliffs: Prentice Hall.

Kvale, S. (1996). *InterViews. An introduction to qualitative research interviewing.* Thousand Oaks, CA: Sage.

Lawler, E. E., Mohrman, A. M. Jr, Mohrman, S. A., Ledford, G. E. Jr, Cummings, T. G., & Associates. (1985). *Doing research that is useful for theory and practice.* San Francisco, CA: Jossey-Bass.

Morgan, G. (1986). *Images of organization.* Thousand Oaks, CA: Sage.

Neilsen, D. H. (1984). *Becoming an OD practitioner.* Englewood Cliffs, NJ: Prentice Hall.

O'Reilly, C., & Chatman, J. (1996). Culture as social control: Corporations, cults and commitment. In B. Staw & L. Cummings (Eds.), *Research in organizational behavior* (pp. 157–200). Greenwich, CT: JAI Press.

Praxis Business School. (n.d.) Retrieved April 27, 2011, from http://praxis.ac.in/about-praxis/

Reason, P., & Bradbury, H. (Eds.). (2001). *Handbook of action research: Participative inquiry & practice.* Thousand Oaks, CA: Sage Publications.

Schein, E. H. (1987a). *The clinical perspective in fieldwork.* (*Sage Qualitative Research Methods Series, Vol. 5).* Thousand Oaks, CA: Sage.

Schein, E. H. (1987b). *Process consultation. Vol. 2. Lessons for managers and consultants.* Reading, MA: Addison-Wesley.

Schein, E. H. (1992). *Organizational culture and leadership* (2nd ed.). San Francisco, CA: Jossey-Bass.

Schön, D. (1983). *The reflective practitioner. How professionals think in action*. New York, NY: Basic Books.

Senge, P. M. (1990). *The fifth discipline. The art and practice of the learning organization*. New York, NY: Doubleday/Currency.

Senge, P. M., Kleiner, A., Roberts, C., Ross, R., & Smith, B. J. (1994). *The fifth discipline fieldbook. Strategies and tools for building a learning organization*. New York, NY: Doubleday/Currency.

Trice, H. M., & Beyer, J. M. (1993). *The cultures of work organizations*. Englewood Cliffs, NJ: Prentice-Hall.

Wilkerson, J. M. (1999). On research relevance, professors' "real world" experience, and management development: Are we closing the gap? *Journal of Management Development, 18*, 598–613.

SECTION IV

SHIFTING IDENTITIES AND CHALLENGES IN MANAGEMENT CONSULTING

CHAPTER 12

A COMPARATIVE IMAGE OF MANAGEMENT CONSULTING THROUGH THE MAGNIFYING GLASS OF ITS MAIN STAKEHOLDERS

Valentin Bejan and Léon de Caluwé

The modern concept of management consulting can be linked to the early decades of the 20th century when companies known today as Booz Allen Hamilton and Arthur D. Little saw a business opportunity out of providing external assistance and expertise to companies. It was thought to be a beneficial opportunity for both the providers of the services and the organizations in need of advice. After more than a century, management consulting grew enormously, diversified in many profiles, became embedded in most aspects of business, and created a world-wide, powerful industry.

Yet, management consulting is still searching for a clear definition, with stronger boundaries around the profession, and it is confronted with an ambiguous image. A few facts show that this search continues to be troublesome. The different estimations of the industry's yearly global revenues

Exploring the Professional Identity of Management Consultants, pages 243–263
Copyright © 2013 by Information Age Publishing
All rights of reproduction in any form reserved.

show an immense gap, revolving at sums between 160 billion Euros (Greiner & Ennsfellner, 2010, p. 72; about 207 billion USD) and 280 billion Euros (Plunkett Research, 2011; about 363 billion USD). At the same time, while several estimations show that the profession employs over one million consultants worldwide, the largest professional association, the International Council of Management Consulting Institutes (ICMCI), counts only 30,000 members. We see these facts as proof of a blurry image.

At the same time, from academia and the media, a more negative image seems to stand out. This image seems to reflect the intensity of the discourse rather than the frequency of critical or negative comments. As an example, van Workum's (2011) Master's thesis revealed that most comments in newspapers about management consultants are not negative. The news of a trading scandal with consultants involved is more likely to make front page news than a story that describes a positive contribution of a consulting firm in a project. Additionally some consulting firms and their clients make it harder to see the joint work—good or bad—because of a strict sphere of confidentiality or even secrecy surrounding the engagement, which further gives room for speculation.

Further contributing to this image is the growing collaboration between academia and business, with expected benefits and synergies that support the closeness (Daniels, 1991; Dodgson, 1993). Academics, as producers of knowledge, and management consultants, as dispersers of knowledge, may be important facilitators in this process. But there are a number of academics who completely exclude the possibility of fructuous collaboration (Kieser & Leiner, 2009) and invoke the unscrupulous reputation of consultants.

Given this context, a team of professors and scholar-consultants with great interest in the professionalization of the industry decided to undertake a stakeholder assessment of the current image of management consultants. The team jointly designed a research study aimed at answering the question: "What is the (comparative) image of management consultants based on the perception of its most important stakeholders—academics, consultants, clients, and the public?

The research follows a mixed approach, which is explained in the methodology section. The chapter also contains a brief review of the literature that captures the diversity of perspectives about management consultants and the need for a clearer image of their role. The data gathering and the analysis of results for each category were part of the Master's program of five students. As the research for the "clients" category is still ongoing, it is not part of this chapter, and will be explored in subsequent articles. The chapter concludes with our reflections on the research, its limitations, and implications.

METHODOLOGY

This section describes the study methodology, drawing out the design of the project and the rationale underlying the questionnaire.

Strategy, Design, Measures, and Validity

A panel consisting of three professors (two of whom are part-time consultants as well) and one assistant professor designed and guided the entire research process. The team of experts leading this study opted for a mixed (quantitative and qualitative) method in the cases of the consultants, academics and clients (the latter of which is not completed) and a quantitative method with the public (see Table 12.1). The mixed method follows the directions of a follow-up sequential explanatory design (Creswell, Plano Clark, Gutman, & Hanson, 2003). This approach was chosen to probe the questionnaire results with explanatory interviews with the participants. The team also considered that given the size and the nature of the sample, it would not be feasible to approach the public through this mixed method.

The chosen research strategy is deductive in nature (Saunders, Lewis, & Thornhill, 2009). As illustrated in Figure 12.1, the design of the questionnaire and the semi-structured interviews followed a rigorous process in order to ensure the validity and relevance of the content. The first step of the process was the selection by the expert panel of a relevant body of literature that is related to the image of management consultants. After the relevant body of literature was chosen, a thorough analysis was done by the same professors, which lead to defining and framing the constructs in the questionnaire: Advice, Roles, Competencies, Personal Characteristics, and Effectiveness.

Content Rationale for the Questionnaire

The research team filtered a high number of academic sources that resulted in the five constructs noted above. Kubr (2002) and Jang and Lee (1998)

TABLE 12.1   Sample Sizes for the Mixed Research Design

	Number of Questionnaires	Number of Interviews
Academics	63	17
Consultants	34	33
Public	400	—

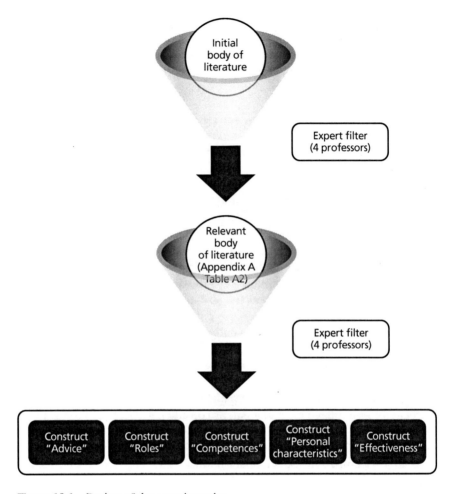

Figure 12.1 Design of the questionnaire.

state that management consulting is synonymous with giving *advice* and that this image dominates the profession. Several authors argue that such advice needs to be independent, based on diagnosis and analysis, and supported by expert knowledge and tools (cf. Greiner & Metzger, 1983; Kubr, 2002; Werr & Stjernberg, 2003; Wood, 2002). The advice can sometimes extend to participating in its implementation (Block 1981; Greiner & Metzger 1983; Kubr 2002), which involves a different *role* and a higher degree of intervention in the organization. Kubr (2002) also mentions that seizing new opportunities is an integral part of the advice given by a management consultant.

Regarding the term *competencies*, we take the definition of de Caluwé and Reitsma (2010) as "something that someone is good at" (p. 21). These two scholars also emphasize a list of six core skills required by the consultant:

stress tolerance, planning abilities, results-orientation, awareness of the organizational context, aptitude to innovate, and coaching. Clark (1995), Huczynski (1996), and Sturdy (1997) argue that listening, persuasion, and conflict mediation skills are also central competencies for the management consulting professional. "Good at selling and marketing" was pointed out as a central skill by the research done by Greiner and Metzger (1983, p. 32), while "recycling solutions" emerged in Werr and Stjernberg's (2003, p. 891) study. As a senior consultant from a top firm noted in that study, the same proposals are adapted and used in several projects.

Among the *personal characteristics* that remained in the newly formed construct, traits like arrogance, superficiality, over-charging clients, and motivated by money also appear in several publications (Buono & Poulfelt, 2009; Pinault, 2001; Redekop & Heath, 2007; Werr & Styhre, 2003). Due to its relative intangibility, the *effectiveness* of the consultant services is not easy to measure (Kipping, 1999). With this challenge in mind, de Caluwé and Stoppelenburg (2004) gathered insights from literature (Gable, 1996; Phillips, 2000; Quinn & Rohrbaugh, 1983) and their own experience, and framed nineteen effectiveness criteria split into three categories:

- *Formal Criteria* (e.g., Has a solution been found? Has the objective been achieved? Were the budget and time paths followed?)
- *Content Criteria* (e.g., Did the system of the client learn and developed? Is the system of the client more effective, efficient and/or better planned?)
- *Process Criteria* (e.g., Has a specific method been used? Did the consultant clearly coordinate and give directions over what needs to be done?)

The complete list of connections between the literature and the final constructs can be found in Table 12.2.

The final items of the questionnaire were chosen to balance content with a questionnaire of reasonable length to maximize participation. In order to increase the validity of the answers, the questionnaire began with two open-ended questions focused on assessing the subject's familiarity level with consultants and consultancies. The independent constructs (Advice, Roles, Competencies, and Personal Characteristics) were linked to the dependent variable (Effectiveness) as a way of examining the connection between several personal attributes and performance.

The questionnaire was administered to four relevant categories of respondents: academics, consultants, the public, and clients of consultants (as noted earlier, only the first three categories are examined in the chapter). The questionnaires were administered by a master degree student for academics and consultants, and by two master students for the public. The

TABLE 12.2   Relevant Literature used in the Design of the Questionnaire

Advice	Literature
3.1 Provide clients with help	Kubr (2002); Schein (1990); Jang & Lee (1998); Wellington & Bryson (2001); Werr & Styhre (2003); Werr & Stjernberg (2003); Werr, Stjernberg & Docherty (1997); Turner (1982); Appelbaum & Steed (2005); Poulfelt & Payne (1994)
3.2 Analyze problems for client	
3.3 Give advice to client	
3.4 Be independent from client	
3.5 Base activities on expertise, tools and methods	
3.6 Implement solutions for/with client	
3.7 Intervening in the client's organization	
3.8 Discuss/solve strategic issues	
3.9 Work in collaboration with client	
3.10 Seize new (market)opportunities for clients	
3.11 Advise about short-term organizational issues	
3.12 Follow established procedures	

Competencies	Literature
5.1 Stress resistant	Appelbaum & Steed (2005); de Caluwé & Reitsma (2010); Sturdy (1997); Werr & Stjernberg (2003); ICMCI (2002); Kubr (2002) ; Clark (1995); Huczynski (1996); Whitley (1994); Fincham (1999); Werr & Styhre (2003); Clark & Salaman (1998); Wellington & Bryson (2001)
5.2 Good at planning	
5.3 Good at selling	
5.4 Results oriented	
5.5 Innovative	
5.6 Analytical	
5.7 Persuasive	
5.8 Able to create a good atmosphere	
5.9 Good at taking decisions	
5.10 Good at coaching	
5.11 Good at being dominant	
5.12 Good at using jargon	
5.13 Good at recycling solutions	
5.14 Good at avoiding accountability for bad advice	
5.15 Good at getting people fired	

Personal Characteristics	Literature
6.1 Is a workaholic	Kubr (2002); Werr & Stjernberg (2003); Bejan & de Man (2011)
6.2 Is curious	
6.3 Is a number cruncher/likes figures	
6.4 Is superficial	
6.5 Is manipulative	
6.6 Is motivated to improve the life of others	
6.7 Has backbone	
6.8 Is very experienced	
6.9 Is reflective	

(continued)

TABLE 12.2   Relevant Literature used in the Design of the Questionnaire (continued)

6.10   Is motivated by money
6.11   Likes variety in his/her work
6.12   Likes challenges
6.13   Likes over charging clients
6.14   Is arrogant
6.15   Is intelligent

Effectiveness	**Literature**
7.1 Helping organizations to grow and improve	Kubr (2002); Werr & Styhre
7.2 Improving financial performance of organizations	(2003); Appelbaum & Steed (2005); de Caluwé &
7.3 Helping with downsizing organizations	Stoppelenburg (2004); Philips
7.4 Fulfilling managers' spiritual needs	(2000); Kipping & Engwal (2002); Poulfelt & Payne (1994);
7.5 Helping with implementation of advice	Gable (1996); Casey (2004)
7.6 Realizing changes of behavior	

analysis of the questionnaires was done through SPSS statistical software. The data gathering and the interpretation of the results were part of the students' master theses. The interviews were recorded, transcribed (academics), or summarized (consultants) and coded for interpretation.

Reliability

Given the smaller sample size for academics and consultants, the assessment of the public's attitudes seems most reliable. The sample size for the public provides a 95% confidence level. The Cronbach's alphas (1951) for each construct are: Advice (0.755) and the value based on the standardized items is the highest achievable; Roles (0.676) on standardized items—after deleting components through SPSS, the alpha was still under 0.7, so we chose to eliminate the construct from our analysis for the time being; Competencies (0.728) based on standardized items with no possibility for improvement; Personal Characteristics (0.611) based on standardized items (through exploratory factor analysis several items were eliminated, leaving us with a component consisting of "superficial," "manipulative," "motivated by money," "likes to overcharge," and "arrogant," with a Cronbach's alpha for the newly created component of 0.858); and finally Effectiveness (0.7) after eliminating "brings spirituality in the organization."

MANAGEMENT CONSULTING: AN AMBIGUOUS IMAGE?

McKenna (2006), noting management consulting as the "the world's newest profession" (p. 163), cites Richard Paget, former partner of Booz Allen Hamilton, in his address to the firm's partners in 1958:

> Today, no one in our kind of work has to explain what he does. There are books written about us, we are the subjects of frequent articles, we have been honoured in numerous cartoons and stories, and serious groups even hold meetings to discuss how we can best be utilized. (p. 63)

Greiner and Ennsfellner (2010) mention that Marvin Bower, the founder of McKinsey & Co, once claimed that being hired by McKinsey gave a label of qualification significant enough for the employee to be called a professional consultant. But the phrases of even the most respected management consultants talking about their own profession are usually taken with a grain of salt.

Is management consulting a profession? Alvesson (1993) defines a profession as characterized by "systematic, scientifically-based theory, long formal education, autonomy, ethical rules, a distinct occupational culture, client-orientation, socially sanctioned and authorized" (p. 31). He concludes that management consulting falls short of these attributes and therefore does not fit the status of a profession. Many others (cf. Greiner & Ennsfellner, 2010; Kinard, 1995; Kubr, 2002; Rassam, 1998; Sahlin-Andersson & Engwall, 2002) disagree and acknowledge that even based on Alvesson's definition, management consulting fits the requirements. A substantial scientific body of knowledge has been formed over the years, with expertise coming from a broad range of fields and disciplines. This knowledge is being disseminated through explicit programs by an increasing number of educational institutions worldwide, such as Vrije Universiteit, Amsterdam, Newcastle University, Grenoble University, Pepperdine University, Erasmus University, and so forth. Furthermore, associations such as the International Council of Management Consulting Institutes (ICMCI) and its national partners are making efforts to formulate the body of knowledge and skills to clearly define the profession and create standards and codes of conduct and ethics.

Being a profession though does not ensure the quality and reliability of all those bearing the title of consultant. As Greiner and Ennsfellner (2010) point out, in the last decades there was an amazingly steep increase in the number of people who call themselves management consultants. Given this rapid increase, it is unlikely that quality stays the same, as there has been a similar increase in people who do not adhere to the standards and full meaning of the profession. Moreover, even being knowledgeable about the standards does not automatically mean following them. There is also no proof that higher professionalization produces better ethical behavior (O'Mahoney, 2010). As a result, it is not surprising that there is a body of literature that presents an unflattering picture of management consultants by using terms like systematic silencers (O'Shea & Madigan, 1998), charlatans (Bloomfield & Danieli, 1995) and demons (Pinault, 2001). Regarding claims of over-charging clients and that consultants can get away with inflating numbers in self-advantageous situations, Redekop and Heath (2007) note that "it is not that consultants are necessarily greedier than anyone else, it is only that they are in a unique position to capitalize on it" (p. 44).

The overall view of management consulting in the literature is more positive than the above and predominantly balanced. For example, McKenna (2006) and Ruef (found in Sahlin-Andersson & Engwall, 2002, p. 74) focus on the history and the important economic role of management consultancy in the 20th century. Milan Kubr (2002), in one of the most long-standing publications on the topic, offers a "guide to the profession," stating that one of the most important purposes of the consultant is to add value to the organization by having a "tangible and measurable contribution to achieving the client's principal purpose," but without forgetting about the ethical and professional guidelines that he needs in order to do so. Maister and his associates (Maister, Green, & Galford, 2000) argue that consultants are most successful when they are seen as "trusted advisors."

Poulfelt and Payne (1994) undertook an extensive analysis of several studies (Gattiker & Larwood, 1985; Greiner & Metzger, 1983; Kubr, 1986; Wilderom, 1990) and characterize the management consultant as having several roles or attributes: external catalyst and mediator, legitimizer, neutral bringer of solutions and resource, and a fresh (expert) pair of eyes. These findings are supported by the results of research done with the help of 87 companies from the *Financial Times'* 500 largest organizations (Wood, 2002). The researchers asked for the reasons why the respective companies used management consultants. At the top of the list was the expert knowledge brought by consultancies, while the remaining reasons are directly connected to Poulfelt and Payne's (1994) previous findings mentioned above. This portion of the literature paints quite a different picture of the management consultant.

Is Image Important for Consultants?

The reputation of a firm or an individual consultant is—among other factors—influenced by the image of the profession they represent. Research by Kipping (1999) and Dawes, Dowling, and Patterson (1992) shows that reputation is one of the main competitive advantages for a consulting firm, one of the main reasons why a particular firm is chosen, and the most important attribute that a consultant can develop in order to enhance his or her own business. Reputation comes from the sum of individual perceptions about the credibility, reliability, trustworthiness, responsibility (Fombrun, 1996, p. 72), and quality of work by the consultant.

A positive image also enhances the advice given by the consultant, leading to a higher degree of legitimacy (Kipping & Armbrüster, 2002), while an ambiguous or negative image can create confusion, skepticism and high resistance to the changes that the consultant proposes. As the image of the consultant is mainly a function of individual perception, a positive and an ambiguous image can coexist within a given case. For example, the top management of an organization can view consultants as expert helpers while the employees can perceive them as hired hands or legitimizers of unpleasant decisions. Whichever the case, the perception of the image of particular consultants can come from individual beliefs or experiences, but it is also influenced by the larger public's image of management consultants and the profession.

RESULTS AND DISCUSSION

This section presents the results of the three stakeholder analyses, drawing out the implications of the most important differences and similarities. The regressions for each category of respondents are reported in Tables 12.3 (Academics), 12.4 (Consultants) and 12.5 (the Public).

Advice

This construct was captured by the question "To what extent do you find the following items as central to the work of a consultant?" and the com-

TABLE 12.3 Regression Analysis: Academics

| | Coefficients[a] | | | | |
| | Unstandardized Coefficients | | Standardized Coefficients | | |
Model	B	Std. Error	Beta	*t*	Sig.
1 (Constant)	.417	.896		.465	.644
Activity Construct_1	.093	.190	.067	.490	.626
Role Construct_1	.424	.162	.419	2.614	.011
Competencies Construct_1	.338	.166	.266	2.038	.046
Personal Characteristics Construct_1	−.217	.171	−.150	−1.265	.211

[a] Dependent variable: Effectiveness

TABLE 12.4 Regression Analysis: Consultants

Model Summary

Model	R	R²	Adjusted R²	Std. Error of the Estimate
1	.657[a]	.432	.353	.47203

	Coefficients[b]				
	Unstandardized Coefficients		Standardized Coefficients		
Model	B	Std. Error	Beta	t	Sig.
1 (Constant)	.831	.765		1.086	.287
Advice	.470	.270	.442	1.744	.092
Roles	.371	.252	.316	1.471	.152
Competencies	−.561	.267	−.444	−2.105	.044
Personal Characteristics	.485	.233	.343	2.079	.047

[a] Predictors: (Constant), Personalcharacteristics, Roles, Competencies, Advice
[b] Dependent variable: Effectiveness

TABLE 12.5 Regression Analysis: Public

Model Summary

Model	R	R²	Adjusted R²	Std. Error of the Estimate
1	.486[a]	.236	.221	.52759

	Coefficients[b]					Collinearity Statistics	
	Unstandardized Coefficients		Standardized Coefficients				
Model	B	Std. Error	Beta	t	Sig.	Tolerance	VIF
1 (Constant)	.829	.401		2.068	.040		
Advice	.320	.095	.271	3.355	.001	.608	1.645
Roles	.263	.095	.217	2.758	.006	.642	1.557
Competencies	.104	.114	.077	.918	.360	.560	1.786
Personal Characteristics	.075	.105	.052	.714	.476	.738	1.355

[a] Dependent variable: Effectiveness

parative mean scores are summarized in Table 12.6. Overall, this construct seemed fairly stable in that there appears to be a relative consensus when it comes to what a consultant's work involves and implies. Providing clients with help and advice (items 3.1, 3.3) and analyzing their problems based on expertise, methods, and tools (items 3.2, 3.5) were the highest

TABLE 12.6 Mean Scores for "Advice"

		Academics	Consultants	Public
3.1	Provide clients with help	4.40	4.53	4.33
3.2	Analyze problems for client	4.43	4.41	4.43
3.3	Give advice to client	4.63	4.65	4.57
3.4	Be independent from client	3.87	4.09	3.75
3.5	Base activities on expertise, tools and methods	4.14	4.06	4.01
3.6	Implement solutions for/with client	3.67	3.56	3.82
3.7	Intervening in the client's organization	3.35	3.50	3.21
3.8	Discuss/solve strategic issues	3.81	3.50	3.76
3.9	Work in collaboration with client	4.05	4.18	3.97
3.10	Seize new (market)opportunities for clients	3.75	2.85	3.43
3.11	Advise about short-term organizational issues	3.89	3.12	3.44
3.12	Follow established procedures	2.75	2.41	2.95

Key: 5-point scale.

scoring activities. Independence, which was considered central to management consulting by eight of the interviewed consultants, as well as in the literature (Greiner & Metzger, 1983; Kubr, 2002) and by the International Council of Management Consulting Institutes (ICMCI), also scored high in this section.

All three categories of respondents scored "following established procedures" (item 3.12) the lowest. Interestingly, the consultants themselves rated it as least describing the service they provide, which suggests that maintaining the status quo does not go hand-in-hand with consultancy work. We can relate this to Clegg et al's (Clegg, Kornberger, & Rhodes, 2004) "parasitic" view on consulting.

There are two areas where we can see the most notable differences in the mean results across the three populations. First, academics consider more than consultants that the advice given goes towards seizing new (market) opportunities for clients (item 3.10). An explanation for this difference could be that the consultants do not see facilitating market opportunities as part of advice giving per se but rather as a potential result. Regarding advice focusing on short-term organizational issues (item 3.11), there is another gap between the opinions of the consultants and the academics. As we see here, academics state that consultants are likely to offer short-term solutions, which are easier to quantify and in many cases are preferred by corporations (Ittner & Larker, 2003). Consultants, in contrast, feel they are less involved in giving short-term advice than external observers think. In both cases, the perception of the public finds itself in the middle.

Competencies

The comparative mean scores for this construct can be seen in Table 12.7. There was a high degree of consensus among the participants about the relevant and required competencies for a consultant. Analytical skills (item 5.6), orientation towards results (5.4), resilience to stress (5.1), and planning abilities (5.2) are seen as of paramount importance by all three stakeholder groups. One of the academic interviewers took the "analytical skills" competence one step further, noting that, in his opinion, "an academic attitude and an academic level of thinking and working... are essential for a consultant." The rigor of a consultant's actions was brought into the discussion by another professor, who described the consultants as "able to adapt quickly" but questioned "whether that has enough depth." While the other items seem intuitive, resilience to stress has been dealt with in the literature. The "ideal" consultant has been described as someone who is able to work long hours, is willing to travel on short notice, and has very little free time for anything but work (cf. Ibarra, 1999; Meriläinen, Tienari, Thomas, & Davies, 2004; Werr, 1999). Kärreman and Alvesson (2004) even claim that working long hours is for many consultants seen as a reflection of "being the best."

Academics also consider sales abilities (item 5.3) to be of a greater importance than consultants. In the interviews, the academics considered communication abilities as very significant in the consultant role. The literature

TABLE 12.7   Mean Scores for "Competencies"

		Academics	Consultants	Public
5.1	Stress resistant	4.13	4.41	4.08
5.2	Good at planning	3.97	4.06	4.05
5.3	Good at selling	3.65	3.12	3.24
5.4	Results oriented	4.37	4.21	4.36
5.5	Innovative	3.95	3.97	4.07
5.6	Analytical	4.44	4.47	4.34
5.7	Persuasive	3.59	3.21	3.29
5.8	Able to create a good atmosphere	3.86	4.03	3.62
5.9	Good at taking decisions	3.48	3.65	3.52
5.10	Good at coaching	4.05	3.85	3.82
5.11	Good at being dominant	2.46	2.18	2.54
5.12	Good at using jargon	2.62	2.09	2.73
5.13	Good at recycling solutions	3.56	2.71	3.36
5.14	Good at avoiding accountability for bad advice	2.87	1.62	2.44
5.15	Good at getting people fired	2.43	1.53	1.74

Key: 5-point scale

also acknowledges rhetoric and sales abilities as an important part of the profession (e.g., Kubr, 2002). However, the reason for which scholars assign a greater importance to this competency may also be found in parts of academic literature. This particular body of literature considers that rhetoric is not only a logical part of the profession but also a tool for turning managers into "victim-buyers" of consulting services (Werr & Styhre, 2003, p. 46).

A similar pattern appears with regard to the more negative traits. Academics assign a considerably higher value to the ability to recycle solutions (item 5.13) and getting people fired (5.15) than the consultants, with the public opinion between the academics and consultants. However, in the case of avoiding accountability (5.14) there is a considerably more negative image from both the public and the academics than the perception of consultants about themselves.

Personal Characteristics

The comparative mean scores for this construct are summarized in Table 12.8. The trend seen in the previous constructs persists here as well with regard to the negative characteristics: academics and the public consider that financial motivation (item 6.3) is important for the people working in the profession. It is therefore not a surprise that "overcharging clients" (item 6.4) is also considered by academics as significant. This opinion is visibly milder than that expressed in literature by other scholars (e.g., Bloomfield & Danieli, 1995; Redekop & Heath, 2007) who consider consultants as charlatans—they are able to overcharge clients because of the intangible nature of their work and the difficulty in valuing it. Another reason for this perception raised by several consultants in the study concerns the lack of transparency. This is a plausible explanation, especially since most top consulting firms have very strict confidentiality policies regarding their clients and their fees. Over the decades, this practice has given birth to countless speculations about extremely high fees, especially when the projects were

TABLE 12.8 Mean Scores for "Personal Characteristics"[a]

		Academics	Consultants	Public
6.1	Is superficial	2.37	1.47	2.05
6.2	Is manipulative	2.21	1.76	2.24
6.3	Is motivated by money	2.67	1.94	2.33
6.4	Likes over charging clients	2.75	1.85	2.14
6.5	Is arrogant	2.52	1.44	1.91

Key: 5-point Scale
[1] New component after item elimination subsequent to EFA.

seen as unsuccessful (e.g., Swissair's Hunter Strategy started by McKinsey, analyzed by Knorr & Arndt, 2003).

It is important to note that difficulties in measuring the value of consulting assignments for their clients cannot only be seen as an advantage for consultants. As Johnston (1963) has observed, it is not unusual that the expected results do not appear because the management of the company did not implement, accept or follow-up on the advice that the consultants were paid for.

Arrogance (item 6.1) and superficiality (6.5) are the last two negative attributes that academics assign to consultants more than the other two respondent groups. This view seems to reflect the distance between universities and practitioners (Gulati, 2007) and the reality that some practitioners exclude completely the possibility of getting information from academic research papers (see Rynes, Colbert, & Brown, 2002; Wenger, McDermott, & Snyder, 2002). In the interviews conducted, one of the academics noted that "from my scientific point of view, reasonably superficial research is being done at consultants."

Drawing on the literature critical of management consulting, Werr and Styhre (2003) point to the presence of "manipulation in order to create impression of value" (p. 49) in several publications. Among the three study populations, the public was most likely to view consultants as "manipulative" (item 6.2). Nevertheless, the value of the item was low enough to question many of the claims of the literature that critique management consulting.

One of the academic interviewees highlighted the fact that "a good consultant should be able to reflect, and with that [reflection] to develop practical coded knowledge." However, the creation of coded knowledge—or theories—is, at the moment, a main characteristic of the business scientist. We can therefore see the emergence of a "hybrid" professional—one who combines the practicality of the business world with the thoroughness of the academic world (Bejan, 2010).

Effectiveness

The comparative mean scores can be seen in Table 12.9. As mentioned before, the effectiveness of management consultants is not always easy to measure, especially when the clients do not engage in the implementation of their advice. According to the majority of the consultants that were interviewed for this study, they underscored that work should always bring value to the client. The "effectiveness" construct shows us in what ways consultants are seen as being most and least effective on bringing value to organizations. The consultants, backed by the public, see themselves as most effective on helping organizations grow and improve (item 7.1), while the

TABLE 12.9 Mean Scores for "Effectiveness"[a]

Effectiveness	Academics	Consultants	Public
7.1 Helping organizations to grow and improve	3.02	4.15	4.04
7.2 Improving financial performance of organizations	2.98	3.21	3.65
7.3 Helping with downsizing organizations	3.33	3.74	3.68
7.4 Helping with implementation of advice	2.94	3.62	3.64
7.5 Realizing changes of behavior	2.79	3.82	3.54

Key: 5-point scale
[a] New component after item elimination subsequent to EFA.

academics considered that "helping with downsizing organizations" (7.3) was the most relevant.

Overall taking all six items into consideration, the consultants and the public have a visibly more positive opinion about the effectiveness of management consultants than scholars. Not surprisingly, the consultants see themselves as being most influential in changing organizations and even people's behaviors (item 7.5).

LIMITATIONS, REFLECTION AND RECOMMENDATIONS

As evidenced by the preceding discussion, the term "management consultant" still lacks a clear definition and clear boundaries. The title itself is often overused, and, as reflected by the questionnaire results, there are highly subjective images of the role and nature of the management consultant.

Limitations

One of the biggest limitations of this joint research project is the different sample size of the categories. The samples for academics (63) and consultants (34) are significantly smaller than the public sample (400). Another limitation is that no distinction was made between the different types of management consultants who participated in the research. A temporary limitation for the overall comparative study is that the research involving the clients is still ongoing. We trust that when that will be complete, the results will reveal a more ample perspective on consultants and their role.

REFLECTION AND RECOMMENDATIONS

The gap between academia and practice is once again obvious through the results of this study. Overall, academics had the worst opinion about consultants. Governments, professional associations and individuals are emphasizing the increasing need for collaboration and knowledge exchange between academia and practice. Yet, although the resulting benefits are promising and they might influence much more than just the two fields, the shift in mutual perception between academics and practitioners is happening very slowly, if at all. Management consulting is a practical, highly-intensive knowledge producing discipline and a diffuser of expertise and knowledge. Academia also produces knowledge, but of a different kind. In order to cooperate effectively, the image that both categories have about each other must improve. The consultants need to be less skeptical about the value of university research and move towards using evidence-based knowledge in their work. On the other hand, academics must create increasingly relevant results and guidance for practice.

In the Netherlands, an increasing number of people are playing a role in both practice and academic science, focusing on management, consultancy, and change. These individuals are referred to as "hybrids." They are closing the practice-scholarship gap in many cases through their ability to pose better questions to their clients, improve the quality of studies in practice, and train and coach their colleagues. But they have been less successful in changing the direction of the scientific community. Through its structure, its specific career model (with strong emphasis on publications in scientific journals), the silos of disciplines and ongoing specialization, the sciences continue to enlarge the gap with practice. There is also skepticism about the motivation of the other group. As one of the academics interviewed for this study noted, "you often notice that they [consultants] want to extract knowledge from you and quickly run off with it. I think that is very annoying!" Thus, the manner of collaboration itself must also improve and attract a less reluctant attitude towards sharing knowledge.

Based on the questionnaire data, it appears that the public's view of consultants is not a negative one. Overall, it is slightly closer to the one that consultants have of themselves than to that of the academics. But this does not need to be taken for granted. One notable exception to this fairly positive view is that, more than the other two stakeholder groups, the public considers consultants as manipulative. In the past year we have seen news of a former executive partner of a top strategy consultancy being arrested on insider charges in the U.S., a large consulting group facing ethical judgments about a confidential public relations contract with the former Libyan ruler, and the prime minister of the Netherlands declaring that the government should rely on less consulting. Management consulting's image—the perceived presence and nature of management consultants—is a critical component of the role that consultants will ultimately play.

REFERENCES

Alvesson, M. (1993). Organizations as rhetoric: Knowledge-intensive firms and the struggle with ambiguity. *Journal of Management Studies, 30*(6), 997–1015.

Appelbaum, S. H., & Steed, A. J. (2005). The critical success factors in the client-consulting relationship. *Journal of Management Development, 24*(1), 68–93.

Bejan, V. (2010). *The role of scholar-consultants in a large scale transformational change: Linking business and science and mapping the knowledge gap.* Unpublished Master's thesis, Vrije Universiteit Amsterdam.

Bejan, V., & de Man, A. P. (2011). De achterhaalde adviseur [The out-dated adviser]. *Management en Consulting, 5*, 15–17.

Block, P. (1981). *Flawless consulting: A guide to getting your expertise used* (1st ed.). Austin, TX: Learning Concepts.

Bloomfield, B. P., & Danieli, A. (1995). The role of management consultants in the development of information technology: The indissoluble nature of socio-political and technical skills. *Journal of Management Studies, 32*(1), 23–46.

Buono, A. F., & Poulfelt F. (Eds.). (2009). *Client-consultant collaboration: Coping with complexity and change.* Charlotte, NC: Information Age Publishing.

Casey, C. (2004). Bureaucracy enchanted? Spirit, experts and authority in organizations. *School of Business and Economics, 11*(1), 59–79.

Clark, T. (1995). *Managing consultants: Consultancy as the management of impressions.* Buckingham: Open University Press.

Clark, T., & Salaman, J. (1996). The management guru as organizational witch doctor. *Organization, 3*(1), 85–107.

Clegg, S. R., Kornberger, M., & Rhodes, C. (2004). Noise, parasites and translation: Theory and practice in management consulting. *Management Learning, 35*(1), 31–44.

Creswell, J. W., Plano Clark, V. L., Gutman, M. L., & Hanson, W. E. (2003). Advanced mixed methods research designs. In A. Tashakkori & C. Teddlie (Eds.), *Handbook of mixed methods in social & behavioral research.* Thousand Oaks, CA: Sage.

Cronbach, L. J. (1951). Coefficient alpha and the interval structure of tests. *Psychometrika, 16*(3), 297–334.

Daniels, J. D. (1991). Relevance in international business research: A need for more linkages. *Journal of International Business Studies, 22*(2), 177–186.

Dawes, P. L., Dowling, G. R., & Patterson, P. G. (1992). Criteria used to select management consultants. *Industrial Marketing Management, 21*(3), 187–193.

de Caluwé, L., & Reitsma, E., (2010). Competencies of management consultants: A research study of senior management consultants. In A. F. Buono & D. W. Jamieson (Eds.), *Consultation for organizational change* (pp. 15–40). Charlotte, NC: Information Age Publishing.

de Caluwé, L., & Stoppelenburg, A. (2004, June). *Developing criteria for effectiveness of consultant's work.* Second International Conference on Management Consulting, Lausanne, Switzerland.

Dodgson, M. (1993). Learning, trust and technological collaboration. *Human Relations, 46*, 77–94.

Fincham, R. (1999). The consultant-client relationship: Critical perspectives on the management of organizational change. *Journal of Management Studies, 36*(3), 335–351.

Fombrun, C. J. (1996). *Reputation: Realizing value from the corporate image.* Boston, MA: Harvard Business School Press.

Gable, G. G. (1996). A multidimensional model of client success when engaging external consultants. *Management Science, 42*(8), 1175–1198.

Gattiker, U. E., & Larwood, L. (1985). Why do clients employ management consultants? *Consultation* (Summer), 119–129.

Greiner, L., & Ennsfellner, I. (2010). Management consultants as professionals, or are they? *Organizational Dynamics, 39*(1), 72–83.

Greiner, L. E., & Metzger, R. O. (1983). *Consulting to management.* Englewood Cliffs, NJ: Prentice-Hall.

Gulati, R. (2007). Tent poles, tribalism, and boundary spanning: The rigor-relevance debate in management research. *Academy of Management Journal, 50*(4), 775–782.

Huczynski, A. A. (1996). *Influencing within organisations.* London: Prentice Hall.

Ibarra, H. (1999). Provisional selves: Experimenting with image and identity in professional adaptation. *Administrative Science Quarterly, 44,* 764–791.

Ittner, C. D., & Larker, D. F. (2003). Coming up short on nonfinancial performance. *Harvard Business Review, 81,* 88–95.

International Council of Management Consulting Institutes. (2002). *The common body of knowledge.* Retrieved from http://www.icmci.org

Jang, Y., & Lee, J. (1998). Factors influencing the success of management consulting projects. *International Journal of Project Management, 16*(2), 67–72.

Johnston, J. (1963). The productivity of management consultants. *Journal of the Royal Statistical Society, 126*(2), 237–249.

Kärreman, D., & Alvesson, M. (2004). Cages in tandem: Management control, social identity, and identification in a knowledge-intensive firm. *Organization, 11,* 149–175.

Kieser, A., & Leiner, L. (2009). Why the rigour & relevance gap in management research is unbridgeable. *Journal of Management Studies, 46*(3), 516–533.

Kinard, J. C. (1995). The management consulting profession and consulting services. In S. W. Barcus & J. W. Wilkinson (Eds.), *Handbook of management consulting services* (pp. 1–20). New York, NY: McGraw-Hill.

Kipping, M. (1999). American management consulting companies in Western Europe, 1920 to 1990: Products, reputation, and relationships. *Business History Review, 73*(2), 190–220.

Kipping, M., & Armbrüster, T. (2002). The burden of otherness: Limits of consultancy interventions in historical case studies. In M. Kipping & L. Engwall (Eds.), *Management consulting: Emergence and dynamics of a knowledge industry.* New York, NY: Oxford University Press.

Kipping, M., & Engwall, L. (Eds.) (2002). *Management consulting: Emergence and dynamics of a knowledge industry.* Oxford: Oxford University Press.

Knorr, A., & Arndt, A. (2003). *Swissair's collapse: An economic analysis.* Bremen: Institute for World Economics and International Management. Retrieved from http://www.iwim.uni-bremen.de/publikationen/pdf/W028.pdf

Kubr, M. (1986). *Management consulting: A guide to the profession* (2nd ed.). Geneva, Switzerland: International Labour Office.

Kubr, M. (2002). *Management consulting: A guide to the profession.* Geneva: International Labour Organization.

Maister D., Green, C., & Galford, R. (2000). *The trusted advisor.* New York, NY: The Free Press.

McKenna, C. D. (2006). *The world's newest profession: Management consulting in the twentieth century.* Cambridge: Cambridge University Press.

Meriläinen, S., Tienari, J., Thomas, R., & Davies, A. (2004). Management consultant talk: A cross-cultural comparison of normalizing discourse and resistance *Organization, 11,* 539–564.

O'Mahoney, J. (2010). *Management consultancy.* New York, NY: Oxford University Press.

O'Shea, J., & Madigan, C. (1998). *Dangerous company: Management consultants and the businesses they save and ruin.* New York, NY: Penguin Books

Philips, J. (2000). *The consultant's scorecard.* New York, NY: McGraw Hill.

Pinault, L. (2001). *Consulting demons: Inside the world of global corporate consulting.* New York, NY: Harper-Collins.

Plunkett Research. (2011). *Industry statistics.* Retrieved from http://www.plunkett research.com/consulting-market-research/industry-statistics

Poulfelt, F., & Payne, A. (1994). Management consultants: Client and consultant perspectives. *Scandinavian Journal of Management, 10*(4), 421–436.

Quinn, R. E., & Rohrbaugh, J. (1983). A spatial model of effectiveness criteria: Towards a competing values approach to organizational analysis. *Management Science, 29*(3), 363–377.

Rassam, C. (1998). Presenting advice and solutions. In P. Sadler (Ed.), *Management consulting: A handbook of best practice.* London: Kogan Page Limited.

Redekop, B. W., & Heath, B. L. (2007). A brief examination of the nature, contexts, and causes of unethical consultant behaviors. *Journal of Practical Consulting, 1*(2), 40–50.

Rynes, S. L., Colbert, A. E., & Brown, K. G. (2002). HR professionals' beliefs about effective human resource practices: Correspondence between research and practice. *Human Resource Management, 41,* 149–174.

Sahlin-Andersson, K., & Engwall, L. (Eds.). (2002). *The expansion of management knowledge.* Palo Alto, CA: Stanford University Press.

Saunders, M., Lewis, P., & Thornhill, A., (2009). *Research methods for business students.* Essex, England: Pearson Education.

Schein, E. H. (1990). A general philosophy of helping: Process consultation. *Sloan Management Review, 31*(3), 57–64.

Sturdy, A. (1997). The consultancy process: An insecure business? *Journal of Management Studies, 34*(3), 389–413.

Turner, J. C. (1982). Towards a cognitive redefinition of the social group. In H. Tajfel (Ed.), *Social identity and intergroup relations.* Cambridge: Cambridge University Press.

Wellington, C., & Bryson, J. (2001). At face value? Image consultancy, emotional labour and professional work. *Sociology, 35*(4), 933–946.

Wenger, E., McDermott, R., & Snyder, W. M. (2002). *Cultivating communities of practice.* Boston, MA: Harvard Business School Press.

Werr, A. (1999). *The language of change: The roles of methods in the work of management consultants.* Unpublished doctoral dissertation, Stockholm, School of Economics/EFI.

Werr, A., & Styhre, A. (2003). Management consultants: Friend or foe? Understanding the ambiguous client-consultant relationship. *International Studies of Management and Organization, 32*(4), 43–66.

Werr, A., & Stjernberg, T. (2003). Exploring management consulting firms as knowledge systems. *Organization Studies, 24*, 881–908.

Werr, A., Stjernberg, T., & Docherty, P. (1997). The functions of methods of change in management consulting. *Journal of Organizational Change Management, 10*(4), 288–307.

Whitley, R. (1994). The internationalisation of firms and markets. *Organization, 1*(1), 101–124.

Wilderom, C. P. M. (1990). Management consulting in Holland: Professional issues and prospects. *Consultation, 9*(1), 51–61.

Wood, P. (2002). The rise of consultancy and the prospect for regions. In T. Clark & R. Fincham (Eds.), *Critical consulting: New perspectives on the management advice industry* (pp. 50–74). Oxford, UK, Blackwell Publishers.

van Workum, R. (2011). *The image of consultants in newspapers.* Unpublished Master's thesis, Vrije Universiteit Amsterdam.

CHAPTER 13

ORGANIZATIONAL IDENTITY CHANGE THROUGH INTERNATIONAL EXPANSION

The Case of a Scandinavian Consulting Firm's Encounter with India

Flemming Poulfelt, Kåre Christiansen, and Irene Skovgaard Smith

Management consulting continues to be a booming global business, despite the industry-wide crisis from 2008 to 2010 that dampened the growth rates experienced the years before. Indeed, it seems that there are prospects for recovery for the consulting arena, as optimism and growth are predicted once again (Management Consultancy Association, n.d.). Today the management consulting industry is a large and worldwide business, with estimated total revenues of more than $250 billion (in 2010) and a promising future as more growth is expected. Among the key drivers for this development are (1) an increased complexity in business, (2) new emergent markets, (3) emphasis on outsourcing and off-shoring, (4) changes driven by technology and deregulation, and (5) major reforms in the public sector.

Exploring the Professional Identity of Management Consultants, pages 265–282
Copyright © 2013 by Information Age Publishing
All rights of reproduction in any form reserved.

When consulting as a business took off after the Second World War, it was primarily domestic expansion. This pattern has changed dramatically, and a significant part of the business today is global in terms of revenues, clients, and the consultants themselves. The major trigger for internationalizing the consulting industry took place during the post-World War II period. As a part of the Marshall Plan, American manufacturing companies began to internationalize their operations by exporting to and setting up subsidiaries in Europe. During these activities, consulting firms also started to move to Europe to be with their clients. For example, when McKinsey & Co. entered Europe in 1950s it was because they wanted to follow their clients and capitalize on Marshall Plan aid, as well as explore new opportunities, which Marvin Bower, the managing partner at that time, referred to as "geographic entrepreneurialism" (Berry, 1988). By 1970, roughly 70 U.S. firms worked in or had established offices in Europe, and as Nees (1986) reflected, "more and more management consulting businesses [were] moving their business abroad, so many in fact, that the consulting industry has become quite international" (p. 18).

During the subsequent period, many consulting firms expanded globally, transforming their practices from a national platform into firms with offices on many continents and creating large global consulting firms. However, the established global players are not the only ones who have embarked on a journey of internationalizing their practices. An abundance of firms of various sizes, across nations and type of businesses, have spent many resources and much energy in their attempt to enter and succeed in the international arena. For many of these firms, the road has been difficult and bumpy, as stretching a business across borders is often far more complicated and demanding than expected. Various cultural differences and traditions impact cooperation between different countries and their organizations. For instance, knowledge sharing and knowledge transfer seem that much more complicated when an international flavor is added (see Werr & Stjernberg, 2003; Hitt, Bierman, Uhlenbruck & Shimizu, 2006). The goals for achieving scale economies have also proven more difficult than expected, thus hurting the level of profitability for a number of consulting firms. This problem could be related to size, as studies show that size is important for success in international markets (Winch, 2008). Finally the issue of trust and the obstacles for developing trust in the process of internationalizing professional service firms has also been a challenge for many firms (Rogers & Tierny, 2004).

Today there is a (new) move as a number of major national firms with a regional presence are expanding their operations in order to be able to support their clients when they move further away or outsource or off-shore activities. Examples include European consulting firms moving to China or India to service their clients in the process of outsourcing operations.

The purpose of this chapter is to explore, illustrate, and reflect on how a Scandinavian consulting firm managed its transition to a new cultural context—in India—examining the ramifications this process has for organizational identity and the internationalization of consulting. The discussion and the analysis are based on a number of assumptions. First it is assumed that the classic type of entry strategy has to be rethought, as consulting is a service business and the resources to be deployed are limited. This dynamic means that the firm has to consider alternative ways of setting up a new practice compared with the traditional models of internationalization. One classic example is the Uppsala School (Johanson & Wiedersheim-Paul, 1975; Johanson & Vahlne, 1977). This framework deals with acquisition, in other words, learning, focusing on how organizations learn and how this learning affects their subsequent investment behavior. Among the assumptions are that firms start to (and continue to) invest in one or a few neighboring countries rather than investing in distant markets and/or several markets simultaneously. Closer markets are those that are perceived to be geographically or conceptually proximate, where the extent of knowledge and the comfort level are higher. Another model of internationalization is by Pearlmutter (1969), who introduces a scheme for categorizing MNC internationalization processes as ethnocentric, polycentric or geocentric. However, the premise in the chapter is that these models do not capture the way in which professional service firms enter a foreign market.

Second, within the focus of our case study, it is assumed that the practice of consulting and the processes involved need to be reconsidered in an Eastern context, as a major driver in consulting is the contextual setting. As such, the idea of "reversed consulting" will be explored as a new way of approaching consulting instead of merely trying to implant a Western/Scandinavian model. The implications of moving away from the traditional focus on the West leading the East will be explored, and the analysis will delve into how integrated approaches can be developed and utilized, which might also inspire and change Western management and consulting models.

Third, it is assumed that the internationalization of a national consulting firm has major implications for organizational identity. An extraordinary event in a firm's history, such as Valcon's entry in India and the changes it involves, are likely to prompt intensified identity work (Jenkins, 2004). Such an event, which represents both rupture and an encounter with cultural "others," triggers key identification processes concerned with who "we" are and how "we" are both similar and different from other consulting firms.

SETTING THE SCENE

Internationalization within consulting has taken place since the early 1950s. At the same time, it is also apparent that a global segmentation process has taken place, with the management consulting industry being classified in three basic tiers of internationalization:

> **Tier 1:** The major global consulting firms (e.g., McKinsey, BCG, Booz Allen, A. T. Kearney, IBM Consulting, Cap Gemini, Accenture)
>
> **Tier 2:** Major national firms with some regional presence
>
> **Tier 3:** Small- and medium-sized national consulting firms with limited or no international outlook

Although Tier 1 firms have been operating on a global scale for years, Tier 2 and Tier 3 firms operate more on a regional and domestic basis. Today, however, there is a move where some Tier 2 firms are expanding their operations internationally in order to be able to support their clients. Valcon, the company that is the focus of the chapter, belongs to this group of Tier 2 firms—and establishing a new office 4,000 miles away in a totally different business context was a big leap in the expansion of the firm.

The Indian Management Consulting Market

The Indian Consulting Industry has been growing at a rapid pace in recent years. This development is largely due to the fact that there has been considerable increase in the number of newcomers in this as well as an increase in the use of consultants by client organizations. In total the Asia Pacific consulting industry generated $33.5 billion as revenues in 2008 and is expected to reach $39.2 billion by 2012—in essence, the industry will grow at a compound annual growth rate of 4% (Consultgenie, 2009). Of these total revenues, India represents 5.4%, equal to $1.8 billion in 2008 and $2.12 billion in 2012. Compared with some of the other Asian consulting markets, for instance Japan and China, the Indian market is still in its premature stage.

Among the services offered, corporate strategy, outsourcing services, human resource management, and operations management have become the prominent business divisions in the Indian consulting market. Regarding strategy consulting, the big and established players dominate the market with nearly three-fourths of the market share, leaving a relatively small share for upcoming firms.

The largest concentration of consultancy organizations is in the four metropolitan cities: Delhi (25.7%) has the highest number of consultancies, followed by Mumbai (25.5%), Chennai (12.1%), and Calcutta (9.1%). The main driver for consulting services has been the growing maturity of Indian industry, which has impacted the expansion of the consulting industry in terms of both size and service offerings. In addition, specialist consulting advice is being sought by Indian clients, further opening the opportunity for a number of specialist organizations to draw on their expert knowledge base and resources to meet the demand for these services (Rathore, 2010). The market itself is characterized by tough competition, and it is more or less a buyer's market, consisting primarily of the big global players and an abundance of local firms of various sizes. When it comes to other types of firms, representation in India is fairly limited, especially regarding firms from Europe.

The major strengths of Indian consulting organizations include professional competence, low cost structure, diverse capabilities, high adaptability, and quick learning capability, whereas its major weaknesses, which has hindered the export growth of the country's consulting sector, are low quality assurance, low local presence overseas, low equity base, lack of market intelligence, and low level of research and development (R&D) (Rathore, 2010). It is in this environment that the Danish consultancy Valcon decided to establish a new operation.

THE VALCON CASE

The following analysis is based on a single case study (Yin, 2003) conducted primarily through participant observation by the second author, documentary and archival information he had access to as a managing partner in the consulting firm (Valcon A/S), and his key role in the establishment of consulting activities in India. The study is aimed at offering an in-depth description of the relatively unexplored and context-specific phenomenon of the internationalization of a Tier 2 consulting firm.

According to Yin (2003), the strengths of using participant observation are related to the fact that events are followed and experienced in real time and in context. It can also provide valuable insight into interpersonal behavior and motives because the researcher is also a participant in the events under study. The strengths of documentary and archival sources (such as emails and other written communication, minutes from meetings, reports, and so forth) are related to their stable and unobtrusive character, potentially broad coverage, detail, and exactness (Yin, 2003). A distinctive feature of our study in relation to both sources of data is the extensive level of access that only a full participant in the role as key decision maker could have achieved in this organizational setting.

The case company Valcon (www.valcon.dk) is a Scandinavian company with offices in Denmark, Sweden, and Norway, and international offices in the Czech Republic, India, and China. The consultancy employs more than 150 people. Value creation is the cornerstone of the firm, and its specialist competencies and experienced consultants lay the foundation for creating solutions that work—and ensure innovation and added value for the customers (see Appendix 1 for additional information about Valcon A/S).

FINDINGS

This part of the chapter explores Valcon's entry and work in India for Danish subsidiaries and local companies. The case description is organized into four sections related to the four main themes identified in the case. Each section concludes with a discussion of the theme in terms of the lessons from Valcon's experience in India.

Client Pull for Internationalization: Entering the Indian Consulting Market

Expanding Valcon's business outside Scandinavia was a topic that was discussed many times in the company. Many of Valcon's customers had established operations abroad, its customers were doing a lot of sourcing work in China, and several clients were setting up manufacturing plants in China. The most advanced activities included the initial outsourcing of white collar work to India. The dilemma for Valcon was obvious—how could the firm advise its customers on their internationalization processes when the company had not gone through that process on its own. The problem was not to answer the "why" question. Significant market potential and cost advantage in both China and India made it rather easy to answer the why question. The real challenge was the "how" question—*how* could the market potential be explored and *how* could the organization benefit from the underlying cost advantages. Finding answers to these "how" questions was not easy—and Valcon gradually realized that it could not provide enough value to their customers without a deeper understanding of China and India. Facilitating strategy projects was seen as simply not good enough. It was clear that hands-on experience was needed—advice based on Google research would fall well short of client expectations and needs.

Valcon knew that starting from scratch was hard work—the firm's members had tried that when entering the Swiss market. Starting in a new market without customers was seen as a definite challenge, so Valcon decided to wait for the opportunity to accompany one of its clients. That chance came. Valcon had worked for a number of years with a large global engineering company headquartered in Denmark. Valcon's role had been to help streamline the firm's Danish engineering operations. The client's strategy called for a significant part of their engineering work to be carried out in India. As such, they had established a large engineering center in India to support the firm's project centers in Europe and the U.S. The work to be carried out in India would be part of the global engineering process.

Having trained the Danish organization in process optimization and lean thinking was suddenly not enough. Valcon had to find ways to develop the Indian organization as well. It was obvious from the start that it was not a project that could be executed in a couple of months—it was conceived as a project where the customer would need support for many years. Sending Danish consultants to India for an extended period, of course, was an option—but it would be very expensive for the client. The other concern was whether Valcon could deploy their "lean box" to India without any real localization.

As a result of these concerns an open discussion with the client both in Denmark and India ensued, and it was agreed that the best option was to set up a legal company in India and build a consultant team there as well. The client offered to help, seemed happy with the decision, and quickly got underway, with localized Valcon services at an Indian cost level.

In reflecting on Valcon's process of entering the Indian consulting market, it is interesting to note the decisive role one particular client played in creating the pull that prompted Valcon to expand its operations. Rather than adopting a conventional internationalization strategy of following one's clients as they globalize, a long-term client requested Valcon's assistance, further supporting the consultancy through the recruitment and development of local consultants. The client not only prompted Valcon to enter the Indian consulting market, but also offered to take on significant responsibilities in the development of Valcon as their Indian consultancy supplier. The client wanted a supplier in India with Valcon's specific mindset and approach, but they also wanted a localized service delivered by Indian consultants and at an Indian cost level.

Valcon's entry strategy became one of recruiting and developing local talent in India in a rare and unique partnership with a client, which set the agenda for Valcon's internationalization in significant ways. Most importantly the client's insistence on localization, compared to the traditional logic of internationalization based on exporting Western consulting services to emerging economies, set the foundation for the evolution of an integrated approach, which would be essentially both Scandinavian and Indian in nature.

"Coming of Age" in India: Learning to Compete for Talent

The second author of the chapter is the Valcon partner who went to India to start the recruitment of consultants as previously mentioned. The recruitment process began in the classic way by defining the required profiles and asking the recruiting company to suggest candidates. When Valcon began the interview process they quickly learned a couple of things. Firstly, that there were extremely qualified people available—people born and educated in India, who had the necessary global profiles from working in international companies. Interviews were carried out with people with rich experience from many years of work in setting up plants and building supply chains for companies like Toyota, Ford, Nokia, Saint Gobain, and so forth. However, Valcon soon realized that they were not the only ones looking for talent.

In Scandinavia, Valcon is a brand, which in essence means that potential new consultants had to "sell" their competences to Valcon. Valcon is the buyer, in other words. In India, the roles were reversed. Valcon had to be sold to potential candidates, which was a new experience. It became clear that Valcon had to answer a different question—instead of simply asking "What can Valcon do for Scandinavian companies in India?" the company had to focus on what Valcon could do for India. A particular incident made it apparent that Valcon had to do a much better job on that exercise.

One of the consultants came to Valcon with a very clear message. The father of his fiancée would not let him marry his daughter, as he did not consider management consulting to be a decent occupation for his future son-in-law. Moreover, he could not see the value in working for a Scandinavian company instead of a large Indian-based corporation. This was a wake-up call—a wake-up call that, in hindsight, Valcon was glad to receive early in the process. It forced a rethinking of the way the "Valcon story" was communicated. To attract and retain talent, the company had to re-image Valcon. The image developed for Scandinavia—the "how" company helping Scandinavian companies to become global leaders—did not work in India.

At that time Valcon decided to participate in the placement program of one of the elite business schools. All the MBA students had working experience prior to joining the MBA program—a perfect place for a "how" oriented professional service company to look for talent. They spent a full day with the students and were asked to give a one-hour lecture in the afternoon. Valcon knew that they were in on a wildcard and had to compete for talent with much bigger and more well-known global consultancy firms.

Deciding on the topic of the lecture was a challenge itself, but it was decided to build it around what Scandinavia as a region is well known for—the ability to innovate. The Scandinavian region—with fewer than 18 million inhabitants—has been able to develop a relatively large number of companies that are world leaders within their fields. It is the story of a small home market being a good incubator for innovation, but also a story about how it forces companies to develop services that have a global relevance if they want to scale. The idea was that the Scandinavia innovation model has a lot to offer other regions in the world and that India as a country could benefit from adopting some of the learning to further boost its export-oriented economy.

In the presentation, Valcon further communicated how innovation was managed in Scandinavia, using the Valcon story as an example of innovation in the professional service segment:

> We communicated how we contribute with something new and how we add value to our customers. We also shared how we developed a very flat organization and a compensation system driven by results rather than titles and roles in the company. Furthermore, we talked about how we stimulate innovation within our own service offering and how consultants are involved in the process.

Thus in essence Valcon focused their story on the things that make a Scandinavian management consultant company different from a U.S. or U.K. based professional service firm.

The lecture was a success. Valcon had a highly interactive session with the students and received great feedback indicating that Valcon had outperformed many of the big consultancy firms in both content and message. Subsequently Valcon received applications from half of the students—as well as from students who did not participate in the lecture but only heard about it.

In reflecting on Valcon's process of learning to attract and recruit Indian talent, we see how it not only resulted in the successful hiring of talented and highly qualified consultants, but also became a "coming of age" experience, which significantly influenced the identity of Valcon as a consulting firm. Valcon learned, changed, and matured as a consequence of the process. Starting up in India was no simple feat for a Scandinavian consulting firm whose usual recruitment strategy was to hire experts with both industry and consulting experience. As opposed to their position in the Scandinavian market, Valcon did not have any brand in India and similarly no references from clients with their own brand of importance. Furthermore, they were competing for talent in a context where the status of the profession and the employer was far more important than in a Scandinavian context. As Valcon found, status plays a crucial role in relation to family acceptance, a particular challenge the company was confronted with in the process of recruiting its first consultant in India.

The encounter with India was beginning to change the identity of Valcon, thus reversing the stereotypical process of internationalization as a one-way initiative, exporting Western products, knowledge, and ideas. As it will become increasingly clear in the following section, a new Valcon emerged that was not only more international, but a company that was also becoming more clearly differentiated and differently positioned in the Scandinavian consulting market. Moreover, it seemed that the most attractive talent—the "biggest brains" within specializations, for instance, in Lean Management—was now found in their Indian subsidiary rather than the head office.

"Valconizing" the Indian Consultants: From Integration to Convergence

As the process of starting up in India continued, a key question emerged concerning how the integration of the newly recruited consultants in India would be managed. Valcon had a standard introduction program for new employees, which was designed for consultants recruited in Denmark. It included sessions where partners in Valcon communicated the values the company was based on and "how we work." A key question was whether this program would be sufficient for their new Indian colleagues. Valcon was doubtful. Valcon also has standard collaborative tools for knowledge sharing that the firm designed to enable sharing of knowledge between consultants. Could this infrastructure stand on its own? Again, Valcon was doubtful.

The Valcon chairman suggested that the introduction process should be rethought with respect to India, and it was decided that more of the partners' time should be invested in the integration. India is far away from Scandinavia—not just in terms of physical distance. To do business in India, Valcon had to invest in understanding the business culture and the people mindset. When the first two consultants recruited in India came to Denmark for the first time, they did not stay in a hotel. They were invited to stay in the private homes of Valcon's top management:

> The purpose was obvious. We wanted to tie stronger personal bonds to our new Indian colleagues. We wanted to establish a strong personal connection between them and the partners in Valcon. This kind of personal engagement in the integration was very different from what we had done before.

Valcon thus attempted to compensate for the lack of geographical proximity with personal proximity. They wanted to ensure that their Indian colleagues felt confident and comfortable with at least one or two partners in Valcon:

> Our Indian consultants should feel comfortable any time to give us a call asking for information or advice. We did it 100%—and we involved our families in the integration process. We did not take them out to dinner—we always

dined in our private homes. In some cases we even involved our Indian colleagues in the preparation of dinner.

This set-up meant a lot of time for talking and listening. Valcon's partners learned a lot, and so did the new Valcon consultants.

The Indian consultants for their part were not used to this kind of personal proximity in business life. They had all worked for large U.S., European, or Japanese corporations. They were used to a hierarchical organizational set-up where you did not mingle privately with your superiors—especially in an extremely flat structure as the one Valcon was based on. Suddenly they found themselves in a new company, and they were invited to stay at the chairman's house. Their reaction was extremely positive—they were very pleased with their introduction to Valcon and to Denmark.

What started out as an experiment had now become a new Valcon standard. All new Valcon Indian consultants were invited to the private homes of Valcon partners. The only adjustment was that the Indian colleagues are now given the option of hotel accommodation. Expecting them to stay in the private homes of one of the partners was probably taking it one step too far. One could ask if this practice was scalable as Valcon grew, in other words, would the company have enough "integration capacity" to scale it? Valcon believed it was possible. In fact several of the Danish Valcon consultants and business unit managers offered to take part in the integration process.

Valcon is still faced with a lot of challenges in its daily operations in India. Sharing knowledge between Scandinavia and India continues to be a challenge due to the fact that most of the project documentation in Valcon is done in Danish. The language challenge is an obstacle in many ways. Translation of the entire document database would be a huge task. It also makes it more difficult to use Indian consultants on Scandinavian projects. These daily challenges remain, but the development of a good personal network has proven to be a good starting point for dealing with them.

In reflecting on Valcon's efforts to integrate their new Indian employees into the firm's culture and mindset, it is interesting to note that the route they chose of creating a very personal encounter between the top people in Valcon and the new consultants in India had several consequences. First, it had a strong and lasting effect on the new consultants. Although it was almost too overwhelming for some, the contact secured an important foundation for a close working relationship between headquarters and subsidiary. Second, the process of integrating "the other" not only affected the Indian employees, but also further contributed to changing Valcon's identity. Although the idea of having new employees stay at the private homes of top management was inspired by the existing values of Valcon as a flat organization, it was also a significant departure from existing practices. In the effort to create a personal encounter with the new Indian consultants and effectively demonstrate the essence of a flat organization, Valcon momentarily "collapsed" its hierarchy completely—something the firm would not have normally done in relation to their Scandinavian employees.

What happened in this process was not just integration or the "Valconization" of the Indian employees. It also created significant learning in Valcon at the top level and continues to do so. The integration goes both ways, and in this sense it can be seen as a *process convergence*, in other words, separate processes of identity change pointing in the same direction with each one taking a different path towards the same common point. As we will continue to explore, this is a point of concurrence where synergies can be created and something new can emerge. Convergence means that an encounter between cultures changes both parties, but it does not mean that they become the same. Both parties change, but in different ways. A space for a productive and innovative encounter is created where there is potential for convergence, while differences are maintained. Thus a changed Valcon is emerging, which is both more international and more "Valcon" than ever before. The positioning in the Scandinavian market vis-à-vis Valcon's competitors is also changing, and Valcon is developing a more distinct identity as they learn from their Indian colleagues, who bring knowledge and experience not previously present in Valcon.

"Reverse Innovation": Bringing Services Developed in India to the Scandinavian Market

Valcon believed that Scandinavia had a lot to offer India, but India also has a lot to offer Scandinavia. India is the world leader in off-shoring of white collar work. The ability to take a business process and package it as a product is world class. India is the global thought leader in this respect. The business process outsourcing/off-shoring industry (BPO) is significant in India. The total revenue is more than USD 50 billion. The Scandinavian region is not a large BPO market for India. Organizations in Scandinavia are in generally not aware of the potential—at least not compared with their U.S. counterparts. The problem is not the large companies. They have identified the potential and the Indian BPO companies know how to deal with them. The problem is with the small- and medium-sized enterprises, which are plentiful in Scandinavia. This is a potential threat to the long-term white collar productivity in Scandinavia.

Valcon decided that it wanted to understand how the outsourcing process worked in India and thus became a client of the Indian BPO industry by encapsulating engineering services from one of the leading BPO companies. In this process Valcon again learned a lot, and decided to develop its own knowledge process outsourcing (KPO) product based on the firm's experience in India. Valcon is one of the leaders in profitability management and has developed and implemented activity-based costing concepts for more than 100 companies. Valcon sets it up—the clients run it. Valcon realized, however, that many of its clients had trouble maintaining the system. Valcon could of course attempt to sell the same consultant project twice—but they also thought about doing it the Indian way, offering to do it on behalf of the client. Valcon developed this new service in India in collaboration with one of the firm's Danish clients. At the time of writing this chapter, roughly six months later, the new service is up and running.

It could be argued that this example is not a true case of reverse innovation (Immelt, Govindarajan, & Trimble, 2009). The service inspired by India was first commercialized in Scandinavia and will then be commercialized in India. However, truly reversed professional service innovations will begin to emerge—developed and commercialized in India, and then commercialized in Scandinavia. Valcon expected that it would start with BPO. Valcon has successfully pioneered the introduction of lean in white collar services in Scandinavia. One obvious opportunity is to develop a lean administration offering, targeting the Indian BPO industry. This product was to be developed and commercialized in India and then later commercialized in Scandinavia. In lean manufacturing, Toyota in Japan has been used as a benchmark. In lean administration, it is as obvious that the benchmarks in terms of productivity, quality, and lead time should be based on the Indian BPO industry. By bringing the product to Scandinavia, Valcon would also be able to take lean administration to the next level. This will allow Valcon's Scandinavian clients to develop and benchmark against world class companies. This is important as many processes are unlikely to be off-shored because of critical mass, proximity, or political reasons (e.g., processes in government controlled organizations servicing the Scandinavian citizens and corporations). Valcon is sure that reverse innovation will play a key role in its future consulting offerings. Scandinavia has a lot to learn from India—and Valcon was planning to play the role as a catalyst.

Thus in this sense both current and future products and concepts developed in India by Indian consultants are being and could potentially be sold both on the Indian and the Scandinavian market. As Valcon is continuously changing and developing through its encounters in India, the firm is beginning to find ways of benefiting from the points of convergence between Scandinavian ways of doing business and Indian ways of doing management. What is particularly striking about this process is that there is nothing predictable or unidirectional about it. As a dynamic learning process, ideas, influences, and inspirations move back and forth, continuously being mixed and transformed. It is as much a case of West meeting East as East meeting West, and in the process new management ideas and concepts are emerging that are neither inherently Eastern or Western.

DISCUSSION AND CONCLUSION

As can be learned from the case study of Valcon's entry into the Indian consulting market, the process not only created a new channel for selling and delivering consulting services in another part of the world, but it also impacted the business, organization, and identity of Valcon. This transformation seemed much more profound than Valcon's partners had initially expected when the new venture was being planned.

From the case study a number of key observations can be emphasized. First, Valcon followed an alternative entry mode Valcon when *setting up* its operation in India. According to traditional internationalization theory, the normal practice would have been to establish a new office or set up a joint venture with a local consultancy to ensure local touch and a viable network. Instead Valcon chose to develop its Indian practice in a joint partnership with a major client. This mode ensured the presence of business and established local relevance in terms of creating innovation and value for clients—a key driver for Valcon.

Second, Valcon had to rethink its "normal" practice and value proposition in a "no name, no brand environment" when the firm started to *recruit*. Just presenting the consulting firm in the traditional way would probably not have gotten anyone to sign up, as Valcon didn't have any well-known client references to present or any convincing consulting story to tell as the audience did not have any insight in the Scandinavian market. The challenge of re-imaging Valcon in a new context turned into a winning formula.

Third, Valcon managed the *integration process* of the new Indian consultants in a non-traditional way. "Valconizing" the new consultants by having them come to Denmark and stay with the partners not only limited the physical distance between them but also created much closer social ties. This move turned out to be a success, although it was met with some hesitations when introduced. However, the impact on the Valcon introduction program was clear, and this new integration mode became a trigger for a new Valcon standard.

Finally, even though Valcon believed the firm had a lot to offer India, it turned out that India also had a lot to offer Scandinavia. In most cases a consulting firm will distribute its services when internationalizing its practice as a part of an economies of scale philosophy. However, it turned out that some of the newly local recruited consultants in India had a cutting-edge competence in specific areas, which led to a service "export" back to Scandinavia of a service, in this case in the area of profitability management and lean management. This dynamic reflects the ways in which advanced knowledge can flow, creating a reverse stream of business.

Our observations indicate that the outcome of Valcon's entry into India impacted the firm far more than expected—in both a positive and disruptive way. This dynamic can be characterized as *reverse consulting*—in a broad sense, the additional value Valcon gained from its entry into India was related to new business and organizational learning, not simply about how to operate in India but also in Scandinavia. Having a newly established practice abroad, operating from the perspective of reverse consulting, adds to the understanding of new ventures in faraway places, and how consulting firms can add more value to their practice by capitalizing on these experiences.

APPENDIX

Valcon A/S: A Brief Description

Consulting Services that Ensure Innovation and Added Value:
- Valcon is a Scandinavian company with offices in Denmark, Sweden and Norway and international offices in the Czech Republic, India and China. We employ more than 150 people.
- Value creation is the aim of everything we do. Our specialist competencies and experience lay the foundation for creating solutions that work—and ensure innovation and added value for our customers.

We Create Results:
- We are highly focused on creating results, the sooner the better. Our experiences enable us to quickly grasp and understand each individual company. We thus rarely need to create long analyses and write thick reports. We prefer attacking the challenges in a direct and pragmatic way. This means that early on in the process, we form a clear opinion and dare voice what challenges are needed.
- All consultants have their own style. Ours is the most direct, practical and engaged one. We are active players on the scene where we create healthy processes and implement solutions that work in practice.

Close Cooperation with the Customer:
- Results and value creation never come as a one-size-fits-all solution. Every client is a unique challenge requiring a unique approach. Valcon is known to have clear attitudes and goal-oriented ambitions on behalf of our clients and us, but our solutions are always created in close cooperation between our consultants and the client organization.
- Consulting services are worthless unless the clients understand and take ownership of the improvements implemented in the company.
- It is not boring to work with us. We challenge, make demands and drive the process. Even though it may be hard work, it is well worth the effort as it is the long-term effects that count. And they are positive.
- The will to make a difference fuels our efforts. We like to challenge our clients in the form of fruitful discussions about solid solutions. Such discussions are always conducted in an atmosphere of mutual respect and help us identify new opportunities. We receive positive feedback showing that our clients appreciate our cooperation. We create analyses which help focus what is important instead of merely what is visible. Our target is to create an open and honest discussion

which takes us directly to the core of the problem and thus to possible solutions.

How:

- Our style is direct, practical and engaged.
- We are direct and ask questions which challenge habitual ways of thinking and old habits.
- We focus on what is important instead of merely what is visible.
- We act and create quick results.
- We go for what can actually be achieved—not for what is best in theory.
- We are part of the solutions all the way from concept to implementation and results.

REFERENCES

Berry, J. (1988). Consulting in Europe and the USA: More alike than not. *Journal of Management Consulting, 4*(3), 39–42.

Consultgenie. (2009). *Consulting industry in India.* [PowerPoint presentation].

Hitt, M., Bierman, L., Uhlenbruck, K., & Shimizu, K. (2006). The importance of resources in the internationalization of professional service firms: The good, the bad and the ugly. *Academy of Management Journal, 49*(6), 1137–1157.

Immelt, J. R., Govindarajan, V., & Trimble, C. (2009). How GE is disrupting itself. *Harvard Business Review, 87,* 56–65.

Jenkins, R. (2004). *Social Identity.* London: Routledge.

Johanson, J. & Wiedersheim-Paul, F. (1975). The internationalization of the firm: Four cases. *Journal of Management Studies, 12,* 305–322.

Johanson, J. & Vahlne, J. -E. (1977). The internationalization process of the firm: A model of knowledge development and increasing foreign market commitments. *Journal of International Business Studies, 8,* 23–32.

Management Consultancy Association. (n.d.). Prospects for recovery. Retrieved from http://www.mca.org.uk/home. 2011

Nees, D. (1986). Building an international practice. *Journal of Management Consulting, 3*(2), 18–25.

Pearlmutter, H. V. (1969). The tortuous evolution of the multinational corporation. *Columbia Journal of World Business, 4*(1), 9–18.

Rathore, S. (2010). *Consulting in India: The present and the future trends.* [PowerPoint presentation]. India Consulting Association.

Rogers, P., & Tierney, T. (2004). Leadership without control. *European Business Journal, 16,* 78.

Segal-Horne, S. (1993). The internationalisation of service firms. *Advances in Strategic Management, 9,* 931–955.

Werr, A., & Stjernberg, T. (2003). Exploring management consulting firms as knowledge systems. *Organization Studies, 24*(6), 881–908.

Winch, G. M. (2008). Internationalisation strategies in the business-to business services: The case of architectural practice. *The Service Industries Journal, 28*(1), 1–13.

Yin, R. K. (2003). *Case study research: Design and methods.* Thousand Oaks, CA: Sage Publications.

CHAPTER 14

EXECUTIVE COACHING

An Emerging Role for Management Consultants[1]

John L. Bennett and Mary Wayne Bush

Arguably, executive coaching is an important
intervention and a competency of consultation.
In addition, it is a role function of the consultant.
—Sperry, 2008, p. 34

One consultant's story:

I was brought in as the process expert, but it became very clear to me early on that this was as much of a leadership issue as it was a process issue. So I ended up developing this relationship with the key general manager of the three facilities, and spent a lot of time one on one with him asking him how he wanted to be presented, how he wanted to be perceived by the organization... There were times where I was coaching him in a group... where I would say, "Is that what we agreed to last week when we had our conversation?" And it became a very powerful combination of driving process change and driving leadership behavior in the same vein, and doing that in an incredibly transparent manner in front of the entire organization where he made very strong public commitments to the organization. That ended up being

Exploring the Professional Identity of Management Consultants, pages 283–301
Copyright © 2013 by Information Age Publishing
All rights of reproduction in any form reserved.

probably one of the most significant work changes I've ever been a part of. (Study Respondent USA005)

Both executive coaching and management consulting are relatively new disciplines, still early in their development as professions. They share ambiguous social status, lack clearly defined and agreed-upon professional standards or accreditation criteria, and low barriers to entry. These issues are current concerns in the field that could form the basis for development of consulting practices, discussions or the starting point for more involved research studies. The use of coaching as a management consulting intervention is also potentially challenging to the distinction of management consulting, further blurring the lines between "skill" and "identity." This chapter explores the dynamic and multiple ways that professional management consultants' identities are being shaped through the application of coaching as a role, at the same time coaching itself is emerging as a discipline (Bennett, 2006; Bennett & Bush, 2009; Bennett & Craig, 2005; Bennett & Martin, 2001; Lane, Stelter, & Rostron, 2010).

In this experience-based chapter we explore how the professional identity of management consultants incorporates or includes a role as executive coach (also referred to as coach), with particular respect to work with organizational change interventions. The authors believe this issue to be a current concern in the field that could form the basis for the development of consulting practices as well as a starting point for more involved research studies. Furthermore, we hope the chapter will be provocative and engaging—leading to further developments in this area.

In this period of constant change, one of the roles that management consultants are called upon to employ is the skill and practice of coaching. Coaching is not currently considered to be a profession; however, it is a valuable skill set. There is already lively discussion among U.S. organization development (OD) practitioners about whether (and how) coaching and OD are similar and different. Our aim is to bring the coaching and consulting communities together, creating a path forward.

With the force of constant change impacting leaders, organizations, and team members, change is indeed the "new normal" in organizational life. The challenge is to lead it, manage it, learn from it, and leverage it as an opportunity for continuous improvement. Executive coaching is a role management consultants can play and an intervention strategy that can be employed to manage change and leverage it at the individual and group levels for the benefit of the entire organization. This chapter explores current thinking about the roles of management consulting and executive coaching, as well as organizational change, and provides evidence-based strategies that can be applied to each stage and role in the organizational change process.

Coaching, of course, is not a new phenomenon. It has been included in the repertoire of many management consultants, formally and informally, for the past several decades. Scott, Murrell, Zintz, and Gallagher (2006) note that,

> For many of us who have been involved with major change interventions, meeting with our clients one-on-one to provide support and guidance on his/ her leadership role is part of our responsibilities.... Increasingly, these roles have been considered coaching (p. 8)

Minahan (2006), asserts that today's consultant "would have a hard time doing an effective OD intervention without a heavy dose of leadership or executive coaching" (p. 6). This statement reminds readers that Marshak (2009), in *Practicing Organization Development*, includes coaching as a role for the professional management consultant.

Current consulting models identify processes for management consulting that build on coaching practices. Yet these models do not specifically call out the role of coaching or point to the skills needed for management consultants to effectively use coaching in an individual or group intervention. By specifically distinguishing executive coaching as a role in management consulting, practitioners can expand their repertoire of resources to help their clients succeed. Steiner (2008, p. 40) asserts that for consultants "looking to shift the way things are done in organizations, coaching can be a very powerful addition to a consultant's toolkit. Most obviously, it's a process or method for you to work with your clients in a way that's supporting, challenging and provocative, the embodiment of what Edgar Schein called 'process consulting.'" Similarly, Storjohann (2006, p. 12) exhorts management consultants to "start to define criteria and competencies that distinguish coaching from an OD consulting perspective as the unique, powerful and timely intervention that it is becoming in this age of human development."

While coaching is a process technology that impacts individuals and teams, this chapter focuses on engagements where coaches work with individuals as the leaders or agents for organizational change. The desired outcome is behavioral and/or cognitive change. In such engagements, our premise is that coaching is the intervention of choice and that management consultants are wise to specifically learn about and incorporate coaching into their repertoires.

This chapter builds on the experiences of eight international management consultants and coaches, as well as our own experiences in this area. These experiences provide a rich set of data from which to establish that coaching needs to be part of the identity of management consultants as professionals.

APPROACH

Using a convenience sampling approach, eight international management consultants and coaches, each with more than 15 years of experience, were recruited for semi-structured telephone interviews. Six participants were from the U.S. and two from Canada; they included three females and five males. A research assistant was oriented to the project and trained to conduct all interviews.

All participants provided their informed consent, and anonymity was promised. Interviews were audio recorded and subsequently transcribed by a professional transcription service. Transcripts were then compared to the audio recordings for accuracy. The two researchers reviewed the transcripts and identified themes, as well as exemplary texts for potential inclusion as findings. These quotes are cited with a unique identifier (e.g., USA001, CAN001). Themes were compared and findings identified. In addition, the authors explored the literature related to coaching, professionalization of coaching, management consulting, and professional identity (cf. Denzin & Lincoln, 2000; Marshall & Rossman, 2011; Maxwell, 2005; Silverman, 2006; Weiss, 1994).

FINDINGS

Based on the experience-focused interviews, eight themes emerged from the data. These themes are related to the distinctions made between coaching and consulting, how and why consultants adopt the role of coach, preparation for the coaching role, role identity, benefits of coaching in consulting, drawbacks of coaching as part of the consulting practice, and concerns about coaching. Each is presented along with quotations from the interview transcripts and references from the related literature.

Distinctions Between Coaching and Consulting

Coaching is described as part of the consulting process by several authors. It is identified as an option for working with executives and senior leaders in organizational contexts. Executive consulting is the term we have adopted for the approach to coaching that is designed to help a senior leader improve on an already successful career. The executive consultant serves as a sounding board who can help a leader anticipate, plan, and think through strategic, political, organizational, and personal issues (Peterson, 1996) with the goal of making the executive as successful as possible (Berman & Bradt, 2006).

Executive coaching is a form of consultation in which a trained professional, mindful of organizational dynamics, functions as a facilitator who forms a collaborative relationship with an executive to improve his or her skills and effectiveness in communicating the corporate vision and goals, fostering better team performance, enhancing organizational productivity, and facilitating professional-personal development. There are three types of such coaching: skill-based, performance-based, and developmental executive coaching (Sperry, 2008).

Stern (2004) offers a "working definition" of executive coaching, referring to it as "an important organizational intervention" (p. 154). This emphasis points to themes very similar to those identified by the study respondents, about both executive coaching and consulting facilitating communication, team performance, organizational effectiveness, personal productivity, and supporting leadership success. The main difference was in the context: the same support and behaviors were seen in coaching and consulting; however, interventions at the individual, personal level, were called "coaching," while those at the group or organizational level were referred to as "consulting."

Overall, respondents defined coaching as an individual, supportive interaction. It is most often used in the context of helping a leader identify and move past fears or personal hurdles and to become empowered to drive a strategy or change. As one of the respondents noted, "coaching is being with people in a way that helps them, . . . I would say unleashes them into action or a new way of being, usually triggered by some sort of a problem situation" (USA002). Similar themes emerged in other comments:

> Coaching is a spoken conversation . . . consulting is more specific. It's more about the organization. To me, consulting at times, I think I'm called on in terms of my expertise. So I tend to share my expertise more so than I would do in a coaching conversation. (CAN002)

> Put another way, I oftentimes think of coaching as observation-based and/or process-based. I think of coaching in two primary realms. One is individual coaching from a development standpoint, from a career standpoint, from an overall effectiveness perspective. . . . Then I think of coaching for business sakes, and I would say that I exclusively reside from a coaching standpoint on the coaching for effectiveness and driving business levers and business change. (USA005)

Respondents identified personal development, insightful and provocative questioning, and the ability to become a trusted advisor as aspects of coaching that they bring to bear in consulting work. "I believe that coaching is supporting, and it's some intentional process to support other people to develop a set of skills that are important to them. It makes no difference if that's management or basketball or music" (USA001). Another offered,

"I think coaching is a process or a methodology for helping leaders, or really anybody I guess. I mostly do it with business leaders, or business owners. Helping them to have some insights that may be invisible to them without some, some kind of provocative questions" (USA004).

The definitions or explanations of consulting from the respondent group were much wider-ranging than those of coaching, including "an extra pair of hands" (CAN001) and being hired for expertise (CAN002). Coaching was seen as one of many roles that consultants employ during engagements:

> In my job I have to wear multiple hats, and I think as a consultant working with organizations you have to do that. You might have a coaching hat that you take on and off. You have an advisor hat that you take on and off. You have a worker bee hat that you take on and off. You know you have a part-psychologist hat that you take on and off. (CAN001)

> It can be to take pressure off clients who have a problem . . . Solving problems and giving objective advice is why I think a lot of clients like working with consultants, because they can hand them an issue and have the consultant work through the issue with the team members and with the people in the organization but then come up with some recommendation or a solution or next steps, whatever it might be in an objective manner. (CAN001)

For another respondent, the focus of consulting is on helping—"helping people, helping organizations with the process of what's going on. Like how people are working together. How things are coordinated. Sort of the human aspect of change" (USA003). This respondent also referred to Peter Block's (2000) description of three types of consulting: process consulting, expert consulting, and "pair of hands."

Several respondents also pointed to consulting as a lever for organizational growth change:

> For me consulting is really enabling the organization to propel itself forward, enabling an organization to grow, enabling an organization to change, and really helping to build capacities within an organization to self-replicate over time. (USA005)

Consulting was also seen as helping to sustain the accomplishments that have been made: ". . . consulting is also making sure that you're enabling the organization to self-sustain itself beyond my departure and beyond the entry, or I should say the exit phase of the OD cycle" (USA005).

In comparing consulting to coaching, one respondent said:

> Consulting is doing the same thing [as coaching] only with a system. It's in a sense having a conversation with an entire system. And that usually takes different forms of meetings, different meetings or workshops or sessions de-

signed to unleash the full potential of the individuals of the system, the organization, and the individuals in that system. (USA002)

These findings echo other writers (Diedrich & Kilburg, 2001; Sperry, 2008; Winum, 1995) who identify coaching as a role within consulting:

> In the early years of consulting psychology, the term consultation prevailed. Unless clearly specified, consultation meant "organizational consultation," the change process wherein the consultee was the entire organization or specific unit of it. When specified it meant "executive consultation," the change process wherein the consultee was an executive. Although executive coaching was recognized in those early years, it was considered as a specific kind of consultation intervention. (Sperry, 2008, p. 34)

In the special issue of *Consulting Psychology Journal on Executive Coaching*, Diedrich and Kilburg (2001) noted that executive coaching remains a "largely ill-defined competency area of consultation" (p. 204), while Winum (1995) catalogued executive coaching as one of nine types of "consultation interventions."

How and Why Consultants Adopt the Role of Coach

Some respondents indicated that they were pulled into the role of coach by their clients' needs or preferences, while others leveraged the role due to their operational beliefs or professional philosophies. One consultant described how he came to adopt the role of coach "... to fully achieve the change goal it is often helpful to also strengthen the capacity of the leader" because "... I believe that leadership is a critical variable in the change project. And in any strategy project, and any work design, and any important development project, the role, the position, the style of leadership makes a difference" (USA001). Another adopted the role of coach out of his belief that senior executive clients need the opportunity to get "honest feedback" in an environment of trust and confidentiality:

> Oh, my clients, because they're so senior, it's very difficult for them to get honest feedback. People don't want to tell their boss the truth. I mean it's just the way it is. And so I can say things that others wouldn't dare to say. That alone can be really helpful, that they can be candid with me. They know nobody else is going to hear about it. They can be vulnerable with me. (USA003)

> Another respondent pointed to the role of coaching as a process step that is a nice contrast to her "other tools" (which can be more methodical). For some of the consultants in the study, the role of coach was a response to the client's request:

I have always used coaching in my work, so each contract that I get, the majority of them require some coaching. . . . And it also encompasses senior people asking me to coach junior people . . . I'm never asked formally to coach. But sometimes I'm brought onboard on a project or in an area where the client has asked me to do some mentoring or coaching or familiarization and those . . . that coaching can take many different forms as you probably know. And it covers a wide area. (CAN001)

Preparation for the Coaching Role

None of the study respondents indicated that they had any formal coaching education or skill training. Most had just incorporated one-on-one conversations as part of the consulting-client work to facilitate the effectiveness of the intervention:

Well, I don't have any official coaching training. . . . And so I never really had the opportunity to integrate it into one body of practice the way a coaching certificate or a coaching education would do. Lacking that, I've been pretty much left up to my own devices through which I've been able to do that. (USA001)

While some respondents indicated interest in developing as a coach, there was also uncertainty about the direction that would take the consulting work, or the acknowledgement that it was not an area of interest:

I don't know what would make me a better coach. I'm sure there's something I need to know about to be a better coach. I'm not particularly interested in coaching people around technical or operational issues . . . So I guess if I could become more interested in the operational or technical stuff, maybe I'd be a more complete coach. (USA002)

Another respondent became aware of the role by having had coaching himself, and posits that if he had had more supervision early on in his career, he would be better enabled to work with clients, noting "... the more feedback I get on how I'm working with clients the better I am working with clients" (USA003).

Other respondents without formal training noticed that their own curiosity and conversational inquiry helped their consulting engagements. While not calling it "coaching," it was still a useful tool or role for them and arose from their own natural curiosity when entering an organizational system:

Being an objective outsider I can provide some observations about things I have noticed . . . and then asking them did they notice those same things? What, how did they feel about that? Did that produce the results that they were intending?...So sometimes it's digging, digging, and digging and digging, asking more questions to help them uncover what's...what's getting them upset that could be getting in the way of effectiveness of their organization. (USA005)

Role Identity

As mentioned above, none of the consultants interviewed saw their primary role or professional identity as coach, exemplified by the comments of one the respondents who underscored, "In fact I don't call myself a coach" (USA003). Part of this clarification is in deference to those who do call themselves coaches:

> So it never occurs to me to actually tell somebody I'm a coach, because the people who I know who are coaches, that's primarily the way they do their work. That's like, that's their whole job. (USA004)

Another aspect is about being very clear about one's own brand as a consultant. As one of the respondents pointed out,

> I don't define myself as a coach. That is not my primary business line...I have never ever had coaching in any of my statements of work for any client. So I am not hired per se as a coach. (CAN001)

Interestingly, an issue that emerged from the data was that out of respect for the client's wishes some of the respondents chose not "advertise" that coaching was taking place in the organization. As one of these individuals argued, "... sometimes clients don't want their staff to know that I am coaching them. They will sort of set it up so I can go in and do the coaching" (CAN001). Another respondent (USA006) does not use the term "coach" in his practice, but tells his clients that he will counsel people if needed within his consultant role.

Consultants are sensitive to situations where the client asks for coaching but does not want to include coaching in the contract, or does not want others in the organization to know that coaching will be part of the consulting engagement.

> Often clients...may not want to put coaching in the statement of work...and I have never ever had coaching in any of my statements of work for any client, so I am not hired per se as a coach. And sometimes clients don't want their staff to know that I am coaching them. They will sort of set it up so I can go in and do the coaching, you know. They will do a soft sell on me going in and, you know, spending time with the personal people involved and helping

them sort through the solutions, and if I can come up with some quick fixes for a few things then I find that there's no problem in going in, in that kind of situation. (CAN001)

Sometimes the coaching is invisible to the people being coached. Although they do generally get the idea after I've been working with them for a while.... so I will have senior people say, "Could you... I'm going to ask my management team to have some sessions with you. Could you give them the benefit of your experience and could you, you know, help them think through some issues?" So sometimes it is explicit in terms of what I'm doing with the people that I'm doing it with, but it's never in my statement of work. (CAN001)

Even if coaching is not an explicit part of the consultant's identity, the roles of consultant and coach are still often seen as intertwined. As one respondent added,

I don't know how you can be an effective consultant without being an effective coach. And I'm thinking that maybe the opposite may be true as well. But I don't sell myself as a coach, so it's never been a problem for me. (USA002)

Benefits of Coaching in Consulting

Respondents identified several ways that coaching benefited their consulting, specifically by helping individuals overcome barriers or obstacles that were negatively influencing organizational effectiveness. Respondent USA006 mentioned the benefit of counseling an individual is to help them with "blocks that are hindering performance or causing issues in the organization's performance." Respondents indicated that by empowering specific leaders to take action or drive change, the consulting engagements were more successful.

One of the consultants we interviewed also noted that working with clients on a daily basis enabled them to leverage coaching to help align and clarify the leader's role and behaviors in a way that facilitated success in consulting:

But I'm also seeing them in action and able to observe them in doing their daily jobs, particularly in relationship to the change or strategy project. And so I'm able to bring some insight and my own observations and feedback about them in their role vis-a-vis the change management project. So typically the 4th to the 7th or 8th sessions are examining their beliefs and assumptions about themselves, their beliefs and assumptions about their work, their belief and assumptions about their jobs, helping them deepen their understanding of themselves, helping them connect the dots between the data from the 360 or the interviews and the ... their own sense of themselves. And see where the alignment is and see where the disconnects are. And helping them work them through [all of this]. (USA001)

Other respondents pointed to using coaching to help everyone in the organizational system. "The smarter the people are around me when I'm trying to help an organization improve itself, the smarter the people are, the more in touch they are with themselves" (USA002). Respondents also pointed to using individual coaching to give bold, pointed feedback to senior clients in a safe, private setting.

Coaching was also seen as a way to help clients deal with the political or organizational culture issues that were negatively impacting their ability to lead or drive results. "What do you do when you've got an alpha person in your unit who is trying to undermine, you know, the management team. How do you handle that?" (CAN001) Another respondent used coaching to foster individual commitment to the results of the consulting work that was done in the organization. "I think coaching is absolutely essential, and I will even go as far as being more specific than that. The inquiry process is absolutely essential to getting clients to own their own stuff" (USA005). As these comments suggest, coaching was seen as an important activity that helps to ensure the gains would be sustained after the consultant disengaged.

Drawbacks of Coaching as Part of Consulting Practice

Despite the benefits noted above, respondents also pointed out several areas of concern about incorporating coaching into their consulting practices. In addition to the lack of formal preparation, or knowledge of the professional role and practices of a coach noted above, there was also concern about personal preference or aptitude for doing work at the individual versus organizational level. Others noted drawbacks including issues about getting too personal, creating role confusion or envy, experiencing the process of coaching as emotionally draining, and not feeling competent or at ease with the role. Another respondent noted the additional concern of having to be aware of, and balance, the use of both roles in engagements with clients.

Where it gets me in trouble is when those issues become personal.... In rare instances, there are times where I can't get past the obstacle of he and she just simply won't work well together, and there are times where I could probably do a better job of, one, understanding those things more proactively, and two, contracting for them differently. (USA005)

I think it's sometimes very challenging to put a coaching hat on and off. It's not so much of a challenge to put a coaching hat on, but it's certainly a challenge to take it off...the only drawback I would say about coaching is that because it's so mental in many ways, psychological and it...I find it quite...I was going to say draining...emotionally draining. (CAN001)

Well, it does...it can...it can create a bit of role envy. Especially with organizations where there are existing coaching programs and where there are...is an existing roster of coaches. I am likely to...often, not always, I'm not on their coaching roster. And so it creates a problem sometimes with HR. It creates a problem sometimes with the coaching program head. It creates a problem sometimes for the contract, because if I'm in there to do a strategy project with kind of a coaching piece of this it's up to the client to decide if I'd need an additional separate contract or if the coaching work can be rolled into the existing strategy or change management project. (USA001)

I think there is a down side potentially in going really deep with these executives when they feel scared because of what they've revealed to the coach. (USA002)

Another example of the drawbacks of coaching included losing consulting business because of the successful impact of coaching:

I've experienced some of those drawbacks. I had this intensive leadership development intensive, oh, experience, it's a three-and-a-half day thing. It's based on the five questions....When I went back to propose a consulting assistance for them, they didn't want to do it....And [the client] said what we did with you is too sacred with this work...we don't want to mess it up by getting you all involved in all this strategic stuff. We want to keep you as almost like the chaplain, like the spiritual chaplain of our organization. (USA002)

However, most of the respondents saw coaching as a value-added tool or resource, an additional way to drive effectiveness and success in organizational engagements:

You know, frankly, I don't see any drawbacks, because I'm not...if maybe my business card said "executive coach," and that's what I was doing all the time, I might see some drawbacks, but I coach when it seems like this is a good thing to do.... It's a resource that I have. I can do it informally or we could even set up weekly meetings, which I've done with some clients. (USA003)

Concerns about Coaching

In addition to findings about the drawbacks of incorporating coaching into consulting engagements, respondents also voiced concerns over coaching itself. Proliferation of coaching, low barrier to entry, and a lack of professionalism and agreed-upon standards and qualifications for coaches were causes for reflection.

> I do have some concern about the popularity of coaching. On one hand it seems like that's a really good thing. But also it's starting to feel a little bit like it's too much flavor-of-the-month, that there are too many people coaching. And one of the real concerns is, just as in consulting, you can coach. And all it takes to be a coach or a consultant is to say, "I'm a coach or a consultant." They don't need to be certified. They don't... and other people are just coaching because they don't know what else to do, and they know how to spell the word so they put it on the business card. And that really... it's always concerned me about the profession I'm in. And it concerns me about the whole coaching area. (USA003)

Also noted among concerns was the importance of dealing with clients in respectful ways, given the level of trust and vulnerability that often attends powerful coaching sessions. Part of this respect is in adequately developing a trusted relationship of permission, or cooperation, with the coachee before embarking on the coaching process. Another aspect is being aware of the level of sensitivity that the person being coached may be experiencing.

> And especially it concerns me, because if you're doing coaching right, I think, people are going to be vulnerable. And when they're vulnerable, I think we have a special responsibility to be sensitive to that. Yeah. I keep using the word vulnerable, but being sensitive to kind of... they've just opened themselves up and I think we need to have the kind of, I don't know, skills and attention and sympathy to be able to work sensitively and effectively with the other person when that's taking place. (USA003)

> So I guess I see drawbacks in the way that some people go about coaching when they don't have permission from the person. And then it ends up creating some upset. And I feel like it only works when somebody is ready, and you have the relationship with them that they can hear it. So I don't have any, I don't see any drawbacks in the way I use it. (USA004)

One respondent brought up the situations where he would *not* do coaching—for performance issues—or where an individual was solely focused on his or her career advancement. The concern here is that coaching, in a consulting context, may damage relationships, while not furthering the overall goals or effectiveness of the organization, and may even take the consulting engagement off track.

> I think there are times where I would not do coaching. I think for performance issues I sometimes get a little angst about coaching people around performance issues directly whenever it's already been declared a performance

issue and [when in all] likelihood the benefit of the doubt for that person has been removed and it's kind of the last ditch effort. So I actually think that can be dangerous, because I think it has an adverse impact on developing positive relationships....I think the two dangerous areas to coach in are for development, directly and exclusively for development, especially whenever it's likely that the decision has been made that this person isn't a good fit, and exclusively coaching people for career advancement, because I have had negative experiences where I've coached people for career advancement and have only manifested some of the negative behaviors and negative impacts they were having on people because their primary concern was getting to the next level. (USA005)

Another respondent commented on a concern about being qualified to coach in technical areas, but not having the skill set to get into the psychological aspects of working with individuals:

I'm qualified to coach on the work related technical day-to-day HR, those kinds of issues. But on the more psychological side, I'm not really...I don't have the skill set to do that as effectively as I think it can be done and I have seen it being done. (CAN001)

Apart from coaching itself, several respondents indicated the need for clearer, up-front contracting in consulting engagements that includes coaching services. As one of these individuals noted:

In hindsight there are lots of times where, and I do a better job at this today, but in hindsight, on numerous initiatives there are times where I wish I would have contracted better on the front end that this isn't just a process issue but, in fact, we're going, it's going to require some behavioral coaching on an ad hoc, as-needed, basis, which I tend to do pretty well today. (USA005)

When Coaching Is Indicated

There are times the consultant initiates coaching in the engagement because of beliefs about how the work should be done or because of deeply-held values. One respondent said "I coach when it seems like this is a good thing to do" (USA003). Another pointed out:

I've had to invite myself in on initiatives because they were deeply personal, and as long as those two people were in the same room or in the same groups that they were in, there would've never been resolutions for the organization itself. (USA005)

A third respondent commented that coaching enables the consultant to add value to the organizational system more directly than with consulting. However, the consultant must be sensitive to the relationships and timing, and check his or her own ego.

> You are not an integral part of the workplace over a long period of time. So you see things differently.... If you can do so in a way that is supportive and encouraging and positive about moving forward or making changes, then I think you can move from sort of tip-toeing around the issue to being more forthright as the issue unfolds for the client and the team.... So it takes time, patience, trust, credibility, positive thinking, supportive language, and generally a, let's say a recognition that as much experience you have as a consultant, you are still learning from other people.... So, you know, you can't be ... you can't be ... your head can't be too big. You've got to keep your ego in check. (CAN001)

Based on the respondents comments, the following are two illustrations where coaching is seen as an important part of a management consulting engagement.

> Quite recently, actually last fall, I was in the UK and I was called by one of my senior clients, and she's a director general of communications, and she said, "I've been asked to go and do an assignment in another department that's having a lot of problems." And she said, "The only way I can go is if you can come in and backfill for me for a couple of months and, you know, be the director general." So this is a little different because if you think of the situation here we've got a team ... a big team, probably about 100 people on the team. They're dealing with public health issues and, you know, outbreaks, disease outbreaks, all that kind of stuff. And all of the sudden they've got as their kind of "go to person," they've got a consultant coming in and running the team. So it was a delicate kind of affair in the sense that as a caretaker, and as a non-public servant, you know, I wasn't in ... I'm not in the bureaucracy, I had to be able to deal with mentoring and coaching the management team and giving them direction whereas, if they had been of a different kind of people that might have been very difficult, and it was challenging. I won't say it was easy. So that was a coaching that was, while not in a statement of work, was pretty explicit that I was there to coach and mentor and help and assist and advise and make sure things stayed on track. (CAN001)

> I'm working with a team that is doing a major change project regarding the government and management and technology of its organization's website. And I went in there with a particular goal to help them with the change of management assignment, and I've been working on that for two years. But within a couple of months it was clear that part of the challenge was that the leader's behavior was getting in the way of her team members' ability to do their jobs. And so I re-contracted with her and included a significant piece on coaching her as a part of the work. (USA001)

REFLECTIONS AND RECOMMENDATIONS

The results of the study indicate that respondents see coaching as an important role within their professional identity as a management consultant but clearly had no interested in reframing their work as "coaching." While none of the respondents indicated a desire to change their professional identity to that of "coach," they did note the importance of the coaching role in supporting the effectiveness of the consulting work that they do.

Respondents pointed to four main ways they incorporated coaching into their consulting:

- Empowering leaders to take action on strategy and drive change.
- Providing a trusted, safe personal relationship within which to give feedback and facilitate reflection and behavior change with individual clients within the organization or project.
- Offering targeted support in a skill area or specific aspect of a project.
- Using coaching as a "process step" in consulting to encourage integration and sustainment of actions that had been taken before moving on to other actions (during or at the end of an engagement).

Several respondents reported situations where they used coaching to inspire and help empower a leader to take a stand, drive change, or take accountability more powerfully in their role within the organization or situation "to not just be a victim, but to be a strong player" (USA004). Respondents reported that the addition of coaching to their consulting added value and impact to their work.

Coaching was also referred to as an important element of ensuring transfer of skill and knowledge to the client at the end of the consulting engagement, to sustain the achievements that came from the consulting intervention. In the role of coach, the consultant can continue dialogue about the change or intervention results, to ensure sustainment, and this process of inquiry can often encourage a sense of ownership and understanding that the client would not have had otherwise. Consultants noted the drawbacks of confusing clients with their professional identity by coaching, as well as bringing in powerful coaching processes and having the client refuse to go back to the original consulting work: "When I went back to propose a consulting assistance for them, they didn't want to do it" (USA002).

Limitations and Future Inquiry

This exploratory, experience-based chapter has a number of limitations. First, it was not designed to provide results for broad application. Due to the process of participant recruitment and selection, the number of participants, and the limited demographic representation of the participants, broad conclusions for generalization should be avoided. In other words, the participant sample was not representative of the general population of management consultants, making it inappropriate to draw definitive conclusions. Second, as an experiential study, attempts were not made to separate the experiences and biases of the authors.

Despite these concerns, the study points to the dynamic interrelationship between coaching and management consulting, even if coaching may not be an explicit part of the consultant's toolkit. Additional opportunities related to this topic include conducting a similar study using a larger sample with a broader geographical distribution of respondents, and comparison of results by country or region. Another opportunity is to explore the topic of the current project with consultants who have changed their professional identity to "coach." As one participant stated,

> I've been thinking about this. Is it possible to be an effective coach without also being an effective consultant? I think the more the coach understands the world, especially if you're working with executives and people in the operational world and day to day alligators biting them, and you know they got politics and finances and all kinds of pressures to deal with...And coaches need to understand that, that person is a part of a system or systems...Well if you're a coach and you don't understand, you can't think systems thinking you're going to end up, I think, not being as useful to your, to your clients as you, as you might. (USA002)

CONCLUSION

This chapter describes the perceptions and experiences of eight management consultants that promote the idea that coaching is an important part of the professional identity of management consultants. We claim, with other writers, that coaching is already a role that is used in consulting interventions, and that consultants would do well to recognize that role and prepare themselves to implement it with expertise as a part of their work. This issue deserves further exploration, examining the two roles and their ramifications for how we intervene in organizations and interact with clients. An academic dialogue on this topic could benefit both the consulting and coaching communities.

While Stern (2004) offers a "working definition" of executive coaching as "an important organizational intervention" (p. 154), Sperry (2008) has underscored it still is not clear whether executive coaching is "an intervention, a role function, or a profession" (p. 35). Referring to the Society of Consulting Psychology, Sperry (2008) goes on to comment:

...it would be more accurate for those in the Society of Consulting Psychology to represent themselves as members of the psychology profession and identify themselves as consulting psychologists who provide such role functions as executive coaching and consultation, rather than as coaches. Because the Society has a major stake in the future and direction of executive coaching, it would seem that it is in its best interest to define and delimit executive coaching in terms of specific functions. Such distinctions have important consequences for theory and research as well as for professional practice. (p. 35)

It is time for those of us who bridge the worlds of practice and scholarship to take on these challenges.

NOTE

1. The authors are grateful for the research assistance provided by Valerie Mc-Murray.

REFERENCES

Bennett, J. L. (2006). An agenda for coaching-related research: A challenge for researchers. *Consulting Psychology Journal: Practice and Research, 58*(4), 240–248.

Bennett, J. L., & Bush, M. W. (2009). Coaching in organizations: Current trends and future opportunities. *OD Practitioner, 41*(1), 2–7.

Bennett, J., & Craig, W. B. (2005). Coaching eye for the OD practitioner. *OD Practitioner, 37*(3), 51–57.

Bennett, J. L., & Martin, D. J. (2001). The next professional wave: Consultant/coach. *Consulting to Management, 12*(3), 6–8.

Berman, W. H., & Bradt, G. (2006). Executive coaching and consulting: 'Different strokes for different folks.' *Professional Psychology: Research and Practice, 37*(3), 244–253.

Block, P. (2000). *Flawless consulting: A guide to getting your expertise used* (2nd ed.). New York, NY: Pfeiffer.

Diedrich, R. C., & Kilburg, R. R. (2001). Further consideration of executive coaching as an emerging competency. *Consulting Psychology Journal, 53*, 203–204.

Denzin, N. K., & Lincoln, Y. S. (Eds.). (2000). *Handbook of qualitative research* (2nd ed.). Thousand Oaks, CA: Sage Publications.

Lane, D., Stelter, R., & Rostron, S. S. (2010). The future of coaching as a profession. In E. Cox, T. Bachkirova, & D. Clutterbuck (Eds.), *The complete handbook of coaching* (pp. 357–368). Thousand Oaks, CA: Sage.

Marshak, R. J. (2009). *Organizational change: Views from the edge*. Bethel, ME: The Lewin Center.

Marshall, C., & Rossman, G. B. (2011). *Designing qualitative research* (5th ed.). Thousand Oaks, CA: Sage.

Maxwell, J. A. (2005). *Qualitative research design: An integrative approach* (2nd ed., Vol. 41). Thousand Oaks, CA: Sage.

Minahan, M. (2006). Coaching roots in OD. *OD Practitioner, 38*(3), 4–7.

Peterson, D. B. (1996). Executive coaching at work: The art of one-on-one change. *Consulting Psychology Journal: Practice and Research,* 48(2), 78–86.

Scott, B., Murrell, L., Zintz, A., & Gallagher, D. (2006). Is coaching OD? *OD Practitioner, 38*(3), 8–11.

Silverman, D. (2006). *Interpreting qualitative data* (3rd ed.). Thousand Oaks, CA: Sage.

Sperry, L. (2008). Executive coaching: An intervention, role function, or profession? *Consulting psychology journal: Practice and research, 6* (1), 33–37.

Steiner, M. B. (2008). OD and coaching. *OD Practitioner, 40*(3), 36–40.

Stern, L. R. (2004). Executive coaching: A working definition. *Consulting Psychology Journal: Practice and Research, 56*(3), 154–162.

Storjohann, G. (2006). This thing called coaching. *OD Practitioner, 38*(3), 12–16.

Thompson, H. B., Bear, D. J., Dennis, D. J., Vickers, M., London, J., & Morrison, C. L. (2008). *Coaching: A global study of successful practices: Trends and future possibilities 2008–2018.* New York, NY: American Management Association.

Weiss, R. S. (1994). *Learning from strangers: The art and method of qualitative interview studies.* New York, NY: The Free Press.

Winum, P. C. (1995). Anatomy of an executive consultation: Three perspectives. *Consulting Psychology Journal, 47,* 114–121.

CHAPTER 15

"MOON SHOTS FOR MANAGEMENT"[1]

Traditional, Systemic or Complementary Consulting for Supporting Management on their Trek to the Moon?

Andreas Drechsler, Peter Kalvelage, and Tobias Trepper

In "Moon Shots for Management," Gary Hamel (2009) called for radical changes to the practice of management in order to address issues like a rapidly changing environment and the need for creativity and flexibility. He referred to these 25 challenges as "moon shots" (hence the title of his article and this chapter). Additionally he initiated an online platform—"Management Innovation eXchange"[2]—to exchange workable ideas on conforming management structures and practices. The amount of usage and apparent acceptance of this online platform by managers—as evident by viewing the site—underline the practical relevance of the suggested approach.

While Hamel and his associates also acknowledge the high level of difficulty in putting the proposed changes into practice, they do not give specific suggestions how this can actually be achieved. One option could include

Exploring the Professional Identity of Management Consultants, pages 303–324
Copyright © 2013 by Information Age Publishing
All rights of reproduction in any form reserved.

hiring external consultants to aid in the transformation process, a common practice in organizational change initiatives (e.g., Buono, Jamieson, Sorensen, & Yaeger, 2010). But since traditional approaches to management consulting are aimed at the current practice of management, the question arises whether these approaches would also be suited to aid management in their "moon shots" and the accompanying transformation efforts.

A fundamentally differing consulting approach with roots in the general theory of social systems by the German sociologist Niklas Luhmann (2008)—called systemic consulting (see Mohe & Seidl, 2009)—appears to be quite close to the characteristics of Hamel's "moon shots" on first glance. Yet the question of the actual extent of this apparent compatibility remains. And last but not least, why not combine the best elements from both consulting paradigms resulting in complementary approaches to consulting (Königswieser, 2008)? This can either be achieved by incorporating systemic elements into traditional consulting approaches or vice-versa.

Either way, the question remains, how, to what extent, and with which kind of approach, can consulting help to support the realization of "moon shots for management" in practice.

GOALS AND OUTCOME

To shed light on this question, we compare the different types of consulting regarding the extent of compatibility to the vision presented in "Moon Shots for Management." As a result, each previously outlined consulting paradigm (traditional, systemic, complementary) will receive a thorough evaluation on whether, and how well, they are suited to introduce one or more "moon shots" in an organization.

This analysis is intended to support managers aiming to transform their management system in choosing an appropriate type of consultant and setting general policies or principles for the change effort. Consultants could extend their methodological portfolio to provide a new type of consulting product, which has a distinct and well-publicized purpose (specifically tackling Hamel's "moon shot" challenges in client organizations) as well as a solid scientific foundation (as outlined in the following sections).

From a researcher's perspective, this evaluation will add a certain purpose to the choice of systemic consulting and therefore extend the perspective beyond just "an alternative way of thinking about interventions in organizations" (Mohe & Seidl, 2009, p. 63). This is especially relevant because systemic and complementary consulting approaches still "almost exclusively [exist] within the German-speaking consulting markets" (Mohe & Seidl, 2009, p. 47). The combination with the "moon shot" initiative— which according to the aforementioned website seems to have gained a certain amount of worldwide attention—could lead to increased interest into systemic consulting in non-German-speaking research communities. Additionally, the results might point towards the possibility of a retroactive construction of theoretical underpinnings of the very practice-driven "moon shots," depending on the actual extent of compatibility to Luhmann's theory of social systems.

METHODOLOGY

To achieve the aforementioned results the authors will first present the fundamentals of the "moon shot" challenges as well as of each consulting approach. In a second step there will be a discussion on the extent of compatibility of each consulting approach to the principles behind the "moon shot" challenges. This discussion will focus both on how compatible each approach is in general to each principle as well as how suitable each consulting approach can be in helping management confronting the "moon shot" challenges in practice. Afterwards, the results will be validated by presenting and discussing specific feedback received from consultants of each approach. In the end, there will be a conclusion on how well each type of consulting fits with Hamel's proposal, their respective strengths and weaknesses, and whether a combined orchestration of the approaches appears promising.

CHARACTERISTICS OF HAMEL'S "MOON SHOTS FOR MANAGEMENT"

Before turning to the analysis, it is necessary to examine the "moon shots for management" themselves. The 25 "moon shot" challenges were developed in a collective process by 35 invited management scholars and practitioners over two days at a conference in California. Although Hamel (2009) deliberately did not want to "condense" their list into a "handful of meta-challenges," viewing and analyzing each of the 25 challenges in detail is beyond the scope of this chapter. However, an introductory document to the aforementioned online platform "Management Innovation Exchange" (2010) arranges them thematically according to six principles. Each principle will be described briefly, in order to lay a foundation for the discussion later.

Principle 1: Mend the Soul of Business

The three challenges behind this first principle aim to "embed the ethos of community and citizenship," "humanize the language of the business," and "focus the work of management on a higher purpose." In other words, the idea is to view and conduct management deliberately embedded in its context in society. Therefore a manager should actively consider consequences of actions for other human beings. And since these human beings possess emotions as well as a rational mind, Hamel and associates propose to modify language to convey strong emotions and virtues, in order to address both aspects together and receive stronger commitments and results. And last but not least, managers' perspectives ideally should grow beyond long-term strategies regarding shareholder value toward an overall and "timeless" purpose guiding all their actions. This principle can therefore be summarized as a call for looking beyond the actual, factual tasks and matters of business and management.

Principle 2: Unleash Human Capabilities

The objectives within this principle are to "increase trust, reduce fear," to "reinvent the means of control," to "amplify imagination" and "enable communities of passion," to "capture the advantages of diversity," and finally to "take the work out of work." In other words, a major duty of management should be to harness the creative and value-creating powers of all personnel to the fullest extent. This principle meshes with the previously mentioned challenge of "focusing on a higher purpose." One recurring issue throughout the challenges in this theme is to eliminate all negative influences of fear and control.

Principle 3: Foster Strategic Renewal

The third principle revolves around "mak[ing] direction bottom up and outside-in," "experiment[ing] more often and more cheaply," "creat[ing] internal markets for ideas, cash and talent," "de-politiciz[ing] decision-making," and "disaggregat[ing] the organization." The underlying idea behind these challenges can be summarized as treating strategy as an emergent and ongoing process (in some ways similar to Mintzberg's (1978) classic perspective on deliberate and emergent strategies). To achieve this, the organization should be tailored in a way so that the full benefits of dealing with these issues directly and openly can be realized. This orientation is opposed to the idea that emergence from the inside or outside is an aberration from plans formulated at the very top of the organization.

Principle 4: Distribute Power

This theme also contains five challenges, such as to "build 'natural,' flexible hierarchies," "redefine the work of leadership," "create a democracy of information," "expand the scope of employee autonomy," and "encourage the dissenters." These challenges all focus on the organization itself, which serves as a backdrop to carry out all other managerial tasks. The general idea is to re-shape the organizational structure and culture to enhance flexibility and dialogue throughout the organization. These changes are intended to provide structural support to the proposed approach to strategy in the last theme. Of particular interest for later discussion is the "moon shot" called "redefine the work of leadership," where Hamel and colleagues call for a drastic change for managers from "heroic decision makers" to "social-systems architects who enable innovation and collaboration" (Hamel, 2009).

Principle 5: Reshape Managerial Minds

The three challenges here focus on the person of the manager itself. The challenges are to "strengthen the right side of the managerial brain," "retool management for an open, borderless world," and "rethink the philosophical foundations of management." This theme provides a counterpart to the previous themes that dealt with issues a manager has to act upon (strategy, structure, etc.), as it focuses on providing managers with the necessary mindset, if not "verbal tools," to be prepared and empowered to carry out these actions. The aforementioned shift towards a social-systems architect could also require a "reshaping" of the managerial mind, so the respective challenge fits here as well.

Principle 6: Seek Balance and Harmony

The three challenges in this principle urge managers to "develop holistic performance measures," "transcend traditional management trade-offs," and "stretch management timeframes and broaden perspectives." Again, similar to the first principle, these challenges (arguably with the exception of the development of holistic performance measures) go deliberately beyond classic management issues, but this time on a less abstract and more "hands-on" level.

In sum, one can find the major part of the challenges dealing with classic themes of management like strategy, organization, and personnel, as well as a theme focusing on the manager as an individual and two themes encouraging new ways of thinking and acting. The themes themselves, while not clearly distinct, indicate a high level of interdependence between the challenges. Hamel himself noted that most of these challenges are not new, but that they are still mostly unsolved in practice, and that overcoming these challenges is necessary to elevate the effectiveness and efficiency of management to a new level in order to enable it to cope with the challenges of the present and the future.

FUNDAMENTALS OF LUHMANN'S THEORY
OF SOCIAL SYSTEMS

Before we discuss the three consulting approaches and their relation to Hamel's "moon shots," we need take a look at an important foundation for the systemic and complementary approaches to consulting. This foundation is the newer general theory of social systems by the German sociologist Niklas Luhmann (2008). This section describes the fundamentals of his theory, which are necessary to distinguish the systemic and complementary consulting approaches from traditional approaches.

There is no single "systems theory." Instead we have a variety of theories that describe actions and impacts in various kinds of systems. There are several different research approaches and theories that can be attributed to a systemic view of the world (Luhmann, 2002). Additionally, some of the research fields of the main representatives of these theories are fundamentally different and yet are complementary in some ways. In general, these theories understand the world as a system consisting of subsystems that interact with each other in more or less strong correlation, which is called "structured coupling" (Kasper, Mayrhofer, & Meyer, 1998).

Although according to Luhmann (1984) the main principles of his theory are valid for all kinds of systems, in this chapter we will focus on social systems, which form the center of his theory. A key principle of his theory rejects the idea that single humans and groups of humans are systems by themselves. Moreover, in his perspective, a human being is an aggregation of several different systems.

Regardless of its type, each system operates and can only exist by doing so continuously. There are two basic principles of operation. On one level, systems just observe, yet a system also differentiates between itself and its environment (Luhmann, 1984). This concept is called autopoiesis. A system is autopoietic if its elements are produced and reproduced by the elements it consists of. There is no input and no output by any objects to and from the system (Luhmann, 2008).

According to Luhmann (1984), the main element a social system consists of, and by which it reproduces itself, is communication, which differentiates that system from other types of systems. This also means that a system is neither a human nor his mind, just communication. It also means that for self-preservation through continuous re-creation (autopoiesis), a continuous flow of communication is necessary. In a case where no more communication takes place inside a social system, its existence is terminated. Furthermore, Luhmann divides the outside of a system into its direct environment and the outer world. Systems can only operate on elements in their direct environment. This means that whenever a system takes a part of the outer world into account during an operation, this part automatically becomes a part of its direct environment. So the difference between the direct environment and the outer world is purely viewed or constructed through the perspective of the system.

Regarding their operations, systems are closed to the outside, the exterior to their boundaries. Only an operation of and within a system can generate new operations. Similarly social systems can only generate new communication through previous communication. Still, systems are not closed to external influences. However, the decision if (and how) an external influence will actually affect the system and its operations is always undertaken by the system itself and cannot be predicted. This openness to the environment allows a structural coupling between systems.

OVERVIEW OF CONSULTING APPROACHES

In preparation for the subsequent discussion, this chapter describes three general consulting approaches, namely the traditional, the systemic, and the complementary approach to consulting. The latter combines elements of both of the aforementioned approaches (Königswieser, Lang, & Wimmer, 2009). Since Hamel's "moon shots" are aimed specifically at managers, we will focus only on topics and issues relevant to management-oriented consulting.

Traditional Consulting Approach

By and large, the aim of traditional management consultants can be summarized as aiding clients in either formulating strategic or organizational initiatives, or in putting them into practice and transforming their organization. They can be employed to solve actual client problems, or to introduce new and promising management concepts (Fink, 2009).

Viewed from a more abstract perspective, this approach of consulting can be characterized as being based upon the behavioristic-positivistic learning theory (Linder, 2006). The consultant sees him or herself as an objective person who occupies an external position, typically assuming that a true reality exists, which can be explored through scientific methods. For every action and decision there is a justification we can influence (Bergknapp, 2007; Cassel & Symon, 1994).

This approach is primary associated with methods of communication through instruction, order, and command (Königswieser & Hillebrand, 2007), or characterized by a "doctor-patient relationship" (Linder, 2006). In practice, these may be communicated under the guise of "suggestions" or "recommendation," but there is the underlying belief by the consultant that these are "correct" and "true," and therefore carry a normative component towards the client (Handler, 2007). Additionally, the traditional consulting approach is said to focus less on sustainability but to place consulting products and practices in companies. Instead of responding to the needs of the client company, consultants following the traditional approach sometimes tend to adjust problems so that they fit to an already found solution (bias-based problem definition towards the "consulting products") (Kolbeck & Wimmer, 2001, p. 11; Raffel, 2006; Walger & Neise, 2005; Walger, 1995). Imitation strategies by other consulting companies contribute to a promotion of industry-wide "management fashions" (Clark, 2004).

Additionally, in other traditional consulting projects the consultants act as decision-makers from the outside. Another point to be mentioned here is the involvement of consultants to justify unpopular decisions, such as mass layoffs (Taylor & Remenyi, 2002).

According to the literature, the traditional consulting industry appears to have undergone significant changes in the last decade. Economic crises and industry scandals, as well as refined customer expectations, have led to a decline in revenue and projects (Buono, 2004; Fink, 2009). While the consulting industry as a whole, according to Fink, has recovered in the meantime, the economic pressure led consultancy firms, according to Buono, to split up, specialize, and explore new ways of meeting client expectations. This includes, for example, change-related interventions (Kerber & Buono, 2004; Sorensen & Yaeger, 2004), approaches from therapy (de Caluwé, Que & Vermaak, 2004; Gebhardt, 2010), and even system-oriented approaches (Mitchell, 2010; Scherer, Lavery, Sullivan, Whitson, & Vales, 2010). All these topics are also relevant in the context of the other two consulting approaches presented subsequently.

Systemic Consulting Approach

The foundation of systemic consulting relies on Luhmann's theory of social systems and builds upon the concept of a complex and dynamic worldview. The advised organization is understood as a system that is closed in itself, but it is also able to interact outwards with other systems. Thus, a direct influence on as well as gaining full insight into the inner workings of this system are not possible. The most important element is no longer the individual, but the communication that occurs in the form of decisions as well as remembered history. By communicating, the organization reproduces itself by relating decisions to decisions (Ellebracht, Lenz, Osterhold, & Schäfer, 2003; Königswieser & Hillebrand, 2007; Kolbeck & Wimmer, 2001; Luhmann, 2006; Linder, 2006).

The consultants themselves, according to Königswieser and Hillebrand (2007), can be seen therefore as a separate social (consultancy) system that interacts with the organization seeking advice, here referred to as client system. This symbiosis results in the consultant-client-system, which in turn differentiates an organization from its environment, but, as noted above, communicates with it. An important point in this regard is the elaboration of a clear contract between the two parties, which states comprehensive roles and targets. In this context the consultant, contrary to the traditional approach, deliberately does not use communication through instruction. This means that he does not transfer knowledge to the client organization and does not offer the client a seemingly complete solution (Wimmer, 2009). Rather, the consultant is a deliberate outsider who brings an exterior view of the client system and can stimulate that system specifically with process know-how and the right methods, for the client system is the true expert in the consulted area (Ellebracht et al., 2003; Königswieser & Hillebrand, 2007; Wimmer, 1999, 2009).

In this context, there are the common terms of intervention and irritation. In systemic consulting, an intervention is a definable, goal-directed action between two systems that aims to achieve a pre-considered action in the target system (Königswieser & Hillebrand, 2007; Wimmer, 1999). Any irritation is also an intervention. However, by using irritations the consultant can create interventions that interfere with the perception, declarations, and behavior of the client system. Interventions are based on consultant observations, which are by definition different from the self-observation of the client system. The interference can lead to a change of the self-observation and self-description of the client system (Walger & Neise, 2005). Whether only the irritation or the bundle of interventions containing irritations is seen as authoritative is not yet clear in the literature. In a commentary on the article by Walger and Neise (2005), Königswieser and Hillebrand (2005) explicitly disagree with the working assertion that only a mere irritation is possible in systemic counseling, and reaffirm their position of using interventions (Königswieser & Hillebrand, 2005).

According to Königswieser and Hillebrand (2007), interventions can be treated on three different levels. On the architectural level, all development decisions in relation to the objective of the consultation are set, the relevant stakeholders are identified, the duration of the project is recognized, and it is determined which symbolism seems to be appropriate. On the design level, the dimensions of specific projects of the top project will be marked out, for example, the framework of a workshop. On the operational level, specific objectives and possible interventions are planned, and expected impacts are forecasted. Thus, the intervention, which also encompasses planning and predictions, goes further than an irritation that simply tries to disturb existing perception patterns and explanatory models of the existing problem (Walger & Neise, 2005).

The main expertise of systemic consulting is the promotion of communication and thus self-initiated development potential of organizations. It is commonly used, for example, to resolve and "unblock" existing communication blockages caused by hierarchies, or by conflicts about power or territory (Wimmer, 2008). That means that one of the main aspects of systemic consulting is the liquefaction of internal organization patterns of cooperation. Therefore, systemic consulting is said to be particularly well suited to support comprehensive development projects for a long time, but without contributing explicit knowledge to the client organization (Königswieser & Hillebrand, 2007). In other words, the systemic approach to consulting generally aims at long-term sustainable learning and renewal processes to initiate continuous change processes in the client organizations and support them in becoming and staying viable, successful, and more efficient.

Complementary Consulting Approaches

Königswieser, Sonuc, and Gebhardt's (2008) book on *Complementary Consulting* contributed to the debate about the future of the consulting business with another approach. Königswieser, Lang, and Wimmer (2009) describe complementary consulting as the integration of technical and process know-how based on a common value system. This approach makes it possible to use the knowledge of both worlds (systemic and traditional consulting) in an integrated way. The background for this step was their personal experience in systemic consulting, which showed the lack of an economic perspective.

As the key success factors of a consulting-system, they mention the three following factors:

1. Complementary skills, context-dependent roles
2. Mutual trust, respect, common base of values
3. Time for reflection, work, and substantive debate

In practice this means that a project team has to be put together contextually, there has to be a foundation of trust among the different team members, and there must be sufficient time for their coordination (Königswieser, 2008). Throughout a consulting project, the use of systemic as well as traditional consulting methods is continuously "oscillating," depending on the situation at hand, and builds on a foundation of a systemic attitude and systemic values.

Wimmer (2008), however, is critical to all this and describes the complementary approach as a transition phenomenon, since the only thing taking place is an additive combination of process-oriented, systemic, and expert-driven traditional consulting. He justifies his critical stance with the thought that social conflicts among the individual consulting philosophies will arise during a consulting project because both sides will try to gain predominance in working with the client. This dynamic occurs because only a certain kind of supremacy secures the retention of the consultant's identity (Wimmer, 2008). Based on these observations, Wimmer aims to develop a completely new understanding of consulting. He calls it the "third way," which can have its "professional roots" in either of the above mentioned forms (Königswieser et al., 2009). In his opinion, the development of a consultant towards this third way varies in difficulty and depends on the individual skills each consultant possesses. According to Wimmer, all professions have one "subject-specific disability" in common, a blind spot that denies them a clear view of the opposed perspective (either traditional or systemic). The idea is to strive to overcome this blind spot by means of regular self-reflection. However, self-reflection is noted as still being inadequately practiced in complementary consulting (Königswieser et al., 2009). Interviews with managers conducted by Handler (2007) support the importance of self-reflection for either type of consultant in practice as well as the potential of combining the best of both worlds in an actual consulting approach.

In conclusion, complementary consulting can be either viewed according to Königswieser as approach integrating the best of both worlds from traditional and systemic consulting, or according to Wimmer as a third way, which tries to build up a fully new understanding of consulting masking out the already known professions. Unfortunately, Wimmer does not delve into further detail on how this could actually be achieved in practice; therefore we will focus on the complementary consulting approach according to Königswieser et al. in the subsequent discussions.

ANALYSIS: WHICH CONSULTING APPROACH FITS MANAGEMENT'S "TREK TO THE MOON"?

After describing the principles behind the "moon shots" as well as the foundations for three consulting approaches, this section take an in-depth look into the general fit between each of the consulting approaches and the "moon shot" principles. The discussion then turns to the suitability of each consulting approach for changing existing management systems in practice, in order to tackle the "moon shot" challenges and, in the end, organization change management practices on a fundamental level.

General Fit between the Consulting Approaches and the "Moon Shot" Principles

The discussion begins with an assessment of the three consulting approaches and the "Moon Shot" principles.

Traditional Consulting

As mentioned in the summarization of the "moon shots," several principles focus on classic management issues—strategy, structure, and personnel. Looking at the challenges in detail, there are tried-and-true consulting approaches for issues like encouraging diversity ("diversity management"), reorganizing organizational hierarchies, disaggregating organizations ("decentralization"), and improving corporate performance management. Even "vision (= purpose) workshops" or "stakeholder relations" (as community and citizenship) are not unheard of among the portfolio of traditional consulting companies. So it could certainly be feasible to take on these and similarly well-known challenges by setting up specialized consulting projects and hiring appropriately skilled and experienced consultants.

Another aspect in favor of traditional consulting approaches is their broad acceptance in the business world (Fink, 2009). Additionally, it is not uncommon, especially for larger organizations, to have in-house consulting departments or long-term partnerships with consultancy firms (Niedereichholz & Niedereichholz, 2006). These consultants also have the advantage (but at the same time the disadvantage) of knowing the inner workings and informal structures of the client organization. Therefore they are potentially able to provide specifically tailored results and suggestions. And the aforementioned "bias-based problem definition" could actually work in favor of a widespread adoption of the "moon shots," if a well-known consultancy firm successfully establishes a consulting product around them and manages to sell it well. This factor could be especially important, since the introduction of new management concepts is one of the key purposes of traditional consultants.

Yet, principles like "mend the soul of business" or "seek balance and harmony" are about topics that do not fit well with the rational and scientific approach to consulting. "Passion," "humanization," "democracy," or even "encouraging dissenters" all go against "mainstream" traditional consulting (and management as well) and are not achievable with tried-and-true, scientific methods or standardized packages. It is difficult to imagine how "rethinking the philosophical foundations of management" can be supported by consultants who supported and advocated the current "state-of-the-art foundations of management" for all their professional life. And it is at least plausible that consultants with well-established relations to and knowledge about their client organization will find it equally difficult to suggest radically new concepts for these organizations, since their "mental image" of them is also well established and difficult to re-imagine, even for themselves. There is also the danger of diluting the "pure idea" behind the "moon shots" as a whole, if they are re-packaged into a one-size-fits-it-all consulting product or "management fashion."

Systemic Consulting

In order to examine the fit between systemic consulting approaches and the "moon shots" challenge, it is useful to look at the relation between the "moon shot" principles and the background of Luhmann's theory of social systems as outlined previously. Since systemic consultants strive to stay separated from the social system (i.e., the organization) they work for, they are uniquely suited to present ideas and concepts that will "irritate" the social system. As mentioned previously, many "moon shot" principles are either contrary to the classic conduct of management ("increase trust, reduce fear," "experiment more often and more cheaply," "encourage the dissenters," etc.) or go beyond it ("create communities of passion," "re-invent means of control," "redefine the work of leadership," etc.). From their deliberately external position, a systemic consultant could give the client suitable irritations or interventions that can lead to an adoption and instantiation of the rather abstract and concise "moon shots" and the underlying principles.

A second perspective of relevance here is the extent of conformity between the "moon shots" and the systemic view of organizations itself. The aforementioned unpredictability and existence of an inner logic in any social system also applies to any managed part of an organization (like a department) as well as the whole organization itself. Viewed through a systemic lens, a manager can effectively only irritate or intervene in an organization he or she is (believed to be) managing. In this perspective, any "control," "steering" or "directing" of an organization is largely the result of the "managed" social system choosing those internal operations on its own, which in retrospect lead to the same results the manager intended (see Drechsler, Kalvelage, & Trepper, 2010 for a more detailed description of principles of systemic management). Systemic management now acknowledges these issues and tries to deal with them deliberately and openly. "Moon shots" like "reinvent the means of control," "make direction bottom-up and outside-in," or "redefine the work of leadership" show a striking similarity to viewing social systems through a (Luhmann-)systemic lens. They can be viewed as instantiations of (usually abstract) principles of systemic management. By "reshaping managerial minds" according to systemic principles, one would certainly not end up far from the underlying ideals of the "moon shots."

The two main disadvantages of systemic consultancy regarding the "moon shots" are acceptance and availability. The issue of acceptance is directly related to its contrast to traditional consulting. The systemic consultant does not act as a teacher who "knows" something or provides state-of-the-art concepts that "work." The one thing they offer as a central principle of this consulting approach is uncertainty, in form of irritations and interventions whose outcomes are deliberately unclear. This deliverable stands in clear contrast to the expectations of a client organization used to working with consultants who follow the traditional approach. It needs a considerable amount of courage from both the one responsible for hiring the consultants as well as the entire organization to face this unfamiliar and deliberate uncertainty and "help themselves" in the process.

Availability is a clear second problem with systemic consulting approaches since they nearly exclusively exist in German-speaking countries (Mohe & Seidl, 2009). Although in this regard, it is striking that at least terminologically similar issues and approaches are discussed in the international literature as well (see last paragraph of the discussion of traditional consulting approaches in general). Since these discussions are not linked to systemic consulting or Luhmann's theory of social systems, further research is needed to arrive at a definite conclusion here.

The previously discussed advantages and disadvantages of familiarity with the client organization as well as the issues about "packaging" the "moon shots" as a consulting product are basically the same as they are for traditional consulting, although the former should be at least critically reflected by systemic consultants.

Complementary Consulting

This consulting approach follows similar ways as systemic consulting, which means that the "moon shots" are addressed to a similar extent with similar advantages and disadvantages. In contrast to a pure systemic approach, the additional application of familiar elements from traditional consulting means a greater familiarity of the client organization with the used consulting approach. It also has the potential to couple specific domain or business knowledge with systemic irritation and intervention techniques.

The disadvantages are directly related to the previously mentioned critiques of complementary consulting itself. Speaking from a strictly systemic perspective, one can either be part of a social system (as traditional consultants are) or be on the outside (as systemic consultants are), so a complementary consultant is prone to the similar advantages or disadvantages, depending where they are effectively "placing themselves" in a given consultancy situation.[3]

Suitability for Changing Existing Management Systems

This section examines the suitability of each consulting approach for putting the challenges into practice, or in other words, conducting "change management" of management.

Traditional Consulting

Traditional consulting firms and consultants typically possess a wide experience and tried-and-true toolsets for large-scale change management efforts (e.g., Gattermayer & Al-Ani, 2001). Since this type of consultancy is also widely accepted, it can lead to having the necessary backing or authority for acceptance of specific advice during a certain change project. This general specificity of advice towards suggested changes is another advantage of traditional consulting approaches. Although in the end this advice can turn out as anywhere between perfect and catastrophic for the client organization, the same is true for any change-related irritation or intervention by a systemic or complementary consultant. Introducing "moon shot management consulting" as a standardized product could even benefit from accumulating experiences from each "moon shot" change project over the years.

The sustainability of such change efforts, however, is often questioned (Schmidt & Strobel, 2005; Niedereichholz & Niedereichholz, 2006). In this specific case, the previously discussed limitations with regard to conformity with the "moon shots" are another disadvantage of traditional consulting approaches. As stated previously, it is at least difficult to, for example, "reinvent the means of control" during an actual change project, when "being an expert in state-of-the-art means of control" has been a major success factor for the consultant in question in the past. It can be theorized that by means of traditional consulting approaches management would only be changed gradually, but not as radically as the whole 25 "moon shots" imply as a necessity for sustained organizational success in the future.

Systemic Consulting

A specialty of systemic consulting approaches is facilitating change in organizations by deliberately refraining from interfering with internal processes of the client organization beyond irritations or interventions. Since the actual solution will be developed by the client organization itself, it might turn out more sustainable and organic than externally prescribed changes. The large amount of conformity between several "moon shots" and Luhmann's theory of social systems enables systemic consulting approaches theoretically to foster even fundamental changes in management structures and culture.

Systemic consultancy, however, appears less suited to introduce changes to the classic areas of management referred to by the "moon shots," since it deliberately refrains from giving factual advice. The previously mentioned issues of general acceptance and availability of the approach itself, the unpredictability of the interventions as well as the downsides of a "product approach" to "moon shot consulting" are equally applicable to bringing organizational change to the client organization.

Complementary Consulting

As the sources in the respective chapter show, complementary consulting is rather new and, more importantly, still not clearly defined, so it is difficult to arrive at a distinct conclusion regarding the suitability of complementary consulting for organizational transformation. The "hybrid" nature of complementary consulting approaches lends itself towards flexibility during a change management effort, and the familiarity of traditional elements will reduce the amount of uncertainty an organization has to face.

This is no guarantee for success, however, since it is up to the experience of the consultant to decide which methods to use and elements of which approach to focus on in a certain situation to change the client organization. This choice is doubly difficult since a complementary consultant is as aware as a systemic consultant about the unpredictability of his client organization, and he or she will never know whether success or failure of a change effort can be attributed to the choice of methods and practices from either approach.

VALIDATION

In order to validate our theoretical analysis laid out in this chapter, we presented the assessment to representatives from three German consulting firms, asking for their critique and comments. The firms and the three respective consultants were selected to represent the traditional, systemic, and complementary approach to consulting.

The consultants' feedback generally indicated a high relevance of the issues mentioned, and there was also a general consensus about most of the discussion about the perceived suitability of each consulting approach for putting the "moon shots" into practice. The apparent paradigm change in the management discipline came up independently in the feedback, but with different perspectives. While one consultant saw evidence of such a paradigm change looming about for quite a while (and not really progressing over the years), another stated that he is not seeing a necessity for radical changes in the management function itself, but rather regarding the person of the manager. The outlined similarities between topics in international and German consulting research were also regarded as striking and of interest for further research regarding their actual extent. Several examples of recent extensions of the traditional consulting approach to go beyond addressing the rational side of managers via PowerPoint presentations were also given.

A suggestion to overcome the (confirmed) lack of broad acceptance of non-traditional approaches to consulting was to clearly communicate and agree on specific targets and deliverables for a consulting project, while still keeping a systemic (or complementary) mindset during the project itself. The aforementioned permanent role-conflicts of a complementary consultant were also confirmed from practical experience, and that acceptance and continuous self-reflection of that "ongoing paradox" throughout the consulting process might be the best way to deal with this issue. A lack of "independent" research and studies about the success of systemic and complementary consulting projects compared to traditional consulting projects was also noted.

It was also noted that the discussion and evaluation of the three approaches to consultancy provided "nothing perceived as substantially new" regarding the consulting approaches themselves. This criticism was directly linked to general criticism towards Hamel's "moon shots" themselves, specifically towards the apparent lack of value in providing "yet another list" of abstract management challenges for the future. It was affirmed that most "moon shots" could serve as a kind of operationalization of usually even more abstract systemic principles. Yet, at the same time the "moon shots" were still found lacking practical applicability. One issue mentioned as missing from the "moon shots" was the necessary handling of the "data/ information overload threat" for managers caused by the availability of an abundance of raw and analyzed data about the corporate situation and performance. It was also noted that the underlying notion on fundamental and permanent change in the "moon shots" would not work well in the typical German medium-sized company, and that the focus on radical and continuous change might even be a culture-specific "American thing." Regarding the accompanying online platform, the value of "solutions that (maybe) worked once in a different company" was also questioned.

At this point, however, the provision of a path towards "hands-on applicability" of the abstract "moon shots" by means of a specifically tailored consulting method or even product was of particular interest to the consultants. One metaphor used was the ideal of a consultant as "battle-hardened and (knowledge-wise) well-trained sparring partner" who does not strive to be the better fighter, but instead aims at the improvement of his partner's prowess and competency. In the respective consultant's opinion, this type of consultant was perceived to be well suited to aid management in putting the "moon shots" into practice.

CONCLUSION AND OUTLOOK

The previous analysis shows that all consulting approaches have some merit for putting the "moon shots for management" into practice. In addition, complementary consulting approaches promise a combination between the advantages of both traditional and systemic consulting, but this combination of potentially incompatible approaches leads to further, not easily solvable problems of its own. The feedback from the consultants from all three consulting approaches largely confirms the findings and, in addition, gives further issues for discussion, both about the "moon shots" themselves as well as each consulting approach. In the end there seemingly needs to be a (hopefully conscious and deliberate) decision between consulting approaches (or any combination thereof), if a manager wants to tackle the "moon shot" challenges in his or her organization with external support. The same can be said regarding the necessity of self-reflection for consultants about their current role(s) during the consulting process.

Based on the shown similarities between systemic principles and the principles behind the "moon shots," it would be interesting to confront the people behind the "moon shots" with Luhmann's theory of social systems and derived principles of systemic management. Of particular interest would be whether their mainly intuitive or experience-based suggestions for "better" management turn out to have a similar foundation to theory-derived principles for systemic management, or whether the similarities are just coincidence or attributable to common sense.

Looking specifically at the discussion of the three consulting approaches, it is striking that there are notions of extending the strictly traditional approach to consulting beyond the mechanistic, positivistic perspective. In this regard it would certainly be interesting to examine more thoroughly whether the extension of traditional consulting towards a systems-oriented view truly corresponds with what the German-speaking market would call "systemic" or "complementary" consulting.

Since changes in organizations are often conducted with the aid of consultants, maybe there also need to be accompanying and complementary "moon shots for consulting," in order to successfully put the "moon shots for management" into widespread and sustained management practice. This challenge might even help to overcome the shortcomings of either consulting approach.

NOTES

1. We would like to thank Mr. Fabian Hoffmann (Systemic Excellence Group), Mr. Andre Voller (excientes Management Consulting GmbH), as well as one experienced consultant from the German division of a large international management consulting company (who has to go unnamed here due to company policies) for their valuable general feedback as well as their specific and insightful comments for the validation section.
2. See http://www.managementexchange.com.
3. Systemically, one could argue that it is impossible to observe oneself objectively and therefore impossible to deem oneself strictly inside or outside of the client system by means of self-observation, but that point will not be explored more fully in this chapter.

REFERENCES

Bergknapp, A., (2007). Zur Logik von Beratungssystemen. Ein methodologischer Ansatz zur Analyse von Beratungsgeschichten [Coaching, Supervision. About the logic of consulting systems (consulting, supervision): A methodological approach for the analysis of consulting stories]. In N. Tomaschek (Ed.), *Perspektiven systemischer Entwicklung und Beratung von Organisationen. Ein Sammelband* [Perspectives of systemic development and consulting of organizations. An anthology] (pp. 95–106). Heidelberg: Carl-Auer-Systeme.

Buono, A. F. (2004). Introduction. In A. F. Buono (Ed.), *Creative Consulting* (pp. vii–xix). Charlotte, NC: Information Age Publishing.

Buono, A. F., Jamieson, D. W., Sorensen, P. & Yaeger, T. (2010). Introduction. In A. F. Buono & D. Jamieson (Eds.), *Consultation for organizational change* (pp. vii–xx). Charlotte, NC: Information Age Publishing.

Cassel, C. & Symon, G. (1994). *Qualitative methods in organizational research: A practical guide.* Thousand Oaks, CA: Sage Publications Ltd.

Clark, T. (2004). Management fashion as collective action. In A. F. Buono (Ed.), *Creative Consulting* (pp. 3–25). Charlotte, NC: Information Age Publishing.

de Caluwé, L., Que, F., & Vermaak, H. (2004). Comparing psychotherapists' and change agents' approaches to change: Reflections on changing people and changing organizations. In A. F. Buono (Ed.), *Creative Consulting* (pp. 267–302). Charlotte, NC: Information Age Publishing.

Drechsler, A., Kalvelage, P., & Trepper, T. (2010). Systemic IT project management: A rational way to manage irrationalities in IT projects? In E. Proper, K. Gaaloul, F. Harmsen, & S. Wrycza (Eds.), *Practice-driven research on enterprise transformation* (pp. 127–155). New York, NY: Springer.

Ellebracht, H., Lenz, G., Osterhold, G., & Schäfer, H. (2003). *Systemische Organisations- und Unternehmensberatung* [Systemic consulting of organizations and businesses]. Wiesbaden: Gabler.

Fink, D. (2009). *Strategische Unternehmensberatung* [Strategic business consulting]. München: Franz Vahlen.

Gattermayer, W. & Al-Ani, A. (2001). *Change Management und Unternehmenserfolg* [Change management and business success]. Wiesbaden: Gabler.

Gebhardt, J. A. (2010). From therapist to executive coach: Insight, intervention and organizational change. In A. F. Buono & D. Jamieson (Eds.), *Consultation for organizational change* (pp.153–181). Charlotte, NC: Information Age Publishing.

Hamel, G. (2009). Moon shots for management. *Harvard Business Review, 87*(2), 91–98.

Handler, G. (2007). *Konzept zur Entwicklung integrierter Beratung: Integration systemischer Elemente in die klassische Beratung* [A concept for the development of integrated consulting: Integration of systemic elements into traditional consulting]. Wiesbaden: Gabler.

Kasper, H., Mayrhofer, W., & Meyer, M. (1998). Managerhandeln—nach der systemtheoretisch-konstruktivistischen Wende [Manager action after the systemic-constructivistic shift]. *Die Betriebswirtschaft, May,* 603–621.

Kerber, K. W. & Buono, A. F. (2004). Intervening in virtual teams: Lessons from practice. In A. F. Buono (Ed.), *Creative consulting* (pp.143–161). Charlotte, NC: Information Age Publishing.

Königswieser, R. (2008). Komplementärberatung: Wenn 1 plus 1 mehr als 2 macht [Complementary consulting. When 1 plus 1 makes more than 2]. *Revue für postheroisches Management* [Revue for post-heroic management], 2, 26–39.

Königswieser, R. & Hillebrand, M. (2005). *Kommentar zu: Die Grenzen der Strategieberatung liegen innen* [Comment to: The limits of strategy consulting lie on the inside]. In D. Seidl, W. Kirsch, & M. Linder, *Grenzen der Strategieberatung* [Limits of strategy consulting] (pp. 116–118). Bern: Haupt Verlag.

Königswieser, R. & Hillebrand, M. (2007). *Einführung in die systemische Organisationsberatung* [Introduction into systemic consulting of organizations]. Heidelberg: Carl-Auer Systeme.

Königswieser, R., Lang, E., & Wimmer, R. (2009). *Komplementärberatung. Quantensprung oder Übergangsphänomen* [Complementary consulting. Quantum leap or transitional phenomenon]. Interview. Organisationsentwicklung, 46–53.

Königswieser, R., Sonuc, E., & Gebhardt, J. (2008). *Komplementärberatung. Das Zusammenspiel zwischen Fach- und Prozeß-know-how* [Complementary consulting. The interplay between expert and process know-how]. Stuttgart: Klett-Cotta.

Kolbeck, C. & Wimmer, R. (2001). *Stößt der Beraterboom an seine Grenzen? Oder: Aufbau und Dekonstruktion von Autorität in Organsationen* [Does the consulting boom reach its limits? Or: Building and deconstructing authority in organizations]. Retrieved on March 31, 2011, from http://www.osb-i.com/sites/default/files/user_upload/Publikationen/Wimmer_Kolbeck_Stoesst_der_Beraterboom_an_seine_Grenzen.pdf

Linder, M. (2006). *Strategische Beratung—eine organisationstheoretische Betrachtung* [Strategic consulting—a perspective from organizational theory]. Herrsching: Barbara Kirsch.

Luhmann, N. (1984). *Soziale Systeme. Grundriß einer allgemeinen Theorie* [Social systems. Outline of a general theory]. Frankfurt: A. M. Suhrkamp.

Luhmann, N. (2002). *Einführung in die Systemtheorie* [Introduction into systems theory]. Heidelberg: Carl-Auer-Systeme Verlag.

Luhmann, N. (2006). *Organisation und Entscheidung* [Organization and decision]. Wiesbaden: Vs Verlag.

Luhmann, N. (2008). *Soziale systeme* [Social systems]. Frankfurt: Suhrkamp.

Management Innovation eXchange. (2010). *The MIX Manifesto.* Retrieved May 27, 2011 from http://www.managementexchange.com/sites/default/files/the_mix_manifesto.pdf

Mitchell, M. D. (2010). Whole system consulting. In A. F. Buono & D. Jamieson (Eds.), *Consultation for organizational change* (pp. 41–55). Charlotte, NC: Information Age Publishing.

Mintzberg, H. (1978). *Patterns in strategy formation.* Management Science, *24*(9), 935–948.

Mohe, M. & Seidl, D. (2009). Systemic concepts of intervention. In A. F. Buono, & F. Poulfelt (Eds.), *Client-consultant collaboration: Coping with complexity and change* (pp. 47–66). Charlotte, NC: Information Age Publishing.

Niedereichholz, C. & Niedereichholz, J. (2006). *Consulting insight.* München: Oldenbourg.

Raffel, T., (2006). *Unternehmensberater in der Politikberatung: Eine empirische Untersuchung zu Aktivitäten, Gründen und Folgen* [Business consultants in politics consulting: An empirical analysis of activities, reasons and consequences]. Wiesbaden: Deutscher Universitäts-Verlag.

Schmidt, A. & Strobel, W. (2005). Strategieberatung—Anspruch und Realität [Strategy consulting – claims and reality]. In D. Seidl, W. Kirsch, & M. Linder, *Grenzen der Strategieberatung* [Limits of strategy consulting] (pp. 21–32). Bern: Haupt Verlag.

Scherer, J. J., Lavery, G., Sullivan, R., Whitson, G., & Vales, E. (2010). Whole system transformation: The consultant's role in creating sustainable results. In A. F. Buono & D. Jamieson (Eds.), *Consultation for organizational change* (pp. 57–77). Charlotte, NC: Information Age Publishing.

Sorensen, P. F. & Yaeger, T. F. (2004). Appreciative inquiry as a large group intervention: An innovation in organizational consulting. In: A. F. Buono (Ed.), *Creative consulting* (pp. 229–242). Charlotte, NC: Information Age Publishing.

Taylor, D. & Remenyi, D. (2002). *How to become a successful IT consultant.* Oxford: Butterworth-Heinemann.

Walger, G. (1995). Idealtypen der Unternehmensberatung [Ideal types of business consulting]. In G. Walger (Ed.), *Formen der Unternehmensberatung. Systemische Unternehmensberatung, Organisationsentwicklung, Expertenberatung und gutachterliche Beratungstätigkeit in Theorie und Praxis* [Forms of business consulting. Systemic consulting, organizational development, expert consulting and independent reviewing in theory and practice] (pp. 1–18). Köln: Otto Schmidt Verlag.

Walger, G. & Neise, R. (2005). Die Grenzen der Strategieberatung liegen innen [The limits of strategy consulting lie on the inside]. In D. Seidl, W. Kirsch, & M. Linder (Eds.), *Grenzen der Strategieberatung* [Limits of strategy consulting] (pp. 87–122). Bern: Haupt Verlag.

Wimmer, R. (1999). *Wozu benötigen wir Berater? Ein aktueller Orientierungsversuch aus systemischer Sicht* [Why do we need consultants? A contemporary attempt of orientation from a systemic perspective]. In G. Walger, H. Achatzi, & W. Benkert (Eds.), *Formen der Unternehmensberatung* [Forms of business consulting] (pp. 1–54). Köln: Otto Schmidt Verlag.

Wimmer, R. (2008). Kommentar zu: Komplementärberatung: Wenn 1 und 1 mehr als 2 macht [Comment to: Complementary consulting: When 1 plus 1 makes more than 2]. *Revue für postheroisches Management/Heft, 2,* 35–39.

Wimmer, R. (2009). *Systemische Organisationsberatung—Organisationsverständnis und künftige Herausforderungen* [Systemic consulting of organizations—Understanding of organizations and future challenges]. In H. Pühl (Ed.), *Handbuch Supervision und Organisationsentwicklung* [Handbook of supervision and organizational development] (pp. 213–230). Wiesbaden: VS Verlag.

ABOUT THE AUTHORS

Susanna Alexius is an assistant professor at Score (the Stockholm Center for Organizational Research) at Stockholm University and Stockholm School of Economics. Her research concerns fundamental aspects of regulation, particularly standard setting and responses to standardization in the management consultancy field. Her current research interests are in the practices of market organization, particularly focused on processes in contested market settings. She also does research on value conflicts in markets, studying how market actors struggle to shape and handle potentially conflicting values such as profitability and responsibility.

Sonja van der Arend is a postdoctoral researcher at Delft University of Technology. In a project running from 2008 until the end of 2011, she studied the implementation of the governance innovations in the EU Water Framework Directive, including public participation and ecological performance measurement. Her teaching activities include a course on professionalization and quality in consultancy. Sonja holds a PhD from the geography department of Utrecht University with a dissertation on the rise and demise of interactive planning in the Netherlands.

Valentin Bejan works for a large consulting firm in the Netherlands as an advisor on various challenges specific to emerging markets. He is Romanian and graduated with a Bachelor in Economics from the Academy of Economic Studies in Bucharest and holds an Master of Science in Business Administration, Management Consulting track, from the Vrije Universiteit Amsterdam. He is a supporter of an evidence-based approach to management consulting and closer cooperation between business and academia.

Exploring the Professional Identity of Management Consultants, pages 325–332
Copyright © 2013 by Information Age Publishing
All rights of reproduction in any form reserved. **325**

John L. Bennett, PCC, CMC, is an assistant professor of behavioral sciences and director of the Master of Science in Executive Coaching program at the McColl School of Business, Queens University of Charlotte. He also serves as president of the Graduate School Alliance for Executive Coaching (GSAEC). In 2010 he was named a fellow of The Lewin Center as well as the Institute of Coaching at Harvard. John is an active executive coach and consultant as well as an educator, researcher, and conference speaker. He earned his PhD in Human and Organizational Systems from Fielding Graduate University.

Liselore Berghman is an assistant professor of strategy at the Department of Organisation Sciences, Faculty of Social Sciences, VU University Amsterdam and an associate professor in the Department of Management, Faculty of Applied Economics, University of Antwerp. She received her PhD in Management from the Erasmus University Rotterdam and has worked as a strategy consultant. Her research focuses on customer relationship management and on intra- and inter-organizational preconditions for disruptive innovation.

Petra den Besten works at the Quality and Risk Management department of Ernst & Young. Her master's thesis focused on the importance of informal client contact, a cross-cultural comparison among seven European countries. She was a research assistant at the VU University for the large international project on the importance of informal client contacts. She received her Master title from the Department of Organisation Sciences, Faculty of Social Sciences, at the VU University Amsterdam.

Bertien Broekhans has had an appointment as assistant professor at Delft University of Technology since 2007. Her research, education, and consulting deal with issues of expertise and governance, and management of uncertainties. Her PhD focused on the birth and growth of environmental science and policy. Her teaching focuses mainly on courses about decision making, and she has recently developed a new course titled "Consultants as Professionals."

Anthony F. Buono, series editor, has a joint appointment as professor of Management and Sociology at Bentley University and is founding coordinator of the Bentley Alliance for Ethics and Social Responsibility. Among his many books and articles are *The Human Side of Mergers and Acquisitions* (Jossey-Bass, 1989; Beard Books, 2003) and *The Changing Paradigm of Consulting* (Information Age Publishing, 2011). His current research and consulting interests focus on organizational change and inter-organizational alliances, with an emphasis on mergers, acquisitions, and strategic partnerships, and developing organizational change capacity. He holds a PhD with a concentration in Industrial and Organizational Sociology from Boston College.

Mary Wayne Bush teaches in the doctorate program in Organization Development and Change at Colorado Technical University and is an executive coach in residence for the Master's of Science in Executive Coaching program at Queens University of Charlotte. In addition to her dissertation research on *Client Perceptions of Effectiveness in Executive Coaching* (2005), she has written articles and book chapters, including *What We Do When We Coach* (2011) and *Diversity in Coaching* (2009). Currently she is a member of the editorial boards of two international coaching journals. Mary Wayne holds a doctorate from Pepperdine University in Organizational Change.

Léon de Caluwé is senior partner with the Twynstra Group of management consultants in Amersfoort (NL) and professor at the Vrije Universiteit in Amsterdam (NL). He is one of The Netherlands' best-known consultants and has undertaken hundreds of assignments in the field of change. He also heads the Center for Research on Consultancy (CRC). He has more than 170 publications to his name, including *Changing Organizations with Gaming/Simulation* (Elsevier, 2000), *Learning to Change* (Sage Publications, 2003), *Intervening and Changing* (Wiley, 2007), and *Why do Games Work?* (Kluwer, 2008). He has received several awards for his work and is an active member of the Academy of Management.

Kåre Groes Christiansen is a partner with Valcon, CEO in Odense Maritime Technology. His core areas of focus include design and engineering, and he is responsible for overseeing Valcon's activities in India. His current responsibilities include building a consultancy unit targeting the global shipbuilding industry. He has an MSc in engineering and a PhD (Product Development) from the Technical University of Denmark.

Karin Derksen is owner of KADE in Arnhem (NL) and associate with EMC Performance in Groenekan (NL). She works as a senior HRD consultant and is a part-time PhD student at the Vrije Universiteit in Amsterdam, at the Faculty of Economics and Business. She is also a supervisor for MBA students working on their theses. Her PhD research focuses on groups working on innovation.

Andreas Drechsler is a PhD candidate and research assistant in the department of Production and Operations Management at the University of Duisburg-Essen, Germany. His current research focuses on how inter- and multidisciplinary approaches (e. g., design science) can enhance the current state-of-the-art in management and consulting, especially in the areas of information systems and information technology.

András Gelei is an associate professor at the Corvinus University of Budapest, and he also works as an independent OD consultant. His research and consulting interests include organization development and learning, interpretive organization theory and hermeneutics, action research and action learning, and the systems-psychodynamics of organizations. In 2011 he co-edited (with Rita Glózer) a book on *Reality Constructions: Interpretive Approaches to the Organizational Meaning-world* published in Hungarian in 2011. He is a member of ISPSO, SCOS and the Hungarian OD Society. He has a PhD in Management and Business Administration from the Corvinus University of Budapest.

Balázs Heidrich is the dean of the faculty of Finance and Accounting at Budapest Business School, where he also heads the Institute of Management and Human Resources. He also works as an OD consultant and trainer for Human Telex Consulting as part of the FLOW Group, mainly working with management teams of local and international organizations. His research focuses on the changes of organizational culture and leadership in transition economies, mainly in Eastern Europe, and also on the human side of the operation models of service organizations. He holds a PhD in Management and Business Administration and a Dr. habil title from the University of Miskolc.

Peter Kalvelage holds a M.Sc. in Business Information Systems ("Wirtschaftsinformatik") from the University of Duisburg-Essen, Germany. Besides his research activities in the domain of systemic IT management, he is head of product management at the CIS GmbH, a German software development company for e-commerce applications. In that role, he applies theoretical findings of systemic management in the areas of agile software development and IT business consulting.

Sebastiaan Meijer is an assistant professor at Delft University of Technology since 2008 and visiting fellow at CSTEP, India. He is responsible for the consultancy minor program of the Faculty of Technology, Policy, and Management. His research focuses on the use of gaming simulation methods for empirical research and testing of designs, particularly in supply chain management, transport systems, and emergency management.

Gergely Németh is a senior consultant at Corporate Values Kft. A qualified organizational and sport psychologist he works in the field of economic psychology. In 2011 he was awarded a CMC certificate and in 2010 received recognition as the "Most Excellent Consultant of the year 2010." In his role as an organizational development consultant, his focus is primarily on organizational philosophy and strategy, and the planning and implementation of development processes aimed at achieving organizational excellence.

Besides being a consultant, he is a senior lecturer in Organization Development and Organizational Psychology. He is writing his doctoral thesis on SME growth crises and possible ways to overcome them.

Frida Pemer is an assistant professor at the Stockholm School of Economics in Sweden. Her research centers on buyer-supplier relationships in professional services and organizational sensemaking. She has written numerous academic papers about how professional services such as management consulting are purchased, organized, constructed and evaluated by buyers and suppliers in the private and public sectors, and her work has been published in journals like *Human Relations* and *Journal of Purchasing and Supply Management*. She holds a PhD with a concentration in Management and Organization from the Stockholm School of Economics.

Flemming Poulfelt is a professor of management and strategy at the Department of Management, Politics, and Philosophy, and vice dean of Research Communication at Copenhagen Business School, Denmark. His current research focuses on strategy, managing knowledge intensive firms, and management consulting. He has published extensively, and his most recent books include *Managing the Knowledge-Intensive Firm, Return on Strategy, Management Consulting Today and Tomorrow: Perspectives and Advice from 27 Leading World Experts, Management Consulting Today and Tomorrow: Casebook Enhancing Skills to Become Better Professionals,* and *Consultant-Client Collaboration: Coping with Complexity and Change.* He is on the editorial boards of leading journals in management and has held visiting positions at various universities in the U.S. and Australia. Flemming has also given seminars and lectures on most continents, is on the board of several companies, and is a practicing consultant.

Elsbeth Reitsma is a partner of C3 consultants and managers in Leusden (the Netherlands). She studied Sociology at the University of Leiden (Master of Science) and followed a postgraduate course on management consultancy and change management. She is preparing a PhD dissertation on professional action and craftsmanship in consulting. Her consulting practice focuses on innovations in healthcare.

Kelly D. B. Rogers is the Executive Director of Harris YMCA with the YMCA of Greater Charlotte in North Carolina. She also serves on the Board of Directors for International Coach Federation Charlotte Area Chapter and consults nonprofits in leadership and organization development. Kelly worked in organizational change for a Fortune 100 company and has spent most of her career in community, organization and individual change and development. She holds a Master of Divinity degree and earned her Master of Science in Organization Development and Executive Coaching Certification at the McColl School of Business at Queens University of Charlotte.

Geert Roovers is a senior consultant at Antea Group, working on organizational issues and decision making processes. He focuses on water management, navigation and spatial planning, and works for public administrations in the Netherlands and Belgium. His current issues are chain management of navigation and the development of long-term river policy strategies. Geert is also working on a PhD project, doing a survey on decision making in river management at Technical University of Delft, Faculty of Technology, Policy and Management. Geert publishes on these issues in various popular journals.

Annika Schilling is an affiliated assistant professor at the Stockholm School of Economics. Her research interests focus mainly on the role of professional identity, human resource management, and embodiment practices of professionals in professional service firms. In 2008 Annika finished her PhD, which studies the role of identity in mergers between consulting firms. Her work has been published in journals like *The Service Industries Journal* and *Service Business*.

P. Robert-Jan Simons is director of the Netherlands School of Educational Management (NSO) and a professor in the field of digital learning at Utrecht University, Faculty of Social Sciences. In 1981 he wrote his PhD on the role of analogies in learning. His articles appear in such journals as *Human Resources Development International, Computers in Human Behaviour, Culture and Psychology, Learning and Instruction*, and *Journal of Educational Psychology*. His work focuses on self-directed learning, social learning, organizational learning, digital learning, and learning communities. His main books are *Learning and Instruction* (with Monique Boekaerts, 1993) and *Learning and Working* (with Sanneke Bolhuis, 1999). He has served as promoter of over 45 PhD students.

Irene Skovgaard Smith is classically trained as a social anthropologist (BA, MSc) with a PhD in organization studies. She is currently affiliated with Copenhagen Business School. Her research interests revolve around the use of anthropological theory and ethnographic methods in the study of organizational activities and relations. Her PhD dissertation was an ethnographic study of management consultants working on change projects in client organizations.

Karen Somerville is an assistant professor of management with the School of Business at Hamline University. Her primary research interests include organizational change, organizational behavior, and human resource management. Her work has been published in *Journal of Change Management* and *Public Administration Quarterly*. Prior to joining academe on a full time basis, for 15 years she was the managing partner of a management consulting firm offering services focused on organizational change and strategic management. Karen holds a PhD in Management from Carleton University and an MBA from the University of Ottawa.

Annemieke Stoppelenburg is an academic supervisor and lecturer in organization studies at Tilburg University in the Netherlands and SIOO, a knowledge community and intellectual space in the field of organizational studies and change management. As a management consultant, she supports organizations in organizational change and development, alternative approaches for strategic decision-making, and implementation. She frequently publishes articles on related topics, like organizational learning, large scale interventions, and the work of management consultants. She is currently conducting research on the quality and effectiveness of consultants' work.

J. Strikwerda is a partner with the consulting firm Nolan, Norton & Co. and director of its Nolan Norton Institute (for thought leadership and innovation). He also has an appointment as professor of organization and change at the Faculty for Economics and Business Administration of the University of Amsterdam. In 2003 he published *Shared Service Centers* (awarded as the best management book of the year) and in 2008 his book on the emergence of multidimensional organizations also received the award for best management book of the year. He publishes on new organization forms and institutional changes as relevant for organizations, including internal governance and corporate governance. His latest book is an iBook published with Apple Store, *Organization Design for the 21st Century: From Structure Follows Strategy to Process Follows Proposition*, which explains the new options for organization that are created by the declining costs of organization and communication. Hans holds a PhD from the University of Tilburg.

Yvette Taminiau is an assistant professor of strategy at the Department of Organisation Sciences, Faculty of Social Sciences, VU University Amsterdam. She received her PhD from the Rotterdam School of Management. Her research focuses on institutional and cultural pressures on the consultancy and accountancy professions and has resulted in a number of publications.

Tobias Trepper is a PhD candidate and research assistant in the department of Production and Operations Management at the University of Duisburg-Essen, Germany. His current research and consulting interests focus on agile and systemic IT project management, with an emphasis on social interactions.

Dawn-Marie Turner is president of Turner Change Management. Her experience includes the development and implementation of change programming, transition planning, and organizational change education. She has also developed the DEAM transition management methodology. Her current consulting and research interest focus on enhancing change readiness and organizational capacity, evidence-based practice, and change leadership. Dawn-Marie holds a PhD in applied management and decision science from Walden University and is a certified management consultant. She founded and chairs the International Council of Organizational Change, a group of scholar practitioners working in a collaborative, non-competitive way to inform and advance the practice of change management worldwide.

Tanja J.M. Verheij holds a position as managing director of Public Administration and Safety at Berenschot BV, a Dutch consultancy firm. Over her career, she has combined her work as a consultant with work as a trainer at the Dutch Interacademic Centre for Organisation & Change Management. Tanja works for (semi)public organizations, on issues of (process) management in interorganizational alliances, public management, and change management. Her current research and consulting interests focus on (de)centralization and strategic partnerships in public administration. Her publications include works on governance in hybrid organizations and the gap between planners and practitioners in the field of safety management.

Ivo Wenzler is a senior expert with Accenture's Management Consulting Organization and an associate professor at the Delft University of Technology. At Accenture he focuses on development and implementation of strategic workforce planning, performance management, change management, and business simulation approaches aimed at helping clients deal with their business transformation challenges. At the university he does research on the next generation of infrastructures and teaches a master's course on simulation game design. Ivo holds a PhD in Simulations and Gaming from the University of Michigan.

Andreas Werr is a professor at the Stockholm School of Economics (SSE) and head of the Center for HRM and Knowledge Work at the SSE Institute for Research. His research interests focus on the acquisition, application. and development of knowledge and expertise in knowledge intensive work. Andreas has carried out extensive research on the use of management consultants and the management of professional service firms. His work has been published in journals like *Organization Studies, Organizational Change Management* and MIT's *Sloan Management Review*.

CPSIA information can be obtained at www.ICGtesting.com
Printed in the USA
LVOW10s1803280214

375588LV00002B/127/P

9 781623 961718